STATE OF WASHINGTON

2013 Washington State Juvenile Disposition Guidelines Manual

CASELOAD FORECAST COUNCIL

John C. Steiger, PhD
Executive Director

State of Washington

CASELOAD FORECAST COUNCIL

Jeannie Darneille, Chair
Washington State Senator

Kevin Parker
Washington State Representative

Kevin Quigley
Secretary, Dept. of Social and Health Services

Andy Hill
Washington State Senator

David Schumacher
Director, Office of Financial Management

Derek Stanford
Washington State Representative

Council Staff

John Steiger
Executive Director

Dave Bendemire
Senior Caseload Forecaster

Matt Bridges
Senior Caseload Forecaster

Gongwei Chen
Senior Caseload Forecaster

Elaine Deschamps
Deputy Director

Jennifer Jones
Research Analyst

Thuy Le
Research Analyst

Duc Luu
Database and Sentencing Administration Manager

Kathleen Turnbow
Confidential Secretary

Ed Vukich
Senior Caseload Forecaster

The Caseload Forecast Council is not liable for errors or omissions in the manual, for sentences that may be inappropriately calculated as a result of a practitioner's or court's reliance on the manual, or for any other written or verbal information related to adult or juvenile sentencing. The scoring sheets are intended to provide assistance in most cases but does not cover all permutations of the scoring rules. If you find any errors or omissions, we encourage you to report them to the Caseload Forecast Council.

ACKNOWLEDGMENTS

The Caseload Forecast Council would like to express a special acknowledgement of council staff John Steiger, Ed Vukich and Jennifer Jones for their work on the manual.

The Caseload Forecast Council would like to express a special acknowledgement for the contributions of Todd Dowell, Kitsap County Senior Deputy Prosecutor. Mr. Dowell provided numerous suggestions for improvements to the manual, and drafted a comprehensive revision and expansion of Section I: Juvenile Disposition Guidelines.

The Council acknowledges the contribution of Judge Ronald Kessler, King County Superior Court. Judge Kessler graciously permitted us to reprint his Caselaw review.

The Council acknowledges the contribution of Washington Defenders Association which graciously permitted us to reprint its publication, "Beyond Juvenile Court."

The Council also appreciates the suggestions for improvements and additions to the manual received from users.

We always welcome suggestions for making the manual easier to use.

© Copyright 2014, State of Washington, Caseload Forecast Council

All rights reserved. Portions of this document may be reproduced without permission for non-commercial purposes.

The Caseload Forecast Council is not liable for errors or omissions in the manual, for sentences that may be inappropriately calculated as a result of a practitioner's or court's reliance on the manual, or for any other written or verbal information related to adult or juvenile sentencing. The scoring sheets are intended to provide assistance in most cases but does not cover all permutations of the scoring rules. If you find any errors or omissions, we encourage you to report them to the Caseload Forecast Council.

FORWARD

The purpose of this manual is to provide a reference for those interested in Washington State's Juvenile Disposition Guidelines. It is not intended to provide legal advice.

The Caseload Forecast Council and its staff are not liable for errors or omissions in the manual, for sentences that may be inappropriately calculated as a result of a practitioner's or court's reliance on the manual, or for any other written or verbal information related to adult or juvenile sentencing. The scoring instructions are intended to provide assistance in most cases but do not cover all permutations of the scoring rules. If you find any errors or omissions, we encourage you to report them to the Caseload Forecast Council.

TABLE OF CONTENTS

Contents

CASELOAD FORECAST COUNCIL iii

ACKNOWLEDGMENTS iv

FORWARD v

TABLE OF CONTENTS vii

SECTION 1 JUVENILE DISPOSITION GUIDELINES 1

   Introduction 1

   Determining the Appropriate Court of Jurisdiction 2
      What is a *Juvenile* for Purposes of Juvenile Court Jurisdiction? 2
      Less Than 18 Years Old 3
      Not Subject to Adult Court Proceedings 3
         1.   Certain "License" Offenses if 16 or 17 Years Old 3
         2.   Exclusive Adult Jurisdiction if 16 or 17 Years Old ("Automatic Adult") 4
         3.   Judicial Decline Hearings for Any Age 5
      When Does Juvenile Court Jurisdiction End? 6

   Washington State Juvenile Disposition Guidelines 7
      Title 13 is the Exclusive Authority for Juvenile Dispositions 7
      Consequences: Local Sanctions vs. Confinement to JRA 7
      Multiple Juvenile Offenses 8
      Disposition Options for Juvenile Adjudications 9
         1.   Standard Range (RCW 13.40.0357 Option A) 9
         2.   Deferred Disposition (RCW 13.40.127) 9
         3.   Manifest Injustice (RCW 13.40.0357 Option D) 9
         4.   Suspended Disposition (four alternatives): 9
      Standard Range (RCW 13.40.0357 Option A) 10
      Current Offense Category 11
      Prior Adjudications 12
      Firearm Enhancement 12
      Motor Vehicle Minimums 13
      Deferred Disposition (RCW 13.40.127) 13
      Manifest Injustice (RCW 13.40.0357 Option D) 14
      Suspended Disposition Alternatives 15
         1.   Suspended Disposition Alternative (Option B) 15
         2.   The Chemical Dependency Disposition Alternative (Option C) 16
         3.   Special Sex Offender Disposition Alternative (RCW 13.40.162 SSODA) 17
         4.   Mental Health Disposition Alternative (RCW 13.40.167) 18

SECTION 2 RCW 13.40: JUVENILE JUSTICE ACT OF 1977, AS AMENDED 21
    RCW 13.40.010 Short title — Intent — Purpose. 21
    RCW 13.40.020 Definitions. 22
    RCW 13.40.030 Security guidelines — Legislative review — Limitations on permissible ranges of confinement 27
    RCW 13.40.0351 Equal application of guidelines and standards. 27
    RCW 13.40.0357 Juvenile offender sentencing standards. (Effective until July 22, 2007.) 28
    JUVENILE SENTENCING STANDARDS 32
    OPTION A: JUVENILE OFFENDER SENTENCING GRID 33
    OPTION B: SUSPENDED DISPOSITION ALTERNATIVE 34
    OPTION C: CHEMICAL DEPENDENCY DISPOSITION ALTERNATIVE 35
    OPTION D: MANIFEST INJUSTICE 35
    RCW 13.40.038 County juvenile detention facilities -- Policy -- Detention and risk assessment standards. ... 36
    RCW 13.40.040 Taking juvenile into custody, grounds — Detention of, grounds — Detention pending disposition — Release on bond, conditions — Bail jumping 36
    13.40.042 Detention of juvenile with mental disorder. 38
    RCW 13.40.045 Escapees — Arrest warrants. 38
    RCW 13.40.050 Detention procedures -- Notice of hearing -- Conditions of release -- Consultation with parent, guardian, or custodian. 39
    RCW 13.40.054 Probation bond or collateral — Modification or revocation of probation bond. 40
    RCW 13.40.056 Nonrefundable bail fee. 41
    RCW 13.40.060 Jurisdiction of actions — Transfer of case and records, when — Change in venue, grounds. 41
    RCW 13.40.070 Complaints — Screening — Filing information — Diversion — Modification of community supervision — Notice to parent or guardian — Probation counselor acting for prosecutor — Referral to mediation or reconciliation programs. 42
    RCW 13.40.077 Recommended prosecuting standards for charging and plea dispositions. 44
    RCW 13.40.080 Diversion agreement -- Scope -- Limitations -- Restitution orders -- Divertee's rights -- Diversion unit's powers and duties -- Interpreters -- Modification -- Fines. 50
    RCW 13.40.085 Diversion services costs — Fees — Payment by parent or legal guardian. 54
    RCW 13.40.087 Youth who have been diverted — Alleged prostitution or prostitution loitering offenses — Services and treatment. 55
    RCW 13.40.090 Prosecuting attorney as party to juvenile court proceedings -- Exception, procedure. 55
    RCW 13.40.100 Summons or other notification issued upon filing of information -- Procedure -- Order to take juvenile into custody -- Contempt of court, when. 55
    RCW 13.40.110 Hearing on question of declining jurisdiction — Held, when — Findings. 56
    RCW 13.40.120 Hearings — Time and place. 57
    RCW 13.40.127 Deferred disposition. 57
    RCW 13.40.130 Procedure upon plea of guilty or not guilty to information allegations — Notice — Adjudicatory and disposition hearing — Disposition standards used in sentencing. 60
    RCW 13.40.135 Sexual motivation special allegation — Procedures. 61
    RCW 13.40.140 Juveniles entitled to usual judicial rights — Notice of — Open court — Privilege against self-incrimination — Waiver of rights, when. 61
    RCW 13.40.145 Payment of fees for legal services by publicly funded counsel — Hearing — Order or decree — Entering and enforcing judgments. 63
    RCW 13.40.150 Disposition hearing — Scope — Factors to be considered prior to entry of dispositional order. 64
    RCW 13.40.160 Disposition order — Court's action prescribed — Disposition outside standard range — Right of appeal — Special sex offender disposition alternative. 66

The Caseload Forecast Council is not liable for errors or omissions in the manual, for sentences that may be inappropriately calculated as a result of a practitioner's or court's reliance on the manual, or for any other written or verbal information related to adult or juvenile sentencing. The scoring sheets are intended to provide assistance in most cases but does not cover all permutations of the scoring rules. If you find any errors or omissions, we encourage you to report them to the Caseload Forecast Council.

RCW 13.40.162 Special sex offender disposition alternative. 68
RCW 13.40.165 Chemical dependency disposition alternative. 71
RCW 13.40.167 Mental health disposition alternative. 74
RCW 13.40.180 Disposition order -- Consecutive terms when two or more offenses – Limitations – Separate disposition order – Concurrent period of community supervision. 76
RCW 13.40.185 Disposition order — Confinement under departmental supervision or in juvenile facility, when. 77
RCW 13.40.190 Disposition order — Restitution for loss — Modification of restitution order. 77
RCW 13.40.192 Legal financial obligations -- Enforceability -- Treatment of obligations upon age of eighteen or conclusion of juvenile court jurisdiction -- Extension of judgment. 77
RCW 13.40.193 Firearms — Length of confinement. 78
RCW 13.40.196 Firearms — Special allegation. 79
RCW 13.40.198 Penalty assessments — Jurisdiction of court. 79
RCW 13.40.200 Violation of order of restitution, community supervision, fines, penalty assessments, or confinement — Modification of order after hearing — Scope — Rights — Use of fines. 79
RCW 13.40.205 Release from physical custody, when — Authorized leaves — Leave plan and order — Notice. 80
RCW 13.40.210 Setting of release date -- Administrative release authorized, when --Parole program, revocation or modification of, scope -- Intensive supervision program -- Parole officer's right of arrest. (Effective until October 1, 2007) 82
RCW 13.40.212 Intensive supervision program — Elements — Report. 85
RCW 13.40.213 Juveniles alleged to have committed offenses of prostitution or prostitution loitering -- Diversion. 86
RCW 13.40.215 Juveniles found to have committed violent or sex offense or stalking — Notification of discharge, parole, leave, release, transfer, or escape — To whom given — School attendance — Definitions. 87
RCW 13.40.217 Juveniles adjudicated of sex offenses — Release of information authorized. 89
RCW 13.40.219 Arrest for prostitution or prostitution loitering – Alleged offender –Victim of severe form of trafficking, commercial sex abuse of a minor. 90
RCW 13.40.220 Costs of support, treatment, and confinement — Order — Contempt of court. 90
RCW 13.40.230 Appeal from order of disposition — Jurisdiction — Procedure — Scope — Release pending appeal. 92
RCW 13.40.240 Construction of RCW references to juvenile delinquents or juvenile delinquency. 93
RCW 13.40.250 Traffic and civil infraction cases. 93
RCW 13.40.265 Firearm, alcohol, and drug violations. 93
RCW 13.40.280 Transfer of juvenile to department of corrections facility — Grounds — Hearing — Term — Retransfer to a facility for juveniles. 94
RCW 13.40.285 Juvenile offender sentenced to terms in juvenile and adult facilities — Transfer to department of corrections — Term of confinement. 95
RCW 13.40.300 Commitment of juvenile beyond age twenty-one prohibited — Jurisdiction of juvenile court after juvenile's eighteenth birthday. 96
RCW 13.40.305 Juvenile offender adjudicated of theft of motor vehicle, possession of stolen vehicle, taking motor vehicle without permission in the first degree, taking motor vehicle without permission in the second degree — Local sanctions — Evaluation. 97
RCW 13.40.308 Juvenile offender adjudicated of taking motor vehicle without permission in the first degree, theft of motor vehicle, possession of a stolen vehicle, taking motor vehicle without permission in the second degree — Minimum sentences. 97
RCW 13.40.310 Transitional treatment program for gang and drug-involved juvenile offenders. 99

The Caseload Forecast Council is not liable for errors or omissions in the manual, for sentences that may be inappropriately calculated as a result of a practitioner's or court's reliance on the manual, or for any other written or verbal information related to adult or juvenile sentencing. The scoring sheets are intended to provide assistance in most cases but does not cover all permutations of the scoring rules. If you find any errors or omissions, we encourage you to report them to the Caseload Forecast Council.

RCW 13.40.320 Juvenile offender basic training camp program. 99
RCW 13.40.400 Applicability of RCW 10.01.040 to chapter. 101
RCW 13.40.430 Disparity in disposition of juvenile offenders — Data collection. 101
RCW 13.40.460 Juvenile rehabilitation programs — Administration. 101
RCW 13.40.462 Reinvesting in youth program. 103
RCW 13.40.464 Reinvesting in youth program — Guidelines. 104
RCW 13.40.466 Reinvesting in youth account. 105
RCW 13.40.468 Juvenile rehabilitation administration — State quality assurance program. 106
RCW 13.40.470 Vulnerable youth committed to residential facilities — Protection from sexually aggressive youth — Assessment process. 106
RCW 13.40.480 Student records and information — Reasons for release — Who may request. 107
RCW 13.40.500 Community juvenile accountability programs — Findings — Purpose. 108
RCW 13.40.510 Community juvenile accountability programs — Establishment — Proposals — Guidelines.
.... 108
RCW 13.40.520 Community juvenile accountability programs — Grants. 110
RCW 13.40.530 Community juvenile accountability programs — Effectiveness standards. 110
RCW 13.40.540 Community juvenile accountability programs — Information collection — Report. 111
RCW 13.40.550 Community juvenile accountability programs — Short title. 111
RCW 13.40.560 Juvenile accountability incentive account. 111
RCW 13.40.570 Sexual misconduct by state employees, contractors. 112
RCW 13.40.580 Youth courts — Diversion. 113
RCW 13.40.590 Youth court programs. 114
RCW 13.40.600 Youth court jurisdiction. 114
RCW 13.40.610 Youth court notification of satisfaction of conditions. 115
RCW 13.40.620 Appearance before youth court with parent, guardian, or legal custodian. 115
RCW 13.40.630 Youth court dispositions. 115
RCW 13.40.640 Youth court nonrefundable fee. 116
RCW 13.40.650 Use of restraints on pregnant youth in custody — Allowed in extraordinary circumstances.
.... 117
RCW 13.40.651 Use of restraints on pregnant youth in custody — Allowed in extraordinary circumstances.
.... 117
RCW 13.40.700 Juvenile gang courts — Minimum requirements — Admission — Individualized plan — Completion. 118
RCW 13.40.710 Juvenile gang courts — Data — Reports. 120
RCW 13.40.900 Construction — Chapter applicable to state registered domestic partnerships — 2009 c 521.
.... 121

SECTION 3 RCW 13.50: KEEPING AND RELEASE OF RECORDS BY JUVENILE JUSTICE OR CARE AGENCIES 123

RCW 13.50.010 Definitions — Conditions when filing petition or information — Duties to maintain accurate records and access. 123
RCW 13.50.050 Records relating to commission of juvenile offenses — Maintenance of, access to, and destruction — Release of information to schools. 125
RCW 13.50.100 Records not relating to commission of juvenile offenses — Maintenance and access — Release of information for child custody hearings — Disclosure of unfounded allegations prohibited. 131
RCW 13.50.140 Disclosure of privileged information to office of the family and children's ombudsman — Privilege not waived as to others. 133
RCW 13.50.150 Confidential records — Expungement to protect due process rights. 133
RCW 13.50.160 Disposition records — Provision to schools. 133

The Caseload Forecast Council is not liable for errors or omissions in the manual, for sentences that may be inappropriately calculated as a result of a practitioner's or court's reliance on the manual, or for any other written or verbal information related to adult or juvenile sentencing. The scoring sheets are intended to provide assistance in most cases but does not cover all permutations of the scoring rules. If you find any errors or omissions, we encourage you to report them to the Caseload Forecast Council.

RCW 13.50.200 Records of motor vehicle operation violation forwarded. 134
RCW 13.50.250 Records chapter applicable to. 134

SECTION 4 JUVENILE CASE LAW REVIEW: 2013 135

Introduction 135
2013 Juvenile Case Law Review Update.. 136
2012 Juvenile Case Law Review 137
Dispositions 157

SECTION 5 JUVENILE REHABILITATION ADMINISTRATION SENTENCING WORKSHEET 179

Sentencing Worksheet Instructions 179
Purpose 179
General Instructions 180
Supply of forms: 181
Instructions for completing each item: 181

APPENDIX A 185

APPENDIX A: 185
   RACE CODES 185
   HISPANIC ORIGIN CODES 185
   COURT CODE 186

APPENDIX B 187

APPENDIX B: JRA OFFENSE CODES BY OFFENSE TITLE... 187

APPENDIX C 211

APPENDIX C: JRA OFFENSE CODES BY OFFENSE CATEGORY.. 211

APPENDIX D 235

APPENDIX D: Beyond Juvenile Court 235
   Acknowledgements 236
   Who should use this Booklet? 237
   Is a Juvenile Adjudication a "Conviction"? 237
   Juvenile Criminal History Records 238
   Immigration 242
   Legal Financial Obligations (LFOs) 245
   Driving 246
   School Issues... 249
   Applying to College... 251
   Federal Student Loans 252
   Right to Possess Firearms 253
   Voting and Jury Service 255
   Military Service 255
   Employment 256
   Employment Discrimination: 259

The Caseload Forecast Council is not liable for errors or omissions in the manual, for sentences that may be inappropriately calculated as a result of a practitioner's or court's reliance on the manual, or for any other written or verbal information related to adult or juvenile sentencing. The scoring sheets are intended to provide assistance in most cases but does not cover all permutations of the scoring rules. If you find any errors or omissions, we encourage you to report them to the Caseload Forecast Council.

Discretionary Bans on Admission: 261
Public Benefits 262
Traveling to Canada 263
Other Countries: 264
Juvenile Sex Offenses 264
End of the Duty to Register as a Sex Offender: 264
Sex Offender Websites 266
Foster Children 267
Parental Responsibility 267

APPENDIX E **269**

APPENDIX E: Juvenile Disposition Summary - Fiscal Year 2013 269
Washington State Juvenile Sentencing Guidelines 269
Current Offense Category 269
Prior Adjudication Score 269
Standard Range: Local Sanctions vs. Confinement to JRA 269
FY2013 Juvenile Court Dispositions 271
Demographics 271
Race/Ethnicity: Dispositions v. State Population 271
County 272
Type of Court Disposition 273
Locus of Sanction 273
Felony Offenses 274
Violent and Non-violent Offenses 275
Sentencing Alternatives 275
Special Sex Offender Disposition Alternative (SSODA) 275
Chemical Dependency Disposition Alternative (CDDA) 276
Option-B Suspended Disposition 276
Mental Health Disposition 276
Manifest Injustice Dispositions 276
Summary 277

The Caseload Forecast Council is not liable for errors or omissions in the manual, for sentences that may be inappropriately calculated as a result of a practitioner's or court's reliance on the manual, or for any other written or verbal information related to adult or juvenile sentencing. The scoring sheets are intended to provide assistance in most cases but does not cover all permutations of the scoring rules. If you find any errors or omissions, we encourage you to report them to the Caseload Forecast Council.

SECTION 1

JUVENILE DISPOSITION GUIDELINES

Introduction

Juveniles who commit criminal offenses in Washington are subject to the provisions of RCW Chapter 13.40, the Juvenile Justice Act of 1977, as amended.

The Act contains guidelines and procedures for the imposition of a presumptive standard range of sanctions commensurate with the offender's age, seriousness of the current offense and prior criminal history.

The Act also specifies a number of sentencing alternatives to the standard range which the court may select if deemed appropriate.

We offer a special note of caution to those practitioners who are familiar with the state's adult felony sentencing guidelines. Washington is perhaps unique in that both adult felony sentencing and juvenile court dispositions are structured by statutorily defined sentencing guidelines. However, while similar in many ways to its adult felony guidelines, the juvenile sentencing guidelines in Washington State differ in significant ways. For example:

- Juveniles sentenced to more than 30 days of confinement are sentenced to a range of confinement, with the actual release date set within the range at the discretion of the state Juvenile Rehabilitation Administration (JRA)[1]; adults are sentenced to a specific sentence within a specified standard range, but may be released early as a result of "earned release time."
- The "seriousness" of juvenile offense, while generally following the state's adult felony classification, is more differentiated and includes adjustments reflecting recognition of the differences between juvenile and adult social development.
- With the exception of supervision time across dispositions, terms of juvenile dispositions are served consecutively; adult sentences are typically run concurrently.

---

[1] In 2013, the DSHS Juvenile Rehabilitation Administration (JRA) was reorganized as the Juvenile Justice and Rehabilitation Administration (JJRA). In this publication, we will continue to reference the Juvenile Rehabilitation Administration (JRA) consistent with current statutory references.

SECTION 1: JUVENILE DISPOSITION GUIDELINES

Determining the Appropriate Court of Jurisdiction

The sentencing guidelines in this manual only apply to cases properly before a juvenile court. Juvenile courts are not separate constitutional courts; rather, they are a statutory division of the superior courts in Washington State.[2]

A juvenile court's constitutional jurisdiction to act derives from the superior court's general jurisdiction set out in Art. IV, §6 of the Washington State Constitution. Terminology such as "juvenile court jurisdiction" and "jurisdiction of the juvenile court" do not refer to a juvenile court's constitutional jurisdiction. Instead, terms related to a juvenile court's jurisdiction refer to the statutory procedures and protections provided in cases before the juvenile court.[3]

Those statutory provisions exclusive to juveniles include a set of sentencing guidelines discussed in this manual. Failure to substantively abide by these statutory provisions violates a juvenile's right to due process, but never deprives the juvenile court of its constitutional authority to act as a division of superior court.[4]

In Washington State, any *juvenile* alleged or found to have committed a criminal offense is subject to the jurisdiction of the juvenile court.[5] With few exceptions, only a *juvenile* is entitled to the statutory sentencing guidelines exclusive to juveniles. Thus, the initial inquiry for sentencing will focus on determining whether the person is a *juvenile* or otherwise remains subject to the jurisdiction of the juvenile court on a residual basis.

What is a *Juvenile* for Purposes of Juvenile Court Jurisdiction?

While commonly thought to encompass anyone under eighteen (18) years of age, for purposes of juvenile jurisdiction, the term *juvenile* is more complex. The Act defines the term *juvenile*.[6] That legal definition contains two primary components, both of which are required for a person to be a *juvenile* for purposes of juvenile court jurisdiction:

1. **The person must be under the age of eighteen (18); and,**

2. **The person must not be subject to adult court proceedings.**

Unless both components are present, the person is not a *juvenile* for purposes of juvenile court jurisdiction, and, with the exception of residual juvenile jurisdiction, may not remain in juvenile court. However, a person who is either a *juvenile* or is subject to the residual jurisdiction of the

---

[2] RCW 13.04.021(1).
[3] *Dillenburg v. Maxwell*, 70 Wn.2d 331, 353, 422 P.2d 783 (1967).
[4] *State v. Posey*, 174 Wn.2d 131, 139-40, 272 P.3d 840 (2012).
[5] RCW 13.04.030(1)
[6] RCW 13.40.020(14).

The Caseload Forecast Council is not liable for errors or omissions in the manual, for sentences that may be inappropriately calculated as a result of a practitioner's or court's reliance on the manual, or for any other written or verbal information related to adult or juvenile sentencing. The scoring sheets are intended to provide assistance in most cases but does not cover all permutations of the scoring rules. If you find any errors or omissions, we encourage you to report them to the Caseload Forecast Council.

SECTION 1: JUVENILE DISPOSITION GUIDELINES

juvenile court is deemed a *"juvenile offender.*[7] A *juvenile offender* must be given a juvenile disposition.

Less Than 18 Years Old

Being less than 18 years of age requires the person remain under age 18 *up to and through adjudication* of a case in juvenile court.[8] A person loses their status as a *juvenile* anytime they turn 18 years old regardless of their age at the time they commit an offense. There are however three exceptions that continue juvenile court jurisdiction past age 18 despite the loss of juvenile status.

The first exception requires the juvenile court to issue a written order extending juvenile court jurisdiction past the person's 18th birthday pre-adjudication.[9]

The second exception extends juvenile court jurisdiction automatically past age 18 for purposes of imposing or supervising a juvenile court disposition.[10]

The third exception extends juvenile court jurisdiction past age 18 for purposes of disposition after failed "exclusive adult jurisdiction", a term discussed later in this manual.[11]

All three exceptions must be in effect prior to the person turning 18, which is why they create residual jurisdiction in the juvenile court even after a juvenile offender turns age 18.

Not Subject to Adult Court Proceedings

Even if a person is under the age of 18, they may not qualify as a *juvenile* if they are subject to proceedings in adult court either by statutory mandate or judicial decision. There are functionally three ways a person under the age of 18 can be subject to adult court:

1. **Certain "License" Offenses if 16 or 17 Years Old**

    For those who are 16 or 17 years old, there are certain "license" type offenses which require prosecution in adult courts of limited jurisdiction (district and municipal courts). These violations involve any "traffic, fish, boating, or game offense, or traffic or civil infraction" that would, if committed by an adult, be heard in a court of limited jurisdiction.[12] They are referred to as "license" offenses because they involve activities which require licensing or adult status, and, therefore, anyone violating them should be

---

[7] RCW 13.40.020(15).
[8] See, RCW 13.40.300; *State v. Calderon*, 102 Wn.2d 348, 351-52. 684 P.2d 1293 (1984).
[9] RCW 13.40.300(1)(a).
[10] RCW 13.40.300(1)(b)&(c).
[11] RCW 13.40.300(1)(d).
[12] RCW 13.04.030(1)(e)(iii).

The Caseload Forecast Council is not liable for errors or omissions in the manual, for sentences that may be inappropriately calculated as a result of a practitioner's or court's reliance on the manual, or for any other written or verbal information related to adult or juvenile sentencing. The scoring sheets are intended to provide assistance in most cases but does not cover all permutations of the scoring rules. If you find any errors or omissions, we encourage you to report them to the Caseload Forecast Council.

SECTION 1: JUVENILE DISPOSITION GUIDELINES

held to the same standard as any adult properly licensed or otherwise authorized to perform the activity.[13]

The person must be 16 or 17 years old when the offense is committed, and, there is an exception made if the license offense is committed in the same incident as another offense which would properly be before the juvenile court (i.e., Driving while License Suspended and Possession of Marijuana for instance). In that case, both the license offense and the juvenile offense may proceed in juvenile court.

2. **Exclusive Adult Jurisdiction if 16 or 17 Years Old ("Automatic Adult")**

   For those who are 16 or 17 years old, there are certain offenses considered so serious they require prosecution in adult court. Generally, they include any serious violent offense, or, any violent offense along with certain criminal history or use of firearms.

   The conditions for exclusive adult jurisdiction are contained in RCW 13.04.030(1)(v), and require the person to be 16 or 17 years of age at the time the offense is committed. Exclusive adult jurisdiction requires one or more enumerated offenses and/or conditions, so it is necessary to examine and be aware of the particular offenses and conditions in the statute.[14]

   Because adult court jurisdiction is primarily based on the offense charged, any alteration of the crime outside of one of the statutorily enumerated offenses, either pre or post adjudication, may subject the person charged to the jurisdiction of the juvenile court for

---

[13] *State v. Kravchuk*, 86 Wn. App. 276, 280, 936 P.2d 1161 (1997).

[14] Exclusive Adult Jurisdiction: The juvenile must be 16 or 17 at the time of the offense and the offense must be:

(1) A serious violent offense as defined in RCW 9.94A.030;

(2) A violent offense as defined in RCW 9.94A.030 and the juvenile has a criminal history consisting of: (I) One or more prior serious violent offenses; (II) two or more prior violent offenses; or (III) three or more of any combination of the following offenses: Any class A felony, any class B felony, vehicular assault, or manslaughter in the second degree, all of which must have been committed after the juvenile's thirteenth birthday and prosecuted separately;

(3) Robbery in the first degree, rape of a child in the first degree, or drive-by shooting, committed on or after July 1, 1997;

(4) Burglary in the first degree committed on or after July 1, 1997, and the juvenile has a criminal history consisting of one or more prior felony or misdemeanor offenses; or

(5) Any violent offense as defined in RCW 9.94A.030 committed on or after July 1, 1997, and the juvenile is alleged to have been armed with a firearm.

See, RCW 13.04.030(1)(v)(A-E)

The Caseload Forecast Council is not liable for errors or omissions in the manual, for sentences that may be inappropriately calculated as a result of a practitioner's or court's reliance on the manual, or for any other written or verbal information related to adult or juvenile sentencing. The scoring sheets are intended to provide assistance in most cases but does not cover all permutations of the scoring rules. If you find any errors or omissions, we encourage you to report them to the Caseload Forecast Council.

SECTION 1: JUVENILE DISPOSITION GUIDELINES

further proceedings, including disposition.[15] This is referred to as failed exclusive adult jurisdiction.

As discussed earlier, there is an exception allowing for residual juvenile jurisdiction for failed exclusive adult jurisdiction where the person turns 18 while pending adult proceedings.[16] For example: A person age 17 pending adult court for Robbery in the First Degree turns 18 years old prior to trial, but is later found guilty in adult court of the lesser included offense of Robbery in the Second Degree, a non-exclusive adult offense. In this example, the case must return to juvenile court for disposition, and, despite the person being over 18, residual juvenile jurisdiction remains to sentence the matter in juvenile court. Once returned, the juvenile court must sentence the individual to the juvenile sentencing guidelines unless a judicial decline hearing determines the case can return to adult court for sentencing.[17]

There is another exception to exclusive adult jurisdiction which allows the parties and the court to agree to send an exclusive adult case from adult court to juvenile court for further proceedings.[18]

3. Judicial Decline Hearings for Any Age

Under certain circumstances, a juvenile court may decide to waive it's jurisdiction over a juvenile and have the juvenile remanded to the jurisdiction of the adult superior court for further proceedings. This is commonly referred to as a judicial "decline hearing" authorized by statute.[19] Decline hearings are done in juvenile court while a person is pending juvenile court proceedings. Judicial decline hearings can be done for any juvenile regardless of age. In certain cases where the juvenile is 16 or 17 years old and charged with certain offenses, a decline hearing is mandatory unless waived by all parties, including the juvenile court.[20]

During the decline hearing, the parties present testimony and evidence to the juvenile court. At the end of the hearing the juvenile court decides to either retain juvenile court jurisdiction, or, to remand the individual to adult court for further proceedings, in which case the person is no longer subject to juvenile court jurisdiction. The court decides the case based on a specific set of factors, often referred to as the eight *Kent* factors.[21]

---

[15] RCW 13.04.030(1)(v)(E)(II); *State v. Mora*, 138 Wn.2d 43, 54, 977 P.2d 564 (1999).
[16] RCW 13.40.300(1)(d) and RCW 13.04.030(1)(v)(E)(II).
[17] RCW 13.04.030(1)(v)(E)(II).
[18] RCW 13.04.030(1)(v)(E)(III).
[19] See, RCW 13.40.110.
[20] RCW 13.40.110(2).
[21] *Kent v. United States*, 383 U.S. 541, 566-67, 86 Sup.Ct. 1045, 16 L.Ed. 2d 84 (1966).

The Caseload Forecast Council is not liable for errors or omissions in the manual, for sentences that may be inappropriately calculated as a result of a practitioner's or court's reliance on the manual, or for any other written or verbal information related to adult or juvenile sentencing. The scoring sheets are intended to provide assistance in most cases but does not cover all permutations of the scoring rules. If you find any errors or omissions, we encourage you to report them to the Caseload Forecast Council.

SECTION 1: JUVENILE DISPOSITION GUIDELINES

If the juvenile court decides to remand an individual under age 18 to adult court, the individual loses his or her *juvenile* status for any and all cases brought thereafter unless the charge remanded to adult court is later reduced or dismissed in adult court.[22] This is sometimes referred to as *"once declined, always declined."*

Judicial decline hearings may be held either pre-adjudication, or in the case of failed exclusive adult jurisdiction, post-adjudication for purposes of adult sentencing.

When Does Juvenile Court Jurisdiction End?

Once it is determined the juvenile court has jurisdiction to impose disposition on a juvenile offender, that jurisdiction will not remain indefinitely. A juvenile court's jurisdiction to impose a disposition order ends when a juvenile offender turns 21 years of age.[23] However, even in rare instances where the juvenile court loses jurisdiction to impose disposition past age 21, the adult superior courts always maintains constitutional jurisdiction to impose a juvenile disposition.[24]

Once disposition is imposed, there are additional time limits on how long the juvenile court maintains procedural jurisdiction to enforce the disposition order. That depends on both the disposition condition as well as the age of the individual subject to the disposition.

With some exceptions, a juvenile court's procedural jurisdiction to enforce a disposition order against a juvenile offender terminates when the supervision period in the disposition order ends.[25] In no case may the juvenile court extend supervision past the offender's 21st birthday.[26] For purposes of enforcing financial obligations such as payment of restitution, a juvenile court maintains jurisdiction for a period of ten years past disposition, or up to the offender's 28th birthday, whichever is less.[27] That period may be extended for an additional 10 years by written order.[28]

---

[22] RCW 13.40.020(14); *State v. Sharon*, 33 Wn. App. 491, 496, 655 P.2d 1193 (1982).
[23] RCW 13.40.300(3).
[24] *State v. Posey*, 174 Wn.2d at 142.
[25] *State v. May*, 80 Wn. App. 711, 716-17, 911 P.2d 399 (1996).
[26] RCW 13.40.300(3).
[27] RCW 13.40.190(1); *In Re Brady*, 154 Wn. App. 189, 198, 224 P.3d 842 (2010).
[28] RCW 13.40.190(1)(d).

The Caseload Forecast Council is not liable for errors or omissions in the manual, for sentences that may be inappropriately calculated as a result of a practitioner's or court's reliance on the manual, or for any other written or verbal information related to adult or juvenile sentencing. The scoring sheets are intended to provide assistance in most cases but does not cover all permutations of the scoring rules. If you find any errors or omissions, we encourage you to report them to the Caseload Forecast Council.

SECTION 1: JUVENILE DISPOSITION GUIDELINES

Washington State Juvenile Disposition Guidelines

Title 13 is the Exclusive Authority for Juvenile Dispositions

RCW 13.04 and RCW 13.40. are the exclusive authority for the adjudication and sentencing of juveniles unless specifically provided in other statutes.[29] This means juvenile courts are not allowed to utilize other disposition options or sentences that don't specifically include juveniles. For instance, the ability to compromise a misdemeanor under RCW 10.22 does not apply to juvenile proceedings.[30] Similarly, unless otherwise stated, enhancements and penalties imposed outside of Title 13 do not apply to juvenile dispositions. Examples include: Mandatory minimum jail sentences, school zone enhancements, gang enhancements, and, most fines and fees.

Rarely, a particular consequence outside of Title 13 will specifically state its application to juvenile cases. For example, the Crime Victim's Compensation (CVC) fine contained in RCW 7.68, and, certain fees for prostitution related crimes contained in RCW 9A.88 apply to juveniles by specific reference.[31]

More often, application of a particular consequence outside of Title 13 depends on whether or not the juvenile is deemed "convicted" of an offense. Like adult convictions, typically juvenile adjudications involve a finding by the juvenile court that a juvenile has committed an offense.[32] However, unless otherwise stated, juvenile adjudications are not "convictions" for purposes of sentencing a juvenile outside Title 13.[33]

Consequences: Local Sanctions vs. Confinement to JRA

In Title 13 there are two general types of consequences for juveniles adjudicated of offenses. The first involves "local Sanctions" or "LS" for short.[34] Local sanctions are community based consequences wherein the juvenile remains in the community, or, is released after a short stay in the local juvenile detention facility. Local sanctions can include up to 30 days of confinement in detention, up to 12 months of community supervision, up to 150 hours of community restitution, and/or up to a $500 fine.

The second involves confinement to a Juvenile Rehabilitation Administration[35] facility or "JRA" for short. In this case the juvenile is confined to the custody of the Dept. of Social and Health

---

[29] RCW 13.04.450.
[30] Id.
[31] See, RCW 7.68.035(1)(b) and 9A.88.120(2).
[32] RCW 13.40.020(15); RCW 13.40.150(3).
[33] RCW 13.04.011(1).
[34] RCW 13.40.020(17).
[35] In 2013, the DSHS Juvenile Rehabilitation Administration was renamed the

The Caseload Forecast Council is not liable for errors or omissions in the manual, for sentences that may be inappropriately calculated as a result of a practitioner's or court's reliance on the manual, or for any other written or verbal information related to adult or juvenile sentencing. The scoring sheets are intended to provide assistance in most cases but does not cover all permutations of the scoring rules. If you find any errors or omissions, we encourage you to report them to the Caseload Forecast Council.

SECTION 1: JUVENILE DISPOSITION GUIDELINES

Services to serve more than 30 days of confinement in a facility operated by JRA.[36] Confinement in JRA is typically done for a number of weeks within a range ordered by the juvenile court.[37] In most instances, JRA will determine the amount of weeks within the range ordered and may provide parole services to the juvenile after release.

Multiple Juvenile Offenses

As stated earlier, the juvenile sentencing structure differs significantly from the adult system. One primary difference is how sentences for multiple offenses within a single disposition order, as well as across multiple disposition orders are served. There are also rules which limit the total amount of time that may be served among multiple offenses.

If a juvenile is sentenced for two or more offenses in a single disposition order, the disposition terms for each offense run consecutive to one another.[38] That includes community supervision, community restitution, and, any confinement imposed. For example: A juvenile sentenced for two assault counts is ordered to serve 6 months of supervision, 16 hours of community restitution, and 1 day of detention on each count. Those terms run consecutive to one another so the juvenile will have a total of 12 months supervision (6 x 2 = 12 months), 32 hours of community service (16 x 2 = 32 hours), and, 2 days of detention (1 x 2 = 2 days) total. Likewise, a juvenile facing two counts, each of which involves commitment to JRA, will serve those consecutively as well. For example, two counts each of which involves a standard range of 15 to 36 weeks at JRA will total a minimum of 30 weeks to a maximum of 72 weeks commitment.

In addition, where multiple offenses each impose less than 30 days of detention, but the aggregate total of all counts exceeds 30 days, the detention may be served at JRA at the discretion of the juvenile court.[39]

There are limitations however. First, the aggregate of all consecutive terms in a single disposition may not exceed three hundred percent (300%) of the term imposed for the most serious offense.[40] This is often referred to as the "300% rule". Keep in mind the rule does not allow for 300% of the maximum which the court *could* presumptively impose; rather, it presumes a total no greater than three times the term *actually imposed* by the court on the most serious offense. Logically, the 300% rule will only be relevant for those dispositions where there are four or more counts sentenced in a single disposition order. Sentencing three or less offenses will avoid application of the rule altogether.

---

[36] RCW 13.40.020(5) and RCW 13.40.185.
[37] RCW 13.40.0357.
[38] RCW 13.40.180(1).
[39] RCW 13.40.185(1).
[40] RCW 13.40.180(1)(b).

The Caseload Forecast Council is not liable for errors or omissions in the manual, for sentences that may be inappropriately calculated as a result of a practitioner's or court's reliance on the manual, or for any other written or verbal information related to adult or juvenile sentencing. The scoring sheets are intended to provide assistance in most cases but does not cover all permutations of the scoring rules. If you find any errors or omissions, we encourage you to report them to the Caseload Forecast Council.

SECTION 1: JUVENILE DISPOSITION GUIDELINES

Second, the aggregate of all consecutive terms of community supervision shall not exceed two years in length, or require payment of more than two hundred dollars in fines or the performance of more than two hundred hours of community restitution.[41]

Third, in very rare cases where multiple offenses are closely related to the same action, the aggregate disposition must not exceed one hundred fifty percent of the total imposed for the most serious offense.[42] This is often referred to as the "150% rule". In order for the 150% rule to apply, the offenses must either be committed through a single act or omission, or, through an act or omission which in itself constitutes one of the offenses and is also an element of the other. Because the 150% rule requires the offenses be similar, the fact patterns for application of the 150% rule are rare, but there are a few cases which discuss the rule's application should one encounter a potential issue.[43]

Finally, there is one exception to concurrent sentencing where a juvenile is sentenced across multiple disposition orders. Amongst multiple disposition orders, all terms will remain consecutive with the exception of supervision, which runs concurrent between separate disposition orders.[44]

Disposition Options for Juvenile Adjudications

There are several statutory options for sentencing a juvenile adjudicated of an offense in Title 13. Some cases may be excluded from a particular option based on the type of case, the juvenile's age, or the potential sentence. The juvenile disposition options are:

1. **Standard Range (RCW 13.40.0357 Option A)**

2. **Deferred Disposition (RCW 13.40.127)**

3. **Manifest Injustice (RCW 13.40.0357 Option D)**

4. **Suspended Disposition (four alternatives):**
   a. Suspended Disposition Alternative (RCW 13.40.0357 Option B)
   b. Chemical Dependency Disposition Alternative (RCW 13.40.0357 Option C)
   c. Special Sexual Offender Disposition Alternative (RCW 13.40.162)
   d. Mental Health Disposition Alternative (RCW 13.40.167)

Each option is explained below beginning with the standard range which should always be calculated first before considering other options.

---

[41] RCW 13.40.180(1)(c).
[42] RCW 13.40.180(1)(a).
[43] See, *State v. Contreras*, 124 P.2d 741, 880 P.2d 1000 (1994); and, *State v. S.S.Y.*, 150 Wn. App. 325, 207 P.3d 1273 (2009), affirmed and remanded. 170 Wn.2d 322, 241 P.3d 781 (2010).
[44] RCW 13.40.180(2).

The Caseload Forecast Council is not liable for errors or omissions in the manual, for sentences that may be inappropriately calculated as a result of a practitioner's or court's reliance on the manual, or for any other written or verbal information related to adult or juvenile sentencing. The scoring sheets are intended to provide assistance in most cases but does not cover all permutations of the scoring rules. If you find any errors or omissions, we encourage you to report them to the Caseload Forecast Council.

SECTION 1: JUVENILE DISPOSITION GUIDELINES

Standard Range (RCW 13.40.0357 Option A)

The standard range, or "Option A" in RCW 13.40.0357, is the most common disposition option in juvenile court. This is considered the presumptive sentence based on a juvenile's age and type of offense committed. Every juvenile offender is subject to imposition of the standard range, which the court must consider before determining a final disposition.[45] Therefore, the standard range should be calculated in every juvenile case regardless of what other disposition options may be available to a juvenile offender. A standard range sentence may not be appealed.[46]

In most cases, calculation of the standard range is done using a statutory grid in RCW 13.40.0357. The grid takes into account three variables: Type of offense, prior criminal history, and, age of the juvenile offender. An example of the grid found in RCW 13.40.0357 is shown below:

			OPTION A **JUVENILE OFFENDER SENTENCING GRID** **STANDARD RANGE**			
	A+	\multicolumn{5}{c}{180 weeks to age 21 for all category A+ offenses}				
	A	\multicolumn{5}{c}{103-129 weeks for all category A offenses}				
CURRENT OFFENSE CATAGORY	A-	15 - 36 WEEKS EXCEPT 30 - 40 WEEKS FOR 15 TO 17 YEAR OLDS	52 – 65 WEEKS	80 – 100 WEEKS	103 – 129 WEEKS	103 – 129 WEEKS
	B+	15 - 36 WEEKS	15 - 36 WEEKS	52 - 65 WEEKS	80 - 100 WEEKS	103 - 129 WEEKS
	B	LS	LS	15 – 36 WEEKS	15 – 36 WEEKS	52 – 65 WEEKS
	C+	LS	LS	LS	15 – 36 WEEKS	15 – 36 WEEKS
	C	LS	LS	LS	LS	15 – 36 WEEKS
	D+	LS	LS	LS	LS	LS
	D	LS	LS	LS	LS	LS
	E	LS	LS	LS	LS	LS
		0	1	2	3	4 or more
		\multicolumn{5}{c}{PRIOR ADJUDICATIONS}				

NOTE: References in the grid to days or weeks mean periods of confinement. "LS" means "local sanctions" as defined in RCW 13.40.020.

The vertical axis of the grid is the "current offense category" which is determined using a list of offenses also found in RCW 13.40.0357. The horizontal axis of the grid is the "prior adjudications" which is determined using the juvenile offender's criminal history. The standard range is found where the vertical and horizontal axes converge for a particular juvenile offender. Depending on where the axes converge, the standard range will consist of one of the two general

---

[45] See, RCW 13.40.150.
[46] RCW 13.40.160(2).

The Caseload Forecast Council is not liable for errors or omissions in the manual, for sentences that may be inappropriately calculated as a result of a practitioner's or court's reliance on the manual, or for any other written or verbal information related to adult or juvenile sentencing. The scoring sheets are intended to provide assistance in most cases but does not cover all permutations of the scoring rules. If you find any errors or omissions, we encourage you to report them to the Caseload Forecast Council.

SECTION 1: JUVENILE DISPOSITION GUIDELINES

consequences previously discussed: Either local sanctions ("LS") or a range of weeks confined to JRA.

Current Offense Category

The vertical axis of the grid sets the juvenile disposition category which is based on each current offense for which the juvenile offender is adjudicated. A short example of the list of current offense categories in RCW 13.40.0357 appears below:

DESCRIPTION AND OFFENSE CATEGORY

JUVENILE DISPOSITION OFFENSE CATEGORY	DESCRIPTION (RCW CITATION)	JUVENILE DISPOSITION CATEGORY FOR ATTEMPT, BAILJUMP, CONSPIRACY, OR SOLICITATION
	Arson and Malicious Mischief	
A	Arson 1 (9A.48.020)	B+
B	Arson 2 (9A.48.030)	C
C	Reckless Burning 1 (9A.48.040)	D
D	Reckless Burning 2 (9A.48.050)	E
B	Malicious Mischief 1 (9A.48.070)	C
C	Malicious Mischief 2 (9A.48.080)	D
D	Malicious Mischief 3 (9A.48.090)	E
E	Tampering with Fire Alarm Apparatus (9.40.100)	E
E	Tampering with Fire Alarm Apparatus with Intent to Commit Arson (9.40.105)	E
A	Possession of Incendiary Device (9.40.120)	B+

The above example shows only a small number of offenses but many more are listed specifically by name in RCW 13.40.0357. In the event the current offense is not listed by name, there is an "other offense" category to include any offense not otherwise listed.

In many cases the disposition category parallels the standard severity of the offense; but not always. For example, while Assault in the Second Degree is a class B felony, for purposes of juvenile disposition it is a B+ current offense category. Likewise, Vehicular Homicide is a class A felony, but a B+ current offense category. Therefore, the current offense category must always be determined using the list of offenses in RCW 13.40.0357.

The list in RCW 13.40.0357 contains two different categories for any offense. The first column to the left of the offense is the category for the principal offense. The second column to the right of the offense lists the category for any anticipatory version (attempt, conspiracy, or solicitation) or calculating bail jump from the same. For example, Arson 1 is a class A felony for disposition, but an attempt of the same crime, or a bail jump from that crime, would be a class B+ felony for disposition.

The Caseload Forecast Council is not liable for errors or omissions in the manual, for sentences that may be inappropriately calculated as a result of a practitioner's or court's reliance on the manual, or for any other written or verbal information related to adult or juvenile sentencing. The scoring sheets are intended to provide assistance in most cases but does not cover all permutations of the scoring rules. If you find any errors or omissions, we encourage you to report them to the Caseload Forecast Council.

SECTION 1: JUVENILE DISPOSITION GUIDELINES

Prior Adjudications

The horizontal axis of the grid is determined using the juvenile offender's criminal history to calculate the number of prior adjudications. Prior adjudications are those alleged offenses found correct by a court prior to commission of the current offense being calculated.[47] In other words, any previous offense for which the juvenile offender was adjudicated before he or she committed the current offense. Prior diversions do not count as prior adjudications because diversions do not involve a finding of guilt by a court. Offenses committed but not adjudicated prior to commission of the current offense do not count as prior adjudications.

Each prior adjudication is given a numbered "point" score depending on whether or not it involved a felony. Each prior felony adjudication counts as 1 whole point. However, if the prior adjudication involved a gross misdemeanor or misdemeanor offense, the adjudication only counts as a ¼ of a point (or .25 points). Points are added together and rounded down to the nearest full number to obtain the final score for all prior adjudications. So, for example, a person with one prior felony and three prior misdemeanors will have a prior adjudication score of 1 (not 1.75). A person with four prior felony adjudications will have a prior adjudication score of 4.

Prior adjudications do not affect the standard range for any current offense that is not a felony. Any current offense that is a misdemeanor or gross misdemeanor will always involve local sanctions regardless of the offender's prior adjudication score.

Finally, prior adjudications are never counted for purposes of determining standard range for a current offense of either Escape in the First Degree, or, Escape in the Second Degree. For each of those offenses the disposition offense category is a C, and, instead of the grid, the standard range is calculated using footnote 1 at the end of the offenses listed in RCW 13.40.0357. The calculation is based on the number of previous escapes or attempted escapes and ranges between 4 weeks and 12 weeks of confinement.

Firearm Enhancement

There are two special juvenile enhancements for firearm crimes. The first involves a disposition for Unlawful Possession of a Firearm where the offender is under 18 years old per RCW 9.41.030(2)(a)(iii). Disposition for that offense requires a minimum of 10 days confinement.[48] The second involves disposition for any current felony offense where there is a special allegation under RCW 13.40.196 alleging the juvenile offender is "armed with a firearm" during commission (except certain offenses where possession of a firearm is an element).[49] In that case there is an additional commitment time period to be served at JRA in addition to other sanctions.

---

[47] See, RCW 13.40.020(7).
[48] RCW 13.40.193(1).
[49] RCW 13.40.193(2)

The Caseload Forecast Council is not liable for errors or omissions in the manual, for sentences that may be inappropriately calculated as a result of a practitioner's or court's reliance on the manual, or for any other written or verbal information related to adult or juvenile sentencing. The scoring sheets are intended to provide assistance in most cases but does not cover all permutations of the scoring rules. If you find any errors or omissions, we encourage you to report them to the Caseload Forecast Council.

SECTION 1: JUVENILE DISPOSITION GUIDELINES

The additional commitment period is based on the level of offense: 6 months for class A offenses, 4 months for class B offenses, and, 2 months for class C offenses.

Motor Vehicle Minimums

There are minimum sentencing requirements for certain crimes involving motor vehicle theft (Theft of a Motor Vehicle, Possession of a Stolen Motor Vehicle, and, Taking a Motor Vehicle Without Owner's Permission). The minimum requirements for disposition of those offenses are set forth in RCW 13.40.308.

Deferred Disposition (RCW 13.40.127)

Deferred Disposition is an option available to many juveniles. This disposition option in RCW 13.40.127 allows an adjudicated juvenile to defer imposition of sentence and instead be placed on conditions of supervision for up to 12 months. The conditions of supervision can include up to 150 hours of community service and up to a $500 fine, but cannot include detention or commitment to JRA.[50] Because deferred disposition is not considered a final juvenile offense disposition or sentence, certain mandatory fines like crime victim's compensation, do not apply.[51] Likewise, because no detention or commitment time is allowed, the mandatory minimum sentences for vehicle crimes and firearms won't apply to deferred dispositions either.

First, the juvenile offender must qualify in order to request deferred disposition. There are a few limitations in the statute requiring the juvenile:

1. Is not charged with a sex or violent offense;
2. Has no prior felony history;
3. Has no prior deferred disposition; and/or,
4. Has no more than one prior adjudication.

Second, the juvenile must move for imposition of the deferred disposition at least 14 days prior to trial unless that time period is shortened for good cause. This limits use of the deferred disposition to cases where the juvenile has not yet been adjudicated guilty by means of a trial. In addition, the court may not impose a deferred disposition unless the juvenile agrees to it.[52]

Third, the juvenile must either stipulate to admission of the law enforcement reports or plead guilty to the offenses. The adjudication is limited to a finding of guilt based on either stipulation to the reports or the plea of guilt.

---

[50] *State v. I.K.C.*, 160 Wn. App. 660, 669, 248 P.3d 145 (2011).
[51] *State v. M.C.*, 148 Wn. App. 968, 972, 201 P.3d 413 (2009).
[52] *State v. Mohamoud*, 159 Wn.App. 753, 765, 246 P.3d 849 (2011).

The Caseload Forecast Council is not liable for errors or omissions in the manual, for sentences that may be inappropriately calculated as a result of a practitioner's or court's reliance on the manual, or for any other written or verbal information related to adult or juvenile sentencing. The scoring sheets are intended to provide assistance in most cases but does not cover all permutations of the scoring rules. If you find any errors or omissions, we encourage you to report them to the Caseload Forecast Council.

SECTION 1: JUVENILE DISPOSITION GUIDELINES

Fourth, should the juvenile offender fail to comply with the terms of the deferred disposition, the court may either treat the violation as a probation violation, or, in the alternative, may revoke the deferred disposition and impose another disposition option.

Finally, full payment of restitution is generally required in order for the court to dismiss and vacate the case later on. There is one exception, however, where the court finds the juvenile made a "good faith" effort to pay restitution, in which case the court may dismiss, vacate the conviction, and impose a new restitution order for any unpaid amount which remains enforceable the same as any other restitution order issued under RCW 13.40.190.

Upon completion of the deferred disposition conditions, the conviction is vacated and the case is dismissed (except for a charge of Animal Cruelty 1° which cannot be vacated). If the conditions are not satisfied by the end of supervision, the court can continue the case an additional 12 months for good cause; however, at any time the court finds the conditions have not been satisfied, the court can revoke the deferred disposition and impose a disposition order under one of the other sentencing options.

In addition to the benefit of having the case dismissed and vacated, so long as restitution is paid or not otherwise required, the dismissed deferred disposition will be subject to sealing at the time the juvenile is 18 years or older. This makes deferred disposition an attractive option for many juveniles.

Manifest Injustice (RCW 13.40.0357 Option D)

Manifest Injustice is a disposition outside of the standard range. In order to impose a manifest injustice disposition, the court must first find the standard range would be *manifestly unjust* either because a standard range sentence would be too excessive, or, too lenient in light of various factors.[53]

A manifest injustice sentence can only be imposed where the court finds by *clear and convincing evidence*[54] the standard range manifestly unjust[55]. In this case "clear and convincing evidence" is equivalent to "beyond a reasonable doubt."[56] The court must support the finding with circumstances applicable to the juvenile.

There is a list of statutory aggravating and mitigating circumstances set out in RCW 13.40.150(3). In addition to the statutory factors, a manifest injustice can be based on any additional "non-

---

[53] RCW 13.40.160(2); and, *State v. M.L.*, 134 Wn.2d 657, 660, 952 P.2d 187 (1998).
[54] *Id.*
[55] *Id.*
[56] *State v. Meade*, 129 Wn. App. 918, 922, 120 P.3d 975 (2005), citing, *State v. Rhoades*, 92 Wn.2d 755, 760, 600 P.2d 1264 (1979).

The Caseload Forecast Council is not liable for errors or omissions in the manual, for sentences that may be inappropriately calculated as a result of a practitioner's or court's reliance on the manual, or for any other written or verbal information related to adult or juvenile sentencing. The scoring sheets are intended to provide assistance in most cases but does not cover all permutations of the scoring rules. If you find any errors or omissions, we encourage you to report them to the Caseload Forecast Council.

SECTION 1: JUVENILE DISPOSITION GUIDELINES

statutory" factors peculiar to the juvenile and any pre-sentence report.[57] Because the court must provide adequate findings, a manifest injustice sentence may be appealed.[58]

A manifest injustice sentence must be determinate, meaning the court sets forth the terms of the sentence. Where a manifest injustice disposition involves local sanctions, the court sets the terms of confinement less than 30 days as well as any terms of community supervision. Likewise, where the manifest injustice would impose a term of confinement greater than 30 days on any offense, the court may set a determinate range of confinement to JRA, the minimum limited only by the security guidelines set out in RCW 13.40.030 (which limits the court to a minimum based on the percentage of the maximum time).[59]

This means a judge may sentence a juvenile to a range where both the maximum and minimum are the same.[60] Where the maximum and minimum are not the same, then the minimum can be any number of weeks so long as the minimum is not lower than that allowed by computation under the security guidelines in RCW 13.40.030.[61]

A manifest injustice can provide authority for a court to supervise, detain, or commit a juvenile up to age 21.[62] However, regardless of that authority, the juvenile may not be detained or committed for a period that is longer than that which an adult would receive for the same offense.[63]

Suspended Disposition Alternatives

There are four "alternative" dispositions which allow a court to impose a sentence, and then suspend that sentence in favor of a community based local sanctions disposition. These four alternatives are based on compliance with appropriate treatment goals. Provided the juvenile maintains compliance, the suspended sentence is not served. However, should the offender violate the community based disposition, the court has the option of revoking the suspended disposition in which case the original sentence goes into effect. Other than the four alternatives mentioned, the court has no authority to suspend imposition of a juvenile sentence.[64]

   1. **Suspended Disposition Alternative (Option B)**

   The Suspended Disposition Alternative is a treatment based suspended sentence set forth under "Option B" of RCW 13.40.0357. The offender must be subject to a standard range disposition involving confinement by JRA and the court must find the offender and community would benefit from the use of a suspended

---

[57] *Rhoads*, 92 Wn.2d at 759, citing, *In Re Luft*, 21 Wn. App. 841, 589 P.2d 314 (1979).
[58] RCW 13.40.160(2).
[59] RCW 13.40.160(2).
[60] *State v. Beaver*, 148 Wn.2d 338, 350, 60 P.3d 586 (2002).
[61] *Id.*
[62] See, RCW 13.40.300.
[63] RCW 13.40.160(11).
[64] RCW 13.40.160(10).

The Caseload Forecast Council is not liable for errors or omissions in the manual, for sentences that may be inappropriately calculated as a result of a practitioner's or court's reliance on the manual, or for any other written or verbal information related to adult or juvenile sentencing. The scoring sheets are intended to provide assistance in most cases but does not cover all permutations of the scoring rules. If you find any errors or omissions, we encourage you to report them to the Caseload Forecast Council.

SECTION 1: JUVENILE DISPOSITION GUIDELINES

disposition. In this case the court may impose the standard range and suspend execution of the disposition on condition the offender comply with one or more local sanctions and any educational or treatment requirement. The treatment programs provided to the offender must be research-based best practice programs.

These programs must qualify as either: a) Programs approved by the Washington State Institute for Public Policy or the Joint Legislative Audit and Review Committee; or, b) In the case of chemical dependency treatment, evidence based or research based best practice programs. Note: These programs will not be available in every county.

If the offender fails to comply with the suspended disposition condition(s), the court may impose sanctions pursuant to RCW 13.40.200 or may revoke the suspended disposition and order the disposition's execution.

An offender is ineligible for SSODA if the offender:

1) Committed a category A+ offense; or,
2) Is fourteen years or older and committed any of the following offenses:
    a) a category A offense (completed and anticipatory) r
    b) Manslaughter in the first degree
    c) Assault in the second degree
    d) Extortion in the first degree
    e) Robbery in the second degree
    f) Residential Burglary
    g) Burglary in the second degree
    h) Drive-by Shooting
    i) Vehicle Homicide (RCW 46.61.520)
    j) Hit and Run Death (RCW 46.52.020(4)(a))
    k) Intimidating a Witness (RCW 9A.72.110)
    l) Violation of the Uniform Controlled Substance Act
    m) Manslaughter2, when the offense includes infliction of bodily harm upon another or when during the commission or immediate withdrawal from the offense the respondent was armed with a deadly weapon
3) Is ordered to serve a disposition for a firearm violation under RCW 13.40.193
4) Committed a sex offense as defined in RCW 9.94A.030.

2. The Chemical Dependency Disposition Alternative (Option C)

The Chemical Dependency Disposition Alternative, a.k.a. "CDDA", is primarily a substance abuse treatment based suspended sentence set forth under "Option

SECTION 1: JUVENILE DISPOSITION GUIDELINES

C" of RCW 13.40.0357 as well as RCW 13.40.165, which contains most of the requirements for this suspended disposition alternative.

The court must consider eligibility for CCDA whenever the offender is subject to a standard range disposition of either local sanctions, or, 15 to 36 weeks of confinement, and, has not committed a category A- or B+ offense. Provided the court finds the offender is chemically dependent and amenable to treatment, the court may either impose a disposition within the standard range, or, where appropriate, impose a manifest injustice sentence (up to 52 weeks or as otherwise limited by that which an adult could receive), and, thereafter suspend that disposition, and, impose a community based disposition including up to 12 months of community supervision, up to 150 hours of community service, up to 30 days of detention, and, payment of restitution. As a condition of supervision, the court must require the offender undergo available inpatient/outpatient drug or alcohol treatment.

The combination of inpatient treatment and confinement may not exceed 90 days. The treatment provider must submit monthly progress reports and the court may schedule treatment review hearings. The suspension may be revoked and the disposition executed (with credit for confinement time served on the same offense) for violating conditions or failing to make satisfactory progress in treatment.

A CCDA disposition is not appealable.[65]

3. Special Sex Offender Disposition Alternative (RCW 13.40.162 SSODA)

The Special Sex Offender Disposition Alternative, a.k.a. "SSODA", is primarily a sexual deviancy treatment based suspended sentence set forth in RCW 13.40.162.

The offender must have committed a sex offense, other than a sex offense that is also a serious violent offense as defined in RCW 9.94A.030, and must have no history of sex offense(s). The court may order an examination to determine whether the offender is amenable to treatment. If, following such an examination, the court determines the offender and the community would benefit from the use of the SSODA, the court may either impose a determinate disposition within the standard range,[66] or, in the alternative, impose a manifest injustice and, thereafter, suspend execution of the disposition and place the

---

[65] RCW 13.40.165(10).
[66] Imposition of the standard range in a SSODA must be a determinate number within the range; not the range itself. *State v. Linssen*, 131 Wn. App. 292, 296, 126 P.3 1287 (2006).

The Caseload Forecast Council is not liable for errors or omissions in the manual, for sentences that may be inappropriately calculated as a result of a practitioner's or court's reliance on the manual, or for any other written or verbal information related to adult or juvenile sentencing. The scoring sheets are intended to provide assistance in most cases but does not cover all permutations of the scoring rules. If you find any errors or omissions, we encourage you to report them to the Caseload Forecast Council.

SECTION 1: JUVENILE DISPOSITION GUIDELINES

offender on community supervision for at least two years. The court may impose conditions of community supervision and other conditions, including up to thirty days of confinement and requirements that the offender:

- Devote time to specific education, employment, or occupation;
- Undergo available outpatient sex offender treatment for up to two years, or inpatient treatment sex offender treatment not to exceed the standard range of confinement for that offense;
- Remain within prescribed geographical boundaries and notify the court or the probation counselor prior to any change of address, educational program or employment;
- Report to the prosecutor and the probation counselor prior to any change in a sex offender treatment provider (Prior approval by the court is required for any change);
- Report as directed to the court and a probation counselor;
- Pay all court-ordered legal financial obligations, perform community service, or any combination thereof;
- Make restitution to the victim for counseling costs reasonably related to the offense;
- Comply with the conditions of any court-ordered probation bond; or
- The court shall order that the offender may not attend the public or approved private elementary, middle or high school attended by the victim or the victim's siblings.

A disposition entered under the SSODA option may not be appealed.[67]

4. Mental Health Disposition Alternative (RCW 13.40.167)

The Mental Health Disposition Alternative, a.k.a. "MHDA", is primarily a mental health treatment based suspended sentence set forth in RCW 13.40.167.

In order to qualify, the offender must be subject to a standard range commitment to JRA (any range). In addition, the offender must have a current diagnosis consistent with the American Psychiatry Association Diagnostic and Statistical Manual of Mental Disorders, of axis I psychiatric disorder, excluding youth that are diagnosed as solely having a conduct disorder, oppositional defiant disorder, substance abuse disorder, paraphilia, or pedophilia. In addition, there must be appropriate treatment available in the local community that can meet the demands and requirements in RCW 13.40.167. Note: many if most Washington

---

[67] RCW 13.40.162(10).

The Caseload Forecast Council is not liable for errors or omissions in the manual, for sentences that may be inappropriately calculated as a result of a practitioner's or court's reliance on the manual, or for any other written or verbal information related to adult or juvenile sentencing. The scoring sheets are intended to provide assistance in most cases but does not cover all permutations of the scoring rules. If you find any errors or omissions, we encourage you to report them to the Caseload Forecast Council.

SECTION 1: JUVENILE DISPOSITION GUIDELINES

State Counties will not have the necessary local treatment due to budgetary restraints.

In addition, an offender is ineligible for the MHDA if:

1) The offender is ordered to serve a disposition for a firearm violation under RCW 13.40.193; or

2) The offense for which the disposition is being considered is:

   (i) An offense category A+, A, or A- offense, or an attempt, conspiracy, or solicitation to commit a class A+, A, or A- offense;

   (ii) Manslaughter in the second degree (RCW 9A.32.070);

   (iii) A sex offense as defined in RCW 9.94A.030; or

   (iv) Any offense category B+ or B offense, when the offense includes infliction of bodily harm upon another or when during the commission or immediate withdrawal from the offense the respondent was armed with a deadly weapon.

There are a number of other specific considerations the court must consider prior to ordering the MHDA, including the opinion of the victim. If qualified, the court may impose conditions of community supervision for up to 12 months, and other conditions, including up to thirty days of confinement and requirements that the offender abide by the treatment plan, including conditions the offender:

- Undergo available treatment in the local community
- Devote time to educational and vocational pursuits.
- Participate in alcohol and chemical dependency assessments to identify co-occurring disorders.
- Report to the court and probation counselor as directed.
- Pay court ordered financial obligations.

SECTION 2

RCW 13.40: JUVENILE JUSTICE ACT OF 1977, AS AMENDED

RCW 13.40.010 Short title — Intent — Purpose.

(1) This chapter shall be known and cited as the Juvenile Justice Act of 1977.

(2) It is the intent of the legislature that a system capable of having primary responsibility for, being accountable for, and responding to the needs of youthful offenders and their victims, as defined by this chapter, be established. It is the further intent of the legislature that youth, in turn, be held accountable for their offenses and that communities, families, and the juvenile courts carry out their functions consistent with this intent. To effectuate these policies, the legislature declares the following to be equally important purposes of this chapter:

(a) Protect the citizenry from criminal behavior;

(b) Provide for determining whether accused juveniles have committed offenses as defined by this chapter;

(c) Make the juvenile offender accountable for his or her criminal behavior;

(d) Provide for punishment commensurate with the age, crime, and criminal history of the juvenile offender;

(e) Provide due process for juveniles alleged to have committed an offense;

(f) Provide necessary treatment, supervision, and custody for juvenile offenders;

(g) Provide for the handling of juvenile offenders by communities whenever consistent with public safety;

(h) Provide for restitution to victims of crime;

(i) Develop effective standards and goals for the operation, funding, and evaluation of all components of the juvenile justice system and related services at the state and local levels;

(j) Provide for a clear policy to determine what types of offenders shall receive punishment,

SECTION 2: RCW 13.40: JUVENILE JUSTICE ACT OF 1977, AS AMENDED

treatment, or both, and to determine the jurisdictional limitations of the courts, institutions, and community services;

(k) Provide opportunities for victim participation in juvenile justice process, including court hearings on juvenile offender matters, and ensure that Article I, section 35 of the Washington state Constitution, the victim bill of rights, is fully observed; and

(l) Encourage the parents, guardian, or custodian of the juvenile to actively participate in the juvenile justice process.

[2004 c 120 § 1; 1997 c 338 § 8; 1992 c 205 § 101; 1977 ex.s. c 291 § 55.]

RCW 13.40.020 Definitions

For the purposes of this chapter:

(1) "Community-based rehabilitation" means one or more of the following: Employment; attendance of information classes; literacy classes; counseling, outpatient substance abuse treatment programs, outpatient mental health programs, anger management classes, education or outpatient treatment programs to prevent animal cruelty, or other services; or attendance at school or other educational programs appropriate for the juvenile as determined by the school district. Placement in community-based rehabilitation programs is subject to available funds;

(2) "Community-based sanctions" may include one or more of the following:

(a) A fine, not to exceed five hundred dollars;

(b) Community restitution not to exceed one hundred fifty hours of community restitution;

(3) "Community restitution" means compulsory service, without compensation, performed for the benefit of the community by the offender as punishment for committing an offense. Community restitution may be performed through public or private organizations or through work crews;

(4) "Community supervision" means an order of disposition by the court of an adjudicated youth not committed to the department or an order granting a deferred disposition. A community supervision order for a single offense may be for a period of up to two years for a sex offense as defined by RCW 9.94A.030 and up to one year for other offenses. As a mandatory condition of any term of community supervision, the court shall order the juvenile to refrain from committing new offenses. As a mandatory condition of community supervision, the court shall order the juvenile to comply with the mandatory school attendance provisions of chapter 28A.225 RCW and to inform the school of the existence of this requirement. Community supervision is an individualized program comprised of one or more of the following:

SECTION 2: RCW 13.40: JUVENILE JUSTICE ACT OF 1977, AS AMENDED

(a) Community-based sanctions;

(b) Community-based rehabilitation;

(c) Monitoring and reporting requirements;

(d) Posting of a probation bond;

(5) "Confinement" means physical custody by the department of social and health services in a facility operated by or pursuant to a contract with the state, or physical custody in a detention facility operated by or pursuant to a contract with any county. The county may operate or contract with vendors to operate county detention facilities. The department may operate or contract to operate detention facilities for juveniles committed to the department. Pretrial confinement or confinement of less than thirty-one days imposed as part of a disposition or modification order may be served consecutively or intermittently, in the discretion of the court;

(6) "Court," when used without further qualification, means the juvenile court judge(s) or commissioner(s);

(7) "Criminal history" includes all criminal complaints against the respondent for which, prior to the commission of a current offense:

(a) The allegations were found correct by a court. If a respondent is convicted of two or more charges arising out of the same course of conduct, only the highest charge from among these shall count as an offense for the purposes of this chapter; or

(b) The criminal complaint was diverted by a prosecutor pursuant to the provisions of this chapter on agreement of the respondent and after an advisement to the respondent that the criminal complaint would be considered as part of the respondent's criminal history. A successfully completed deferred adjudication that was entered before July 1, 1998, or a deferred disposition shall not be considered part of the respondent's criminal history;

(8) "Department" means the department of social and health services;

(9) "Detention facility" means a county facility, paid for by the county, for the physical confinement of a juvenile alleged to have committed an offense or an adjudicated offender subject to a disposition or modification order. "Detention facility" includes county group homes, inpatient substance abuse programs, juvenile basic training camps, and electronic monitoring;

(10) "Diversion unit" means any probation counselor who enters into a diversion agreement with an alleged youthful offender, or any other person, community accountability board, youth court under the supervision of the juvenile court, or other entity except a law enforcement official or

SECTION 2: RCW 13.40: JUVENILE JUSTICE ACT OF 1977, AS AMENDED

entity, with whom the juvenile court administrator has contracted to arrange and supervise such agreements pursuant to RCW 13.40.080, or any person, community accountability board, or other entity specially funded by the legislature to arrange and supervise diversion agreements in accordance with the requirements of this chapter. For purposes of this subsection, "community accountability board" means a board comprised of members of the local community in which the juvenile offender resides. The superior court shall appoint the members. The boards shall consist of at least three and not more than seven members. If possible, the board should include a variety of representatives from the community, such as a law enforcement officer, teacher or school administrator, high school student, parent, and business owner, and should represent the cultural diversity of the local community;

(11) "Foster care" means temporary physical care in a foster family home or group care facility as defined in RCW 74.15.020 and licensed by the department, or other legally authorized care;

(12) "Institution" means a juvenile facility established pursuant to chapters 72.05 and 72.16 through 72.20 RCW;

(13) "Intensive supervision program" means a parole program that requires intensive supervision and monitoring, offers an array of individualized treatment and transitional services, and emphasizes community involvement and support in order to reduce the likelihood a juvenile offender will commit further offenses;

(14) "Juvenile," "youth," and "child" mean any individual who is under the chronological age of eighteen years and who has not been previously transferred to adult court pursuant to RCW 13.40.110, unless the individual was convicted of a lesser charge or acquitted of the charge for which he or she was previously transferred pursuant to RCW 13.40.110 or who is not otherwise under adult court jurisdiction;

(15) "Juvenile offender" means any juvenile who has been found by the juvenile court to have committed an offense, including a person eighteen years of age or older over whom jurisdiction has been extended under RCW 13.40.300;

(16) "Labor" means the period of time before a birth during which contractions are of sufficient frequency, intensity, and duration to bring about effacement and progressive dilation of the cervix;

(17) "Local sanctions" means one or more of the following: (a) 0-30 days of confinement; (b) 0-12 months of community supervision; (c) 0-150 hours of community restitution; or (d) $0-$500 fine;

(18) "Manifest injustice" means a disposition that would either impose an excessive penalty on the juvenile or would impose a serious, and clear danger to society in light of the purposes of this chapter;

The Caseload Forecast Council is not liable for errors or omissions in the manual, for sentences that may be inappropriately calculated as a result of a practitioner's or court's reliance on the manual, or for any other written or verbal information related to adult or juvenile sentencing. The scoring sheets are intended to provide assistance in most cases but does not cover all permutations of the scoring rules. If you find any errors or omissions, we encourage you to report them to the Caseload Forecast Council.

SECTION 2: RCW 13.40: JUVENILE JUSTICE ACT OF 1977, AS AMENDED

(19) "Monitoring and reporting requirements" means one or more of the following: Curfews; requirements to remain at home, school, work, or court-ordered treatment programs during specified hours; restrictions from leaving or entering specified geographical areas; requirements to report to the probation officer as directed and to remain under the probation officer's supervision; and other conditions or limitations as the court may require which may not include confinement;

(20) "Offense" means an act designated a violation or a crime if committed by an adult under the law of this state, under any ordinance of any city or county of this state, under any federal law, or under the law of another state if the act occurred in that state;

(21) "Physical restraint" means the use of any bodily force or physical intervention to control a juvenile offender or limit a juvenile offender's freedom of movement in a way that does not involve a mechanical restraint. Physical restraint does not include momentary periods of minimal physical restriction by direct person-to-person contact, without the aid of mechanical restraint, accomplished with limited force and designed to:

(a) Prevent a juvenile offender from completing an act that would result in potential bodily harm to self or others or damage property;

(b) Remove a disruptive juvenile offender who is unwilling to leave the area voluntarily; or

(c) Guide a juvenile offender from one location to another;

(22) "Postpartum recovery" means (a) the entire period a woman or youth is in the hospital, birthing center, or clinic after giving birth and (b) an additional time period, if any, a treating physician determines is necessary for healing after the youth leaves the hospital, birthing center, or clinic;

(23) "Probation bond" means a bond, posted with sufficient security by a surety justified and approved by the court, to secure the offender's appearance at required court proceedings and compliance with court-ordered community supervision or conditions of release ordered pursuant to RCW 13.40.040 or 13.40.050. It also means a deposit of cash or posting of other collateral in lieu of a bond if approved by the court;

(24) "Respondent" means a juvenile who is alleged or proven to have committed an offense;

(25) "Restitution" means financial reimbursement by the offender to the victim, and shall be limited to easily ascertainable damages for injury to or loss of property, actual expenses incurred for medical treatment for physical injury to persons, lost wages resulting from physical injury, and costs of the victim's counseling reasonably related to the offense. Restitution shall not include reimbursement for damages for mental anguish, pain and suffering, or other intangible

SECTION 2: RCW 13.40: JUVENILE JUSTICE ACT OF 1977, AS AMENDED

losses. Nothing in this chapter shall limit or replace civil remedies or defenses available to the victim or offender;

(26) "Restorative justice" means practices, policies, and programs informed by and sensitive to the needs of crime victims that are designed to encourage offenders to accept responsibility for repairing the harm caused by their offense by providing safe and supportive opportunities for voluntary participation and communication between the victim, the offender, their families, and relevant community members;

(27) "Restraints" means anything used to control the movement of a person's body or limbs and includes:

(a) Physical restraint; or

(b) Mechanical device including but not limited to: Metal handcuffs, plastic ties, ankle restraints, leather cuffs, other hospital-type restraints, tasers, or batons;

(28) "Secretary" means the secretary of the department of social and health services. "Assistant secretary" means the assistant secretary for juvenile rehabilitation for the department;

(29) "Services" means services which provide alternatives to incarceration for those juveniles who have pleaded or been adjudicated guilty of an offense or have signed a diversion agreement pursuant to this chapter;

(30) "Sex offense" means an offense defined as a sex offense in RCW 9.94A.030;

(31) "Sexual motivation" means that one of the purposes for which the respondent committed the offense was for the purpose of his or her sexual gratification;

(32) "Surety" means an entity licensed under state insurance laws or by the state department of licensing, to write corporate, property, or probation bonds within the state, and justified and approved by the superior court of the county having jurisdiction of the case;

(33) "Transportation" means the conveying, by any means, of an incarcerated pregnant youth from the institution or detention facility to another location from the moment she leaves the institution or detention facility to the time of arrival at the other location, and includes the escorting of the pregnant incarcerated youth from the institution or detention facility to a transport vehicle and from the vehicle to the other location;

(34) "Violation" means an act or omission, which if committed by an adult, must be proven beyond a reasonable doubt, and is punishable by sanctions which do not include incarceration;

(35) "Violent offense" means a violent offense as defined in RCW 9.94A.030;

SECTION 2: RCW 13.40: JUVENILE JUSTICE ACT OF 1977, AS AMENDED

(36) "Youth court" means a diversion unit under the supervision of the juvenile court.

[2012 c 201 § 1; 2010 c 181 § 10; 2009 c 454 § 2; 2004 c 120 § 2. Prior: 2002 c 237 § 7; 2002 c 175 § 19; 1997 c 338 § 10; (1997 c 338 § 9 expired July 1, 1998); prior: 1995 c 395 § 2; 1995 c 134 § 1; prior: 1994 sp.s. c 7 § 520; 1994 c 271 § 803; 1994 c 261 § 18; 1993 c 373 § 1; 1990 1st ex.s. c 12 § 1; 1990 c 3 § 301; 1989 c 407 § 1; 1988 c 145 § 17; 1983 c 191 § 7; 1981 c 299 § 2; 1979 c 155 § 54; 1977 ex.s. c 291 § 56.]

RCW 13.40.030 Security guidelines — Legislative review — Limitations on permissible ranges of confinement

(1) The secretary shall submit guidelines pertaining to the nature of the security to be imposed on youth placed in his or her custody based on the age, offense(s), and criminal history of the juvenile offender. Such guidelines shall be submitted to the legislature for its review no later than November 1st of each year. The department shall include security status definitions in the security guidelines it submits to the legislature pursuant to this section.

(2) The permissible ranges of confinement resulting from a finding of manifest injustice under RCW

13.40.0357 are subject to the following limitations:

(a) Where the maximum term in the range is ninety days or less, the minimum term in the range may be no less than fifty percent of the maximum term in the range;

(b) Where the maximum term in the range is greater than ninety days but not greater than one year, the minimum term in the range may be no less than seventy-five percent of the maximum term in the range; and

(c) Where the maximum term in the range is more than one year, the minimum term in the range may be no less than eighty percent of the maximum term in the range.

[2003 c 207 § 5; 1996 c 232 § 5; 1989 c 407 § 3; 1985 c 73 § 1; 1983 c 191 § 6; 1981 c 299 § 5; 1979 c 155 § 55; 1977 ex.s. c 291 § 57.]

RCW 13.40.0351 Equal application of guidelines and standards.

The sentencing guidelines and prosecuting standards apply equally to juvenile offenders in all parts of the state, without discrimination as to any element that does not relate to the crime or the previous record of the offender.

The Caseload Forecast Council is not liable for errors or omissions in the manual, for sentences that may be inappropriately calculated as a result of a practitioner's or court's reliance on the manual, or for any other written or verbal information related to adult or juvenile sentencing. The scoring sheets are intended to provide assistance in most cases but does not cover all permutations of the scoring rules. If you find any errors or omissions, we encourage you to report them to the Caseload Forecast Council.

SECTION 2: RCW 13.40: JUVENILE JUSTICE ACT OF 1977, AS AMENDED

[1989 c 407 § 5.]

RCW 13.40.0357 Juvenile offender sentencing standards. (Effective until July 22, 2007.)

JUVENILE DISPOSITION OFFENSE CATEGORY	DESCRIPTION (RCW CITATION)	JUVENILE DISPOSITION CATEGORY FOR ATTEMPT, BAILJUMP, CONSPIRACY, OR SOLICITATION
Arson and Malicious Mischief		
A	Arson 1 (9A.48.020)	B+
B	Arson 2 (9A.48.030)	C
B	Malicious Mischief 1 (9A.48.070)	C
C	Malicious Mischief 2 (9A.48.080)	D
D	Malicious Mischief 3 (9A.48.090)	E
A	Possession of Incendiary Device (9.40.120)	B+
C	Reckless Burning 1 (9A.48.040)	D
D	Reckless Burning 2 (9A.48.050)	E
E	Tampering with Fire Alarm Apparatus (9.40.100)	E
E	Tampering with Fire Alarm Apparatus with Intent to Commit Arson (9.40.105)	E
Assault and Other Crimes Involving Physical Harm		
A	Assault 1 (9A.36.011)	B+
B+	Assault 2 (9A.36.021)	C+
C+	Assault 3 (9A.36.031)	D+
D+	Assault 4 (9A.36.041)	E
D+	Coercion (9A.36.070)	E
C+	Custodial Assault (9A.36.100)	D+
B+	Drive-By Shooting (9A.36.045)	C+
C+	Promoting Suicide Attempt (9A.36.060)	D+
D+	Reckless Endangerment (9A.36.050)	E
Burglary and Trespass		
B+	Burglary 1 (9A.52.020)	C+
B	Burglary 2 (9A.52.030)	C

The Caseload Forecast Council is not liable for errors or omissions in the manual, for sentences that may be inappropriately calculated as a result of a practitioner's or court's reliance on the manual, or for any other written or verbal information related to adult or juvenile sentencing. The scoring sheets are intended to provide assistance in most cases but does not cover all permutations of the scoring rules. If you find any errors or omissions, we encourage you to report them to the Caseload Forecast Council.

SECTION 2: RCW 13.40: JUVENILE JUSTICE ACT OF 1977, AS AMENDED

D	Burglary Tools (Possession of) (9A.52.060)	E
D	Criminal Trespass 1 (9A.52.070)	E
E	Criminal Trespass 2 (9A.52.080)	E
C	Mineral Trespass (78.44.330)	C
B	Residential Burglary (9A.52.025)	C
C	Vehicle Prowling 1 (9A.52.095)	D
D	Vehicle Prowling 2 (9A.52.100)	E

Drugs

C	Fraudulently Obtaining Controlled Substance (69.50.403)	C
C	Illegally Obtaining Legend Drug (69.41.020)	D
E	Possession of Legend Drug (69.41.030(2)(b))	E
E	Possession of Marihuana <40 grams (69.50.4014)	E
E	Possession/Consumption of Alcohol (66.44.270)	E
C+	Sale of Controlled Substance for Profit (69.50.410)	C+
C+	Sale, Delivery, Possession of Legend Drug with Intent to Sell (69.41.030(2)(a))	D+
E	Unlawful Inhalation (9.47A.020)	E
B	Violation of Uniform Controlled Substances Act - Narcotic, Methamphetamine, or Flunitrazepam Counterfeit Substances (69.50.4011(2) (a) or (b))	B
B+	Violation of Uniform Controlled Substances Act - Narcotic, Methamphetamine, or Flunitrazepam Sale (69.50.401(2) (a) or (b))	B+
C	Violation of Uniform Controlled Substances Act - Nonnarcotic Counterfeit Substances (69.50.4011(2) (c), (d), or (e))	C
C	Violation of Uniform Controlled Substances Act - Nonnarcotic Sale (69.50.401(2)(c))	C
C	Violation of Uniform Controlled Substances Act - Possession of a Controlled Substance (69.50.4012)	C
C	Violation of Uniform Controlled Substances Act - Possession of a Controlled Substance (69.50.4013)	C

Firearms and Weapons

E	Carrying Loaded Pistol Without Permit (9.41.050)	E
D	Intimidating Another Person by use of Weapon (9.41.270)	E
D+	Possession of Dangerous Weapon (9.41.250)	E
C	Possession of Firearms by Minor (<18) (9.41.040(2)(a)(iii))	C

The Caseload Forecast Council is not liable for errors or omissions in the manual, for sentences that may be inappropriately calculated as a result of a practitioner's or court's reliance on the manual, or for any other written or verbal information related to adult or juvenile sentencing. The scoring sheets are intended to provide assistance in most cases but does not cover all permutations of the scoring rules. If you find any errors or omissions, we encourage you to report them to the Caseload Forecast Council.

SECTION 2: RCW 13.40: JUVENILE JUSTICE ACT OF 1977, AS AMENDED

B	Possession of Stolen Firearm (9A.56.310)	C
B	Theft of Firearm (9A.56.300)	C
	Homicide	
B+	Manslaughter 1 (9A.32.060)	C+
C+	Manslaughter 2 (9A.32.070)	D+
A+	Murder 1 (9A.32.030)	A
A+	Murder 2 (9A.32.050)	B+
B+	Vehicular Homicide (46.61.520)	C+
	Kidnapping	
A	Kidnap 1 (9A.40.020)	B+
B+	Kidnap 2 (9A.40.030)	C+
C+	Unlawful Imprisonment (9A.40.040)	D+
	Obstructing Governmental Operation	
B+	Intimidating a Public Servant (9A.76.180)	C+
B+	Intimidating a Witness (9A.72.110)	C+
B	Introducing Contraband 1 (9A.76.140)	C
C	Introducing Contraband 2 (9A.76.150)	D
E	Introducing Contraband 3 (9A.76.160)	E
D	Obstructing a Law Enforcement Officer (9A.76.020)	E
E	Resisting Arrest (9A.76.040)	E
	Public Disturbance	
E	Disorderly Conduct (9A.84.030)	E
E	Failure to Disperse (9A.84.020)	E
C+	Riot with Weapon (9A.84.010(2)(b)) [before 1/1/2014]	D+
D+	Riot Without Weapon (9A.84.010(2)(a)) [before 1/1/2014]	E
C+	Criminal Mischief with Weapon (9A.84.010(2)(b)) [as of 1/1/2014]	D+
D+	Criminal Mischief Without Weapon (9A.84.010(2)(a)) [as of 1/1/2014]	E
	Sex Crimes	
A-	Child Molestation 1 (9A.44.083)	B+
B	Child Molestation 2 (9A.44.086)	C+
B	Incest 1 (9A.64.020(1))	C
C	Incest 2 (9A.64.020(2))	D
D+	Indecent Exposure (Victim <14) (9A.88.010)	E
E	Indecent Exposure (Victim 14 or over) (9A.88.010)	E
B+	Indecent Liberties (9A.44.100)	C+

The Caseload Forecast Council is not liable for errors or omissions in the manual, for sentences that may be inappropriately calculated as a result of a practitioner's or court's reliance on the manual, or for any other written or verbal information related to adult or juvenile sentencing. The scoring sheets are intended to provide assistance in most cases but does not cover all permutations of the scoring rules. If you find any errors or omissions, we encourage you to report them to the Caseload Forecast Council.

SECTION 2: RCW 13.40: JUVENILE JUSTICE ACT OF 1977, AS AMENDED

E	O & A (Prostitution) (9A.88.030)	E
B+	Promoting Prostitution 1 (9A.88.070)	C+
C+	Promoting Prostitution 2 (9A.88.080)	D+
A	Rape 1 (9A.44.040)	B+
A-	Rape 2 (9A.44.050)	B+
C+	Rape 3 (9A.44.060)	D+
A-	Rape of a Child 1 (9A.44.073)	B+
B+	Rape of a Child 2 (9A.44.076)	C+

Theft, Robbery, Extortion, and Forgery

B+	Extortion 1 (9A.56.120)	C+
C+	Extortion 2 (9A.56.130)	D+
C	Forgery (9A.60.020)	D
C	Identity Theft 1 (9.35.020(2))	D
D	Identity Theft 2 (9.35.020(3))	E
D	Improperly Obtaining Financial Information (9.35.010)	E
B	Possession of a Stolen Vehicle (9A.56.068)	C
B	Possession of Stolen Property 1 (9A.56.150)	C
C	Possession of Stolen Property 2 (9A.56.160)	D
D	Possession of Stolen Property 3 (9A.56.170)	E
A	Robbery 1 (9A.56.200)	B+
B+	Robbery 2 (9A.56.210)	C+
B	Theft 1 (9A.56.030)	C
C	Theft 2 (9A.56.040)	D
D	Theft 3 (9A.56.050)	E
B	Theft of Livestock 1 and 2 (9A.56.080 and 9A.56.083)	C

Motor Vehicle Related Crimes

C	Attempting to Elude Pursuing Police Vehicle (46.61.024)	D
D	Driving While Under the Influence (46.61.502 and 46.61.504)	E
E	Driving Without a License (46.20.005)	E
B+	Hit and Run - Death (46.52.020(4)(a))	C+
C	Hit and Run - Injury (46.52.020(4)(b))	D
D	Hit and Run-Attended (46.52.020(5))	E
E	Hit and Run-Unattended (46.52.010)	E
E	Reckless Driving (46.61.500)	E
C	Vehicular Assault (46.61.522)	D

Other

The Caseload Forecast Council is not liable for errors or omissions in the manual, for sentences that may be inappropriately calculated as a result of a practitioner's or court's reliance on the manual, or for any other written or verbal information related to adult or juvenile sentencing. The scoring sheets are intended to provide assistance in most cases but does not cover all permutations of the scoring rules. If you find any errors or omissions, we encourage you to report them to the Caseload Forecast Council.

SECTION 2: RCW 13.40: JUVENILE JUSTICE ACT OF 1977, AS AMENDED

B	Animal Cruelty 1 (16.52.205)	C
B	Bomb Threat (9.61.160)	C
C	Escape 1¹ (9A.76.110)	C
C	Escape 2¹ (9A.76.120)	C
D	Escape 3 (9A.76.130)	E
E	Obscene, Harassing, Etc., Phone Calls (9.61.230)	E
A	Other Offense Equivalent to an Adult Class A Felony	B+
B	Other Offense Equivalent to an Adult Class B Felony	C
C	Other Offense Equivalent to an Adult Class C Felony	D
D	Other Offense Equivalent to an Adult Gross Misdemeanor	E

[1] Escape 1 and 2 and Attempted Escape 1 and 2 are classed as C offenses and the standard range is established as follows:

1st escape or attempted escape during 12-month period - 4 weeks confinement
2nd escape or attempted escape during 12-month period - 8 weeks confinement
3rd and subsequent escape or attempted escape during 12-month period - 12 weeks confinement

[2] If the court finds that a respondent has violated terms of an order, it may impose a penalty of up to 30 days of confinement.

JUVENILE SENTENCING STANDARDS

This schedule must be used for juvenile offenders. The court may select sentencing option A, B, C, D, or RCW 13.40.167.

SECTION 2: RCW 13.40: JUVENILE JUSTICE ACT OF 1977, AS AMENDED

OPTION A: JUVENILE OFFENDER SENTENCING GRID

STANDARD RANGE

CURRENT OFFENSE CATEGORY

	0	1	2	3	4 or more
A+	180 weeks to age 21 for all category A+ offenses				
A	103 - 129 weeks for all category A offenses				
A-	15 - 36 weeks Except 30 – 40 weeks for 15 to 17 year olds	52 - 65 weeks	80 - 100 weeks	103 - 129 weeks	103 - 129 weeks
B+	15 - 36 weeks	15 – 36 weeks	52 - 65 weeks	80 - 100 weeks	103 - 129 weeks
B	LS	LS	15 - 36 weeks	15 - 36 weeks	52 - 65 weeks
C+	LS	LS	LS	15 - 36 weeks	15 - 36 weeks
C	LS	LS	LS	LS	15 - 36 weeks
D+	LS	LS	LS	LS	LS
D	LS	LS	LS	LS	LS
E	LS	LS	LS	LS	LS

PRIOR ADJUDICATIONS

NOTE: References in the grid to days or weeks mean periods of confinement. "LS" means "local sanctions" as defined in RCW 13.40.020.

(1) The vertical axis of the grid is the current offense category. The current offense category is determined by the offense of adjudication.

(2) The horizontal axis of the grid is the number of prior adjudications included in the juvenile's criminal history. Each prior felony adjudication shall count as one point. Each prior violation, misdemeanor, and gross misdemeanor adjudication shall count as 1/4 point. Fractional points shall be rounded down.

The Caseload Forecast Council is not liable for errors or omissions in the manual, for sentences that may be inappropriately calculated as a result of a practitioner's or court's reliance on the manual, or for any other written or verbal information related to adult or juvenile sentencing. The scoring sheets are intended to provide assistance in most cases but does not cover all permutations of the scoring rules. If you find any errors or omissions, we encourage you to report them to the Caseload Forecast Council.

SECTION 2: RCW 13.40: JUVENILE JUSTICE ACT OF 1977, AS AMENDED

(3) The standard range disposition for each offense is determined by the intersection of the column defined by the prior adjudications and the row defined by the current offense category.

(4) RCW 13.40.180 applies if the offender is being sentenced for more than one offense.

(5) A current offense that is a violation is equivalent to an offense category of E. However, a disposition for a violation shall not include confinement.

OR

OPTION B: SUSPENDED DISPOSITION ALTERNATIVE

(1) If the offender is subject to a standard range disposition involving confinement by the department, the court may impose the standard range and suspend the disposition on condition that the offender comply with one or more local sanctions and any educational or treatment requirement. The treatment programs provided to the offender must be either research-based best practice programs as identified by the Washington state institute for public policy or the joint legislative audit and review committee, or for chemical dependency treatment programs or services, they must be evidence-based or research-based best practice programs. For the purposes of this subsection:

(a) "Evidence-based" means a program or practice that has had multiple site random controlled trials across heterogeneous populations demonstrating that the program or practice is effective for the population; and

(b) "Research-based" means a program or practice that has some research demonstrating effectiveness, but that does not yet meet the standard of evidence-based practices.

(2) If the offender fails to comply with the suspended disposition, the court may impose sanctions pursuant to RCW 13.40.200 or may revoke the suspended disposition and order the disposition's execution.

(3) An offender is ineligible for the suspended disposition option under this section if the offender is:

(a) Adjudicated of an A+ offense;

(b) Fourteen years of age or older and is adjudicated of one or more of the following offenses:

(i) A class A offense, or an attempt, conspiracy, or solicitation to commit a class A offense;

(ii) Manslaughter in the first degree (RCW 9A.32.060); or

SECTION 2: RCW 13.40: JUVENILE JUSTICE ACT OF 1977, AS AMENDED

(iii) Assault in the second degree (RCW 9A.36.021), extortion in the first degree (RCW 9A.56.120), kidnapping in the second degree (RCW 9A.40.030), robbery in the second degree (RCW 9A.56.210), residential burglary (RCW 9A.52.025), burglary in the second degree (RCW 9A.52.030), drive-by shooting (RCW 9A.36.045), vehicular homicide (RCW 46.61.520), hit and run death (RCW 46.52.020(4)(a)), intimidating a witness (RCW 9A.72.110), violation of the uniform controlled substances act (RCW 69.50.401 (2)(a) and (b)), or manslaughter 2 (RCW 9A.32.070), when the offense includes infliction of bodily harm upon another or when during the commission or immediate withdrawal from the offense the respondent was armed with a deadly weapon;

(c) Ordered to serve a disposition for a firearm violation under RCW 13.40.193; or

(d) Adjudicated of a sex offense as defined in RCW 9.94A.030.

OR

OPTION C: CHEMICAL DEPENDENCY DISPOSITION ALTERNATIVE

If the juvenile offender is subject to a standard range disposition of local sanctions or 15 to 36 weeks of confinement and has not committed an A- or B+ offense, the court may impose a disposition under RCW 13.40.160(4) and 13.40.165.

OR

OPTION D: MANIFEST INJUSTICE

If the court determines that a disposition under option A, B, or C would effectuate a manifest injustice, the court shall impose a disposition outside the standard range under RCW 13.40.160(2).

[2012 c 177 § 4. Prior: 2008 c 230 § 3; 2008 c 158 § 1; 2007 c 199 § 11; 2006 c 73 § 14; 2004 c 117 § 1; prior: 2003 c 378 § 2; 2003 c 335 § 6; 2003 c 53 § 97; prior: 2002 c 324 § 3; 2002 c 175 § 20; 2001 c 217 § 13; 2000 c 66 § 3; 1998 c 290 § 5; prior: 1997 c 338 § 12; (1997 c 338 § 11 expired July 1, 1998); 1997 c 66 § 6; 1996 c 205 § 6; 1995 c 395 § 3; 1994 sp.s. c 7 § 522; 1989 c 407 § 7.]

The Caseload Forecast Council is not liable for errors or omissions in the manual, for sentences that may be inappropriately calculated as a result of a practitioner's or court's reliance on the manual, or for any other written or verbal information related to adult or juvenile sentencing. The scoring sheets are intended to provide assistance in most cases but does not cover all permutations of the scoring rules. If you find any errors or omissions, we encourage you to report them to the Caseload Forecast Council.

SECTION 2: RCW 13.40: JUVENILE JUSTICE ACT OF 1977, AS AMENDED

RCW 13.40.038 County juvenile detention facilities -- Policy -- Detention and risk assessment standards.

(1) It is the policy of this state that all county juvenile detention facilities provide a humane, safe, and rehabilitative environment and that unadjudicated youth remain in the community whenever possible, consistent with public safety and the provisions of chapter 13.40 RCW.

(2) The counties shall develop and implement detention intake standards and risk assessment standards to determine whether detention is warranted, whether the juvenile is developmentally disabled, and if detention is warranted, whether the juvenile should be placed in secure, nonsecure, or home detention to implement the goals of this section.

(3) Inability to pay for a less restrictive detention placement shall not be a basis for denying a respondent a less restrictive placement in the community.

(4) The assessment standards to determine whether a juvenile entering detention is developmentally disabled must be developed and implemented no later than December 31, 2012.

[2012 c 120 § 1; 1992 c 205 § 105; 1986 c 288 § 7.]

RCW 13.40.040 Taking juvenile into custody, grounds — Detention of, grounds — Detention pending disposition — Release on bond, conditions — Bail jumping

(1) A juvenile may be taken into custody:

(a) Pursuant to a court order if a complaint is filed with the court alleging, and the court finds probable cause to believe, that the juvenile has committed an offense or has violated terms of a disposition order or release order; or

(b) Without a court order, by a law enforcement officer if grounds exist for the arrest of an adult in identical circumstances. Admission to, and continued custody in, a court detention facility shall be governed by subsection (2) of this section; or

(c) Pursuant to a court order that the juvenile be held as a material witness; or

(d) Where the secretary or the secretary's designee has suspended the parole of a juvenile offender.

(2) A juvenile may not be held in detention unless there is probable cause to believe that:

(a) The juvenile has committed an offense or has violated the terms of a disposition order; and

SECTION 2: RCW 13.40: JUVENILE JUSTICE ACT OF 1977, AS AMENDED

(i) The juvenile will likely fail to appear for further proceedings; or

(ii) Detention is required to protect the juvenile from himself or herself; or

(iii) The juvenile is a threat to community safety; or

(iv) The juvenile will intimidate witnesses or otherwise unlawfully interfere with the administration of justice; or

(v) The juvenile has committed a crime while another case was pending; or

(b) The juvenile is a fugitive from justice; or

(c) The juvenile's parole has been suspended or modified; or

(d) The juvenile is a material witness.

(3) Notwithstanding subsection (2) of this section, and within available funds, a juvenile who has been found guilty of one of the following offenses shall be detained pending disposition: Rape in the first or second degree (RCW 9A.44.040 and 9A.44.050); or rape of a child in the first degree (RCW 9A.44.073).

(4) Upon a finding that members of the community have threatened the health of a juvenile taken into custody, at the juvenile's request the court may order continued detention pending further order of the court.

(5) Except as provided in RCW 9.41.280, a juvenile detained under this section may be released upon posting a probation bond set by the court. The juvenile's parent or guardian may sign for the probation bond. A court authorizing such a release shall issue an order containing a statement of conditions imposed upon the juvenile and shall set the date of his or her next court appearance. The court shall advise the juvenile of any conditions specified in the order and may at any time amend such an order in order to impose additional or different conditions of release upon the juvenile or to return the juvenile to custody for failing to conform to the conditions imposed. In addition to requiring the juvenile to appear at the next court date, the court may condition the probation bond on the juvenile's compliance with conditions of release. The juvenile's parent or guardian may notify the court that the juvenile has failed to conform to the conditions of release or the provisions in the probation bond. If the parent notifies the court of the juvenile's failure to comply with the probation bond, the court shall notify the surety. As provided in the terms of the bond, the surety shall provide notice to the court of the offender's noncompliance. A juvenile may be released only to a responsible adult or the department of social and health services. Failure to appear on the date scheduled by the court pursuant to this section shall constitute the crime of bail jumping.

The Caseload Forecast Council is not liable for errors or omissions in the manual, for sentences that may be inappropriately calculated as a result of a practitioner's or court's reliance on the manual, or for any other written or verbal information related to adult or juvenile sentencing. The scoring sheets are intended to provide assistance in most cases but does not cover all permutations of the scoring rules. If you find any errors or omissions, we encourage you to report them to the Caseload Forecast Council.

SECTION 2: RCW 13.40: JUVENILE JUSTICE ACT OF 1977, AS AMENDED

[2002 c 171 § 2; 1999 c 167 § 2; 1997 c 338 § 13; 1995 c 395 § 4; 1979 c 155 § 57; 1977 ex.s. c 291 § 58.]

13.40.042 Detention of juvenile with mental disorder.

(1) When a police officer has reasonable cause to believe that a juvenile has committed acts constituting a nonfelony crime that is not a serious offense as identified in RCW 10.77.092, and the officer believes that the juvenile suffers from a mental disorder, and the local prosecutor has entered into an agreement with law enforcement regarding the detention of juveniles who may have a mental disorder, the arresting officer, instead of taking the juvenile to the local juvenile detention facility, may take the juvenile to:

(a) An evaluation and treatment facility as defined in RCW 71.34.020 if the facility has been identified as an alternative location by agreement of the prosecutor, law enforcement, and the mental health provider;

(b) A facility or program identified by agreement of the prosecutor and law enforcement; or

(c) A location already identified and in use by law enforcement for the purpose of mental health diversion.

(2) For the purposes of this section, an "alternative location" means a facility or program that has the capacity to evaluate a youth and, if determined to be appropriate, develop a behavioral health intervention plan and initiate treatment.

(3) If a juvenile is taken to any location described in subsection (1)(a) or (b) of this section, the juvenile may be held for up to twelve hours and must be examined by a mental health professional within three hours of arrival.

(4) The authority provided pursuant to this section is in addition to existing authority under RCW 10.31.110.

[2013 c 179 § 2.]

RCW 13.40.045 Escapees — Arrest warrants.

The secretary, assistant secretary, or the secretary's designee shall issue arrest warrants for juveniles who escape from department residential custody. The secretary, assistant secretary, or the secretary's designee may issue arrest warrants for juveniles who abscond from parole supervision or fail to meet conditions of parole. These arrest warrants shall authorize any law enforcement, probation and parole, or peace officer of this state, or any other state where the juvenile is located, to arrest the juvenile and to place the juvenile in physical custody pending the juvenile's return to confinement in a state juvenile rehabilitation facility.

The Caseload Forecast Council is not liable for errors or omissions in the manual, for sentences that may be inappropriately calculated as a result of a practitioner's or court's reliance on the manual, or for any other written or verbal information related to adult or juvenile sentencing. The scoring sheets are intended to provide assistance in most cases but does not cover all permutations of the scoring rules. If you find any errors or omissions, we encourage you to report them to the Caseload Forecast Council.

SECTION 2: RCW 13.40: JUVENILE JUSTICE ACT OF 1977, AS AMENDED

[1997 c 338 § 14; 1994 sp.s. c 7 § 518.]

RCW 13.40.050 Detention procedures -- Notice of hearing -- Conditions of release -- Consultation with parent, guardian, or custodian.

(1) When a juvenile taken into custody is held in detention:

(a) An information, a community supervision modification or termination of diversion petition, or a parole modification petition shall be filed within seventy-two hours, Saturdays, Sundays, and holidays excluded, or the juvenile shall be released; and

(b) A detention hearing, a community supervision modification or termination of diversion petition, or a parole modification petition shall be held within seventy-two hours, Saturdays, Sundays, and holidays excluded, from the time of filing the information or petition, to determine whether continued detention is necessary under RCW 13.40.040.

(2) Notice of the detention hearing, stating the time, place, and purpose of the hearing, stating the right to counsel, and requiring attendance shall be given to the parent, guardian, or custodian if such person can be found and shall also be given to the juvenile if over twelve years of age.

(3) At the commencement of the detention hearing, the court shall advise the parties of their rights under this chapter and shall appoint counsel as specified in this chapter.

(4) The court shall, based upon the allegations in the information, determine whether the case is properly before it or whether the case should be treated as a diversion case under RCW 13.40.080. If the case is not properly before the court the juvenile shall be ordered released.

(5) Notwithstanding a determination that the case is properly before the court and that probable cause exists, a juvenile shall at the detention hearing be ordered released on the juvenile's personal recognizance pending further hearing unless the court finds detention is necessary under RCW 13.40.040.

(6) If detention is not necessary under RCW 13.40.040, the court shall impose the most appropriate of the following conditions or, if necessary, any combination of the following conditions:

(a) Place the juvenile in the custody of a designated person agreeing to supervise such juvenile;

(b) Place restrictions on the travel of the juvenile during the period of release;

(c) Require the juvenile to report regularly to and remain under the supervision of the juvenile court;

SECTION 2: RCW 13.40: JUVENILE JUSTICE ACT OF 1977, AS AMENDED

(d) Impose any condition other than detention deemed reasonably necessary to assure appearance as required;

(e) Require that the juvenile return to detention during specified hours; or

(f) Require the juvenile to post a probation bond set by the court under terms and conditions as provided in *RCW 13.40.040(4).

(7) A juvenile may be released only to a responsible adult or the department.

(8) If the parent, guardian, or custodian of the juvenile in detention is available, the court shall consult with them prior to a determination to further detain or release the juvenile or treat the case as a diversion case under RCW 13.40.080.

(9) A person notified under this section who fails without reasonable cause to appear and abide by the order of the court may be proceeded against as for contempt of court. In determining whether a parent, guardian, or custodian had reasonable cause not to appear, the court may consider all factors relevant to the person's ability to appear as summoned.

[1997 c 338 § 15; 1995 c 395 § 5; 1992 c 205 § 106; 1979 c 155 § 58; 1977 ex.s. c 291 § 59.]

RCW 13.40.054 Probation bond or collateral — Modification or revocation of probation bond.

(1) As provided in this chapter, the court may order a juvenile to post a probation bond as defined in RCW

13.40.020 or to deposit cash or post other collateral in lieu of a probation bond, to enhance public safety, increase the likelihood that a respondent will appear as required to respond to charges, and increase compliance with community supervision imposed under various alternative disposition options. The parents or guardians of the juvenile may sign for a probation bond on behalf of the juvenile or deposit cash or other collateral in lieu of a bond if approved by the court.

(2) A parent or guardian who has signed for a probation bond, deposited cash, or posted other collateral on behalf of a juvenile has the right to notify the court if the juvenile violates any of the terms and conditions of the bond. The parent or guardian who signed for a probation bond may move the court to modify the terms of the bond or revoke the bond without penalty to the surety or parent. The court shall notify the surety if a parent or guardian notifies the court that the juvenile has violated conditions of the probation bond and has requested modification or revocation of the bond. At a hearing on the motion, the court may consider the nature and seriousness of the violation or violations and may either keep the bond in effect, modify the

SECTION 2: RCW 13.40: JUVENILE JUSTICE ACT OF 1977, AS AMENDED

terms of the bond with the consent of the parent or guardian and surety, or revoke the bond. If the court revokes the bond the court may require full payment of the face amount of the bond. In the alternative, the court may revoke the bond and impose a partial payment for less than the full amount of the bond or may revoke the bond without imposing any penalty. In reaching its decision, the court may consider the timeliness of the parent's or guardian's notification to the court and the efforts of the parent and surety to monitor the offender's compliance with conditions of the bond and release. A surety shall have the same obligations and rights as provided sureties in adult criminal cases. Rules of forfeiture and revocation of bonds issued in adult criminal cases shall apply to forfeiture and revocation of probation bonds issued under this chapter except as specifically provided in this subsection.

[1995 c 395 § 1.]

RCW 13.40.056 Nonrefundable bail fee.

When a juvenile charged with an offense posts a probation bond or deposits cash or posts other collateral in lieu of a bond, ten dollars of the total amount required to be posted as bail shall be paid in cash as a nonrefundable bail fee. The bail fee shall be distributed to the county for costs associated with implementing chapter 395, Laws of 1995.

[1995 c 395 § 9.]

RCW 13.40.060 Jurisdiction of actions — Transfer of case and records, when — Change in venue, grounds.

(1) All actions under this chapter shall be commenced and tried in the county where any element of the offense was committed except as otherwise specially provided by statute. In cases in which diversion is provided by statute, venue is in the county in which the juvenile resides or in the county in which any element of the offense was committed.

(2)(a) The court upon motion of any party or upon its own motion may, at any time, transfer a proceeding to another juvenile court when there is reason to believe that an impartial proceeding cannot be held in the county in which the proceeding was begun; and

(b) A court may transfer a proceeding to another juvenile court following disposition for the purposes of supervision and enforcement of the disposition order.

(3) If the court orders a transfer of the proceeding pursuant to subsection (2)(b) of this section:

(a) The case and copies of only those legal and social documents pertaining thereto shall be transferred to the county in which the juvenile resides, without regard to whether or not his or her custodial parent resides there, for supervision and enforcement of the disposition order.

SECTION 2: RCW 13.40: JUVENILE JUSTICE ACT OF 1977, AS AMENDED

(b) If any restitution is yet to be determined, the originating court shall transfer the case to the new county with the exception of the restitution. Venue over restitution shall be retained by the originating court for purposes of establishing a restitution order. Once restitution is determined, the originating county shall then transfer venue over modification and enforcement of the restitution to the new county.

(c) The court of the receiving county may modify and enforce the disposition order, including restitution.

(d) The clerk of the originating county shall maintain the account receivable in the judicial information system and all payments shall be made to the clerk of the originating county.

(e) Any collection of the offender legal financial obligation shall be managed by the juvenile probation department of the new county while the offender is under juvenile probation supervision, or by the clerk of the original county at the conclusion of supervision by juvenile probation. The probation department of the new county shall notify the clerk of the originating county when they end supervision of the offender.

(f) In cases where a civil judgment has already been established, venue may not be transferred to another county.

[2005 c 165 § 1; 1997 c 338 § 16; 1989 c 71 § 1; 1981 c 299 § 6; 1979 c 155 § 59; 1977 ex.s. c 291 § 60.]

RCW 13.40.070 Complaints — Screening — Filing information — Diversion — Modification of community supervision — Notice to parent or guardian — Probation counselor acting for prosecutor — Referral to mediation or reconciliation programs.

(1) Complaints referred to the juvenile court alleging the commission of an offense shall be referred directly to the prosecutor. The prosecutor, upon receipt of a complaint, shall screen the complaint to determine whether:

(a) The alleged facts bring the case within the jurisdiction of the court; and

(b) On a basis of available evidence there is probable cause to believe that the juvenile did commit the offense.

(2) If the identical alleged acts constitute an offense under both the law of this state and an ordinance of any city or county of this state, state law shall govern the prosecutor's screening and charging decision for both filed and diverted cases.

(3) If the requirements of subsections (1)(a) and (b) of this section are met, the prosecutor shall

SECTION 2: RCW 13.40: JUVENILE JUSTICE ACT OF 1977, AS AMENDED

either file an information in juvenile court or divert the case, as set forth in subsections (5), (6), and (8) of this section. If the prosecutor finds that the requirements of subsection (1)(a) and (b) of this section are not met, the prosecutor shall maintain a record, for one year, of such decision and the reasons therefor. In lieu of filing an information or diverting an offense a prosecutor may file a motion to modify community supervision where such offense constitutes a violation of community supervision.

(4) An information shall be a plain, concise, and definite written statement of the essential facts constituting the offense charged. It shall be signed by the prosecuting attorney and conform to chapter 10.37 RCW.

(5) Except as provided in RCW 13.40.213 and subsection (7) of this section, where a case is legally sufficient, the prosecutor shall file an information with the juvenile court if:

(a) An alleged offender is accused of a class A felony, a class B felony, an attempt to commit a class B felony, a class C felony listed in RCW 9.94A.411(2) as a crime against persons or listed in RCW 9A.46.060 as a crime of harassment, or a class C felony that is a violation of RCW 9.41.080 or 9.41.040(2)(a)(iii); or

(b) An alleged offender is accused of a felony and has a criminal history of any felony, or at least two gross misdemeanors, or at least two misdemeanors; or

(c) An alleged offender has previously been committed to the department; or

(d) An alleged offender has been referred by a diversion unit for prosecution or desires prosecution instead of diversion; or

(e) An alleged offender has two or more diversion agreements on the alleged offender's criminal history; or

(f) A special allegation has been filed that the offender or an accomplice was armed with a firearm when the offense was committed.

(6) Where a case is legally sufficient the prosecutor shall divert the case if the alleged offense is a misdemeanor or gross misdemeanor or violation and the alleged offense is the offender's first offense or violation. If the alleged offender is charged with a related offense that must or may be filed under subsections (5) and (8) of this section, a case under this subsection may also be filed.

(7) Where a case is legally sufficient to charge an alleged offender with either prostitution or prostitution loitering and the alleged offense is the offender's first prostitution or prostitution loitering offense, the prosecutor shall divert the case.

(8) Where a case is legally sufficient and falls into neither subsection (5) nor (6) of this section, it

The Caseload Forecast Council is not liable for errors or omissions in the manual, for sentences that may be inappropriately calculated as a result of a practitioner's or court's reliance on the manual, or for any other written or verbal information related to adult or juvenile sentencing. The scoring sheets are intended to provide assistance in most cases but does not cover all permutations of the scoring rules. If you find any errors or omissions, we encourage you to report them to the Caseload Forecast Council.

SECTION 2: RCW 13.40: JUVENILE JUSTICE ACT OF 1977, AS AMENDED

may be filed or diverted. In deciding whether to file or divert an offense under this section the prosecutor shall be guided only by the length, seriousness, and recency of the alleged offender's criminal history and the circumstances surrounding the commission of the alleged offense.

(9) Whenever a juvenile is placed in custody or, where not placed in custody, referred to a diversion interview, the parent or legal guardian of the juvenile shall be notified as soon as possible concerning the allegation made against the juvenile and the current status of the juvenile. Where a case involves victims of crimes against persons or victims whose property has not been recovered at the time a juvenile is referred to a diversion unit, the victim shall be notified of the referral and informed how to contact the unit.

(10) The responsibilities of the prosecutor under subsections (1) through (9) of this section may be performed by a juvenile court probation counselor for any complaint referred to the court alleging the commission of an offense which would not be a felony if committed by an adult, if the prosecutor has given sufficient written notice to the juvenile court that the prosecutor will not review such complaints.

(11) The prosecutor, juvenile court probation counselor, or diversion unit may, in exercising their authority under this section or RCW 13.40.080, refer juveniles to mediation or victim offender reconciliation programs. Such mediation or victim offender reconciliation programs shall be voluntary for victims.

[2010 c 289 § 7; 2009 c 252 § 3; 2003 c 53 § 98; 2001 c 175 § 2; 1997 c 338 § 17; 1994 sp.s. c 7 § 543; 1992 c 205 § 107; 1989 c 407 § 9; 1983 c 191 § 18; 1981 c 299 § 7; 1979 c 155 § 60; 1977 ex.s. c 291 § 61.]

RCW 13.40.077 Recommended prosecuting standards for charging and plea dispositions.

INTRODUCTION: These standards are intended solely for the guidance of prosecutors in the state of Washington. They are not intended to, do not, and may not be relied upon to create a right or benefit, substantive or procedural, enforceable at law by a party in litigation with the state.

Evidentiary sufficiency.

(1) Decision not to prosecute.

STANDARD: A prosecuting attorney may decline to prosecute, even though technically sufficient evidence to prosecute exists, in situations where prosecution would serve no public purpose, would defeat the underlying purpose of the law in question, or would result in decreased respect for the law. The decision not to prosecute or divert shall not be influenced by the race, gender, religion, or creed of the suspect.

SECTION 2: RCW 13.40: JUVENILE JUSTICE ACT OF 1977, AS AMENDED

GUIDELINES/COMMENTARY:

Examples

The following are examples of reasons not to prosecute which could satisfy the standard.

(a) Contrary to Legislative Intent - It may be proper to decline to charge where the application of criminal sanctions would be clearly contrary to the intent of the legislature in enacting the particular statute.

(b) Antiquated Statute - It may be proper to decline to charge where the statute in question is antiquated in that:

(i) It has not been enforced for many years;

(ii) Most members of society act as if it were no longer in existence;

(iii) It serves no deterrent or protective purpose in today's society; and

(iv) The statute has not been recently reconsidered by the legislature.

This reason is not to be construed as the basis for declining cases because the law in question is unpopular or because it is difficult to enforce.

(c) De Minimis Violation - It may be proper to decline to charge where the violation of law is only technical or insubstantial and where no public interest or deterrent purpose would be served by prosecution.

(d) Confinement on Other Charges - It may be proper to decline to charge because the accused has been sentenced on another charge to a lengthy period of confinement; and

(i) Conviction of the new offense would not merit any additional direct or collateral punishment;

(ii) The new offense is either a misdemeanor or a felony which is not particularly aggravated; and

(iii) Conviction of the new offense would not serve any significant deterrent purpose.

(e) Pending Conviction on Another Charge - It may be proper to decline to charge because the accused is facing a pending prosecution in the same or another county; and

(i) Conviction of the new offense would not merit any additional direct or collateral punishment;

SECTION 2: RCW 13.40: JUVENILE JUSTICE ACT OF 1977, AS AMENDED

(ii) Conviction in the pending prosecution is imminent;

(iii) The new offense is either a misdemeanor or a felony which is not particularly aggravated; and

(iv) Conviction of the new offense would not serve any significant deterrent purpose.

(f) High Disproportionate Cost of Prosecution - It may be proper to decline to charge where the cost of locating or transporting, or the burden on, prosecution witnesses is highly disproportionate to the importance of prosecuting the offense in question. The reason should be limited to minor cases and should not be relied upon in serious cases.

(g) Improper Motives of Complainant - It may be proper to decline charges because the motives of the complainant are improper and prosecution would serve no public purpose, would defeat the underlying purpose of the law in question, or would result in decreased respect for the law.

(h) Immunity - It may be proper to decline to charge where immunity is to be given to an accused in order to prosecute another where the accused information or testimony will reasonably lead to the conviction of others who are responsible for more serious criminal conduct or who represent a greater danger to the public interest.

(i) Victim Request - It may be proper to decline to charge because the victim requests that no criminal charges be filed and the case involves the following crimes or situations:

(i) Assault cases where the victim has suffered little or no injury;

(ii) Crimes against property, not involving violence, where no major loss was suffered;

(iii) Where doing so would not jeopardize the safety of society.

Care should be taken to insure that the victim's request is freely made and is not the product of threats or pressure by the accused.

The presence of these factors may also justify the decision to dismiss a prosecution which has been commenced.

Notification

The prosecutor is encouraged to notify the victim, when practical, and the law enforcement personnel, of the decision not to prosecute.

(2) Decision to prosecute.

SECTION 2: RCW 13.40: JUVENILE JUSTICE ACT OF 1977, AS AMENDED

STANDARD:

Crimes against persons will be filed if sufficient admissible evidence exists, which, when considered with the most plausible, reasonably foreseeable defense that could be raised under the evidence, would justify conviction by a reasonable and objective fact finder. With regard to offenses prohibited by RCW 9A.44.040, 9A.44.050, 9A.44.073, 9A.44.076, 9A.44.079, 9A.44.083, 9A.44.086, 9A.44.089, and 9A.64.020 the prosecutor should avoid prefiling agreements or diversions intended to place the accused in a program of treatment or counseling, so that treatment, if determined to be beneficial, can be proved under *RCW 13.40.160(4).

Crimes against property/other crimes will be filed if the admissible evidence is of such convincing force as to make it probable that a reasonable and objective fact finder would convict after hearing all the admissible evidence and the most plausible defense that could be raised.

The categorization of crimes for these charging standards shall be the same as found in RCW 9.94A.411(2).

The decision to prosecute or use diversion shall not be influenced by the race, gender, religion, or creed of the respondent.

(3) Selection of Charges/Degree of Charge

(a) The prosecutor should file charges which adequately describe the nature of the respondent's conduct. Other offenses may be charged only if they are necessary to ensure that the charges:

(i) Will significantly enhance the strength of the state's case at trial; or

(ii) Will result in restitution to all victims.

(b) The prosecutor should not overcharge to obtain a guilty plea. Overcharging includes:

(i) Charging a higher degree;

(ii) Charging additional counts.

This standard is intended to direct prosecutors to charge those crimes which demonstrate the nature and seriousness of a respondent's criminal conduct, but to decline to charge crimes which are not necessary to such an indication. Crimes which do not merge as a matter of law, but which arise from the same course of conduct, do not all have to be charged.

(4) Police Investigation

A prosecuting attorney is dependent upon law enforcement agencies to conduct the necessary

SECTION 2: RCW 13.40: JUVENILE JUSTICE ACT OF 1977, AS AMENDED

factual investigation which must precede the decision to prosecute. The prosecuting attorney shall ensure that a thorough factual investigation has been conducted before a decision to prosecute is made. In ordinary circumstances the investigation should include the following:

(a) The interviewing of all material witnesses, together with the obtaining of written statements whenever possible;

(b) The completion of necessary laboratory tests; and

(c) The obtaining, in accordance with constitutional requirements, of the suspect's version of the events.

If the initial investigation is incomplete, a prosecuting attorney should insist upon further investigation before a decision to prosecute is made, and specify what the investigation needs to include.

(5) Exceptions

In certain situations, a prosecuting attorney may authorize filing of a criminal complaint before the investigation is complete if:

(a) Probable cause exists to believe the suspect is guilty; and

(b) The suspect presents a danger to the community or is likely to flee if not apprehended; or

(c) The arrest of the suspect is necessary to complete the investigation of the crime.

In the event that the exception to the standard is applied, the prosecuting attorney shall obtain a commitment from the law enforcement agency involved to complete the investigation in a timely manner. If the subsequent investigation does not produce sufficient evidence to meet the normal charging standard, the complaint should be dismissed.

(6) Investigation Techniques

The prosecutor should be fully advised of the investigatory techniques that were used in the case investigation including:

(a) Polygraph testing;

(b) Hypnosis;

(c) Electronic surveillance;

SECTION 2: RCW 13.40: JUVENILE JUSTICE ACT OF 1977, AS AMENDED

(d) Use of informants.

(7) Prefiling Discussions with Defendant

Discussions with the defendant or his or her representative regarding the selection or disposition of charges may occur prior to the filing of charges, and potential agreements can be reached.

(8) Plea dispositions:

STANDARD

(a) Except as provided in subsection (2) of this section, a respondent will normally be expected to plead guilty to the charge or charges which adequately describe the nature of his or her criminal conduct or go to trial.

(b) In certain circumstances, a plea agreement with a respondent in exchange for a plea of guilty to a charge or charges that may not fully describe the nature of his or her criminal conduct may be necessary and in the public interest. Such situations may include the following:

(i) Evidentiary problems which make conviction of the original charges doubtful;

(ii) The respondent's willingness to cooperate in the investigation or prosecution of others whose criminal conduct is more serious or represents a greater public threat;

(iii) A request by the victim when it is not the result of pressure from the respondent;

(iv) The discovery of facts which mitigate the seriousness of the respondent's conduct;

(v) The correction of errors in the initial charging decision;

(vi) The respondent's history with respect to criminal activity;

(vii) The nature and seriousness of the offense or offenses charged;

(viii) The probable effect of witnesses.

(c) No plea agreement shall be influenced by the race, gender, religion, or creed of the respondent. This includes but is not limited to the prosecutor's decision to utilize such disposition alternatives as the Special Sex Offender Disposition Alternative, the Chemical Dependency Disposition Alternative, and manifest injustice.

(9) Disposition recommendations:

SECTION 2: RCW 13.40: JUVENILE JUSTICE ACT OF 1977, AS AMENDED

STANDARD

The prosecutor may reach an agreement regarding disposition recommendations.

The prosecutor shall not agree to withhold relevant information from the court concerning the plea agreement.

[1997 c 338 § 18; 1996 c 9 § 1.]

RCW 13.40.080 Diversion agreement -- Scope -- Limitations -- Restitution orders -- Divertee's rights -- Diversion unit's powers and duties -- Interpreters -- Modification -- Fines.

(1) A diversion agreement shall be a contract between a juvenile accused of an offense and a diversion unit whereby the juvenile agrees to fulfill certain conditions in lieu of prosecution. Such agreements may be entered into only after the prosecutor, or probation counselor pursuant to this chapter, has determined that probable cause exists to believe that a crime has been committed and that the juvenile committed it. Such agreements shall be entered into as expeditiously as possible.

(2) A diversion agreement shall be limited to one or more of the following:

(a) Community restitution not to exceed one hundred fifty hours, not to be performed during school hours if the juvenile is attending school;

(b) Restitution limited to the amount of actual loss incurred by any victim;

(c) Attendance at up to ten hours of counseling and/or up to twenty hours of educational or informational sessions at a community agency. The educational or informational sessions may include sessions relating to respect for self, others, and authority; victim awareness; accountability; self-worth; responsibility; work ethics; good citizenship; literacy; and life skills. For purposes of this section, "community agency" may also mean a community-based nonprofit organization, if approved by the diversion unit. The state shall not be liable for costs resulting from the diversion unit exercising the option to permit diversion agreements to mandate attendance at up to ten hours of counseling and/or up to twenty hours of educational or informational sessions;

(d) A fine, not to exceed one hundred dollars;

(e) Requirements to remain during specified hours at home, school, or work, and restrictions on leaving or entering specified geographical areas; and

(f) Upon request of any victim or witness, requirements to refrain from any contact with victims or witnesses of offenses committed by the juvenile.

SECTION 2: RCW 13.40: JUVENILE JUSTICE ACT OF 1977, AS AMENDED

(3) Notwithstanding the provisions of subsection (2) of this section, youth courts are not limited to the conditions imposed by subsection (2) of this section in imposing sanctions on juveniles pursuant to RCW 13.40.630.

(4) In assessing periods of community restitution to be performed and restitution to be paid by a juvenile who has entered into a diversion agreement, the court officer to whom this task is assigned shall consult with the juvenile's custodial parent or parents or guardian. To the extent possible, the court officer shall advise the victims of the juvenile offender of the diversion process, offer victim impact letter forms and restitution claim forms, and involve members of the community. Such members of the community shall meet with the juvenile and advise the court officer as to the terms of the diversion agreement and shall supervise the juvenile in carrying out its terms.

(5)(a) A diversion agreement may not exceed a period of six months and may include a period extending beyond the eighteenth birthday of the divertee.

(b) If additional time is necessary for the juvenile to complete restitution to a victim, the time period limitations of this subsection may be extended by an additional six months.

(c) If the juvenile has not paid the full amount of restitution by the end of the additional six-month period, then the juvenile shall be referred to the juvenile court for entry of an order establishing the amount of restitution still owed to the victim. In this order, the court shall also determine the terms and conditions of the restitution, including a payment plan extending up to ten years if the court determines that the juvenile does not have the means to make full restitution over a shorter period. For the purposes of this subsection (5)(c), the juvenile shall remain under the court's jurisdiction for a maximum term of ten years after the juvenile's eighteenth birthday. Prior to the expiration of the initial ten-year period, the juvenile court may extend the judgment for restitution an additional ten years. The court may relieve the juvenile of the requirement to pay full or partial restitution if the juvenile reasonably satisfies the court that he or she does not have the means to make full or partial restitution and could not reasonably acquire the means to pay the restitution over a ten-year period. If the court relieves the juvenile of the requirement to pay full or partial restitution, the court may order an amount of community restitution that the court deems appropriate. The county clerk shall make disbursements to victims named in the order. The restitution to victims named in the order shall be paid prior to any payment for other penalties or monetary assessments. A juvenile under obligation to pay restitution may petition the court for modification of the restitution order.

(6) The juvenile shall retain the right to be referred to the court at any time prior to the signing of the diversion agreement.

(7) Divertees and potential divertees shall be afforded due process in all contacts with a diversion unit regardless of whether the juveniles are accepted for diversion or whether the diversion

SECTION 2: RCW 13.40: JUVENILE JUSTICE ACT OF 1977, AS AMENDED

program is successfully completed. Such due process shall include, but not be limited to, the following:

(a) A written diversion agreement shall be executed stating all conditions in clearly understandable language;

(b) Violation of the terms of the agreement shall be the only grounds for termination;

(c) No divertee may be terminated from a diversion program without being given a court hearing, which hearing shall be preceded by:

(i) Written notice of alleged violations of the conditions of the diversion program; and

(ii) Disclosure of all evidence to be offered against the divertee;

(d) The hearing shall be conducted by the juvenile court and shall include:

(i) Opportunity to be heard in person and to present evidence;

(ii) The right to confront and cross-examine all adverse witnesses;

(iii) A written statement by the court as to the evidence relied on and the reasons for termination, should that be the decision; and

(iv) Demonstration by evidence that the divertee has substantially violated the terms of his or her diversion agreement.

(e) The prosecutor may file an information on the offense for which the divertee was diverted:

(i) In juvenile court if the divertee is under eighteen years of age; or

(ii) In superior court or the appropriate court of limited jurisdiction if the divertee is eighteen years of age or older.

(8) The diversion unit shall, subject to available funds, be responsible for providing interpreters when juveniles need interpreters to effectively communicate during diversion unit hearings or negotiations.

(9) The diversion unit shall be responsible for advising a divertee of his or her rights as provided in this chapter.

(10) The diversion unit may refer a juvenile to a restorative justice program, community-based counseling, or treatment programs.

The Caseload Forecast Council is not liable for errors or omissions in the manual, for sentences that may be inappropriately calculated as a result of a practitioner's or court's reliance on the manual, or for any other written or verbal information related to adult or juvenile sentencing. The scoring sheets are intended to provide assistance in most cases but does not cover all permutations of the scoring rules. If you find any errors or omissions, we encourage you to report them to the Caseload Forecast Council.

SECTION 2: RCW 13.40: JUVENILE JUSTICE ACT OF 1977, AS AMENDED

(11) The right to counsel shall inure prior to the initial interview for purposes of advising the juvenile as to whether he or she desires to participate in the diversion process or to appear in the juvenile court. The juvenile may be represented by counsel at any critical stage of the diversion process, including intake interviews and termination hearings. The juvenile shall be fully advised at the intake of his or her right to an attorney and of the relevant services an attorney can provide. For the purpose of this section, intake interviews mean all interviews regarding the diversion agreement process.

The juvenile shall be advised that a diversion agreement shall constitute a part of the juvenile's criminal history as defined by RCW 13.40.020(7). A signed acknowledgment of such advisement shall be obtained from the juvenile, and the document shall be maintained by the diversion unit together with the diversion agreement, and a copy of both documents shall be delivered to the prosecutor if requested by the prosecutor. The supreme court shall promulgate rules setting forth the content of such advisement in simple language.

(12) When a juvenile enters into a diversion agreement, the juvenile court may receive only the following information for dispositional purposes:

(a) The fact that a charge or charges were made;

(b) The fact that a diversion agreement was entered into;

(c) The juvenile's obligations under such agreement;

(d) Whether the alleged offender performed his or her obligations under such agreement; and

(e) The facts of the alleged offense.

(13) A diversion unit may refuse to enter into a diversion agreement with a juvenile. When a diversion unit refuses to enter a diversion agreement with a juvenile, it shall immediately refer such juvenile to the court for action and shall forward to the court the criminal complaint and a detailed statement of its reasons for refusing to enter into a diversion agreement. The diversion unit shall also immediately refer the case to the prosecuting attorney for action if such juvenile violates the terms of the diversion agreement.

(14) A diversion unit may, in instances where it determines that the act or omission of an act for which a juvenile has been referred to it involved no victim, or where it determines that the juvenile referred to it has no prior criminal history and is alleged to have committed an illegal act involving no threat of or instance of actual physical harm and involving not more than fifty dollars in property loss or damage and that there is no loss outstanding to the person or firm suffering such damage or loss, counsel and release or release such a juvenile without entering into a diversion agreement. A diversion unit's authority to counsel and release a juvenile under

---

The Caseload Forecast Council is not liable for errors or omissions in the manual, for sentences that may be inappropriately calculated as a result of a practitioner's or court's reliance on the manual, or for any other written or verbal information related to adult or juvenile sentencing. The scoring sheets are intended to provide assistance in most cases but does not cover all permutations of the scoring rules. If you find any errors or omissions, we encourage you to report them to the Caseload Forecast Council.

SECTION 2: RCW 13.40: JUVENILE JUSTICE ACT OF 1977, AS AMENDED

this subsection includes the authority to refer the juvenile to community-based counseling or treatment programs or a restorative justice program. Any juvenile released under this subsection shall be advised that the act or omission of any act for which he or she had been referred shall constitute a part of the juvenile's criminal history as defined by RCW 13.40.020(7). A signed acknowledgment of such advisement shall be obtained from the juvenile, and the document shall be maintained by the unit, and a copy of the document shall be delivered to the prosecutor if requested by the prosecutor. The supreme court shall promulgate rules setting forth the content of such advisement in simple language. A juvenile determined to be eligible by a diversion unit for release as provided in this subsection shall retain the same right to counsel and right to have his or her case referred to the court for formal action as any other juvenile referred to the unit.

(15) A diversion unit may supervise the fulfillment of a diversion agreement entered into before the juvenile's eighteenth birthday and which includes a period extending beyond the divertee's eighteenth birthday.

(16) If a fine required by a diversion agreement cannot reasonably be paid due to a change of circumstance, the diversion agreement may be modified at the request of the divertee and with the concurrence of the diversion unit to convert an unpaid fine into community restitution. The modification of the diversion agreement shall be in writing and signed by the divertee and the diversion unit. The number of hours of community restitution in lieu of a monetary penalty shall be converted at the rate of the prevailing state minimum wage per hour.

(17) Fines imposed under this section shall be collected and paid into the county general fund in accordance with procedures established by the juvenile court administrator under RCW 13.04.040 and may be used only for juvenile services. In the expenditure of funds for juvenile services, there shall be a maintenance of effort whereby counties exhaust existing resources before using amounts collected under this section.

[2012 c 201 § 2; 2004 c 120 § 3. Prior: 2002 c 237 § 8; 2002 c 175 § 21; 1999 c 91 § 1; 1997 c 338 § 70; 1997 c 121 § 8; 1996 c 124 § 1; 1994 sp.s. c 7 § 544; 1992 c 205 § 108; 1985 c 73 § 2; 1983 c 191 § 16; 1981 c 299 § 8; 1979 c 155 § 61; 1977 ex.s. c 291 § 62.]

RCW 13.40.085 Diversion services costs — Fees — Payment by parent or legal guardian.

The county legislative authority may authorize juvenile court administrators to establish fees to cover the costs of the administration and operation of diversion services provided under this chapter. The parent or legal guardian of a juvenile who receives diversion services must pay for the services based on the parent's or guardian's ability to pay. The juvenile court administrators shall develop a fair and equitable payment schedule. No juvenile who is eligible for diversion as provided in this chapter may be denied diversion services based on an inability to pay for the services.

SECTION 2: RCW 13.40: JUVENILE JUSTICE ACT OF 1977, AS AMENDED

[1993 c 171 § 1.]

RCW 13.40.087 Youth who have been diverted — Alleged prostitution or prostitution loitering offenses — Services and treatment.

Within available funding, when a youth who has been diverted under RCW 13.40.070 for an alleged offense of prostitution or prostitution loitering is referred to the department, the department shall connect that youth with the services and treatment specified in RCW *74.14B.060 and 74.14B.070 .

[2010 c 289 § 5.]

RCW 13.40.090 Prosecuting attorney as party to juvenile court proceedings -- Exception, procedure.

The county prosecuting attorney shall be a party to all juvenile court proceedings involving juvenile offenders or alleged juvenile offenders.

The prosecuting attorney may, after giving appropriate notice to the juvenile court, decline to represent the state of Washington in juvenile court matters except felonies unless requested by the court on an individual basis to represent the state at an adjudicatory hearing in which case he or she shall participate. When the prosecutor declines to represent the state, then such function may be performed by the juvenile court probation counselor authorized by the court or local court rule to serve as the prosecuting authority.

If the prosecuting attorney elects not to participate, the prosecuting attorney shall file with the county clerk each year by the first Monday in July notice of intent not to participate. In a county wherein the prosecuting attorney has elected not to participate in juvenile court, he or she shall not thereafter until the next filing date participate in juvenile court proceedings unless so requested by the court on an individual basis, in which case the prosecuting attorney shall participate.

[1977 ex.s. c 291 § 63.]

RCW 13.40.100 Summons or other notification issued upon filing of information -- Procedure -- Order to take juvenile into custody -- Contempt of court, when.

(1) Upon the filing of an information the alleged offender shall be notified by summons, warrant, or other method approved by the court of the next required court appearance.

(2) If notice is by summons, the clerk of the court shall issue a summons directed to the juvenile, if the juvenile is twelve or more years of age, and another to the parents, guardian, or custodian,

SECTION 2: RCW 13.40: JUVENILE JUSTICE ACT OF 1977, AS AMENDED

and such other persons as appear to the court to be proper or necessary parties to the proceedings, requiring them to appear personally before the court at the time fixed to hear the petition. Where the custodian is summoned, the parent or guardian or both shall also be served with a summons.

(3) A copy of the information shall be attached to each summons.

(4) The summons shall advise the parties of the right to counsel.

(5) The judge may endorse upon the summons an order directing the parents, guardian, or custodian having the custody or control of the juvenile to bring the juvenile to the hearing.

(6) If it appears from affidavit or sworn statement presented to the judge that there is probable cause for the issuance of a warrant of arrest or that the juvenile needs to be taken into custody pursuant to RCW 13.34.050, the judge may endorse upon the summons an order that an officer serving the summons shall at once take the juvenile into custody and take the juvenile to the place of detention or shelter designated by the court.

(7) Service of summons may be made under the direction of the court by any law enforcement officer or probation counselor.

(8) If the person summoned as herein provided fails without reasonable cause to appear and abide the order of the court, the person may be proceeded against as for contempt of court. In determining whether a parent, guardian, or custodian had reasonable cause not to appear, the court may consider all factors relevant to the person's ability to appear as summoned.

[1997 c 338 § 19; 1979 c 155 § 62; 1977 ex.s. c 291 § 64.]

RCW 13.40.110 Hearing on question of declining jurisdiction — Held, when — Findings.

(1) Discretionary decline hearing - The prosecutor, respondent, or the court on its own motion may, before a hearing on the information on its merits, file a motion requesting the court to transfer the respondent for adult criminal prosecution and the matter shall be set for a hearing on the question of declining jurisdiction.

(2) Mandatory decline hearing - Unless waived by the court, the parties, and their counsel, a decline hearing shall be held when:

(a) The respondent is sixteen or seventeen years of age and the information alleges a class A felony or an attempt, solicitation, or conspiracy to commit a class A felony;

(b) The respondent is seventeen years of age and the information alleges assault in the second degree, extortion in the first degree, indecent liberties, child molestation in the second degree, kidnapping in the second degree, or robbery in the second degree; or

---

The Caseload Forecast Council is not liable for errors or omissions in the manual, for sentences that may be inappropriately calculated as a result of a practitioner's or court's reliance on the manual, or for any other written or verbal information related to adult or juvenile sentencing. The scoring sheets are intended to provide assistance in most cases but does not cover all permutations of the scoring rules. If you find any errors or omissions, we encourage you to report them to the Caseload Forecast Council.

SECTION 2: RCW 13.40: JUVENILE JUSTICE ACT OF 1977, AS AMENDED

(c) The information alleges an escape by the respondent and the respondent is serving a minimum juvenile sentence to age twenty-one.

(3) The court after a decline hearing may order the case transferred for adult criminal prosecution upon a finding that the declination would be in the best interest of the juvenile or the public. The court shall consider the relevant reports, facts, opinions, and arguments presented by the parties and their counsel.

(4) When the respondent is transferred for criminal prosecution or retained for prosecution in juvenile court, the court shall set forth in writing its finding which shall be supported by relevant facts and opinions produced at the hearing.

[2009 c 454 § 3; 1997 c 338 § 20; 1990 c 3 § 303; 1988 c 145 § 18; 1979 c 155 § 63; 1977 ex.s. c 291 § 65.]

RCW 13.40.120 Hearings — Time and place.

All hearings may be conducted at any time or place within the limits of the judicial district, and such cases may not be heard in conjunction with other business of any other division of the superior court.

[1981 c 299 § 9; 1979 c 155 § 64; 1977 ex.s. c 291 § 66.]

RCW 13.40.127 Deferred disposition.

(1) A juvenile is eligible for deferred disposition unless he or she:

(a) Is charged with a sex or violent offense;

(b) Has a criminal history which includes any felony;

(c) Has a prior deferred disposition or deferred adjudication; or

(d) Has two or more adjudications.

(2) The juvenile court may, upon motion at least fourteen days before commencement of trial and, after consulting the juvenile's custodial parent or parents or guardian and with the consent of the juvenile, continue the case for disposition for a period not to exceed one year from the date the juvenile is found guilty. The court shall consider whether the offender and the community will benefit from a deferred disposition before deferring the disposition. The court may waive the fourteen-day period any time before the commencement of trial for good cause.

The Caseload Forecast Council is not liable for errors or omissions in the manual, for sentences that may be inappropriately calculated as a result of a practitioner's or court's reliance on the manual, or for any other written or verbal information related to adult or juvenile sentencing. The scoring sheets are intended to provide assistance in most cases but does not cover all permutations of the scoring rules. If you find any errors or omissions, we encourage you to report them to the Caseload Forecast Council.

SECTION 2: RCW 13.40: JUVENILE JUSTICE ACT OF 1977, AS AMENDED

(3) Any juvenile who agrees to a deferral of disposition shall:

(a) Stipulate to the admissibility of the facts contained in the written police report;

(b) Acknowledge that the report will be entered and used to support a finding of guilt and to impose a disposition if the juvenile fails to comply with terms of supervision;

(c) Waive the following rights to: (i) A speedy disposition; and (ii) call and confront witnesses; and

(d) Acknowledge the direct consequences of being found guilty and the direct consequences that will happen if an order of disposition is entered.

The adjudicatory hearing shall be limited to a reading of the court's record.

(4) Following the stipulation, acknowledgment, waiver, and entry of a finding or plea of guilt, the court shall defer entry of an order of disposition of the juvenile.

(5) Any juvenile granted a deferral of disposition under this section shall be placed under community supervision. The court may impose any conditions of supervision that it deems appropriate including posting a probation bond. Payment of restitution under RCW 13.40.190 shall be a condition of community supervision under this section.

The court may require a juvenile offender convicted of animal cruelty in the first degree to submit to a mental health evaluation to determine if the offender would benefit from treatment and such intervention would promote the safety of the community. After consideration of the results of the evaluation, as a condition of community supervision, the court may order the offender to attend treatment to address issues pertinent to the offense.

(6) A parent who signed for a probation bond has the right to notify the counselor if the juvenile fails to comply with the bond or conditions of supervision. The counselor shall notify the court and surety of any failure to comply. A surety shall notify the court of the juvenile's failure to comply with the probation bond. The state shall bear the burden to prove, by a preponderance of the evidence, that the juvenile has failed to comply with the terms of community supervision.

(7)(a) Any time prior to the conclusion of the period of supervision, the prosecutor or the juvenile's juvenile court community supervision counselor may file a motion with the court requesting the court revoke the deferred disposition based on the juvenile's lack of compliance or treat the juvenile's lack of compliance as a violation pursuant to RCW 13.40.200.

(b) If the court finds the juvenile failed to comply with the terms of the deferred disposition, the

SECTION 2: RCW 13.40: JUVENILE JUSTICE ACT OF 1977, AS AMENDED

court may:

(i) Revoke the deferred disposition and enter an order of disposition; or

(ii) Impose sanctions for the violation pursuant to RCW 13.40.200.

(8) At any time following deferral of disposition the court may, following a hearing, continue supervision for an additional one-year period for good cause.

(9)(a) At the conclusion of the period of supervision, the court shall determine whether the juvenile is entitled to dismissal of the deferred disposition only when the court finds:

(i) The deferred disposition has not been previously revoked;

(ii) The juvenile has completed the terms of supervision;

(iii) There are no pending motions concerning lack of compliance pursuant to subsection (7) of this section; and

(iv) The juvenile has either paid the full amount of restitution, or, made a good faith effort to pay the full amount of restitution during the period of supervision.

(b) If the court finds the juvenile is entitled to dismissal of the deferred disposition pursuant to (a) of this subsection, the juvenile's conviction shall be vacated and the court shall dismiss the case with prejudice, except that a conviction under RCW 16.52.205 shall not be vacated. Whenever a case is dismissed with restitution still owing, the court shall enter a restitution order pursuant to RCW 13.40.190 for any unpaid restitution. Jurisdiction to enforce payment and modify terms of the restitution order shall be the same as those set forth in RCW 13.40.190.

(c) If the court finds the juvenile is not entitled to dismissal of the deferred disposition pursuant to (a) of this subsection, the court shall revoke the deferred disposition and enter an order of disposition. A deferred disposition shall remain a conviction unless the case is dismissed and the conviction is vacated pursuant to (b) of this subsection or sealed pursuant to RCW 13.50.050.

(10)(a)(i) Any time the court vacates a conviction pursuant to subsection (9) of this section, if the juvenile is eighteen years of age or older and the full amount of restitution ordered has been paid, the court shall enter a written order sealing the case.

(ii) Any time the court vacates a conviction pursuant to subsection (9) of this section, if the juvenile is not eighteen years of age or older and full restitution ordered has been paid, the court shall schedule an administrative sealing hearing to take place no later than thirty days after the respondent's eighteenth birthday, at which time the court shall enter a written order sealing the case. The respondent's presence at the administrative sealing hearing is not required.

SECTION 2: RCW 13.40: JUVENILE JUSTICE ACT OF 1977, AS AMENDED

(iii) Any deferred disposition vacated prior to June 7, 2012, is not subject to sealing under this subsection.

(b) Nothing in this subsection shall preclude a juvenile from petitioning the court to have the records of his or her deferred dispositions sealed under RCW 13.50.050 (11) and (12).

(c) Records sealed under this provision shall have the same legal status as records sealed under RCW 13.50.050.

[2012 c 177 § 1; 2009 c 236 § 1; 2004 c 117 § 2; 2001 c 175 § 3; 1997 c 338 § 21.]

RCW 13.40.130 Procedure upon plea of guilty or not guilty to information allegations — Notice — Adjudicatory and disposition hearing — Disposition standards used in sentencing.

(1) The respondent shall be advised of the allegations in the information and shall be required to plead guilty or not guilty to the allegation(s). The state or the respondent may make preliminary motions up to the time of the plea.

(2) If the respondent pleads guilty, the court may proceed with disposition or may continue the case for a dispositional hearing. If the respondent denies guilt, an adjudicatory hearing date shall be set. The court shall notify the parent, guardian, or custodian who has custody of a juvenile described in the charging document of the dispositional or adjudicatory hearing and shall require attendance.

(3) At the adjudicatory hearing it shall be the burden of the prosecution to prove the allegations of the information beyond a reasonable doubt.

(4) The court shall record its findings of fact and shall enter its decision upon the record. Such findings shall set forth the evidence relied upon by the court in reaching its decision.

(5) If the respondent is found not guilty he or she shall be released from detention.

(6) If the respondent is found guilty the court may immediately proceed to disposition or may continue the case for a dispositional hearing. Notice of the time and place of the continued hearing may be given in open court. If notice is not given in open court to a party, the party and the parent, guardian, or custodian who has custody of the juvenile shall be notified by mail of the time and place of the continued hearing.

(7) The court following an adjudicatory hearing may request that a predisposition study be prepared to aid the court in its evaluation of the matters relevant to disposition of the case.

(8) The disposition hearing shall be held within fourteen days after the adjudicatory hearing or

---

The Caseload Forecast Council is not liable for errors or omissions in the manual, for sentences that may be inappropriately calculated as a result of a practitioner's or court's reliance on the manual, or for any other written or verbal information related to adult or juvenile sentencing. The scoring sheets are intended to provide assistance in most cases but does not cover all permutations of the scoring rules. If you find any errors or omissions, we encourage you to report them to the Caseload Forecast Council.

SECTION 2: RCW 13.40: JUVENILE JUSTICE ACT OF 1977, AS AMENDED

plea of guilty unless good cause is shown for further delay, or within twenty-one days if the juvenile is not held in a detention facility, unless good cause is shown for further delay.

(9) In sentencing an offender, the court shall use the disposition standards in effect on the date of the offense.

(10) A person notified under this section who fails without reasonable cause to appear and abide by the order of the court may be proceeded against as for contempt of court. In determining whether a parent, guardian, or custodian had reasonable cause not to appear, the court may consider all factors relevant to the person's ability to appear as summoned.

[1997 c 338 § 22; 1981 c 299 § 10; 1979 c 155 § 65; 1977 ex.s. c 291 § 67.]

RCW 13.40.135 Sexual motivation special allegation — Procedures.

(1) The prosecuting attorney shall file a special allegation of sexual motivation in every juvenile offense other than sex offenses as defined in RCW

9.94A.030 when sufficient admissible evidence exists, which, when considered with the most plausible, reasonably consistent defense that could be raised under the evidence, would justify a finding of sexual motivation by a reasonable and objective fact finder.

(2) In a juvenile case wherein there has been a special allegation the state shall prove beyond a reasonable doubt that the juvenile committed the offense with a sexual motivation. The court shall make a finding of fact of whether or not the sexual motivation was present at the time of the commission of the offense. This finding shall not be applied to sex offenses as defined in RCW 9.94A.030.

(3) The prosecuting attorney shall not withdraw the special allegation of "sexual motivation" without approval of the court through an order of dismissal. The court shall not dismiss the special allegation unless it finds that such an order is necessary to correct an error in the initial charging decision or unless there are evidentiary problems which make proving the special allegation doubtful.

[2009 c 28 § 33; 1997 c 338 § 23; 1990 c 3 § 604.]

RCW 13.40.140 Juveniles entitled to usual judicial rights — Notice of — Open court — Privilege against self-incrimination — Waiver of rights, when.

(1) A juvenile shall be advised of his or her rights when appearing before the court.

(2) A juvenile and his or her parent, guardian, or custodian shall be advised by the court or its

SECTION 2: RCW 13.40: JUVENILE JUSTICE ACT OF 1977, AS AMENDED

representative that the juvenile has a right to be represented by counsel at all critical stages of the proceedings. Unless waived, counsel shall be provided to a juvenile who is financially unable to obtain counsel without causing substantial hardship to himself or herself or the juvenile's family, in any proceeding where the juvenile may be subject to transfer for criminal prosecution, or in any proceeding where the juvenile may be in danger of confinement. The ability to pay part of the cost of counsel does not preclude assignment. In no case may a juvenile be deprived of counsel because of a parent, guardian, or custodian refusing to pay therefor. The juvenile shall be fully advised of his or her right to an attorney and of the relevant services an attorney can provide.

(3) The right to counsel includes the right to the appointment of experts necessary, and the experts shall be required pursuant to the procedures and requirements established by the supreme court.

(4) Upon application of a party, the clerk of the court shall issue, and the court on its own motion may issue, subpoenas requiring attendance and testimony of witnesses and production of records, documents, or other tangible objects at any hearing, or such subpoenas may be issued by an attorney of record.

(5) All proceedings shall be transcribed verbatim by means which will provide an accurate record.

(6) The general public and press shall be permitted to attend any hearing unless the court, for good cause, orders a particular hearing to be closed. The presumption shall be that all such hearings will be open.

(7) In all adjudicatory proceedings before the court, all parties shall have the right to adequate notice, discovery as provided in criminal cases, opportunity to be heard, confrontation of witnesses except in such cases as this chapter expressly permits the use of hearsay testimony, findings based solely upon the evidence adduced at the hearing, and an unbiased fact finder.

(8) A juvenile shall be accorded the same privilege against self-incrimination as an adult. An extrajudicial statement which would be constitutionally inadmissible in a criminal proceeding may not be received in evidence at an adjudicatory hearing over objection. Evidence illegally seized or obtained may not be received in evidence over objection at an adjudicatory hearing to prove the allegations against the juvenile if the evidence would be inadmissible in an adult criminal proceeding. An extrajudicial admission or confession made by the juvenile out of court is insufficient to support a finding that the juvenile committed the acts alleged in the information unless evidence of a corpus delicti is first independently established in the same manner as required in an adult criminal proceeding.

(9) Waiver of any right which a juvenile has under this chapter must be an express waiver intelligently made by the juvenile after the juvenile has been fully informed of the right being

---

The Caseload Forecast Council is not liable for errors or omissions in the manual, for sentences that may be inappropriately calculated as a result of a practitioner's or court's reliance on the manual, or for any other written or verbal information related to adult or juvenile sentencing. The scoring sheets are intended to provide assistance in most cases but does not cover all permutations of the scoring rules. If you find any errors or omissions, we encourage you to report them to the Caseload Forecast Council.

SECTION 2: RCW 13.40: JUVENILE JUSTICE ACT OF 1977, AS AMENDED

waived.

(10) Whenever this chapter refers to waiver or objection by a juvenile, the word juvenile shall be construed to refer to a juvenile who is at least twelve years of age. If a juvenile is under twelve years of age, the juvenile's parent, guardian, or custodian shall give any waiver or offer any objection contemplated by this chapter.

[1981 c 299 § 11; 1979 c 155 § 66; 1977 ex.s. c 291 § 68.]

RCW 13.40.145 Payment of fees for legal services by publicly funded counsel — Hearing — Order or decree — Entering and enforcing judgments.

Upon disposition or at the time of a modification or at the time an appellate court remands the case to the trial court following a ruling in favor of the state the court may order the juvenile or a parent or another person legally obligated to support the juvenile to appear, and the court may inquire into the ability of those persons to pay a reasonable sum representing in whole or in part the fees for legal services provided by publicly funded counsel and the costs incurred by the public in producing a verbatim report of proceedings and clerk's papers for use in the appellate courts.

If, after hearing, the court finds the juvenile, parent, or other legally obligated person able to pay part or all of the attorney's fees and costs incurred on appeal, the court may enter such order or decree as is equitable and may enforce the order or decree by execution, or in any way in which a court of equity may enforce its decrees.

In no event may the court order an amount to be paid for attorneys' fees that exceeds the average per case fee allocation for juvenile proceedings in the county where the services have been provided or the average per case fee allocation for juvenile appeals established by the Washington supreme court.

In any case in which there is no compliance with an order or decree of the court requiring a juvenile, parent, or other person legally obligated to support the juvenile to pay for legal services provided by publicly funded counsel, the court may, upon such person or persons being properly summoned or voluntarily appearing, proceed to inquire into the amount due upon the order or decree and enter judgment for that amount against the defaulting party or parties. Judgment shall be docketed in the same manner as are other judgments for the payment of money.

The county in which such judgments are entered shall be denominated the judgment creditor, and the judgments may be enforced by the prosecuting attorney of that county. Any moneys recovered thereon shall be paid into the registry of the court and shall be disbursed to such person, persons, agency, or governmental entity as the court finds entitled thereto.

Such judgments shall remain valid and enforceable for a period of ten years subsequent to entry.

The Caseload Forecast Council is not liable for errors or omissions in the manual, for sentences that may be inappropriately calculated as a result of a practitioner's or court's reliance on the manual, or for any other written or verbal information related to adult or juvenile sentencing. The scoring sheets are intended to provide assistance in most cases but does not cover all permutations of the scoring rules. If you find any errors or omissions, we encourage you to report them to the Caseload Forecast Council.

SECTION 2: RCW 13.40: JUVENILE JUSTICE ACT OF 1977, AS AMENDED

When the juvenile reaches the age of eighteen or at the conclusion of juvenile court jurisdiction, whichever occurs later, the superior court clerk must docket the remaining balance of the juvenile's legal financial obligations in the same manner as other judgments for the payment of money. The judgment remains valid and enforceable until ten years from the date of its imposition. The clerk of superior court may seek extension of the judgment for legal financial obligations, including crime victims' assessments, in the same manner as RCW

6.17.020 for purposes of collection as allowed under RCW 36.18.190.

[1997 c 121 § 6; 1995 c 275 § 4; 1984 c 86 § 1.]

RCW 13.40.150 Disposition hearing — Scope — Factors to be considered prior to entry of dispositional order.

(1) In disposition hearings all relevant and material evidence, including oral and written reports, may be received by the court and may be relied upon to the extent of its probative value, even though such evidence may not be admissible in a hearing on the information. The youth or the youth's counsel and the prosecuting attorney shall be afforded an opportunity to examine and controvert written reports so received and to cross-examine individuals making reports when such individuals are reasonably available, but sources of confidential information need not be disclosed. The prosecutor and counsel for the juvenile may submit recommendations for disposition.

(2) For purposes of disposition:

(a) Violations which are current offenses count as misdemeanors;

(b) Violations may not count as part of the offender's criminal history;

(c) In no event may a disposition for a violation include confinement.

(3) Before entering a dispositional order as to a respondent found to have committed an offense, the court shall hold a disposition hearing, at which the court shall:

(a) Consider the facts supporting the allegations of criminal conduct by the respondent;

(b) Consider information and arguments offered by parties and their counsel;

(c) Consider any predisposition reports;

(d) Consult with the respondent's parent, guardian, or custodian on the appropriateness of

SECTION 2: RCW 13.40: JUVENILE JUSTICE ACT OF 1977, AS AMENDED

dispositional options under consideration and afford the respondent and the respondent's parent, guardian, or custodian an opportunity to speak in the respondent's behalf;

(e) Allow the victim or a representative of the victim and an investigative law enforcement officer to speak;

(f) Determine the amount of restitution owing to the victim, if any, or set a hearing for a later date not to exceed one hundred eighty days from the date of the disposition hearing to determine the amount, except that the court may continue the hearing beyond the one hundred eighty days for good cause;

(g) Determine the respondent's offender score;

(h) Consider whether or not any of the following mitigating factors exist:

(i) The respondent's conduct neither caused nor threatened serious bodily injury or the respondent did not contemplate that his or her conduct would cause or threaten serious bodily injury;

(ii) The respondent acted under strong and immediate provocation;

(iii) The respondent was suffering from a mental or physical condition that significantly reduced his or her culpability for the offense though failing to establish a defense;

(iv) Prior to his or her detection, the respondent compensated or made a good faith attempt to compensate the victim for the injury or loss sustained; and

(v) There has been at least one year between the respondent's current offense and any prior criminal offense;

(i) Consider whether or not any of the following aggravating factors exist:

(i) In the commission of the offense, or in flight therefrom, the respondent inflicted or attempted to inflict serious bodily injury to another;

(ii) The offense was committed in an especially heinous, cruel, or depraved manner;

(iii) The victim or victims were particularly vulnerable;

(iv) The respondent has a recent criminal history or has failed to comply with conditions of a recent dispositional order or diversion agreement;

(v) The current offense included a finding of sexual motivation pursuant to RCW 13.40.135;

The Caseload Forecast Council is not liable for errors or omissions in the manual, for sentences that may be inappropriately calculated as a result of a practitioner's or court's reliance on the manual, or for any other written or verbal information related to adult or juvenile sentencing. The scoring sheets are intended to provide assistance in most cases but does not cover all permutations of the scoring rules. If you find any errors or omissions, we encourage you to report them to the Caseload Forecast Council.

SECTION 2: RCW 13.40: JUVENILE JUSTICE ACT OF 1977, AS AMENDED

(vi) The respondent was the leader of a criminal enterprise involving several persons;

(vii) There are other complaints which have resulted in diversion or a finding or plea of guilty but which are not included as criminal history; and

(viii) The standard range disposition is clearly too lenient considering the seriousness of the juvenile's prior adjudications.

(4) The following factors may not be considered in determining the punishment to be imposed:

(a) The sex of the respondent;

(b) The race or color of the respondent or the respondent's family;

(c) The creed or religion of the respondent or the respondent's family;

(d) The economic or social class of the respondent or the respondent's family; and

(e) Factors indicating that the respondent may be or is a dependent child within the meaning of this chapter.

(5) A court may not commit a juvenile to a state institution solely because of the lack of facilities, including treatment facilities, existing in the community.

[1998 c 86 § 1; 1997 c 338 § 24; 1995 c 268 § 5; 1992 c 205 § 109; 1990 c 3 § 605; 1981 c 299 § 12; 1979 c 155 § 67; 1977 ex.s. c 291 § 69.]

RCW 13.40.160 Disposition order — Court's action prescribed — Disposition outside standard range — Right of appeal — Special sex offender disposition alternative.

(1) The standard range disposition for a juvenile adjudicated of an offense is determined according to RCW 13.40.0357.

(a) When the court sentences an offender to a local sanction as provided in RCW 13.40.0357 option A, the court shall impose a determinate disposition within the standard ranges, except as provided in subsection (2), (3), (4), (5), or (6) of this section. The disposition may be comprised of one or more local sanctions.

(b) When the court sentences an offender to a standard range as provided in RCW 13.40.0357 option A that includes a term of confinement exceeding thirty days, commitment shall be to the department for the standard range of confinement, except as provided in subsection (2), (3), (4), (5), or (6) of this section.

The Caseload Forecast Council is not liable for errors or omissions in the manual, for sentences that may be inappropriately calculated as a result of a practitioner's or court's reliance on the manual, or for any other written or verbal information related to adult or juvenile sentencing. The scoring sheets are intended to provide assistance in most cases but does not cover all permutations of the scoring rules. If you find any errors or omissions, we encourage you to report them to the Caseload Forecast Council.

SECTION 2: RCW 13.40: JUVENILE JUSTICE ACT OF 1977, AS AMENDED

(2) If the court concludes, and enters reasons for its conclusion, that disposition within the standard range would effectuate a manifest injustice the court shall impose a disposition outside the standard range, as indicated in option D of RCW 13.40.0357. The court's finding of manifest injustice shall be supported by clear and convincing evidence.

A disposition outside the standard range shall be determinate and shall be comprised of confinement or community supervision, or a combination thereof. When a judge finds a manifest injustice and imposes a sentence of confinement exceeding thirty days, the court shall sentence the juvenile to a maximum term, and the provisions of RCW 13.40.030(2) shall be used to determine the range. A disposition outside the standard range is appealable under RCW 13.40.230 by the state or the respondent. A disposition within the standard range is not appealable under RCW 13.40.230.

(3) If a juvenile offender is found to have committed a sex offense, other than a sex offense that is also a serious violent offense as defined by RCW 9.94A.030, and has no history of a prior sex offense, the court may impose the special sex offender disposition alternative under RCW 13.40.162.

(4) If the juvenile offender is subject to a standard range disposition of local sanctions or 15 to 36 weeks of confinement and has not committed an A- or B+ offense, the court may impose the disposition alternative under RCW 13.40.165.

(5) If a juvenile is subject to a commitment of 15 to 65 weeks of confinement, the court may impose the disposition alternative under RCW 13.40.167.

(6) When the offender is subject to a standard range commitment of 15 to 36 weeks and is ineligible for a suspended disposition alternative, a manifest injustice disposition below the standard range, special sex offender disposition alternative, chemical dependency disposition alternative, or mental health disposition alternative, the court in a county with a pilot program under *RCW 13.40.169 may impose the disposition alternative under *RCW 13.40.169.

(7) RCW 13.40.193 shall govern the disposition of any juvenile adjudicated of possessing a firearm in violation of RCW 9.41.040(2)(a)(iii) or any crime in which a special finding is entered that the juvenile was armed with a firearm.

(8) RCW 13.40.308 shall govern the disposition of any juvenile adjudicated of theft of a motor vehicle as defined under RCW 9A.56.065, possession of a stolen motor vehicle as defined under RCW 9A.56.068, taking a motor vehicle without permission in the first degree under RCW 9A.56.070, and taking a motor vehicle without permission in the second degree under RCW 9A.56.075.

(9) Whenever a juvenile offender is entitled to credit for time spent in detention prior to a

---

The Caseload Forecast Council is not liable for errors or omissions in the manual, for sentences that may be inappropriately calculated as a result of a practitioner's or court's reliance on the manual, or for any other written or verbal information related to adult or juvenile sentencing. The scoring sheets are intended to provide assistance in most cases but does not cover all permutations of the scoring rules. If you find any errors or omissions, we encourage you to report them to the Caseload Forecast Council.

SECTION 2: RCW 13.40: JUVENILE JUSTICE ACT OF 1977, AS AMENDED

dispositional order, the dispositional order shall specifically state the number of days of credit for time served.

(10) Except as provided under subsection (3), (4), (5), or (6) of this section, or option B of RCW 13.40.0357, or RCW 13.40.127, the court shall not suspend or defer the imposition or the execution of the disposition.

(11) In no case shall the term of confinement imposed by the court at disposition exceed that to which an adult could be subjected for the same offense.

[2011 c 338 § 2; 2007 c 199 § 14. Prior: 2004 c 120 § 4; 2004 c 38 § 11; prior: 2003 c 378 § 3; 2003 c 53 § 99; 2002 c 175 § 22; 1999 c 91 § 2; prior: 1997 c 338 § 25; 1997 c 265 § 1; 1995 c 395 § 7; 1994 sp.s. c 7 § 523; 1992 c 45 § 6; 1990 c 3 § 302; 1989 c 407 § 4; 1983 c 191 § 8; 1981 c 299 § 13; 1979 c 155 § 68; 1977 ex.s. c 291 § 70.]

RCW 13.40.162 Special sex offender disposition alternative.

(1) A juvenile offender is eligible for the special sex offender disposition alternative when:

(a) The offender is found to have committed a sex offense, other than a sex offense that is also a serious violent offense as defined by RCW 9.94A.030; and

(b) The offender has no history of a prior sex offense.

(2) If the court finds the offender is eligible for this alternative, the court, on its own motion or the motion of the state or the respondent, may order an examination to determine whether the respondent is amenable to treatment.

(a) The report of the examination shall include at a minimum the following:

(i) The respondent's version of the facts and the official version of the facts;

(ii) The respondent's offense history;

(iii) An assessment of problems in addition to alleged deviant behaviors;

(iv) The respondent's social, educational, and employment situation;

(v) Other evaluation measures used.

The report shall set forth the sources of the evaluator's information.

(b) The examiner shall assess and report regarding the respondent's amenability to treatment and

SECTION 2: RCW 13.40: JUVENILE JUSTICE ACT OF 1977, AS AMENDED

relative risk to the community. A proposed treatment plan shall be provided and shall include, at a minimum:

(i) The frequency and type of contact between the offender and therapist;

(ii) Specific issues to be addressed in the treatment and description of planned treatment modalities;

(iii) Monitoring plans, including any requirements regarding living conditions, lifestyle requirements, and monitoring by family members, legal guardians, or others;

(iv) Anticipated length of treatment; and

(v) Recommended crime-related prohibitions.

(c) The court on its own motion may order, or on a motion by the state shall order, a second examination regarding the offender's amenability to treatment. The evaluator shall be selected by the party making the motion. The defendant shall pay the cost of any second examination ordered unless the court finds the defendant to be indigent in which case the state shall pay the cost.

(3) After receipt of reports of the examination, the court shall then consider whether the offender and the community will benefit from use of this special sex offender disposition alternative and consider the victim's opinion whether the offender should receive a treatment disposition under this section. If the court determines that this special sex offender disposition alternative is appropriate, then the court shall impose a determinate disposition within the standard range for the offense, or if the court concludes, and enters reasons for its conclusions, that such disposition would cause a manifest injustice, the court shall impose a disposition under option D, and the court may suspend the execution of the disposition and place the offender on community supervision for at least two years.

(4) As a condition of the suspended disposition, the court may impose the conditions of community supervision and other conditions, including up to thirty days of confinement and requirements that the offender do any one or more of the following:

(a) Devote time to a specific education, employment, or occupation;

(b) Undergo available outpatient sex offender treatment for up to two years, or inpatient sex offender treatment not to exceed the standard range of confinement for that offense. A community mental health center may not be used for such treatment unless it has an appropriate program designed for sex offender treatment. The respondent shall not change sex offender treatment providers or treatment conditions without first notifying the prosecutor, the probation counselor, and the court, and shall not change providers without court approval after a hearing if

SECTION 2: RCW 13.40: JUVENILE JUSTICE ACT OF 1977, AS AMENDED

the prosecutor or probation counselor object to the change;

(c) Remain within prescribed geographical boundaries and notify the court or the probation counselor prior to any change in the offender's address, educational program, or employment;

(d) Report to the prosecutor and the probation counselor prior to any change in a sex offender treatment provider. This change shall have prior approval by the court;

(e) Report as directed to the court and a probation counselor;

(f) Pay all court-ordered legal financial obligations, perform community restitution, or any combination thereof;

(g) Make restitution to the victim for the cost of any counseling reasonably related to the offense;

or

(h) Comply with the conditions of any court-ordered probation bond.

(5) If the court orders twenty-four hour, continuous monitoring of the offender while on probation, the court shall include the basis for this condition in its findings.

(6)(a) The court must order the offender not to attend the public or approved private elementary, middle, or high school attended by the victim or the victim's siblings.

(b) The parents or legal guardians of the offender are responsible for transportation or other costs associated with the offender's change of school that would otherwise be paid by the school district.

(c) The court shall send notice of the disposition and restriction on attending the same school as the victim or victim's siblings to the public or approved private school the juvenile will attend, if known, or if unknown, to the approved private schools and the public school district board of directors of the district in which the juvenile resides or intends to reside. This notice must be sent at the earliest possible date but not later than ten calendar days after entry of the disposition.

(7)(a) The sex offender treatment provider shall submit quarterly reports on the respondent's progress in treatment to the court and the parties. The reports shall reference the treatment plan and include at a minimum the following: Dates of attendance, respondent's compliance with requirements, treatment activities, the respondent's relative progress in treatment, and any other material specified by the court at the time of the disposition.

(b) At the time of the disposition, the court may set treatment review hearings as the court considers appropriate.

SECTION 2: RCW 13.40: JUVENILE JUSTICE ACT OF 1977, AS AMENDED

(c) Except as provided in this subsection, examinations and treatment ordered pursuant to this subsection shall only be conducted by certified sex offender treatment providers or certified affiliate sex offender treatment providers under chapter 18.155 RCW.

(d) A sex offender therapist who examines or treats a juvenile sex offender pursuant to this subsection does not have to be certified by the department of health pursuant to chapter 18.155 RCW if the court finds that: (i) The offender has already moved to another state or plans to move to another state for reasons other than circumventing the certification requirements; (ii) no certified sex offender treatment providers or certified affiliate sex offender treatment providers are available for treatment within a reasonable geographical distance of the offender's home; and (iii) the evaluation and treatment plan comply with this subsection and the rules adopted by the department of health.

(8)(a) If the offender violates any condition of the disposition or the court finds that the respondent is failing to make satisfactory progress in treatment, the court may revoke the suspension and order execution of the disposition or the court may impose a penalty of up to thirty days confinement for violating conditions of the disposition.

(b) The court may order both execution of the disposition and up to thirty days confinement for the violation of the conditions of the disposition.

(c) The court shall give credit for any confinement time previously served if that confinement was for the offense for which the suspension is being revoked.

(9) For purposes of this section, "victim" means any person who has sustained emotional, psychological, physical, or financial injury to person or property as a direct result of the crime charged. "Victim" may also include a known parent or guardian of a victim who is a minor child unless the parent or guardian is the perpetrator of the offense.

(10) A disposition entered under this section is not appealable under RCW 13.40.230.

[2011 c 338 § 3.]

RCW 13.40.165 Chemical dependency disposition alternative.

(1) The purpose of this disposition alternative is to ensure that successful treatment options to reduce recidivism are available to eligible youth, pursuant to RCW 70.96A.520. The court must consider eligibility for the chemical dependency disposition alternative when a juvenile offender is subject to a standard range disposition of local sanctions or 15 to 36 weeks of confinement and has not committed an A- or B+ offense, other than a first time B+ offense under chapter 69.50 RCW. The court, on its own motion or the motion of the state or the respondent if the evidence shows that the offender may be chemically dependent or substance abusing, may order an

SECTION 2: RCW 13.40: JUVENILE JUSTICE ACT OF 1977, AS AMENDED

examination by a chemical dependency counselor from a chemical dependency treatment facility approved under chapter 70.96A RCW to determine if the youth is chemically dependent or substance abusing. The offender shall pay the cost of any examination ordered under this subsection unless the court finds that the offender is indigent and no third party insurance coverage is available, in which case the state shall pay the cost.

(2) The report of the examination shall include at a minimum the following: The respondent's version of the facts and the official version of the facts, the respondent's offense history, an assessment of drug-alcohol problems and previous treatment attempts, the respondent's social, educational, and employment situation, and other evaluation measures used. The report shall set forth the sources of the examiner's information.

(3) The examiner shall assess and report regarding the respondent's relative risk to the community. A proposed treatment plan shall be provided and shall include, at a minimum:

(a) Whether inpatient and/or outpatient treatment is recommended;

(b) Availability of appropriate treatment;

(c) Monitoring plans, including any requirements regarding living conditions, lifestyle requirements, and monitoring by family members, legal guardians, or others;

(d) Anticipated length of treatment; and

(e) Recommended crime-related prohibitions.

(4) The court on its own motion may order, or on a motion by the state or the respondent shall order, a second examination. The evaluator shall be selected by the party making the motion. The requesting party shall pay the cost of any examination ordered under this subsection unless the requesting party is the offender and the court finds that the offender is indigent and no third party insurance coverage is available, in which case the state shall pay the cost.

(5)(a) After receipt of reports of the examination, the court shall then consider whether the offender and the community will benefit from use of this chemical dependency disposition alternative and consider the victim's opinion whether the offender should receive a treatment disposition under this section.

(b) If the court determines that this chemical dependency disposition alternative is appropriate, then the court shall impose the standard range for the offense, or if the court concludes, and enters reasons for its conclusion, that such disposition would effectuate a manifest injustice, the court shall impose a disposition above the standard range as indicated in option D of RCW 13.40.0357 if the disposition is an increase from the standard range and the confinement of the offender does not exceed a maximum of fifty-two weeks, suspend execution of the disposition,

---

The Caseload Forecast Council is not liable for errors or omissions in the manual, for sentences that may be inappropriately calculated as a result of a practitioner's or court's reliance on the manual, or for any other written or verbal information related to adult or juvenile sentencing. The scoring sheets are intended to provide assistance in most cases but does not cover all permutations of the scoring rules. If you find any errors or omissions, we encourage you to report them to the Caseload Forecast Council.

SECTION 2: RCW 13.40: JUVENILE JUSTICE ACT OF 1977, AS AMENDED

and place the offender on community supervision for up to one year. As a condition of the suspended disposition, the court shall require the offender to undergo available outpatient drug/alcohol treatment and/or inpatient drug/alcohol treatment. For purposes of this section, inpatient treatment may not exceed ninety days. As a condition of the suspended disposition, the court may impose conditions of community supervision and other sanctions, including up to thirty days of confinement, one hundred fifty hours of community restitution, and payment of legal financial obligations and restitution.

(6) The drug/alcohol treatment provider shall submit monthly reports on the respondent's progress in treatment to the court and the parties. The reports shall reference the treatment plan and include at a minimum the following: Dates of attendance, respondent's compliance with requirements, treatment activities, the respondent's relative progress in treatment, and any other material specified by the court at the time of the disposition.

At the time of the disposition, the court may set treatment review hearings as the court considers appropriate.

If the offender violates any condition of the disposition or the court finds that the respondent is failing to make satisfactory progress in treatment, the court may impose sanctions pursuant to RCW 13.40.200 or revoke the suspension and order execution of the disposition. The court shall give credit for any confinement time previously served if that confinement was for the offense for which the suspension is being revoked.

(7) For purposes of this section, "victim" means any person who has sustained emotional, psychological, physical, or financial injury to person or property as a direct result of the offense charged. "Victim" may also include a known parent or guardian of a victim who is a minor child or is not a minor child but is incapacitated, incompetent, disabled, or deceased.

(8) Whenever a juvenile offender is entitled to credit for time spent in detention prior to a dispositional order, the dispositional order shall specifically state the number of days of credit for time served.

(9) In no case shall the term of confinement imposed by the court at disposition exceed that to which an adult could be subjected for the same offense.

(10) A disposition under this section is not appealable under RCW 13.40.230.

[2004 c 120 § 5; 2003 c 378 § 6. Prior: 2002 c 175 § 23; 2002 c 42 § 1; 2001 c 164 § 1; 1997 c 338 § 26.]

SECTION 2: RCW 13.40: JUVENILE JUSTICE ACT OF 1977, AS AMENDED

RCW 13.40.167 Mental health disposition alternative.

(1) When an offender is subject to a standard range disposition involving confinement by the department, the court may:

(a) Impose the standard range; or

(b) Suspend the standard range disposition on condition that the offender complies with the terms of this mental health disposition alternative.

(2) The court may impose this disposition alternative when the court finds the following:

(a) The offender has a current diagnosis, consistent with the American psychiatry association diagnostic and statistical manual of mental disorders, of axis I psychiatric disorder, excluding youth that are diagnosed as solely having a conduct disorder, oppositional defiant disorder, substance abuse disorder, paraphilia, or pedophilia;

(b) An appropriate treatment option is available in the local community;

(c) The plan for the offender identifies and addresses requirements for successful participation and completion of the treatment intervention program including: Incentives and graduated sanctions designed specifically for amenable youth, including the use of detention, detoxication, and inpatient or outpatient substance abuse treatment and psychiatric hospitalization, and structured community support consisting of mental health providers, probation, educational and vocational advocates, child welfare services, and family and community support. For any mental health treatment ordered for an offender under this section, the treatment option selected shall be chosen from among programs which have been successful in addressing mental health needs of juveniles and successful in mental health treatment of juveniles and identified as research-based best practice programs. A list of programs which meet these criteria shall be agreed upon by: The Washington association of juvenile court administrators, the juvenile rehabilitation administration of the department of social and health services, a representative of the division of public behavioral health and justice policy at the University of Washington, and the Washington institute for public policy. The list of programs shall be created not later than July 1, 2003. The group shall provide the list to all superior courts, its own membership, the legislature, and the governor. The group shall meet annually and revise the list as appropriate; and

(d) The offender, offender's family, and community will benefit from use of the mental health disposition alternative.

(3) The court on its own motion may order, or on motion by either party, shall order a comprehensive mental health evaluation to determine if the offender has a designated mental disorder. The court may also order a chemical dependency evaluation to determine if the offender also has a co-occurring chemical dependency disorder. The evaluation shall include at a

SECTION 2: RCW 13.40: JUVENILE JUSTICE ACT OF 1977, AS AMENDED

minimum the following: The offender's version of the facts and the official version of the facts, the offender's offense, an assessment of the offender's mental health and drug-alcohol problems and previous treatment attempts, and the offender's social, criminal, educational, and employment history and living situation.

(4) The evaluator shall determine if the offender is amenable to research-based treatment. A proposed case management and treatment plan shall include at a minimum:

(a) The availability of treatment;

(b) Anticipated length of treatment;

(c) Whether one or more treatment interventions are proposed and the anticipated sequence of those treatment interventions;

(d) The education plan;

(e) The residential plan; and

(f) The monitoring plan.

(5) The court on its own motion may order, or on motion by either party, shall order a second mental health or chemical dependency evaluation. The party making the motion shall select the evaluator. The requesting party shall pay the cost of any examination ordered under this subsection and subsection (3) of this section unless the court finds the offender is indigent and no third party insurance coverage is available, in which case the state shall pay the cost.

(6) Upon receipt of the assessments, evaluations, and reports the court shall consider whether the offender and the community will benefit from use of the mental health disposition alternative. The court shall consider the victim's opinion whether the offender should receive the option.

(7) If the court determines that the mental health disposition alternative is appropriate, the court shall impose a standard range disposition, suspend execution of the disposition, and place the offender on community supervision up to one year and impose one or more other local sanctions. Confinement in a secure county detention facility, other than county group homes, inpatient psychiatric treatment facilities, and substance abuse programs, shall be limited to thirty days. As a condition of a suspended disposition, the court shall require the offender to participate in the recommended treatment interventions.

(8) The treatment providers shall submit monthly reports to the court and parties on the offender's progress in treatment. The report shall reference the treatment plan and include at a minimum the following: Dates of attendance, offender's compliance with requirements, treatment activities, medication management, the offender's relative progress in treatment, and

SECTION 2: RCW 13.40: JUVENILE JUSTICE ACT OF 1977, AS AMENDED

any other material specified by the court at the time of the disposition.

(9) If the offender fails to comply with the suspended disposition, the court may impose sanctions pursuant to RCW 13.40.200 or may revoke the suspended disposition and order the disposition's execution.

(10) An offender is ineligible for the mental health disposition option under this section if:

(a) The offender is ordered to serve a disposition for a firearm violation under RCW 13.40.193; or

(b) The offense for which the disposition is being considered is:

(i) An offense category A+, A, or A- offense, or an attempt, conspiracy, or solicitation to commit a class A+, A, or A- offense;

(ii) Manslaughter in the second degree (RCW 9A.32.070);

(iii) A sex offense as defined in RCW 9.94A.030; or

(iv) Any offense category B+ or B offense, when the offense includes infliction of bodily harm upon another or when during the commission or immediate withdrawal from the offense the respondent was armed with a deadly weapon.

(11) Subject to funds appropriated for this specific purpose, the costs incurred by the juvenile courts for the mental health and chemical dependency evaluations, treatment, and costs of supervision required under this section shall be paid by the department's juvenile rehabilitation administration.

[2005 c 508 § 1; 2003 c 378 § 4.]

RCW 13.40.180 Disposition order -- Consecutive terms when two or more offenses – Limitations – Separate disposition order – Concurrent period of community supervision.

(1) Where a disposition in a single disposition order is imposed on a youth for two or more offenses, the terms shall run consecutively, subject to the following limitations:

(a) Where the offenses were committed through a single act or omission, omission, or through an act or omission which in itself constituted one of the offenses and also was an element of the other, the aggregate of all the terms shall not exceed one hundred fifty percent of the term imposed for the most serious offense;

(b) The aggregate of all consecutive terms shall not exceed three hundred percent of the term

SECTION 2: RCW 13.40: JUVENILE JUSTICE ACT OF 1977, AS AMENDED

imposed for the most serious offense; and

(c) The aggregate of all consecutive terms of community supervision shall not exceed two years in length, or require payment of more than two hundred dollars in fines or the performance of more than two hundred hours of community restitution.

(2) Where disposition in separate disposition orders is imposed on a youth, the periods of community supervision contained in separate orders, if any, shall run concurrently. All other terms contained in separate disposition orders shall run consecutively.

[2012 c 177 § 3; 2002 c 175 § 24; 1981 c 299 § 14; 1977 ex.s. c 291 § 72.]

RCW 13.40.185 Disposition order — Confinement under departmental supervision or in juvenile facility, when.

(1) Any term of confinement imposed for an offense which exceeds thirty days shall be served under the supervision of the department. If the period of confinement imposed for more than one offense exceeds thirty days but the term imposed for each offense is less than thirty days, the confinement may, in the discretion of the court, be served in a juvenile facility operated by or pursuant to a contract with the state or a county.

(2) Whenever a juvenile is confined in a detention facility or is committed to the department, the court may not directly order a juvenile into a particular county or state facility. The juvenile court administrator and the secretary, assistant secretary, or the secretary's designee, as appropriate, has the sole discretion to determine in which facility a juvenile should be confined or committed. The counties may operate a variety of detention facilities as determined by the county legislative authority subject to available funds.

[1994 sp.s. c 7 § 524; 1981 c 299 § 15.]

RCW 13.40.190 Disposition order — Restitution for loss — Modification of restitution order.

RCW 13.40.192 Legal financial obligations -- Enforceability -- Treatment of obligations upon age of eighteen or conclusion of juvenile court jurisdiction -- Extension of judgment.

If a juvenile is ordered to pay legal financial obligations, including fines, penalty assessments, attorneys' fees, court costs, and restitution, the money judgment remains enforceable for a period of ten years. When the juvenile reaches the age of eighteen years or at the conclusion of juvenile court jurisdiction, whichever occurs later, the superior court clerk must docket the remaining balance of the juvenile's legal financial obligations in the same manner as other judgments for the payment of money. The judgment remains valid and enforceable until ten years from the date

SECTION 2: RCW 13.40: JUVENILE JUSTICE ACT OF 1977, AS AMENDED

of its imposition. The clerk of the superior court may seek extension of the judgment for legal financial obligations, including crime victims' assessments, in the same manner as RCW 6.17.020 for purposes of collection as allowed under RCW 36.18.190.

[1997 c 121 § 7.]

RCW 13.40.193 Firearms -- Length of confinement.

(1) If a respondent is found to have been in possession of a firearm in violation of RCW 9.41.040(2)(a)(iii), the court shall impose a minimum disposition of ten days of confinement. If the offender's standard range of disposition for the offense as indicated in RCW 13.40.0357 is more than thirty days of confinement, the court shall commit the offender to the department for the standard range disposition. The offender shall not be released until the offender has served a minimum of ten days in confinement.

(2) If the court finds that the respondent or an accomplice was armed with a firearm, the court shall determine the standard range disposition for the offense pursuant to RCW 13.40.160. If the offender or an accomplice was armed with a firearm when the offender committed any felony other than possession of a machine gun, possession of a stolen firearm, drive-by shooting, theft of a firearm, unlawful possession of a firearm in the first and second degree, or use of a machine gun in a felony, the following periods of total confinement must be added to the sentence: For a class A felony, six months; for a class B felony, four months; and for a class C felony, two months. The additional time shall be imposed regardless of the offense's juvenile disposition offense category as designated in RCW 13.40.0357.

(3) When a disposition under this section would effectuate a manifest injustice, the court may impose another disposition. When a judge finds a manifest injustice and imposes a disposition of confinement exceeding thirty days, the court shall commit the juvenile to a maximum term, and the provisions of RCW 13.40.030(2) shall be used to determine the range. When a judge finds a manifest injustice and imposes a disposition of confinement less than thirty days, the disposition shall be comprised of confinement or community supervision or both.

(4) Any term of confinement ordered pursuant to this section shall run consecutively to any term of confinement imposed in the same disposition for other offenses.

[2003 c 53 § 100; 1997 c 338 § 30; 1994 sp.s. c 7 § 525.]

The Caseload Forecast Council is not liable for errors or omissions in the manual, for sentences that may be inappropriately calculated as a result of a practitioner's or court's reliance on the manual, or for any other written or verbal information related to adult or juvenile sentencing. The scoring sheets are intended to provide assistance in most cases but does not cover all permutations of the scoring rules. If you find any errors or omissions, we encourage you to report them to the Caseload Forecast Council.

SECTION 2: RCW 13.40: JUVENILE JUSTICE ACT OF 1977, AS AMENDED

RCW 13.40.196 Firearms — Special allegation.

A prosecutor may file a special allegation that the offender or an accomplice was armed with a firearm when the offender committed the alleged offense. If a special allegation has been filed and the court finds that the offender committed the alleged offense, the court shall also make a finding whether the offender or an accomplice was armed with a firearm when the offender committed the offense.

[1994 sp.s. c 7 § 526.]

RCW 13.40.198 Penalty assessments — Jurisdiction of court.

If a respondent is ordered to pay a penalty assessment pursuant to a dispositional order entered under this chapter, he or she shall remain under the court's jurisdiction for a maximum term of ten years after the respondent's eighteenth birthday. Prior to the expiration of the ten-year period, the juvenile court may extend the judgment for the payment of a penalty assessment for an additional ten years.

[2000 c 71 § 1.]

RCW 13.40.200 Violation of order of restitution, community supervision, fines, penalty assessments, or confinement — Modification of order after hearing — Scope — Rights — Use of fines.

(1) When a respondent fails to comply with an order of restitution, community supervision, penalty assessments, or confinement of less than thirty days, the court upon motion of the prosecutor or its own motion, may modify the order after a hearing on the violation.

(2) The hearing shall afford the respondent the same due process of law as would be afforded an adult probationer. The court may issue a summons or a warrant to compel the respondent's appearance. The state shall have the burden of proving by a preponderance of the evidence the fact of the violation. The respondent shall have the burden of showing that the violation was not a willful refusal to comply with the terms of the order. If a respondent has failed to pay a fine, penalty assessments, or restitution or to perform community restitution hours, as required by the court, it shall be the respondent's burden to show that he or she did not have the means and could not reasonably have acquired the means to pay the fine, penalty assessments, or restitution or perform community restitution.

(3) If the court finds that a respondent has willfully violated the terms of an order pursuant to subsections (1) and (2) of this section, it may impose a penalty of up to thirty days' confinement. Penalties for multiple violations occurring prior to the hearing shall not be aggregated to exceed thirty days' confinement. Regardless of the number of times a respondent is brought to court for

SECTION 2: RCW 13.40: JUVENILE JUSTICE ACT OF 1977, AS AMENDED

violations of the terms of a single disposition order, the combined total number of days spent by the respondent in detention shall never exceed the maximum term to which an adult could be sentenced for the underlying offense.

(4) If a respondent has been ordered to pay a fine or monetary penalty and due to a change of circumstance cannot reasonably comply with the order, the court, upon motion of the respondent, may order that the unpaid fine or monetary penalty be converted to community restitution unless the monetary penalty is the crime victim penalty assessment, which cannot be converted, waived, or otherwise modified, except for schedule of payment. The number of hours of community restitution in lieu of a monetary penalty or fine shall be converted at the rate of the prevailing state minimum wage per hour. The monetary penalties or fines collected shall be deposited in the county general fund. A failure to comply with an order under this subsection shall be deemed a failure to comply with an order of community supervision and may be proceeded against as provided in this section.

(5) When a respondent has willfully violated the terms of a probation bond, the court may modify, revoke, or retain the probation bond as provided in RCW 13.40.054.

[2004 c 120 § 7; 2002 c 175 § 25; 1997 c 338 § 31; 1995 c 395 § 8; 1986 c 288 § 5; 1983 c 191 § 15; 1979 c 155 § 70; 1977 ex.s. c 291 § 74.]

RCW 13.40.205 Release from physical custody, when — Authorized leaves — Leave plan and order — Notice.

(1) A juvenile sentenced to a term of confinement to be served under the supervision of the department shall not be released from the physical custody of the department prior to the release date established under RCW

13.40.210 except as otherwise provided in this section.

(2) A juvenile serving a term of confinement under the supervision of the department may be released on authorized leave from the physical custody of the department only if consistent with public safety and if:

(a) Sixty percent of the minimum term of confinement has been served; and

(b) The purpose of the leave is to enable the juvenile:

(i) To visit the juvenile's family for the purpose of strengthening or preserving family relationships;

(ii) To make plans for parole or release which require the juvenile's personal appearance in the

SECTION 2: RCW 13.40: JUVENILE JUSTICE ACT OF 1977, AS AMENDED

community and which will facilitate the juvenile's reintegration into the community; or

(iii) To make plans for a residential placement out of the juvenile's home which requires the juvenile's personal appearance in the community.

(3) No authorized leave may exceed seven consecutive days. The total of all pre-minimum term authorized leaves granted to a juvenile prior to final discharge from confinement shall not exceed thirty days.

(4) Prior to authorizing a leave, the secretary shall require a written leave plan, which shall detail the purpose of the leave and how it is to be achieved, the address at which the juvenile shall reside, the identity of the person responsible for supervising the juvenile during the leave, and a statement by such person acknowledging familiarity with the leave plan and agreeing to supervise the juvenile and to notify the secretary immediately if the juvenile violates any terms or conditions of the leave. The leave plan shall include such terms and conditions as the secretary deems appropriate and shall be signed by the juvenile.

(5) Upon authorizing a leave, the secretary shall issue to the juvenile an authorized leave order which shall contain the name of the juvenile, the fact that the juvenile is on leave from a designated facility, the time period of the leave, and the identity of an appropriate official of the department to contact when necessary. The authorized leave order shall be carried by the juvenile at all times while on leave.

(6) Prior to the commencement of any authorized leave, the secretary shall give notice of the leave to the appropriate law enforcement agency in the jurisdiction in which the juvenile will reside during the leave period. The notice shall include the identity of the juvenile, the time period of the leave, the residence of the juvenile during the leave, and the identity of the person responsible for supervising the juvenile during the leave.

(7) The secretary may authorize a leave, which shall not exceed forty-eight hours plus travel time, to meet an emergency situation such as a death or critical illness of a member of the juvenile's family. The secretary may authorize a leave, which shall not exceed the period of time medically necessary, to obtain medical care not available in a juvenile facility maintained by the department. In cases of emergency or medical leave the secretary may waive all or any portions of subsections (2)(a), (3), (4), (5), and (6) of this section.

(8) If requested by the juvenile's victim or the victim's immediate family, the secretary shall give notice of any leave to the victim or the victim's immediate family.

(9) A juvenile who violates any condition of an authorized leave plan may be taken into custody and returned to the department in the same manner as an adult in identical circumstances.

(10) Notwithstanding the provisions of this section, a juvenile placed in minimum security status

The Caseload Forecast Council is not liable for errors or omissions in the manual, for sentences that may be inappropriately calculated as a result of a practitioner's or court's reliance on the manual, or for any other written or verbal information related to adult or juvenile sentencing. The scoring sheets are intended to provide assistance in most cases but does not cover all permutations of the scoring rules. If you find any errors or omissions, we encourage you to report them to the Caseload Forecast Council.

SECTION 2: RCW 13.40: JUVENILE JUSTICE ACT OF 1977, AS AMENDED

may participate in work, educational, community restitution, or treatment programs in the community up to twelve hours a day if approved by the secretary. Such a release shall not be deemed a leave of absence.

(11) Subsections (6), (7), and (8) of this section do not apply to juveniles covered by RCW 13.40.215.

[2002 c 175 § 26; 1990 c 3 § 103; 1983 c 191 § 10.]

RCW 13.40.210 Setting of release date -- Administrative release authorized, when --Parole program, revocation or modification of, scope -- Intensive supervision program -- Parole officer's right of arrest. (Effective until October 1, 2007)

(1) The secretary shall set a release date for each juvenile committed to its custody. The release date shall be within the prescribed range to which a juvenile has been committed under RCW 13.40.0357 or 13.40.030 except as provided in RCW 13.40.320 concerning offenders the department determines are eligible for the juvenile offender basic training camp program. Such dates shall be determined prior to the expiration of sixty percent of a juvenile's minimum term of confinement included within the prescribed range to which the juvenile has been committed. The secretary shall release any juvenile committed to the custody of the department within four calendar days prior to the juvenile's release date or on the release date set under this chapter. Days spent in the custody of the department shall be tolled by any period of time during which a juvenile has absented himself or herself from the department's supervision without the prior approval of the secretary or the secretary's designee.

(2) The secretary shall monitor the average daily population of the state's juvenile residential facilities. When the secretary concludes that in-residence population of residential facilities exceeds one hundred five percent of the rated bed capacity specified in statute, or in absence of such specification, as specified by the department in rule, the secretary may recommend reductions to the governor. On certification by the governor that the recommended reductions are necessary, the secretary has authority to administratively release a sufficient number of offenders to reduce in-residence population to one hundred percent of rated bed capacity. The secretary shall release those offenders who have served the greatest proportion of their sentence. However, the secretary may deny release in a particular case at the request of an offender, or if the secretary finds that there is no responsible custodian, as determined by the department, to whom to release the offender, or if the release of the offender would pose a clear danger to society. The department shall notify the committing court of the release at the time of release if any such early releases have occurred as a result of excessive in-residence population. In no event shall an offender adjudicated of a violent offense be granted release under the provisions of this subsection.

SECTION 2: RCW 13.40: JUVENILE JUSTICE ACT OF 1977, AS AMENDED

(3)(a) Following the release of any juvenile under subsection (1) of this section, the secretary may require the juvenile to comply with a program of parole to be administered by the department in his or her community which shall last no longer than eighteen months, except that in the case of a juvenile sentenced for rape in the first or second degree, rape of a child in the first or second degree, child molestation in the first degree, or indecent liberties with forcible compulsion, the period of parole shall be twenty-four months and, in the discretion of the secretary, may be up to thirty-six months when the secretary finds that an additional period of parole is necessary and appropriate in the interests of public safety or to meet the ongoing needs of the juvenile. A parole program is mandatory for offenders released under subsection (2) of this section and for offenders who receive a juvenile residential commitment sentence of theft of a motor vehicle, possession of a stolen motor vehicle, or taking a motor vehicle without permission 1. The decision to place an offender on parole shall be based on an assessment by the department of the offender's risk for reoffending upon release. The department shall prioritize available parole resources to provide supervision and services to offenders at moderate to high risk for reoffending.

(b) The secretary shall, for the period of parole, facilitate the juvenile's reintegration into his or her community and to further this goal shall require the juvenile to refrain from possessing a firearm or using a deadly weapon and refrain from committing new offenses and may require the juvenile to: (i) Undergo available medical, psychiatric, drug and alcohol, sex offender, mental health, and other offense-related treatment services; (ii) report as directed to a parole officer and/or designee; (iii) pursue a course of study, vocational training, or employment; (iv) notify the parole officer of the current address where he or she resides; (v) be present at a particular address during specified hours; (vi) remain within prescribed geographical boundaries; (vii) submit to electronic monitoring; (viii) refrain from using illegal drugs and alcohol, and submit to random urinalysis when requested by the assigned parole officer; (ix) refrain from contact with specific individuals or a specified class of individuals; (x) meet other conditions determined by the parole officer to further enhance the juvenile's reintegration into the community; (xi) pay any court-ordered fines or restitution; and (xii) perform community restitution. Community restitution for the purpose of this section means compulsory service, without compensation, performed for the benefit of the community by the offender. Community restitution may be performed through public or private organizations or through work crews.

(c) The secretary may further require up to twenty-five percent of the highest risk juvenile offenders who are placed on parole to participate in an intensive supervision program. Offenders participating in an intensive supervision program shall be required to comply with all terms and conditions listed in (b) of this subsection and shall also be required to comply with the following additional terms and conditions: (i) Obey all laws and refrain from any conduct that threatens public safety; (ii) report at least once a week to an assigned community case manager; and (iii) meet all other requirements imposed by the community case manager related to participating in the intensive supervision program. As a part of the intensive supervision program, the secretary may require day reporting.

The Caseload Forecast Council is not liable for errors or omissions in the manual, for sentences that may be inappropriately calculated as a result of a practitioner's or court's reliance on the manual, or for any other written or verbal information related to adult or juvenile sentencing. The scoring sheets are intended to provide assistance in most cases but does not cover all permutations of the scoring rules. If you find any errors or omissions, we encourage you to report them to the Caseload Forecast Council.

SECTION 2: RCW 13.40: JUVENILE JUSTICE ACT OF 1977, AS AMENDED

(d) After termination of the parole period, the juvenile shall be discharged from the department's supervision.

(4)(a) The department may also modify parole for violation thereof. If, after affording a juvenile all of the due process rights to which he or she would be entitled if the juvenile were an adult, the secretary finds that a juvenile has violated a condition of his or her parole, the secretary shall order one of the following which is reasonably likely to effectuate the purpose of the parole and to protect the public: (i) Continued supervision under the same conditions previously imposed; (ii) intensified supervision with increased reporting requirements; (iii) additional conditions of supervision authorized by this chapter; (iv) except as provided in (a)(v) and (vi) of this subsection, imposition of a period of confinement not to exceed thirty days in a facility operated by or pursuant to a contract with the state of Washington or any city or county for a portion of each day or for a certain number of days each week with the balance of the days or weeks spent under supervision; (v) the secretary may order any of the conditions or may return the offender to confinement for the remainder of the sentence range if the offense for which the offender was sentenced is rape in the first or second degree, rape of a child in the first or second degree, child molestation in the first degree, indecent liberties with forcible compulsion, or a sex offense that is also a serious violent offense as defined by RCW 9.94A.030; and (vi) the secretary may order any of the conditions or may return the offender to confinement for the remainder of the sentence range if the youth has completed the basic training camp program as described in RCW 13.40.320.

(b) The secretary may modify parole and order any of the conditions or may return the offender to confinement for up to twenty-four weeks if the offender was sentenced for a sex offense as defined under *RCW 9A.44.130 and is known to have violated the terms of parole. Confinement beyond thirty days is intended to only be used for a small and limited number of sex offenders. It shall only be used when other graduated sanctions or interventions have not been effective or the behavior is so egregious it warrants the use of the higher level intervention and the violation: (i) Is a known pattern of behavior consistent with a previous sex offense that puts the youth at high risk for reoffending sexually; (ii) consists of sexual behavior that is determined to be predatory as defined in RCW 71.09.020; or (iii) requires a review under chapter 71.09 RCW, due to a recent overt act. The total number of days of confinement for violations of parole conditions during the parole period shall not exceed the number of days provided by the maximum sentence imposed by the disposition for the underlying offense pursuant to RCW 13.40.0357. The department shall not aggregate multiple parole violations that occur prior to the parole revocation hearing and impose consecutive twenty-four week periods of confinement for each parole violation. The department is authorized to engage in rule making pursuant to chapter 34.05 RCW, to implement this subsection, including narrowly defining the behaviors that could lead to this higher level intervention.

(c) If the department finds that any juvenile in a program of parole has possessed a firearm or used a deadly weapon during the program of parole, the department shall modify the parole under (a) of this subsection and confine the juvenile for at least thirty days. Confinement shall be

SECTION 2: RCW 13.40: JUVENILE JUSTICE ACT OF 1977, AS AMENDED

in a facility operated by or pursuant to a contract with the state or any county.

(5) A parole officer of the department of social and health services shall have the power to arrest a juvenile under his or her supervision on the same grounds as a law enforcement officer would be authorized to arrest the person.

(6) If so requested and approved under chapter 13.06 RCW, the secretary shall permit a county or group of counties to perform functions under subsections (3) through (5) of this section.

[2009 c 187 § 1. Prior: 2007 c 203 § 1; 2007 c 199 § 13; 2002 c 175 § 27; prior: 2001 c 137 § 2; 2001 c 51 § 1; 1997 c 338 § 32; 1994 sp.s. c 7 § 527; 1990 c 3 § 304; 1987 c 505 § 4; 1985 c 287 § 1; 1985 c 257 § 4; 1983 c 191 § 11; 1979 c 155 § 71; 1977 ex.s. c 291 § 75.]

RCW 13.40.212 Intensive supervision program — Elements — Report.

(1) The department shall, no later than January 1, 1999, implement an intensive supervision program as a part of its parole services that includes, at a minimum, the following program elements:

(a) A process of case management involving coordinated and comprehensive planning, information exchange, continuity and consistency, service provision and referral, and monitoring. The components of the case management system shall include assessment, classification, and selection criteria; individual case planning that incorporates a family and community perspective; a mixture of intensive surveillance and services; a balance of incentives and graduated consequences coupled with the imposition of realistic, enforceable conditions; and service brokerage with community resources and linkage with social networks;

(b) Administration of transition services that transcend traditional agency boundaries and professional interests and include courts, institutions, aftercare, education, social and mental health services, substance abuse treatment, and employment and vocational training; and

(c) A plan for information management and program evaluation that maintains close oversight over implementation and quality control, and determines the effectiveness of both the processes and outcomes of the program.

(2) The department shall report annually to the legislature, beginning December 1, 1999, on the department's progress in meeting the intensive supervision program evaluation goals required under subsection (1)(c) of this section.

[1997 c 338 § 34.]

The Caseload Forecast Council is not liable for errors or omissions in the manual, for sentences that may be inappropriately calculated as a result of a practitioner's or court's reliance on the manual, or for any other written or verbal information related to adult or juvenile sentencing. The scoring sheets are intended to provide assistance in most cases but does not cover all permutations of the scoring rules. If you find any errors or omissions, we encourage you to report them to the Caseload Forecast Council.

SECTION 2: RCW 13.40: JUVENILE JUSTICE ACT OF 1977, AS AMENDED

RCW 13.40.213 Juveniles alleged to have committed offenses of prostitution or prostitution loitering -- Diversion.

(1) When a juvenile is alleged to have committed the offenses of prostitution or prostitution loitering, and the allegation, if proved, would not be the juvenile's first offense, a prosecutor may divert the offense if the county in which the offense is alleged to have been committed has a comprehensive program that provides:

(a) Safe and stable housing;

(b) Comprehensive on-site case management;

(c) Integrated mental health and chemical dependency services, including specialized trauma recovery services;

(d) Education and employment training delivered on-site; and

(e) Referrals to off-site specialized services, as appropriate.

(2) A prosecutor may divert a case for prostitution or prostitution loitering into the comprehensive program described in this section, notwithstanding the filing criteria set forth in RCW 13.40.070(5).

(3) A diversion agreement under this section may extend to twelve months.

(4)(a) The administrative office of the courts shall compile data regarding:

(i) The number of juveniles whose cases are diverted into the comprehensive program described in this section;

(ii) Whether the juveniles complete their diversion agreements under this section; and

(iii) Whether juveniles whose cases have been diverted under this section have been subsequently arrested or committed subsequent offenses.

(b) An annual report of the data compiled shall be provided to the governor and the appropriate committee of the legislature. The first report is due by November 1, 2010.

[2010 c 289 § 8; 2009 c 252 § 2.]

The Caseload Forecast Council is not liable for errors or omissions in the manual, for sentences that may be inappropriately calculated as a result of a practitioner's or court's reliance on the manual, or for any other written or verbal information related to adult or juvenile sentencing. The scoring sheets are intended to provide assistance in most cases but does not cover all permutations of the scoring rules. If you find any errors or omissions, we encourage you to report them to the Caseload Forecast Council.

SECTION 2: RCW 13.40: JUVENILE JUSTICE ACT OF 1977, AS AMENDED

RCW 13.40.215 Juveniles found to have committed violent or sex offense or stalking — Notification of discharge, parole, leave, release, transfer, or escape — To whom given — School attendance — Definitions.

(1)(a) Except as provided in subsection (2) of this section, at the earliest possible date, and in no event later than thirty days before discharge, parole, or any other authorized leave or release, or before transfer to a community residential facility, the secretary shall send written notice of the discharge, parole, authorized leave or release, or transfer of a juvenile found to have committed a violent offense, a sex offense, or stalking, to the following:

(i) The chief of police of the city, if any, in which the juvenile will reside;

(ii) The sheriff of the county in which the juvenile will reside; and

(iii) The approved private schools and the common school district board of directors of the district in which the juvenile intends to reside or the approved private school or public school district in which the juvenile last attended school, whichever is appropriate, except when it has been determined by the department that the juvenile is twenty-one years old or will be in the community for less than seven consecutive days on approved leave and will not be attending school during that time.

(b) After July 25, 1999, the department shall send a written notice to approved private and public schools under the same conditions identified in subsection (1)(a)(iii) of this section when a juvenile adjudicated of any offense is transferred to a community residential facility, discharged, paroled, released, or granted a leave. The community residential facility shall provide written notice of the offender's criminal history to any school that the offender attends while residing at the community residential facility and to any employer that employs the offender while residing at the community residential facility.

(c) The same notice as required by (a) of this subsection shall be sent to the following, if such notice has been requested in writing about a specific juvenile:

(i) The victim of the offense for which the juvenile was found to have committed or the victim's next of kin if the crime was a homicide;

(ii) Any witnesses who testified against the juvenile in any court proceedings involving the offense; and

(iii) Any person specified in writing by the prosecuting attorney.

Information regarding victims, next of kin, or witnesses requesting the notice, information regarding any other person specified in writing by the prosecuting attorney to receive the notice, and the notice are confidential and shall not be available to the juvenile. The notice to the chief

---

The Caseload Forecast Council is not liable for errors or omissions in the manual, for sentences that may be inappropriately calculated as a result of a practitioner's or court's reliance on the manual, or for any other written or verbal information related to adult or juvenile sentencing. The scoring sheets are intended to provide assistance in most cases but does not cover all permutations of the scoring rules. If you find any errors or omissions, we encourage you to report them to the Caseload Forecast Council.

SECTION 2: RCW 13.40: JUVENILE JUSTICE ACT OF 1977, AS AMENDED

of police or the sheriff shall include the identity of the juvenile, the residence where the juvenile will reside, the identity of the person, if any, responsible for supervising the juvenile, and the time period of any authorized leave.

(d) The thirty-day notice requirements contained in this subsection shall not apply to emergency medical furloughs.

(e) The existence of the notice requirements in this subsection will not require any extension of the release date in the event the release plan changes after notification.

(2)(a) If a juvenile found to have committed a violent offense, a sex offense, or stalking escapes from a facility of the department, the secretary shall immediately notify, by the most reasonable and expedient means available, the chief of police of the city and the sheriff of the county in which the juvenile resided immediately before the juvenile's arrest. If previously requested, the secretary shall also notify the witnesses and the victim of the offense which the juvenile was found to have committed or the victim's next of kin if the crime was a homicide. If the juvenile is recaptured, the secretary shall send notice to the persons designated in this subsection as soon as possible but in no event later than two working days after the department learns of such recapture.

(b) The secretary may authorize a leave, for a juvenile found to have committed a violent offense, a sex offense, or stalking, which shall not exceed forty-eight hours plus travel time, to meet an emergency situation such as a death or critical illness of a member of the juvenile's family. The secretary may authorize a leave, which shall not exceed the time medically necessary, to obtain medical care not available in a juvenile facility maintained by the department. Prior to the commencement of an emergency or medical leave, the secretary shall give notice of the leave to the appropriate law enforcement agency in the jurisdiction in which the juvenile will be during the leave period. The notice shall include the identity of the juvenile, the time period of the leave, the residence of the juvenile during the leave, and the identity of the person responsible for supervising the juvenile during the leave. If previously requested, the department shall also notify the witnesses and victim of the offense which the juvenile was found to have committed or the victim's next of kin if the offense was a homicide.

In case of an emergency or medical leave the secretary may waive all or any portion of the requirements for leaves pursuant to RCW 13.40.205 (2)(a), (3), (4), and (5).

(3) If the victim, the victim's next of kin, or any witness is under the age of sixteen, the notice required by this section shall be sent to the parents or legal guardian of the child.

(4) The secretary shall send the notices required by this chapter to the last address provided to the department by the requesting party. The requesting party shall furnish the department with a current address.

SECTION 2: RCW 13.40: JUVENILE JUSTICE ACT OF 1977, AS AMENDED

(5) Upon discharge, parole, transfer to a community residential facility, or other authorized leave or release, a convicted juvenile sex offender shall not attend a public or approved private elementary, middle, or high school that is attended by a victim or a sibling of a victim of the sex offender. The parents or legal guardians of the convicted juvenile sex offender shall be responsible for transportation or other costs associated with or required by the sex offender's change in school that otherwise would be paid by a school district. Upon discharge, parole, transfer to a community residential facility, or other authorized leave or release of a convicted juvenile sex offender, the secretary shall send written notice of the discharge, parole, or other authorized leave or release and the requirements of this subsection to the common school district board of directors of the district in which the sex offender intends to reside or the district in which the sex offender last attended school, whichever is appropriate. The secretary shall send a similar notice to any approved private school the juvenile will attend, if known, or if unknown, to the approved private schools within the district the juvenile resides or intends to reside.

(6) For purposes of this section the following terms have the following meanings:

(a) "Violent offense" means a violent offense under RCW 9.94A.030;

(b) "Sex offense" means a sex offense under RCW 9.94A.030;

(c) "Stalking" means the crime of stalking as defined in RCW 9A.46.110;

(d) "Next of kin" means a person's spouse, parents, siblings, and children.

[1999 c 198 § 1; 1997 c 265 § 2; 1995 c 324 § 1. Prior: 1994 c 129 § 6; 1994 c 78 § 1; 1993 c 27 § 1; 1990 c 3 § 101.]

RCW 13.40.217 Juveniles adjudicated of sex offenses — Release of information authorized.

(1) In addition to any other information required to be released under this chapter, the department is authorized, pursuant to RCW 4.24.550, to release relevant information that is necessary to protect the public concerning juveniles adjudicated of sex offenses.

(2) In order for public agencies to have the information necessary for notifying the public about sex offenders as authorized in RCW 4.24.550, the secretary shall issue to appropriate law enforcement agencies narrative notices regarding the pending release of sex offenders from the department's juvenile rehabilitation facilities. The narrative notices shall, at a minimum, describe the identity and criminal history behavior of the offender and shall include the department's risk level classification for the offender. For sex offenders classified as either risk level II or III, the narrative notices shall also include the reasons underlying the classification.

(3) For the purposes of this section, the department shall classify as risk level I those offenders whose risk assessments indicate a low risk of reoffense within the community at large. The

SECTION 2: RCW 13.40: JUVENILE JUSTICE ACT OF 1977, AS AMENDED

department shall classify as risk level II those offenders whose risk assessments indicate a moderate risk of reoffense within the community at large. The department shall classify as risk level III those offenders whose risk assessments indicate a high risk of reoffense within the community at large.

[1997 c 364 § 2; 1990 c 3 § 102.]

RCW 13.40.219 Arrest for prostitution or prostitution loitering – Alleged offender –Victim of severe form of trafficking, commercial sex abuse of a minor.

In any proceeding under this chapter related to an arrest for prostitution or prostitution loitering, there is a presumption that the alleged offender meets the criteria for a certification as a victim of a severe form of trafficking in persons as defined in section 7105 of Title 22 of the United States code, and that the alleged offender is also a victim of commercial sex abuse of a minor.

[2010 c 289 § 9.]

RCW 13.40.220 Costs of support, treatment, and confinement — Order — Contempt of court.

(1) Whenever legal custody of a child is vested in someone other than his or her parents, under this chapter, and not vested in the department of social and health services, after due notice to the parents or other persons legally obligated to care for and support the child, and after a hearing, the court may order and decree that the parent or other legally obligated person shall pay in such a manner as the court may direct a reasonable sum representing in whole or in part the costs of support, treatment, and confinement of the child after the decree is entered.

(2) If the parent or other legally obligated person willfully fails or refuses to pay such sum, the court may proceed against such person for contempt.

(3) Whenever legal custody of a child is vested in the department under this chapter, the parents or other persons legally obligated to care for and support the child shall be liable for the costs of support, treatment, and confinement of the child, in accordance with the department's reimbursement of cost schedule. The department shall adopt a reimbursement of cost schedule based on the costs of providing such services, and shall determine an obligation based on the responsible parents' or other legally obligated person's ability to pay. The department is authorized to adopt additional rules as appropriate to enforce this section.

(4) To enforce subsection (3) of this section, the department shall serve on the parents or other person legally obligated to care for and support the child a notice and finding of financial responsibility requiring the parents or other legally obligated person to appear and show cause in an adjudicative proceeding why the finding of responsibility and/or the amount thereof is

SECTION 2: RCW 13.40: JUVENILE JUSTICE ACT OF 1977, AS AMENDED

incorrect and should not be ordered. This notice and finding shall relate to the costs of support, treatment, and confinement of the child in accordance with the department's reimbursement of cost schedule adopted under this section, including periodic payments to be made in the future. The hearing shall be held pursuant to chapter 34.05 RCW, the Administrative Procedure Act, and the rules of the department.

(5) The notice and finding of financial responsibility shall be served in the same manner prescribed for the service of a summons in a civil action or may be served on the parent or legally obligated person by certified mail, return receipt requested. The receipt shall be prima facie evidence of service.

(6) If the parents or other legally obligated person objects to the notice and finding of financial responsibility, then an application for an adjudicative hearing may be filed within twenty days of the date of service of the notice. If an application for an adjudicative proceeding is filed, the presiding or reviewing officer shall determine the past liability and responsibility, if any, of the parents or other legally obligated person and shall also determine the amount of periodic payments to be made in the future. If the parents or other legally responsible person fails to file an application within twenty days, the notice and finding of financial responsibility shall become a final administrative order.

(7) Debts determined pursuant to this section are subject to collection action without further necessity of action by a presiding or reviewing officer. The department may collect the debt in accordance with RCW 43.20B.635, 43.20B.640, 74.20A.060, and 74.20A.070. The department shall exempt from payment parents receiving adoption support under *RCW 74.13.100 through 74.13.145, parents eligible to receive adoption support under *RCW 74.13.150, and a parent or other legally obligated person when the parent or other legally obligated person, or such person's child, spouse, or spouse's child, was the victim of the offense for which the child was committed.

(8) An administrative order entered pursuant to this section shall supersede any court order entered prior to June 13, 1994.

(9) The department shall be subrogated to the right of the child and his or her parents or other legally responsible person to receive support payments for the benefit of the child from any parent or legally obligated person pursuant to a support order established by a superior court or pursuant to RCW 74.20A.055. The department's right of subrogation under this section is limited to the liability established in accordance with its cost schedule for support, treatment, and confinement, except as addressed in subsection (10) of this section.

(10) Nothing in this section precludes the department from recouping such additional support payments from the child's parents or other legally obligated person as required to qualify for receipt of federal funds. The department may adopt such rules dealing with liability for recoupment of support, treatment, or confinement costs as may become necessary to entitle the state to participate in federal funds unless such rules would be expressly prohibited by law. If

SECTION 2: RCW 13.40: JUVENILE JUSTICE ACT OF 1977, AS AMENDED

any law dealing with liability for recoupment of support, treatment, or confinement costs is ruled to be in conflict with federal requirements which are a prescribed condition of the allocation of federal funds, such conflicting law is declared to be inoperative solely to the extent of the conflict.

[1995 c 300 § 1; 1994 sp.s. c 7 § 529; 1993 c 466 § 1; 1977 ex.s. c 291 § 76.]

RCW 13.40.230 Appeal from order of disposition — Jurisdiction — Procedure — Scope — Release pending appeal.

(1) Dispositions reviewed pursuant to RCW 13.40.160 shall be reviewed in the appropriate division of the court of appeals.

An appeal under this section shall be heard solely upon the record that was before the disposition court. No written briefs may be required, and the appeal shall be heard within thirty days following the date of sentencing and a decision rendered within fifteen days following the argument. The supreme court shall promulgate any necessary rules to effectuate the purposes of this section.

(2) To uphold a disposition outside the standard range, the court of appeals must find (a) that the reasons supplied by the disposition judge are supported by the record which was before the judge and that those reasons clearly and convincingly support the conclusion that a disposition within the range would constitute a manifest injustice, and (b) that the sentence imposed was neither clearly excessive nor clearly too lenient.

(3) If the court does not find subsection (2)(a) of this section it shall remand the case for disposition within the standard range.

(4) If the court finds subsection (2)(a) but not subsection (2)(b) of this section it shall remand the case with instructions for further proceedings consistent with the provisions of this chapter.

(5) The disposition court may impose conditions on release pending appeal as provided in RCW *13.40.040(4) and 13.40.050(6).

(6) Appeal of a disposition under this section does not affect the finality or appeal of the underlying adjudication of guilt.

[1997 c 338 § 35; 1981 c 299 § 16; 1979 c 155 § 72; 1977 ex.s. c 291 § 77.]

SECTION 2: RCW 13.40: JUVENILE JUSTICE ACT OF 1977, AS AMENDED

RCW 13.40.240 Construction of RCW references to juvenile delinquents or juvenile delinquency.

All references to juvenile delinquents or juvenile delinquency in other chapters of the Revised Code of Washington shall be construed as meaning juvenile offenders or the commitment of an offense by juveniles as defined by this chapter.

[1977 ex.s. c 291 § 78.]

RCW 13.40.250 Traffic and civil infraction cases.

A traffic or civil infraction case involving a juvenile under the age of sixteen may be diverted in accordance with the provisions of this chapter or filed in juvenile court.

(1) If a notice of a traffic or civil infraction is filed in juvenile court, the juvenile named in the notice shall be afforded the same due process afforded to adult defendants in traffic infraction cases.

(2) A monetary penalty imposed upon a juvenile under the age of sixteen who is found to have committed a traffic or civil infraction may not exceed one hundred dollars. At the juvenile's request, the court may order performance of a number of hours of community restitution in lieu of a monetary penalty, at the rate of the prevailing state minimum wage per hour.

(3) A diversion agreement entered into by a juvenile referred pursuant to this section shall be limited to thirty hours of community restitution, or educational or informational sessions.

(4) Traffic or civil infractions referred to a youth court pursuant to this section are subject to the conditions imposed by RCW 13.40.630.

(5) If a case involving the commission of a traffic or civil infraction or offense by a juvenile under the age of sixteen has been referred to a diversion unit, an abstract of the action taken by the diversion unit may be forwarded to the department of licensing in the manner provided for in RCW 46.20.270(2).

[2002 c 237 § 19; 2002 c 175 § 28; 1997 c 338 § 36; 1980 c 128 § 16.]

RCW 13.40.265 Firearm, alcohol, and drug violations.

(1)(a) If a juvenile thirteen years of age or older is found by juvenile court to have committed an offense while armed with a firearm or an offense that is a violation of RCW

SECTION 2: RCW 13.40: JUVENILE JUSTICE ACT OF 1977, AS AMENDED

9.41.040(2)(a)(iii) or chapter 66.44, 69.41, 69.50, or 69.52 RCW, the court shall notify the department of licensing within twenty-four hours after entry of the judgment.

(b) Except as otherwise provided in (c) of this subsection, upon petition of a juvenile who has been found by the court to have committed an offense that is a violation of chapter 66.44, 69.41, 69.50, or 69.52 RCW, the court may at any time the court deems appropriate notify the department of licensing that the juvenile's driving privileges should be reinstated.

(c) If the offense is the juvenile's first violation of chapter 66.44, 69.41, 69.50, or 69.52 RCW, the juvenile may not petition the court for reinstatement of the juvenile's privilege to drive revoked pursuant to RCW 46.20.265 until ninety days after the date the juvenile turns sixteen or ninety days after the judgment was entered, whichever is later. If the offense is the juvenile's second or subsequent violation of chapter 66.44, 69.41, 69.50, or 69.52 RCW, the juvenile may not petition the court for reinstatement of the juvenile's privilege to drive revoked pursuant to RCW 46.20.265 until the date the juvenile turns seventeen or one year after the date judgment was entered, whichever is later.

(2)(a) If a juvenile enters into a diversion agreement with a diversion unit pursuant to RCW 13.40.080 concerning an offense that is a violation of chapter 66.44, 69.41, 69.50, or 69.52 RCW, the diversion unit shall notify the department of licensing within twenty-four hours after the diversion agreement is signed.

(b) If a diversion unit has notified the department pursuant to (a) of this subsection, the diversion unit shall notify the department of licensing when the juvenile has completed the agreement.

[2003 c 53 § 101; 1997 c 338 § 37; 1994 sp.s. c 7 § 435; 1989 c 271 § 116; 1988 c 148 § 2.]

RCW 13.40.280 Transfer of juvenile to department of corrections facility — Grounds — Hearing — Term — Retransfer to a facility for juveniles.

(1) The secretary, with the consent of the secretary of the department of corrections, has the authority to transfer a juvenile presently or hereafter committed to the department of social and health services to the department of corrections for appropriate institutional placement in accordance with this section.

(2) The secretary of the department of social and health services may, with the consent of the secretary of the department of corrections, transfer a juvenile offender to the department of corrections if it is established at a hearing before a review board that continued placement of the juvenile offender in an institution for juvenile offenders presents a continuing and serious threat to the safety of others in the institution. The department of social and health services shall establish rules for the conduct of the hearing, including provision of counsel for the juvenile offender.

SECTION 2: RCW 13.40: JUVENILE JUSTICE ACT OF 1977, AS AMENDED

(3) Assaults made against any staff member at a juvenile corrections institution that are reported to a local law enforcement agency shall require a hearing held by the department of social and health services review board within ten judicial working days. The board shall determine whether the accused juvenile offender represents a continuing and serious threat to the safety of others in the institution.

(4) Upon conviction in a court of law for custodial assault as defined in RCW

9A.36.100, the department of social and health services review board shall conduct a second hearing, within five judicial working days, to recommend to the secretary of the department of social and health services that the convicted juvenile be transferred to an adult correctional facility if the review board has determined the juvenile offender represents a continuing and serious threat to the safety of others in the institution.

The juvenile has the burden to show cause why the transfer to an adult correctional facility should not occur.

(5) A juvenile offender transferred to an institution operated by the department of corrections shall not remain in such an institution beyond the maximum term of confinement imposed by the juvenile court.

(6) A juvenile offender who has been transferred to the department of corrections under this section may, in the discretion of the secretary of the department of social and health services and with the consent of the secretary of the department of corrections, be transferred from an institution operated by the department of corrections to a facility for juvenile offenders deemed appropriate by the secretary.

[1989 c 410 § 2; 1989 c 407 § 8; 1983 c 191 § 22.]

RCW 13.40.285 Juvenile offender sentenced to terms in juvenile and adult facilities — Transfer to department of corrections — Term of confinement.

A juvenile offender ordered to serve a term of confinement with the department of social and health services who is subsequently sentenced to the department of corrections may, with the consent of the department of corrections, be transferred by the secretary of social and health services to the department of corrections to serve the balance of the term of confinement ordered by the juvenile court. The juvenile and adult sentences shall be served consecutively. In no case shall the secretary credit time served as a result of an adult conviction against the term of confinement ordered by the juvenile court.

[1983 c 191 § 23.]

The Caseload Forecast Council is not liable for errors or omissions in the manual, for sentences that may be inappropriately calculated as a result of a practitioner's or court's reliance on the manual, or for any other written or verbal information related to adult or juvenile sentencing. The scoring sheets are intended to provide assistance in most cases but does not cover all permutations of the scoring rules. If you find any errors or omissions, we encourage you to report them to the Caseload Forecast Council.

SECTION 2: RCW 13.40: JUVENILE JUSTICE ACT OF 1977, AS AMENDED

RCW 13.40.300 Commitment of juvenile beyond age twenty-one prohibited — Jurisdiction of juvenile court after juvenile's eighteenth birthday.

(1) In no case may a juvenile offender be committed by the juvenile court to the department of social and health services for placement in a juvenile correctional institution beyond the juvenile offender's twenty-first birthday. A juvenile may be under the jurisdiction of the juvenile court or the authority of the department of social and health services beyond the juvenile's eighteenth birthday only if prior to the juvenile's eighteenth birthday:

(a) Proceedings are pending seeking the adjudication of a juvenile offense and the court by written order setting forth its reasons extends jurisdiction of juvenile court over the juvenile beyond his or her eighteenth birthday;

(b) The juvenile has been found guilty after a fact finding or after a plea of guilty and an automatic extension is necessary to allow for the imposition of disposition;

(c) Disposition has been held and an automatic extension is necessary to allow for the execution and enforcement of the court's order of disposition. If an order of disposition imposes commitment to the department, then jurisdiction is automatically extended to include a period of up to twelve months of parole, in no case extending beyond the offender's twenty-first birthday; or

(d) While proceedings are pending in a case in which jurisdiction has been transferred to the adult criminal court pursuant to RCW

13.04.030, the juvenile turns eighteen years of age and is subsequently found not guilty of the charge for which he or she was transferred, or is convicted in the adult criminal court of a lesser included offense, and an automatic extension is necessary to impose the disposition as required by RCW 13.04.030(1)(e)(v)(E).

(2) If the juvenile court previously has extended jurisdiction beyond the juvenile offender's eighteenth birthday and that period of extension has not expired, the court may further extend jurisdiction by written order setting forth its reasons.

(3) In no event may the juvenile court have authority to extend jurisdiction over any juvenile offender beyond the juvenile offender's twenty-first birthday except for the purpose of enforcing an order of restitution or penalty assessment.

(4) Notwithstanding any extension of jurisdiction over a person pursuant to this section, the juvenile court has no jurisdiction over any offenses alleged to have been committed by a person eighteen years of age or older.

The Caseload Forecast Council is not liable for errors or omissions in the manual, for sentences that may be inappropriately calculated as a result of a practitioner's or court's reliance on the manual, or for any other written or verbal information related to adult or juvenile sentencing. The scoring sheets are intended to provide assistance in most cases but does not cover all permutations of the scoring rules. If you find any errors or omissions, we encourage you to report them to the Caseload Forecast Council.

SECTION 2: RCW 13.40: JUVENILE JUSTICE ACT OF 1977, AS AMENDED

[2005 c 238 § 2; 2000 c 71 § 2; 1994 sp.s. c 7 § 530; 1986 c 288 § 6; 1983 c 191 § 17; 1981 c 299 § 17; 1979 c 155 § 73; 1975 1st ex.s. c 170 § 1. Formerly RCW 13.04.260.]

RCW 13.40.305 Juvenile offender adjudicated of theft of motor vehicle, possession of stolen vehicle, taking motor vehicle without permission in the first degree, taking motor vehicle without permission in the second degree — Local sanctions — Evaluation.

If a juvenile is adjudicated of theft of a motor vehicle under RCW 9A.56.065, possession of a stolen vehicle under RCW 9A.56.068, taking a motor vehicle without permission in the first degree as defined in RCW 9A.56.070(1), or taking a motor vehicle without permission in the second degree as defined in RCW 9A.56.075(1) and is sentenced to local sanctions, the juvenile's disposition shall include an evaluation to determine whether the juvenile is in need of community-based rehabilitation services and to complete any treatment recommended by the evaluation.

[2007 c 199 § 12.]

RCW 13.40.308 Juvenile offender adjudicated of taking motor vehicle without permission in the first degree, theft of motor vehicle, possession of a stolen vehicle, taking motor vehicle without permission in the second degree — Minimum sentences.

(1) If a respondent is adjudicated of taking a motor vehicle without permission in the first degree as defined in RCW 9A.56.070, the court shall impose the following minimum sentence, in addition to any restitution the court may order payable to the victim:

(a) Juveniles with a prior criminal history score of zero to one-half points shall be sentenced to a standard range sentence that includes no less than three months of community supervision, forty-five hours of community restitution, a two hundred dollar fine, and a requirement that the juvenile remain at home such that the juvenile is confined to a private residence for no less than five days. The juvenile may be subject to electronic monitoring where available. If the juvenile is enrolled in school, the confinement shall be served on non-school days;

(b) Juveniles with a prior criminal history score of three-quarters to one and one-half points shall be sentenced to a standard range sentence that includes six months of community supervision, no less than ten days of detention, ninety hours of community restitution, and a four hundred dollar fine; and

(c) Juveniles with a prior criminal history score of two or more points shall be sentenced to no less than fifteen to thirty-six weeks commitment to the juvenile rehabilitation administration, four months of parole supervision, ninety hours of community restitution, and a four hundred dollar fine.

The Caseload Forecast Council is not liable for errors or omissions in the manual, for sentences that may be inappropriately calculated as a result of a practitioner's or court's reliance on the manual, or for any other written or verbal information related to adult or juvenile sentencing. The scoring sheets are intended to provide assistance in most cases but does not cover all permutations of the scoring rules. If you find any errors or omissions, we encourage you to report them to the Caseload Forecast Council.

SECTION 2: RCW 13.40: JUVENILE JUSTICE ACT OF 1977, AS AMENDED

(2) If a respondent is adjudicated of theft of a motor vehicle as defined under RCW 9A.56.065, or possession of a stolen vehicle as defined under RCW 9A.56.068, the court shall impose the following minimum sentence, in addition to any restitution the court may order payable to the victim:

(a) Juveniles with a prior criminal history score of zero to one-half points shall be sentenced to a standard range sentence that includes no less than three months of community supervision, forty-five hours of community restitution, a two hundred dollar fine, and either ninety hours of community restitution or a requirement that the juvenile remain at home such that the juvenile is confined in a private residence for no less than five days. The juvenile may be subject to electronic monitoring where available;

(b) Juveniles with a prior criminal history score of three-quarters to one and one-half points shall be sentenced to a standard range sentence that includes no less than six months of community supervision, no less than ten days of detention, ninety hours of community restitution, and a four hundred dollar fine; and

(c) Juveniles with a prior criminal history score of two or more points shall be sentenced to no less than fifteen to thirty-six weeks commitment to the juvenile rehabilitation administration, four months of parole supervision, ninety hours of community restitution, and a four hundred dollar fine.

(3) If a respondent is adjudicated of taking a motor vehicle without permission in the second degree as defined in RCW 9A.56.075, the court shall impose a standard range as follows:

(a) Juveniles with a prior criminal history score of zero to one-half points shall be sentenced to a standard range sentence that includes three months of community supervision, fifteen hours of community restitution, and a requirement that the juvenile remain at home such that the juvenile is confined in a private residence for no less than one day. If the juvenile is enrolled in school, the confinement shall be served on non-school days. The juvenile may be subject to electronic monitoring where available;

(b) Juveniles with a prior criminal history score of three-quarters to one and one-half points shall be sentenced to a standard range sentence that includes no less than one day of detention, three months of community supervision, thirty hours of community restitution, a one hundred fifty dollar fine, and a requirement that the juvenile remain at home such that the juvenile is confined in a private residence for no less than two days. If the juvenile is enrolled in school, the confinement shall be served on non-school days. The juvenile may be subject to electronic monitoring where available; and

(c) Juveniles with a prior criminal history score of two or more points shall be sentenced to no less than three days of detention, six months of community supervision, forty-five hours of community restitution, a one hundred fifty dollar fine, and a requirement that the juvenile remain

---

The Caseload Forecast Council is not liable for errors or omissions in the manual, for sentences that may be inappropriately calculated as a result of a practitioner's or court's reliance on the manual, or for any other written or verbal information related to adult or juvenile sentencing. The scoring sheets are intended to provide assistance in most cases but does not cover all permutations of the scoring rules. If you find any errors or omissions, we encourage you to report them to the Caseload Forecast Council.

SECTION 2: RCW 13.40: JUVENILE JUSTICE ACT OF 1977, AS AMENDED

at home such that the juvenile is confined in a private residence for no less than seven days. If the juvenile is enrolled in school, the confinement shall be served on non-school days. The juvenile may be subject to electronic monitoring where available.

[2009 c 454 § 4; 2007 c 199 § 15.]

RCW 13.40.310 Transitional treatment program for gang and drug-involved juvenile offenders.

(1) The department of social and health services may contract with a community-based nonprofit organization to establish a three-step transitional treatment program for gang and drug-involved juvenile offenders committed to the custody of the department under chapter

13.40 RCW. Any such program shall provide six to twenty-four months of treatment. The program shall emphasize the principles of self-determination, unity, collective work and responsibility, cooperative economics, and creativity. The program shall be culturally relevant and appropriate and shall include:

(a) A culturally relevant and appropriate institution-based program that provides comprehensive drug and alcohol services, individual and family counseling, and a wilderness experience of constructive group living, rigorous physical exercise, and academic studies;

(b) A culturally relevant and appropriate community-based structured group living program that focuses on individual goals, positive community involvement, coordinated drug and alcohol treatment, coordinated individual and family counseling, academic and vocational training, and employment in apprenticeship, internship, and entrepreneurial programs; and

(c) A culturally relevant and appropriate transitional group living program that provides support services, academic services, and coordinated individual and family counseling.

(2) Participation in any such program shall be on a voluntary basis.

(3) The department shall adopt rules as necessary to implement any such program.

[1991 c 326 § 4.]

RCW 13.40.320 Juvenile offender basic training camp program.

(1) The department of social and health services shall establish a medium security juvenile offender basic training camp program. This program for juvenile offenders serving a term of confinement under the supervision of the department is exempt from the licensing requirements of chapter 74.15 RCW.

SECTION 2: RCW 13.40: JUVENILE JUSTICE ACT OF 1977, AS AMENDED

(2) The department may contract under this chapter with private companies, the national guard, or other federal, state, or local agencies to operate the juvenile offender basic training camp.

(3) The juvenile offender basic training camp shall be a structured and regimented model emphasizing the building up of an offender's self-esteem, confidence, and discipline. The juvenile offender basic training camp program shall provide participants with basic education, prevocational training, work-based learning, work experience, work ethic skills, conflict resolution counseling, substance abuse intervention, anger management counseling, and structured intensive physical training. The juvenile offender basic training camp program shall have a curriculum training and work schedule that incorporates a balanced assignment of these or other rehabilitation and training components for no less than sixteen hours per day, six days a week.

The department shall develop standards for the safe and effective operation of the juvenile offender basic training camp program, for an offender's successful program completion, and for the continued after-care supervision of offenders who have successfully completed the program.

(4) Offenders eligible for the juvenile offender basic training camp option shall be those with a disposition of not more than sixty-five weeks. Violent and sex offenders shall not be eligible for the juvenile offender basic training camp program.

(5) If the court determines that the offender is eligible for the juvenile offender basic training camp option, the court may recommend that the department place the offender in the program. The department shall evaluate the offender and may place the offender in the program. The evaluation shall include, at a minimum, a risk assessment developed by the department and designed to determine the offender's suitability for the program. No juvenile who is assessed as a high risk offender or suffers from any mental or physical problems that could endanger his or her health or drastically affect his or her performance in the program shall be admitted to or retained in the juvenile offender basic training camp program.

(6) All juvenile offenders eligible for the juvenile offender basic training camp sentencing option shall spend one hundred twenty days of their disposition in a juvenile offender basic training camp. This period may be extended for up to forty days by the secretary if a juvenile offender requires additional time to successfully complete the basic training camp program. If the juvenile offender's activities while in the juvenile offender basic training camp are so disruptive to the juvenile offender basic training camp program, as determined by the secretary according to standards developed by the department, as to result in the removal of the juvenile offender from the juvenile offender basic training camp program, or if the offender cannot complete the juvenile offender basic training camp program due to medical problems, the secretary shall require that the offender be committed to a juvenile institution to serve the entire remainder of his or her disposition, less the amount of time already served in the juvenile offender basic training camp program.

The Caseload Forecast Council is not liable for errors or omissions in the manual, for sentences that may be inappropriately calculated as a result of a practitioner's or court's reliance on the manual, or for any other written or verbal information related to adult or juvenile sentencing. The scoring sheets are intended to provide assistance in most cases but does not cover all permutations of the scoring rules. If you find any errors or omissions, we encourage you to report them to the Caseload Forecast Council.

SECTION 2: RCW 13.40: JUVENILE JUSTICE ACT OF 1977, AS AMENDED

(7) All offenders who successfully graduate from the juvenile offender basic training camp program shall spend the remainder of their disposition on parole in a juvenile rehabilitation administration intensive aftercare program in the local community. Violation of the conditions of parole is subject to sanctions specified in RCW 13.40.210(4). The program shall provide for the needs of the offender based on his or her progress in the aftercare program as indicated by ongoing assessment of those needs and progress. The intensive aftercare program shall monitor post program juvenile offenders and assist them to successfully reintegrate into the community. In addition, the program shall develop a process for closely monitoring and assessing public safety risks. The intensive aftercare program shall be designed and funded by the department of social and health services.

(8) The department shall also develop and maintain a database to measure recidivism rates specific to this incarceration program. The database shall maintain data on all juvenile offenders who complete the juvenile offender basic training camp program for a period of two years after they have completed the program. The database shall also maintain data on the criminal activity, educational progress, and employment activities of all juvenile offenders who participated in the program.

[2002 c 354 § 234; 2001 c 137 § 1; 1997 c 338 § 38; 1995 c 40 § 1; 1994 sp.s. c 7 § 532.]

RCW 13.40.400 Applicability of RCW 10.01.040 to chapter.

The provisions of RCW 10.01.040 apply to chapter 13.40 RCW.

[1979 c 155 § 74.]

RCW 13.40.430 Disparity in disposition of juvenile offenders — Data collection.

The administrative office of the courts shall collect such data as may be necessary to monitor any disparity in processing or disposing of cases involving juvenile offenders due to economic, gender, geographic, or racial factors that may result from implementation of section 1, chapter 373, Laws of 1993. The administrative office of the courts may, in consultation with juvenile courts, determine a format for the collection of such data and a schedule for the reporting of such data and shall keep a minimum of five years of data at any given time.

[2005 c 282 § 27; 2003 c 207 § 13; 1993 c 373 § 2.]

RCW 13.40.460 Juvenile rehabilitation programs — Administration.

The secretary, assistant secretary, or the secretary's designee shall manage and administer the department's juvenile rehabilitation responsibilities, including but not limited to the operation of

SECTION 2: RCW 13.40: JUVENILE JUSTICE ACT OF 1977, AS AMENDED

all state institutions or facilities used for juvenile rehabilitation.

The secretary or assistant secretary shall:

(1) Prepare a biennial budget request sufficient to meet the confinement and rehabilitative needs of the juvenile rehabilitation program, as forecast by the office of financial management;

(2) Create by rule a formal system for inmate classification. This classification system shall consider:

(a) Public safety;

(b) Internal security and staff safety;

(c) Rehabilitative resources both within and outside the department;

(d) An assessment of each offender's risk of sexually aggressive behavior as provided in RCW 13.40.470; and

(e) An assessment of each offender's vulnerability to sexually aggressive behavior as provided in RCW 13.40.470;

(3) Develop agreements with local jurisdictions to develop regional facilities with a variety of custody levels;

(4) Adopt rules establishing effective disciplinary policies to maintain order within institutions;

(5) Develop a comprehensive diagnostic evaluation process to be used at intake, including but not limited to evaluation for substance addiction or abuse, literacy, learning disabilities, fetal alcohol syndrome or effect, attention deficit disorder, and mental health;

(6) Develop placement criteria:

(a) To avoid assigning youth who present a moderate or high risk of sexually aggressive behavior to the same sleeping quarters as youth assessed as vulnerable to sexual victimization under RCW 13.40.470(1)(c); and

(b) To avoid placing a juvenile offender on parole status who has been assessed as a moderate to high risk for sexually aggressive behavior in a department community residential program with another child who is: (i) Dependent under chapter 13.34 RCW, or an at-risk youth or child in need of services under chapter 13.32A RCW; and (ii) not also a juvenile offender on parole status;

The Caseload Forecast Council is not liable for errors or omissions in the manual, for sentences that may be inappropriately calculated as a result of a practitioner's or court's reliance on the manual, or for any other written or verbal information related to adult or juvenile sentencing. The scoring sheets are intended to provide assistance in most cases but does not cover all permutations of the scoring rules. If you find any errors or omissions, we encourage you to report them to the Caseload Forecast Council.

SECTION 2: RCW 13.40: JUVENILE JUSTICE ACT OF 1977, AS AMENDED

(7) Develop a plan to implement, by July 1, 1995:

(a) Substance abuse treatment programs for all state juvenile rehabilitation facilities and institutions;

(b) Vocational education and instruction programs at all state juvenile rehabilitation facilities and institutions; and

(c) An educational program to establish self-worth and responsibility in juvenile offenders. This educational program shall emphasize instruction in character-building principles such as: Respect for self, others, and authority; victim awareness; accountability; work ethics; good citizenship; and life skills; and

(8)(a) The juvenile rehabilitation administration shall develop uniform policies related to custodial assaults consistent with RCW 72.01.045 and 9A.36.100 that are to be followed in all juvenile rehabilitation administration facilities; and

(b) The juvenile rehabilitation administration will report assaults in accordance with the policies developed in (a) of this subsection.

[2003 c 229 § 1; 1999 c 372 § 2; 1997 c 386 § 54; 1994 sp.s. c 7 § 516.]

RCW 13.40.462 Reinvesting in youth program.

(1) The department of social and health services juvenile rehabilitation administration shall establish a reinvesting in youth program that awards grants to counties for implementing research-based early intervention services that target juvenile justice-involved youth and reduce crime, subject to the availability of amounts appropriated for this specific purpose.

(2) Effective July 1, 2007, any county or group of counties may apply for participation in the reinvesting in youth program.

(3) Counties that participate in the reinvesting in youth program shall have a portion of their costs of serving youth through the research-based intervention service models paid for with moneys from the reinvesting in youth account established pursuant to RCW 13.40.466.

(4) The department of social and health services juvenile rehabilitation administration shall review county applications for funding through the reinvesting in youth program and shall select the counties that will be awarded grants with funds appropriated to implement this program. The department, in consultation with the Washington state institute for public policy, shall develop guidelines to determine which counties will be awarded funding in accordance with the reinvesting in youth program. At a minimum, counties must meet the following criteria in order to participate in the reinvesting in youth program:

SECTION 2: RCW 13.40: JUVENILE JUSTICE ACT OF 1977, AS AMENDED

(a) Counties must match state moneys awarded for research-based early intervention services with nonstarter resources that are at least proportional to the expected local government share of state and local government cost avoidance that would result from the implementation of such services;

(b) Counties must demonstrate that state funds allocated pursuant to this section are used only for the intervention service models authorized pursuant to RCW 13.40.464;

(c) Counties must participate fully in the state quality assurance program established in RCW 13.40.468 to ensure fidelity of program implementation. If no state quality assurance program is in effect for a particular selected research-based service, the county must submit a quality assurance plan for state approval with its grant application. Failure to demonstrate continuing compliance with quality assurance plans shall be grounds for termination of state funding; and

(d) Counties that submit joint applications must submit for approval by the department of social and health services juvenile rehabilitation administration multicounty plans for efficient program delivery.

[2011 1st sp.s. c 32 § 4; 2006 c 304 § 2.]

RCW 13.40.464 Reinvesting in youth program — Guidelines.

(1)(a) In order to receive funding through the reinvesting in youth program established pursuant to RCW 13.40.462, intervention service models must meet the following minimum criteria:

(i) There must be scientific evidence from at least one rigorous evaluation study of the specific service model that measures recidivism reduction;

(ii) There must be evidence that the specific service model's results can be replicated outside of an academic research environment;

(iii) The evaluation or evaluations of the service model must permit dollar cost estimates of both benefits and costs so that the benefit-cost ratio of the model can be calculated; and

(iv) The public taxpayer benefits to all levels of state and local government must exceed the service model costs.

(b) In calendar year 2006, for use beginning in fiscal year 2008, the Washington state institute for public policy shall publish a list of service models that are eligible for reimbursement through the investing in youth program. As authorized by the board of the institute and to the extent necessary to respond to new research and information, the institute shall periodically update the list of service models. The institute shall use the technical advisory committee established in

SECTION 2: RCW 13.40: JUVENILE JUSTICE ACT OF 1977, AS AMENDED

*RCW 13.40.462(5) to review and provide comments on the list of service models that are eligible for reimbursement.

(2) In calendar year 2006, for use beginning in fiscal year 2008, the Washington state institute for public policy shall review and update the methodology for calculating cost savings resulting from implementation of this program. As authorized by the board of the institute and to the extent necessary to respond to new research and information, the institute shall periodically further review and update the methodology. As authorized by the board of the institute, when the institute reviews and updates the methodology for calculating cost savings, the institute shall provide an estimate of savings and avoided costs resulting from this program, along with a projection of future savings and avoided costs, to the appropriate committees of the legislature. The institute shall use the technical advisory committee established in *RCW 13.40.462(5) to review and provide comments on its methodology and cost calculations.

(3) In calendar year 2006, for use beginning in fiscal year 2008, the department of social and health services' juvenile rehabilitation administration shall establish a distribution formula to provide funding to local governments that implement research-based intervention services pursuant to this program. The department shall periodically update the distribution formula. The distribution formula shall require that the state allocation to local governments be proportional to the expected state government share of state and local government cost avoidance that would result from the implementation of such services based on the methodology maintained by the Washington state institute for public policy pursuant to subsection (2) of this section. The department shall use the technical advisory committee established in *RCW 13.40.462(5) to review and provide comments on its proposed distribution formula.

(4) The department of social and health services juvenile rehabilitation administration shall provide a report to the legislature on the initial cost savings calculation methodology and distribution formula by October 1, 2006.

[2006 c 304 § 3.]

RCW 13.40.466 Reinvesting in youth account.

(1) The reinvesting in youth account is created in the state treasury. Moneys in the account shall be spent only after appropriation. Expenditures from the account may be used to reimburse local governments for the implementation of the reinvesting in youth program established in RCW 13.40.462 and 13.40.464.

(2) Revenues to the reinvesting in youth account consist of revenues appropriated to or deposited in the account.

(3) The department of social and health services juvenile rehabilitation administration shall review and monitor the expenditures made by any county or group of counties that is funded, in

SECTION 2: RCW 13.40: JUVENILE JUSTICE ACT OF 1977, AS AMENDED

whole or in part, with funds provided through the reinvesting in youth account. Counties shall repay any funds that are not spent in accordance with RCW 13.40.462 and 13.40.464.

[2006 c 304 § 4.]

RCW 13.40.468 Juvenile rehabilitation administration — State quality assurance program.

The department of social and health services juvenile rehabilitation administration shall establish a state quality assurance program. The juvenile rehabilitation administration shall monitor the implementation of intervention services funded pursuant to RCW 13.40.466 and shall evaluate adherence to service model design and service completion rate.

[2006 c 304 § 6.]

RCW 13.40.470 Vulnerable youth committed to residential facilities — Protection from sexually aggressive youth — Assessment process.

(1) The department shall implement a policy for protecting youth committed to state-operated or state-funded residential facilities under this chapter who are vulnerable to sexual victimization by other youth committed to those facilities who are sexually aggressive. The policy shall include, at a minimum, the following elements:

(a) Development and use of an assessment process for identifying youth, within thirty days of commitment to the department, who present a moderate or high risk of sexually aggressive behavior for the purposes of this section. The assessment process need not require that every youth who is adjudicated or convicted of a sex offense as defined in RCW 9.94A.030 be determined to be sexually aggressive, nor shall a sex offense adjudication or conviction be required in order to determine a youth is sexually aggressive. Instead, the assessment process shall consider the individual circumstances of the youth, including his or her age, physical size, sexual abuse history, mental and emotional condition, and other factors relevant to sexual aggressiveness. The definition of "sexually aggressive youth" in RCW 74.13.075 does not apply to this section to the extent that it conflicts with this section;

(b) Development and use of an assessment process for identifying youth, within thirty days of commitment to the department, who may be vulnerable to victimization by youth identified under (a) of this subsection as presenting a moderate or high risk of sexually aggressive behavior. The assessment process shall consider the individual circumstances of the youth, including his or her age, physical size, sexual abuse history, mental and emotional condition, and other factors relevant to vulnerability;

(c) Development and use of placement criteria to avoid assigning youth who present a moderate or high risk of sexually aggressive behavior to the same sleeping quarters as youth assessed as

---

The Caseload Forecast Council is not liable for errors or omissions in the manual, for sentences that may be inappropriately calculated as a result of a practitioner's or court's reliance on the manual, or for any other written or verbal information related to adult or juvenile sentencing. The scoring sheets are intended to provide assistance in most cases but does not cover all permutations of the scoring rules. If you find any errors or omissions, we encourage you to report them to the Caseload Forecast Council.

SECTION 2: RCW 13.40: JUVENILE JUSTICE ACT OF 1977, AS AMENDED

vulnerable to sexual victimization, except that they may be assigned to the same multiple-person sleeping quarters if those sleeping quarters are regularly monitored by visual surveillance equipment or staff checks;

(d) Development and use of procedures for minimizing, within available funds, unsupervised contact in state-operated or state-funded residential facilities between youth presenting moderate to high risk of sexually aggressive behavior and youth assessed as vulnerable to sexual victimization. The procedures shall include taking reasonable steps to prohibit any youth committed under this chapter who present a moderate to high risk of sexually aggressive behavior from entering any sleeping quarters other than the one to which they are assigned, unless accompanied by an authorized adult.

(2) For the purposes of this section, the following terms have the following meanings:

(a) "Sleeping quarters" means the bedrooms or other rooms within a residential facility where youth are assigned to sleep.

(b) "Unsupervised contact" means contact occurring outside the sight or hearing of a responsible adult for more than a reasonable period of time under the circumstances.

[1997 c 386 § 50.]

RCW 13.40.480 Student records and information — Reasons for release — Who may request.

(1) Pursuant to RCW 28A.600.475, and to the extent permitted by the family educational and privacy rights act of 1974, 20 U.S.C. Sec. 1232g(b), and in order to serve the juvenile while in detention and to prepare any post-conviction services, schools shall make all student records and information necessary for risk assessment, security classification, and placement available to court personnel and the department within three working days of a request under this section.

(2)(a) When a juvenile has one or more prior convictions, a request for records shall be made by the county prosecuting attorney, or probation department if available, to the school not more than ten days following the juvenile's arrest or detention, whichever occurs later, and prior to trial. The request may be made by subpoena.

(b) Where a juvenile has no prior conviction, a request to release records shall be made by subpoena upon the juvenile's conviction. When the request for a juvenile's student records and information is made by subpoena following conviction, the court or other issuing agency shall order the school on which the subpoena is served not to disclose to any person the existence or contents of the subpoena or any information furnished in response to the subpoena. When the court or issuing agency so orders, the school shall not provide notice to the juvenile or his or her parents.

The Caseload Forecast Council is not liable for errors or omissions in the manual, for sentences that may be inappropriately calculated as a result of a practitioner's or court's reliance on the manual, or for any other written or verbal information related to adult or juvenile sentencing. The scoring sheets are intended to provide assistance in most cases but does not cover all permutations of the scoring rules. If you find any errors or omissions, we encourage you to report them to the Caseload Forecast Council.

SECTION 2: RCW 13.40: JUVENILE JUSTICE ACT OF 1977, AS AMENDED

[1998 c 269 § 12.]

RCW 13.40.500 Community juvenile accountability programs — Findings — Purpose.

The legislature finds that meaningful community involvement is vital to the juvenile justice system's ability to respond to the serious problem of juvenile crime. Citizens and crime victims need to be active partners in responding to crime, in the management of resources, and in the disposition decisions regarding juvenile offenders in their community. Involvement of citizens and crime victims increase offender accountability and build healthier communities, which will reduce recidivism and crime rates in Washington state.

The legislature also finds that local governments are in the best position to develop, coordinate, and manage local community prevention, intervention, and corrections programs for juvenile offenders, and to determine local resource priorities. Local community management will build upon local values and increase local control of resources, encourage the use of a comprehensive range of community-based intervention strategies.

The primary purpose of RCW 13.40.500 through 13.40.540, the community juvenile accountability act, is to provide a continuum of community-based programs that emphasize the juvenile offender's accountability for his or her actions while assisting him or her in the development of skills necessary to function effectively and positively in the community in a manner consistent with public safety.

[1997 c 338 § 60.]

RCW 13.40.510 Community juvenile accountability programs — Establishment — Proposals — Guidelines.

(1) In order to receive funds under RCW 13.40.500 through 13.40.540, local governments may, through their respective agencies that administer funding for consolidated juvenile services, submit proposals that establish community juvenile accountability programs within their communities. These proposals must be submitted to the juvenile rehabilitation administration of the department of social and health services for certification.

(2) The proposals must:

(a) Demonstrate that the proposals were developed with the input of the local law and justice councils established under RCW 72.09.300;

(b) Describe how local community groups or members are involved in the implementation of the programs funded under RCW 13.40.500 through 13.40.540;

SECTION 2: RCW 13.40: JUVENILE JUSTICE ACT OF 1977, AS AMENDED

(c) Include a description of how the grant funds will contribute to the expected outcomes of the program and the reduction of youth violence and juvenile crime in their community. Data approaches are not required to be replicated if the networks have information that addresses risks in the community for juvenile offenders.

(3) A local government receiving a grant under this section shall agree that any funds received must be used efficiently to encourage the use of community-based programs that reduce the reliance on secure confinement as the sole means of holding juvenile offenders accountable for their crimes. The local government shall also agree to account for the expenditure of all funds received under the grant and to submit to audits for compliance with the grant criteria developed under RCW 13.40.520.

(4) The juvenile rehabilitation administration, in consultation with the Washington association of juvenile court administrators and the state law and justice advisory council, shall establish guidelines for programs that may be funded under RCW 13.40.500 through 13.40.540. The guidelines must:

(a) Target diverted and adjudicated juvenile offenders;

(b) Include assessment methods to determine services, programs, and intervention strategies most likely to change behaviors and norms of juvenile offenders;

(c) Provide maximum structured supervision in the community. Programs should use natural surveillance and community guardians such as employers, relatives, teachers, clergy, and community mentors to the greatest extent possible;

(d) Promote good work ethic values and educational skills and competencies necessary for the juvenile offender to function effectively and positively in the community;

(e) Maximize the efficient delivery of treatment services aimed at reducing risk factors associated with the commission of juvenile offenses;

(f) Maximize the reintegration of the juvenile offender into the community upon release from confinement;

(g) Maximize the juvenile offender's opportunities to make full restitution to the victims and amends to the community;

(h) Support and encourage increased court discretion in imposing community-based intervention strategies;

(i) Be compatible with research that shows which prevention and early intervention strategies work with juvenile offenders;

SECTION 2: RCW 13.40: JUVENILE JUSTICE ACT OF 1977, AS AMENDED

(j) Be outcome-based in that it describes what outcomes will be achieved or what outcomes have already been achieved;

(k) Include an evaluation component; and

(l) Recognize the diversity of local needs.

(5) The state law and justice advisory council may provide support and technical assistance to local governments for training and education regarding community-based prevention and intervention strategies.

[2010 1st sp.s. c 7 § 62; 1997 c 338 § 61.]

RCW 13.40.520 Community juvenile accountability programs — Grants.

(1) The state may make grants to local governments for the provision of community-based programs for juvenile offenders. The grants must be made under a grant formula developed by the juvenile rehabilitation administration, in consultation with the Washington association of juvenile court administrators.

(2) Upon certification by the juvenile rehabilitation administration that a proposal satisfies the application and selection criteria, grant funds will be distributed to the local government agency that administers funding for consolidated juvenile services.

[1997 c 338 § 62.]

RCW 13.40.530 Community juvenile accountability programs — Effectiveness standards.

The legislature recognizes the importance of evaluation and outcome measurements of programs serving juvenile offenders in order to ensure cost-effective use of public funds.

The Washington state institute for public policy shall develop standards for measuring the effectiveness of juvenile accountability programs established and approved under RCW 13.40.510. The standards must be developed and presented to the governor and legislature not later than January 1, 1998. The standards must include methods for measuring success factors following intervention. Success factors include, but are not limited to, continued use of alcohol or controlled substances, arrests, violations of terms of community supervision, convictions for subsequent offenses, and restitution to victims.

[1997 c 338 § 63.]

SECTION 2: RCW 13.40: JUVENILE JUSTICE ACT OF 1977, AS AMENDED

RCW 13.40.540 Community juvenile accountability programs — Information collection — Report.

(1) Each community juvenile accountability program approved and funded under RCW 13.40.500 through 13.40.540 shall comply with the information collection requirements in subsection (2) of this section and the reporting requirements in subsection (3) of this section.

(2) The information collected by each community juvenile accountability program must include, at a minimum for each juvenile participant: (a) The name, date of birth, gender, social security number, and, when available, the juvenile information system (JUVIS) control number; (b) an initial intake assessment of each juvenile participating in the program; (c) a list of all juveniles who completed the program; and (d) an assessment upon completion or termination of each juvenile, including outcomes and, where applicable, reasons for termination.

(3) The juvenile rehabilitation administration shall annually compile the data and report to the legislature on: (a) The programs funded under RCW 13.40.500 through 13.40.540; (b) the total cost for each funded program and cost per juvenile; and (c) the essential elements of the program.

[1997 c 338 § 64.]

RCW 13.40.550 Community juvenile accountability programs — Short title.

RCW 13.40.500 through 13.40.540 may be known as the community juvenile accountability act.

[1997 c 338 § 66.]

RCW 13.40.560 Juvenile accountability incentive account.

The juvenile accountability incentive account is created in the custody of the state treasurer. Federal awards for juvenile accountability incentives received by the secretary of the department of social and health services shall be deposited into the account. Interest earned from the inception of the trust account shall be deposited in the account. Expenditures from the account may be used only for the purposes specified in the federal award or awards. Moneys in the account may be spent only after appropriation.

[1999 c 182 § 1.]

SECTION 2: RCW 13.40: JUVENILE JUSTICE ACT OF 1977, AS AMENDED

RCW 13.40.570 Sexual misconduct by state employees, contractors.

(1) When the secretary has reasonable cause to believe that sexual intercourse or sexual contact between an employee and an offender has occurred, notwithstanding any rule adopted under chapter

41.06 RCW the secretary shall immediately suspend the employee.

(2) The secretary shall immediately institute proceedings to terminate the employment of any person:

(a) Who is found by the department, based on a preponderance of the evidence, to have had sexual intercourse or sexual contact with the offender; or

(b) Upon a guilty plea or conviction for any crime specified in chapter 9A.44 RCW when the victim was an offender.

(3) When the secretary has reasonable cause to believe that sexual intercourse or sexual contact between the employee of a contractor and an offender has occurred, the secretary shall require the employee of a contractor to be immediately removed from any employment position which would permit the employee to have any access to any offender.

(4) The secretary shall disqualify for employment with a contractor in any position with access to an offender, any person:

(a) Who is found by the department, based on a preponderance of the evidence, to have had sexual intercourse or sexual contact with the offender; or

(b) Upon a guilty plea or conviction for any crime specified in chapter 9A.44 RCW when the victim was an offender.

(5) The secretary, when considering the renewal of a contract with a contractor who has taken action under subsection (3) or (4) of this section, shall require the contractor to demonstrate that there has been significant progress made in reducing the likelihood that any of its employees will have sexual intercourse or sexual contact with an offender. The secretary shall examine whether the contractor has taken steps to improve hiring, training, and monitoring practices and whether the employee remains with the contractor. The secretary shall not renew a contract unless he or she determines that significant progress has been made.

(6)(a) For the purposes of RCW 50.20.060, a person terminated under this section shall be considered discharged for misconduct.

SECTION 2: RCW 13.40: JUVENILE JUSTICE ACT OF 1977, AS AMENDED

(b)(i) The department may, within its discretion or upon request of any member of the public, release information to an individual or to the public regarding any person or contract terminated under this section.

(ii) An appointed or elected public official, public employee, or public agency as defined in RCW 4.24.470 is immune from civil liability for damages for any discretionary release of relevant and necessary information, unless it is shown that the official, employee, or agency acted with gross negligence or in bad faith. The immunity provided under this section applies to the release of relevant and necessary information to other public officials, public employees, or public agencies, and to the public.

(iii) Except as provided in chapter 42.56 RCW, or elsewhere, nothing in this section shall impose any liability upon a public official, public employee, or public agency for failing to release information authorized under this section. Nothing in this section implies that information regarding persons designated in subsection (2) of this section is confidential except as may otherwise be provided by law.

> (1) The department shall adopt rules to implement this section. The rules shall reflect the legislative intent that this section prohibits individuals who are employed by the department or a contractor of the department from having sexual intercourse or sexual contact with offenders. The rules shall also reflect the legislative intent that when a person is employed by the department or a contractor of the department, and has sexual intercourse or sexual contact with an offender against the employed person's will, the termination provisions of this section shall not be invoked.
>
> (2) (8) As used in this section:
>
> (3) (a) "Contractor" includes all subcontractors of a contractor;
>
>> (b) "Offender" means a person under the jurisdiction or supervision of the department; and
>>
>> (c) "Sexual intercourse" and "sexual contact" have the meanings provided in RCW 9A.44.010.

[2005 c 274 § 210; 1999 c 72 § 1.]

RCW 13.40.580 Youth courts — Diversion.

Youth courts provide a diversion for cases involving juvenile offenders, in which participants, under the supervision of an adult coordinator, may serve in various capacities within the program, acting in the role of jurors, lawyers, bailiffs, clerks, and judges. Youths who appear before youth courts are youths eligible for diversion pursuant to *RCW 13.40.070 (6) and (7).

SECTION 2: RCW 13.40: JUVENILE JUSTICE ACT OF 1977, AS AMENDED

Youth courts have no jurisdiction except as provided for in chapter 237, Laws of 2002. Youth courts are diversion units and not courts established under Article IV of the state Constitution.

[2002 c 237 § 9.]

RCW 13.40.590 Youth court programs.

(1) The administrative office of the courts shall encourage the juvenile courts to work with cities and counties to implement, expand, or use youth court programs for juveniles who commit diversion-eligible offenses, civil, or traffic infractions. Program operations of youth court programs may be funded by government and private grants. Youth court programs are limited to those that:

(a) Are developed using the guidelines for creating and operating youth court programs developed by nationally recognized experts in youth court projects;

(b) Target offenders age eight through seventeen; and

(c) Emphasize the following principles:

(i) Youth must be held accountable for their problem behavior;

(ii) Youth must be educated about the impact their actions have on themselves and others including their victims, their families, and their community;

(iii) Youth must develop skills to resolve problems with their peers more effectively; and

(iv) Youth should be provided a meaningful forum to practice and enhance newly developed skills.

(2) Youth court programs under this section may be established by private nonprofit organizations and schools, upon prior approval and under the supervision of juvenile court.

[2002 c 237 § 10.]

RCW 13.40.600 Youth court jurisdiction.

(1) Youth courts have authority over juveniles ages eight through seventeen who:

(a) Along with their parent, guardian, or legal custodian, voluntarily and in writing request youth court involvement;

SECTION 2: RCW 13.40: JUVENILE JUSTICE ACT OF 1977, AS AMENDED

(b) Admit they have committed the offense they are referred for;

(c) Along with their parent, guardian, or legal custodian, waive any privilege against self-incrimination concerning the offense; and

(d) Along with their parent, guardian, or legal custodian, agree to comply with the youth court disposition of the case.

(2) Youth courts shall not exercise authority over youth who are under the continuing jurisdiction of the juvenile court for law violations, including a youth with a matter pending before the juvenile court but which has not yet been adjudicated.

(3) Youth courts may decline to accept a youth for youth court disposition for any reason and may terminate a youth from youth court participation at any time.

(4) A youth or his or her parent, guardian, or legal custodian may withdraw from the youth court process at any time.

(5) Youth courts shall give any victims of a juvenile the opportunity to be notified, present, and heard in any youth court proceeding.

[2002 c 237 § 11.]

RCW 13.40.610 Youth court notification of satisfaction of conditions.

Youth court may not notify the juvenile court of satisfaction of conditions until all ordered restitution has been paid.

[2002 c 237 § 12.]

RCW 13.40.620 Appearance before youth court with parent, guardian, or legal custodian.

Every youth appearing before a youth court shall be accompanied by his or her parent, guardian, or legal custodian.

[2002 c 237 § 13.]

RCW 13.40.630 Youth court dispositions.

(1) Youth court dispositional options include those delineated in RCW 13.40.080, and may also include:

SECTION 2: RCW 13.40: JUVENILE JUSTICE ACT OF 1977, AS AMENDED

(a) Participating in law-related education classes, appropriate counseling, treatment, or other education [educational] programs;

(b) Providing periodic reports to the youth court;

(c) Participating in mentoring programs;

(d) Serving as a participant in future youth court proceedings;

(e) Writing apology letters; or

(f) Writing essays.

(2) Youth courts shall not impose a term of confinement or detention. Youth courts may require that the youth pay reasonable fees to participate in youth court and in classes, counseling, treatment, or other educational programs that are the disposition of the youth court.

(3) A youth court disposition shall be completed within one hundred eighty days from the date of referral.

(4) Pursuant to RCW 13.40.080(1), a youth court disposition shall be reduced to writing and signed by the youth and his or her parent, guardian, or legal custodian accepting the disposition terms.

(5) [A] youth court shall notify the juvenile court upon successful or unsuccessful completion of the disposition.

(6) [A] youth court shall notify the prosecutor or probation counselor of a failure to successfully complete the youth court disposition.

[2002 c 237 § 14.]

RCW 13.40.640 Youth court nonrefundable fee.

A youth court may require that a youth pay a nonrefundable fee, not exceeding thirty dollars, to cover the costs of administering the program. The fee may be reduced or waived for a participant. Fees shall be paid to and accounted for by the youth court.

[2002 c 237 § 15.]

SECTION 2: RCW 13.40: JUVENILE JUSTICE ACT OF 1977, AS AMENDED

RCW 13.40.650 Use of restraints on pregnant youth in custody — Allowed in extraordinary circumstances.

(1) Except in extraordinary circumstances, no restraints of any kind may be used on any pregnant youth in an institution or detention facility covered by this chapter during transportation to and from visits to medical providers and court proceedings during the third trimester of her pregnancy, or during postpartum recovery. For purposes of this section, "extraordinary circumstances" exist where an employee at an institution or detention facility makes an individualized determination that restraints are necessary to prevent an incarcerated pregnant youth from escaping, or from injuring herself, medical or correctional personnel, or others. In the event the employee of the institution or detention facility determines that extraordinary circumstances exist and restraints are used, the employee of the institution or detention facility must fully document in writing the reasons that he or she determined such extraordinary circumstances existed such that restraints were used. As part of this documentation, the employee of the institution or detention facility must also include the kind of restraints used and the reasons those restraints were considered the least restrictive available and the most reasonable under the circumstances.

(2) While the pregnant youth is in labor or in childbirth no restraints of any kind may be used. Nothing in this section affects the use of hospital restraints requested for the medical safety of a patient by treating physicians licensed under Title 18 RCW.

(3) Anytime restraints are permitted to be used on a pregnant youth, the restraints must be the least restrictive available and the most reasonable under the circumstances, but in no case shall leg irons or waist chains be used on any youth known to be pregnant.

(4) No employee of the institution or detention facility shall be present in the room during the pregnant youth's labor or childbirth, unless specifically requested by medical personnel. If the employee's presence is requested by medical personnel, the employee should be female, if practicable.

(5) If the doctor, nurse, or other health professional treating the pregnant youth requests that restraints not be used, the employee of the institution or detention facility accompanying the pregnant youth shall immediately remove all restraints.

[2010 c 181 § 11.]

RCW 13.40.651 Use of restraints on pregnant youth in custody — Allowed in extraordinary circumstances.

(1) Except in extraordinary circumstances, no restraints of any kind may be used on any pregnant youth in an institution or detention facility covered by this chapter during transportation to and

SECTION 2: RCW 13.40: JUVENILE JUSTICE ACT OF 1977, AS AMENDED

from visits to medical providers and court proceedings during the third trimester of her pregnancy, or during postpartum recovery. For purposes of this section, "extraordinary circumstances" exist where an employee at an institution or detention facility makes an individualized determination that restraints are necessary to prevent an incarcerated pregnant youth from escaping, or from injuring herself, medical or correctional personnel, or others. In the event the employee of the institution or detention facility determines that extraordinary circumstances exist and restraints are used, the employee of the institution or detention facility must fully document in writing the reasons that he or she determined such extraordinary circumstances existed such that restraints were used. As part of this documentation, the employee of the institution or detention facility must also include the kind of restraints used and the reasons those restraints were considered the least restrictive available and the most reasonable under the circumstances.

(2) While the pregnant youth is in labor or in childbirth no restraints of any kind may be used. Nothing in this section affects the use of hospital restraints requested for the medical safety of a patient by treating physicians licensed under Title 18 RCW.

(3) Anytime restraints are permitted to be used on a pregnant youth, the restraints must be the least restrictive available and the most reasonable under the circumstances, but in no case shall leg irons or waist chains be used on any youth known to be pregnant.

(4) No employee of the institution or detention facility shall be present in the room during the pregnant youth's labor or childbirth, unless specifically requested by medical personnel. If the employee's presence is requested by medical personnel, the employee should be female, if practicable.

(5) If the doctor, nurse, or other health professional treating the pregnant youth requests that restraints not be used, the employee of the institution or detention facility accompanying the pregnant youth shall immediately remove all restraints.

[2010 c 181 § 11.]

RCW 13.40.700 Juvenile gang courts — Minimum requirements — Admission — Individualized plan — Completion.

(1) Counties may establish and operate juvenile gang courts.

(2) For the purposes of this section, "juvenile gang court" means a court that has special calendars or dockets designed to achieve a reduction in gang-related offenses among juvenile offenders by increasing their likelihood for successful rehabilitation through early, continuous, and judicially supervised and integrated evidence-based services proven to reduce juvenile recidivism and gang involvement or through the use of research-based or promising practices identified by the Washington state partnership council on juvenile justice.

The Caseload Forecast Council is not liable for errors or omissions in the manual, for sentences that may be inappropriately calculated as a result of a practitioner's or court's reliance on the manual, or for any other written or verbal information related to adult or juvenile sentencing. The scoring sheets are intended to provide assistance in most cases but does not cover all permutations of the scoring rules. If you find any errors or omissions, we encourage you to report them to the Caseload Forecast Council.

SECTION 2: RCW 13.40: JUVENILE JUSTICE ACT OF 1977, AS AMENDED

(3) Any county that establishes a juvenile gang court pursuant to this section shall establish minimum requirements for the participation of offenders in the program. The juvenile gang court may adopt local requirements that are more stringent than the minimum. The minimum requirements are:

(a) The juvenile offender participates in gang activity, is repeatedly in the company of known gang members, or openly admits that he or she has been admitted to a gang;

(b) The juvenile offender has not previously been convicted of a serious violent offense or sex offense as defined in RCW 9.94A.030; and

(c) The juvenile offender is not currently charged with an offense:

(i) That is a class A felony offense;

(ii) That is a sex offense;

(iii) During which the juvenile offender intentionally discharged, threatened to discharge, or attempted to discharge a firearm in furtherance of the offense;

(iv) That subjects the juvenile offender to adult court original jurisdiction pursuant to RCW 13.04.030(1)(e)(v); or

(v) That constitutes assault of a child in the second degree.

(4) The court, the prosecutor, and the juvenile must agree to the juvenile's admission to a gang court created under this section.

(5) For the purposes of chapter 146, Laws of 2012, a "gang" means a group which consists of three or more persons; has identifiable leadership; and on an ongoing basis, regularly conspires and acts in concert mainly for criminal purposes.

(6) The juvenile offender who is admitted to juvenile gang court must:

(a) Stipulate to the admissibility of the facts contained in the written police report;

(b) Acknowledge that the report will be entered and used to support a finding of guilt and to impose a disposition if the juvenile fails to comply with the requirements of the juvenile gang court; and

(c) Waive the following rights to: (i) A speedy disposition; and (ii) call and confront witnesses.

SECTION 2: RCW 13.40: JUVENILE JUSTICE ACT OF 1977, AS AMENDED

(7) The adjudicatory hearing shall be limited to a reading of the court's record.

(8) Following the stipulation to the facts in the police report, acknowledgment, waiver, and entry of a finding or plea of guilt, the court shall defer entry of an order of disposition of the juvenile.

(9) Upon admission to juvenile gang court, an individualized plan shall be developed for the juvenile, identifying goals for the juvenile and a team to support the juvenile, which may include mental health and chemical dependency treatment providers, a probation officer, teachers, defense counsel, the prosecuting attorney, law enforcement, guardians or family members, and other participants deemed appropriate by the court. The individualized plan shall include a requirement that the juvenile remain in the gang court program for at least twelve months. At least one member of the support team must have daily contact with the juvenile.

(10) Upon successful completion of the juvenile gang court requirements, the conviction entered by the court shall be vacated and the charge shall be dismissed with prejudice.

(11) A juvenile may only be admitted to juvenile gang court once. If the juvenile fails to complete the requirements of gang court after being admitted, or successfully completes the requirements of gang court after being admitted, the juvenile may not be admitted again.

(12) If the juvenile fails to complete the juvenile gang court requirements, the court shall enter an order of disposition pursuant to RCW 13.40.0357.

[2012 c 146 § 2.]

RCW 13.40.710 Juvenile gang courts — Data — Reports.

(1) Counties that create a juvenile gang court pursuant to RCW

13.40.700 shall track and document data regarding the criteria that led to a juvenile's admission to gang court, the successful and unsuccessful completion of juvenile gang court requirements, and any subsequent criminal charges of juvenile gang court participants and provide such data to the administrative office of the courts.

(2) Subject to the availability of funds appropriated for this purpose, the administrative office of the courts shall study the data provided by the counties pursuant to subsection (1) of this section and report to the appropriate legislative committees regarding the recidivism outcomes for juvenile gang court participants. A preliminary report shall be completed by December 1, 2013. A final report shall be completed by December 1, 2015.

[2012 c 146 § 3.]

The Caseload Forecast Council is not liable for errors or omissions in the manual, for sentences that may be inappropriately calculated as a result of a practitioner's or court's reliance on the manual, or for any other written or verbal information related to adult or juvenile sentencing. The scoring sheets are intended to provide assistance in most cases but does not cover all permutations of the scoring rules. If you find any errors or omissions, we encourage you to report them to the Caseload Forecast Council.

SECTION 2: RCW 13.40: JUVENILE JUSTICE ACT OF 1977, AS AMENDED

RCW 13.40.900 Construction — Chapter applicable to state registered domestic partnerships — 2009 c 521.

For the purposes of this chapter, the terms spouse, marriage, marital, husband, wife, widow, widower, next of kin, and family shall be interpreted as applying equally to state registered domestic partnerships or individuals in state registered domestic partnerships as well as to marital relationships and married persons, and references to dissolution of marriage shall apply equally to state registered domestic partnerships that have been terminated, dissolved, or invalidated, to the extent that such interpretation does not conflict with federal law. Where necessary to implement chapter 521, Laws of 2009, gender-specific terms such as husband and wife used in any statute, rule, or other law shall be construed to be gender neutral, and applicable to individuals in state registered domestic partnerships.

[2009 c 521 § 43.]

SECTION 3

RCW 13.50: KEEPING AND RELEASE OF RECORDS BY JUVENILE JUSTICE OR CARE AGENCIES

RCW 13.50.010 Definitions — Conditions when filing petition or information — Duties to maintain accurate records and access.

(1) For purposes of this chapter:

(a) "Juvenile justice or care agency" means any of the following: Police, diversion units, court, prosecuting attorney, defense attorney, detention center, attorney general, the legislative children's oversight committee, the office of the family and children's ombudsman, the department of social and health services and its contracting agencies, schools; persons or public or private agencies having children committed to their custody; and any placement oversight committee created under RCW 72.05.415;

(b) "Official juvenile court file" means the legal file of the juvenile court containing the petition or information, motions, memorandums, briefs, findings of the court, and court orders;

(c) "Records" means the official juvenile court file, the social file, and records of any other juvenile justice or care agency in the case;

(d) "Social file" means the juvenile court file containing the records and reports of the probation counselor.

(2) Each petition or information filed with the court may include only one juvenile and each petition or information shall be filed under a separate docket number. The social file shall be filed separately from the official juvenile court file.

(3) It is the duty of any juvenile justice or care agency to maintain accurate records. To this end:

(a) The agency may never knowingly record inaccurate information. Any information in records maintained by the department of social and health services relating to a petition filed pursuant to chapter 13.34 RCW that is found by the court to be false or inaccurate shall be corrected or expunged from such records by the agency;

(b) An agency shall take reasonable steps to assure the security of its records and prevent

SECTION 3: RCW 13.50: KEEPING AND RELEASE OF RECORDS BY JUVENILE JUSTICE OR CARE AGENCIES

tampering with them; and

(c) An agency shall make reasonable efforts to insure the completeness of its records, including action taken by other agencies with respect to matters in its files.

(4) Each juvenile justice or care agency shall implement procedures consistent with the provisions of this chapter to facilitate inquiries concerning records.

(5) Any person who has reasonable cause to believe information concerning that person is included in the records of a juvenile justice or care agency and who has been denied access to those records by the agency may make a motion to the court for an order authorizing that person to inspect the juvenile justice or care agency record concerning that person. The court shall grant the motion to examine records unless it finds that in the interests of justice or in the best interests of the juvenile the records or parts of them should remain confidential.

(6) A juvenile, or his or her parents, or any person who has reasonable cause to believe information concerning that person is included in the records of a juvenile justice or care agency may make a motion to the court challenging the accuracy of any information concerning the moving party in the record or challenging the continued possession of the record by the agency. If the court grants the motion, it shall order the record or information to be corrected or destroyed.

(7) The person making a motion under subsection (5) or (6) of this section shall give reasonable notice of the motion to all parties to the original action and to any agency whose records will be affected by the motion.

(8) The court may permit inspection of records by, or release of information to, any clinic, hospital, or agency which has the subject person under care or treatment. The court may also permit inspection by or release to individuals or agencies, including juvenile justice advisory committees of county law and justice councils, engaged in legitimate research for educational, scientific, or public purposes. The court shall release to the caseload forecast council records needed for its research and data-gathering functions. Access to records or information for research purposes shall be permitted only if the anonymity of all persons mentioned in the records or information will be preserved. Each person granted permission to inspect juvenile justice or care agency records for research purposes shall present a notarized statement to the court stating that the names of juveniles and parents will remain confidential.

(9) Juvenile detention facilities shall release records to the caseload forecast council upon request. The commission shall not disclose the names of any juveniles or parents mentioned in the records without the named individual's written permission.

(10) Requirements in this chapter relating to the court's authority to compel disclosure shall not

---

The Caseload Forecast Council is not liable for errors or omissions in the manual, for sentences that may be inappropriately calculated as a result of a practitioner's or court's reliance on the manual, or for any other written or verbal information related to adult or juvenile sentencing. The scoring sheets are intended to provide assistance in most cases but does not cover all permutations of the scoring rules. If you find any errors or omissions, we encourage you to report them to the Caseload Forecast Council.

SECTION 3: RCW 13.50: KEEPING AND RELEASE OF RECORDS BY JUVENILE JUSTICE OR CARE AGENCIES

apply to the legislative children's oversight committee or the office of the family and children's ombudsman.

(11) For the purpose of research only, the administrative office of the courts shall maintain an electronic research copy of all records in the judicial information system related to juveniles. Access to the research copy is restricted to the Washington state center for court research. The Washington state center for court research shall maintain the confidentiality of all confidential records and shall preserve the anonymity of all persons identified in the research copy. The research copy may not be subject to any records retention schedule and must include records destroyed or removed from the judicial information system pursuant to RCW 13.50.050 (17) and (18) and 13.50.100(3).

(12) The court shall release to the Washington state office of public defense records needed to implement the agency's oversight, technical assistance, and other functions as required by RCW 2.70.020. Access to the records used as a basis for oversight, technical assistance, or other agency functions is restricted to the Washington state office of public defense. The Washington state office of public defense shall maintain the confidentiality of all confidential information included in the records.

[2011 1st sp.s. c 40 § 30; 2010 c 150 § 3; 2009 c 440 § 1; 1998 c 269 § 4. Prior: 1997 c 386 § 21; 1997 c 338 § 39; 1996 c 232 § 6; 1994 sp.s. c 7 § 541; 1993 c 374 § 1; 1990 c 246 § 8; 1986 c 288 § 11; 1979 c 155 § 8.]

RCW 13.50.050 Records relating to commission of juvenile offenses — Maintenance of, access to, and destruction — Release of information to schools.

(1) This section governs records relating to the commission of juvenile offenses, including records relating to diversions.

(2) The official juvenile court file of any alleged or proven juvenile offender shall be open to public inspection, unless sealed pursuant to subsection (12) of this section.

(3) All records other than the official juvenile court file are confidential and may be released only as provided in this section, RCW 13.50.010, 13.40.215, and 4.24.550.

(4) Except as otherwise provided in this section and RCW 13.50.010, records retained or produced by any juvenile justice or care agency may be released to other participants in the juvenile justice or care system only when an investigation or case involving the juvenile in question is being pursued by the other participant or when that other participant is assigned the responsibility for supervising the juvenile.

(5) Except as provided in RCW 4.24.550, information not in an official juvenile court file

SECTION 3: RCW 13.50: KEEPING AND RELEASE OF RECORDS BY JUVENILE JUSTICE OR CARE AGENCIES

concerning a juvenile or a juvenile's family may be released to the public only when that information could not reasonably be expected to identify the juvenile or the juvenile's family.

(6) Notwithstanding any other provision of this chapter, the release, to the juvenile or his or her attorney, of law enforcement and prosecuting attorneys' records pertaining to investigation, diversion, and prosecution of juvenile offenses shall be governed by the rules of discovery and other rules of law applicable in adult criminal investigations and prosecutions.

(7) Upon the decision to arrest or the arrest, law enforcement and prosecuting attorneys may cooperate with schools in releasing information to a school pertaining to the investigation, diversion, and prosecution of a juvenile attending the school. Upon the decision to arrest or the arrest, incident reports may be released unless releasing the records would jeopardize the investigation or prosecution or endanger witnesses. If release of incident reports would jeopardize the investigation or prosecution or endanger witnesses, law enforcement and prosecuting attorneys may release information to the maximum extent possible to assist schools in protecting other students, staff, and school property.

(8) The juvenile court and the prosecutor may set up and maintain a central recordkeeping system which may receive information on all alleged juvenile offenders against whom a complaint has been filed pursuant to RCW 13.40.070 whether or not their cases are currently pending before the court. The central recordkeeping system may be computerized. If a complaint has been referred to a diversion unit, the diversion unit shall promptly report to the juvenile court or the prosecuting attorney when the juvenile has agreed to diversion. An offense shall not be reported as criminal history in any central recordkeeping system without notification by the diversion unit of the date on which the offender agreed to diversion.

(9) Upon request of the victim of a crime or the victim's immediate family, the identity of an alleged or proven juvenile offender alleged or found to have committed a crime against the victim and the identity of the alleged or proven juvenile offender's parent, guardian, or custodian and the circumstance of the alleged or proven crime shall be released to the victim of the crime or the victim's immediate family.

(10) Subject to the rules of discovery applicable in adult criminal prosecutions, the juvenile offense records of an adult criminal defendant or witness in an adult criminal proceeding shall be released upon request to prosecution and defense counsel after a charge has actually been filed. The juvenile offense records of any adult convicted of a crime and placed under the supervision of the adult corrections system shall be released upon request to the adult corrections system.

(11) In any case in which an information has been filed pursuant to RCW 13.40.100 or a complaint has been filed with the prosecutor and referred for diversion pursuant to RCW 13.40.070, the person the subject of the information or complaint may file a motion with the court to have the court vacate its order and findings, if any, and, subject to subsection (23) of this

SECTION 3: RCW 13.50: KEEPING AND RELEASE OF RECORDS BY JUVENILE JUSTICE OR CARE AGENCIES

section, order the sealing of the official juvenile court file, the social file, and records of the court and of any other agency in the case.

(12)(a) The court shall not grant any motion to seal records for class A offenses made pursuant to subsection (11) of this section that is filed on or after July 1, 1997, unless:

(i) Since the last date of release from confinement, including full-time residential treatment, if any, or entry of disposition, the person has spent five consecutive years in the community without committing any offense or crime that subsequently results in an adjudication or conviction;

(ii) No proceeding is pending against the moving party seeking the conviction of a juvenile offense or a criminal offense;

(iii) No proceeding is pending seeking the formation of a diversion agreement with that person;

(iv) The person is no longer required to register as a sex offender under RCW 9A.44.130 or has been relieved of the duty to register under RCW 9A.44.143 if the person was convicted of a sex offense;

(v) The person has not been convicted of rape in the first degree, rape in the second degree, or indecent liberties that was actually committed with forcible compulsion; and

(vi) Full restitution has been paid.

(b) The court shall not grant any motion to seal records for class B, C, gross misdemeanor and misdemeanor offenses and diversions made under subsection (11) of this section unless:

(i) Since the date of last release from confinement, including full-time residential treatment, if any, entry of disposition, or completion of the diversion agreement, the person has spent two consecutive years in the community without being convicted of any offense or crime;

(ii) No proceeding is pending against the moving party seeking the conviction of a juvenile offense or a criminal offense;

(iii) No proceeding is pending seeking the formation of a diversion agreement with that person;

(iv) The person is no longer required to register as a sex offender under RCW 9A.44.130 or has been relieved of the duty to register under RCW 9A.44.143 if the person was convicted of a sex offense; and

(v) Full restitution has been paid.

The Caseload Forecast Council is not liable for errors or omissions in the manual, for sentences that may be inappropriately calculated as a result of a practitioner's or court's reliance on the manual, or for any other written or verbal information related to adult or juvenile sentencing. The scoring sheets are intended to provide assistance in most cases but does not cover all permutations of the scoring rules. If you find any errors or omissions, we encourage you to report them to the Caseload Forecast Council.

SECTION 3: RCW 13.50: KEEPING AND RELEASE OF RECORDS BY JUVENILE JUSTICE OR CARE AGENCIES

(c) Notwithstanding the requirements in (a) or (b) of this subsection, the court shall grant any motion to seal records of any deferred disposition vacated under RCW 13.40.127(9) prior to June 7, 2012, if restitution has been paid and the person is eighteen years of age or older at the time of the motion.

(13) The person making a motion pursuant to subsection (11) of this section shall give reasonable notice of the motion to the prosecution and to any person or agency whose files are sought to be sealed.

(14)(a) If the court grants the motion to seal made pursuant to subsection (11) of this section, it shall, subject to subsection (23) of this section, order sealed the official juvenile court file, the social file, and other records relating to the case as are named in the order. Thereafter, the proceedings in the case shall be treated as if they never occurred, and the subject of the records may reply accordingly to any inquiry about the events, records of which are sealed. Any agency shall reply to any inquiry concerning confidential or sealed records that records are confidential, and no information can be given about the existence or nonexistence of records concerning an individual.

(b) In the event the subject of the juvenile records receives a full and unconditional pardon, the proceedings in the matter upon which the pardon has been granted shall be treated as if they never occurred, and the subject of the records may reply accordingly to any inquiry about the events upon which the pardon was received. Any agency shall reply to any inquiry concerning the records pertaining to the events for which the subject received a pardon that records are confidential, and no information can be given about the existence or nonexistence of records concerning an individual.

(15) Inspection of the files and records included in the order to seal may thereafter be permitted only by order of the court upon motion made by the person who is the subject of the information or complaint, except as otherwise provided in RCW 13.50.010(8) and subsection (23) of this section.

(16) Any adjudication of a juvenile offense or a crime subsequent to sealing has the effect of nullifying the sealing order. Any charging of an adult felony subsequent to the sealing has the effect of nullifying the sealing order for the purposes of chapter 9.94A RCW. The administrative office of the courts shall ensure that the superior court judicial information system provides prosecutors access to information on the existence of sealed juvenile records.

(17)(a)(i) Subject to subsection (23) of this section, all records maintained by any court or law enforcement agency, including the juvenile court, local law enforcement, the Washington state patrol, and the prosecutor's office, shall be automatically destroyed within ninety days of becoming eligible for destruction. Juvenile records are eligible for destruction when:

SECTION 3: RCW 13.50: KEEPING AND RELEASE OF RECORDS BY JUVENILE JUSTICE OR CARE AGENCIES

(A) The person who is the subject of the information or complaint is at least eighteen years of age;

(B) His or her criminal history consists entirely of one diversion agreement or counsel and release entered on or after June 12, 2008;

(C) Two years have elapsed since completion of the agreement or counsel and release;

(D) No proceeding is pending against the person seeking the conviction of a criminal offense; and

(E) There is no restitution owing in the case.

(ii) No less than quarterly, the administrative office of the courts shall provide a report to the juvenile courts of those individuals whose records may be eligible for destruction. The juvenile court shall verify eligibility and notify the Washington state patrol and the appropriate local law enforcement agency and prosecutor's office of the records to be destroyed. The requirement to destroy records under this subsection is not dependent on a court hearing or the issuance of a court order to destroy records.

(iii) The state and local governments and their officers and employees are not liable for civil damages for the failure to destroy records pursuant to this section.

(b) All records maintained by any court or law enforcement agency, including the juvenile court, local law enforcement, the Washington state patrol, and the prosecutor's office, shall be automatically destroyed within thirty days of being notified by the governor's office that the subject of those records received a full and unconditional pardon by the governor.

(c) A person eighteen years of age or older whose criminal history consists entirely of one diversion agreement or counsel and release entered prior to June 12, 2008, may request that the court order the records in his or her case destroyed. The request shall be granted, subject to subsection (23) of this section, if the court finds that two years have elapsed since completion of the agreement or counsel and release.

(d) A person twenty-three years of age or older whose criminal history consists of only referrals for diversion may request that the court order the records in those cases destroyed. The request shall be granted, subject to subsection (23) of this section, if the court finds that all diversion agreements have been successfully completed and no proceeding is pending against the person seeking the conviction of a criminal offense.

(18) If the court grants the motion to destroy records made pursuant to subsection (17)(c) or (d)

SECTION 3: RCW 13.50: KEEPING AND RELEASE OF RECORDS BY JUVENILE JUSTICE OR CARE AGENCIES

of this section, it shall, subject to subsection (23) of this section, order the official juvenile court file, the social file, and any other records named in the order to be destroyed.

(19) The person making the motion pursuant to subsection (17)(c) or (d) of this section shall give reasonable notice of the motion to the prosecuting attorney and to any agency whose records are sought to be destroyed.

(20) Any juvenile to whom the provisions of this section may apply shall be given written notice of his or her rights under this section at the time of his or her disposition hearing or during the diversion process.

(21) Nothing in this section may be construed to prevent a crime victim or a member of the victim's family from divulging the identity of the alleged or proven juvenile offender or his or her family when necessary in a civil proceeding.

(22) Any juvenile justice or care agency may, subject to the limitations in subsection (23) of this section and (a) and (b) of this subsection, develop procedures for the routine destruction of records relating to juvenile offenses and diversions.

(a) Records may be routinely destroyed only when the person the subject of the information or complaint has attained twenty-three years of age or older or pursuant to subsection (17)(a) of this section.

(b) The court may not routinely destroy the official juvenile court file or recordings or transcripts of any proceedings.

(23) Except for subsection (17)(b) of this section, no identifying information held by the Washington state patrol in accordance with chapter 43.43 RCW is subject to destruction or sealing under this section. For the purposes of this subsection, identifying information includes photographs, fingerprints, palm prints, soleprints, toe prints and any other data that identifies a person by physical characteristics, name, birthdate or address, but does not include information regarding criminal activity, arrest, charging, diversion, conviction or other information about a person's treatment by the criminal justice system or about the person's behavior.

(24) Information identifying child victims under age eighteen who are victims of sexual assaults by juvenile offenders is confidential and not subject to release to the press or public without the permission of the child victim or the child's legal guardian. Identifying information includes the child victim's name, addresses, location, photographs, and in cases in which the child victim is a relative of the alleged perpetrator, identification of the relationship between the child and the alleged perpetrator. Information identifying a child victim of sexual assault may be released to law enforcement, prosecutors, judges, defense attorneys, or private or governmental agencies that provide services to the child victim of sexual assault.

The Caseload Forecast Council is not liable for errors or omissions in the manual, for sentences that may be inappropriately calculated as a result of a practitioner's or court's reliance on the manual, or for any other written or verbal information related to adult or juvenile sentencing. The scoring sheets are intended to provide assistance in most cases but does not cover all permutations of the scoring rules. If you find any errors or omissions, we encourage you to report them to the Caseload Forecast Council.

SECTION 3: RCW 13.50: KEEPING AND RELEASE OF RECORDS BY JUVENILE JUSTICE OR CARE AGENCIES

[2012 c 177 § 2. Prior: 2011 c 338 § 4; 2011 c 333 § 4; 2010 c 150 § 2; 2008 c 221 § 1; 2004 c 42 § 1; prior: 2001 c 175 § 1; 2001 c 174 § 1; 2001 c 49 § 2; 1999 c 198 § 4; 1997 c 338 § 40; 1992 c 188 § 7; 1990 c 3 § 125; 1987 c 450 § 8; 1986 c 257 § 33; 1984 c 43 § 1; 1983 c 191 § 19; 1981 c 299 § 19; 1979 c 155 § 9.]

RCW 13.50.100 Records not relating to commission of juvenile offenses — Maintenance and access — Release of information for child custody hearings — Disclosure of unfounded allegations prohibited.

(1) This section governs records not covered by RCW 13.50.050.

(2) Records covered by this section shall be confidential and shall be released only pursuant to this section and RCW 13.50.010.

(3) Records retained or produced by any juvenile justice or care agency may be released to other participants in the juvenile justice or care system only when an investigation or case involving the juvenile in question is being pursued by the other participant or when that other participant is assigned the responsibility of supervising the juvenile. Records covered under this section and maintained by the juvenile courts which relate to the official actions of the agency may be entered in the statewide judicial information system. However, truancy records associated with a juvenile who has no other case history, and records of a juvenile's parents who have no other case history, shall be removed from the judicial information system when the juvenile is no longer subject to the compulsory attendance laws in chapter 28A.225 RCW. A county clerk is not liable for unauthorized release of this data by persons or agencies not in his or her employ or otherwise subject to his or her control, nor is the county clerk liable for inaccurate or incomplete information collected from litigants or other persons required to provide identifying data pursuant to this section.

(4) Subject to (a) of this subsection, the department of social and health services may release information retained in the course of conducting child protective services investigations to a family or juvenile court hearing a petition for custody under chapter 26.10 RCW.

(a) Information that may be released shall be limited to information regarding investigations in which: (i) The juvenile was an alleged victim of abandonment or abuse or neglect; or (ii) the petitioner for custody of the juvenile, or any individual aged sixteen or older residing in the petitioner's household, is the subject of a founded or currently pending child protective services investigation made by the department subsequent to October 1, 1998.

(b) Additional information may only be released with the written consent of the subject of the investigation and the juvenile alleged to be the victim of abandonment or abuse and neglect, or the parent, custodian, guardian, or personal representative of the juvenile, or by court order obtained with notice to all interested parties.

SECTION 3: RCW 13.50: KEEPING AND RELEASE OF RECORDS BY JUVENILE JUSTICE OR CARE AGENCIES

(5) Any disclosure of records or information by the department of social and health services pursuant to this section shall not be deemed a waiver of any confidentiality or privilege attached to the records or information by operation of any state or federal statute or regulation, and any recipient of such records or information shall maintain it in such a manner as to comply with such state and federal statutes and regulations and to protect against unauthorized disclosure.

(6) A contracting agency or service provider of the department of social and health services that provides counseling, psychological, psychiatric, or medical services may release to the office of the family and children's ombudsman information or records relating to services provided to a juvenile who is dependent under chapter 13.34 RCW without the consent of the parent or guardian of the juvenile, or of the juvenile if the juvenile is under the age of thirteen years, unless such release is otherwise specifically prohibited by law.

(7) A juvenile, his or her parents, the juvenile's attorney and the juvenile's parent's attorney, shall, upon request, be given access to all records and information collected or retained by a juvenile justice or care agency which pertain to the juvenile except:

(a) If it is determined by the agency that release of this information is likely to cause severe psychological or physical harm to the juvenile or his or her parents the agency may withhold the information subject to other order of the court: PROVIDED, That if the court determines that limited release of the information is appropriate, the court may specify terms and conditions for the release of the information; or

(b) If the information or record has been obtained by a juvenile justice or care agency in connection with the provision of counseling, psychological, psychiatric, or medical services to the juvenile, when the services have been sought voluntarily by the juvenile, and the juvenile has a legal right to receive those services without the consent of any person or agency, then the information or record may not be disclosed to the juvenile's parents without the informed consent of the juvenile unless otherwise authorized by law; or

(c) That the department of social and health services may delete the name and identifying information regarding persons or organizations who have reported alleged child abuse or neglect.

(8) A juvenile or his or her parent denied access to any records following an agency determination under subsection (7) of this section may file a motion in juvenile court requesting access to the records. The court shall grant the motion unless it finds access may not be permitted according to the standards found in subsection (7)(a) and (b) of this section.

(9) The person making a motion under subsection (8) of this section shall give reasonable notice of the motion to all parties to the original action and to any agency whose records will be affected by the motion.

The Caseload Forecast Council is not liable for errors or omissions in the manual, for sentences that may be inappropriately calculated as a result of a practitioner's or court's reliance on the manual, or for any other written or verbal information related to adult or juvenile sentencing. The scoring sheets are intended to provide assistance in most cases but does not cover all permutations of the scoring rules. If you find any errors or omissions, we encourage you to report them to the Caseload Forecast Council.

SECTION 3: RCW 13.50: KEEPING AND RELEASE OF RECORDS BY JUVENILE JUSTICE OR CARE AGENCIES

(10) Subject to the rules of discovery in civil cases, any party to a proceeding seeking a declaration of dependency or a termination of the parent-child relationship and any party's counsel and the guardian ad litem of any party, shall have access to the records of any natural or adoptive child of the parent, subject to the limitations in subsection (7) of this section. A party denied access to records may request judicial review of the denial. If the party prevails, he or she shall be awarded attorneys' fees, costs, and an amount not less than five dollars and not more than one hundred dollars for each day the records were wrongfully denied.

(11) No unfounded allegation of child abuse or neglect as defined in *RCW 26.44.020(12) may be disclosed to a child-placing agency, private adoption agency, or any other licensed provider.

[2003 c 105 § 2; 2001 c 162 § 2; 2000 c 162 § 18; 1999 c 390 § 3; 1997 c 386 § 22; 1995 c 311 § 16; 1990 c 246 § 9; 1983 c 191 § 20; 1979 c 155 § 10.]

RCW 13.50.140 Disclosure of privileged information to office of the family and children's ombudsman — Privilege not waived as to others.

Any communication or advice privileged under RCW 5.60.060 that is disclosed by the office of the attorney general or the department of social and health services to the office of the family and children's ombudsman may not be deemed to be a waiver of the privilege as to others.

[1999 c 390 § 8.]

RCW 13.50.150 Confidential records — Expungement to protect due process rights.

Nothing in this chapter shall be construed to prevent the expungement of any juvenile record ordered expunged by a court to preserve the due process rights of its subject.

[1977 ex.s. c 291 § 13. Formerly RCW 13.04.276, see 1979 c 155 § 12.]

RCW 13.50.160 Disposition records — Provision to schools.

Records of disposition for a juvenile offense must be provided to schools as provided in RCW 13.04.155.

[1997 c 266 § 8.]

SECTION 3: RCW 13.50: KEEPING AND RELEASE OF RECORDS BY JUVENILE JUSTICE OR CARE AGENCIES

RCW 13.50.200 Records of motor vehicle operation violation forwarded.

Notwithstanding any other provision of this chapter, whenever a child is arrested for a violation of any law, including municipal ordinances, regulating the operation of vehicles on the public highways, a copy of the traffic citation and a record of the action taken by the court shall be forwarded by the juvenile court to the department of licensing in the same manner as provided in RCW 46.20.270.

[1979 c 155 § 13; 1977 ex.s. c 291 § 14. Formerly RCW 13.04.278.]

RCW 13.50.250 Records chapter applicable to.

This chapter applies to all juvenile justice or care agency records created on or after July 1, 1978.

[1979 c 155 § 11.]

SECTION 4

JUVENILE CASE LAW REVIEW: 2013

Introduction

The following review of juvenile case law was provided by Judge Ronald Kessler, King County Superior Court. The cases listed under "2013 Review" were added in a 2013 update. It is copyrighted by Judge Kessler and is used with permission.

SECTION 4: JUVENILE CASE LAW REVIEW: 2013

2013 Juvenile Case Law Review Update

State v. W.S., 176 Wn.App. 231 (2013)
    Following adjudication, juvenile court may issue a domestic violence no contact order for the maximum period of the offense which may extend beyond respondent's 18th or 21st birthday; I.

State v. R.G.P., 175 Wn.App. 131 (2013)
    Juvenile court must order full restitution and may not consider respondent's ability to pay, *State v. A.M.R.*, 147 Wn.2d 91, 96 (2002), including a restitution order following a deferred disposition; II.

State v. Sanchez, 172 Wn.App. 678 (2012)
    Juvenile's trial date is not set within fifteen days of arraignment, JuCR 7.8(d)(1), at a pretrial hearing the case is not called, prosecutor is not present, respondent and counsel leave court without notifying the judge, respondent is tried months later; held: dismissal is only a remedy for failure to try a case within the time limits, thus failure to set a date within fifteen days of arraignment, while a violation of the rule, does not require dismissal, *see: State v. Parris, 30 Wn.App. 268 (1981)*; an appearance requires respondent's physical presence plus notification to the prosecutor of presence and presence must be contemporaneously noted on the record, JuCR 7.8(2)(iii), thus amended rule overrules definition of appearance in *State v. Ledenko*, 87 Wn.App. 39 (1997); III.

State v. Lowe, 173 Wn.App. 390 (2013)
    Sentencing court includes in offender score a juvenile conviction where juvenile court had dismissed a deferred disposition because prosecutor neglected to seek revocation prior to the end the deferral period but juvenile court did not vacate the disposition as respondent had not fully complied; held: juvenile court is not required to vacate a conviction at the conclusion of a deferred disposition where motion to revoke has been untimely; juvenile court lacks authority to vacate a conviction unless it affirmatively finds full compliance with the conditions, RCW 13.40.127 (2009), *State v. D.P.G.*, 169 Wn.App. 396, 400-01 (2012); I.

State v. Benitez, 175 Wn.App. 116, 122-23 (2013)
    A juvenile adjudication of a sex offense is a prior conviction for purposes of enhancing **indecent exposure**, RCW 9A.88.010(2)(c) (2003), from a misdemeanor to a felony; II.

SECTION 4: JUVENILE CASE LAW REVIEW: 2013

2012 Juvenile Case Law Review

Nelson v. Seattle Municipal Court, 29 Wn.App. 7 (1981)
    Where a juvenile willfully deceives an adult court into believing she is more than 18 years old she waives her right to be tried as a juvenile, *see:* *Dillenburg v. Maxwell*, 70 Wn.2d 331, 354-56 (1967), *State v. Mendoza-Lopez*, 105 Wn.App. 382 (2001); I.

State v. Lawley, 32 Wn.App. 337 (1982)
    Where court commissioner issues a ruling, and state seeks revision, RCW 2.24.050, speedy trial rule is stayed pending decision by superior court judge; III.

State v. Tidwell, 32 Wn.App. 971 (1982)
    Juvenile court lacks jurisdiction over federal crimes (civil rights violation cross burning); I.

In re Smiley, 96 Wn.2d 950 (1982)
    Defendant, committed by juvenile court, escapes and commits a new offense, which juvenile court declines, and for which Superior Court sentences to jail, following which he is returned to the juvenile facility to complete the juvenile court commitment; held that decline does not nullify the former juvenile court commitment; adult sentence can run concurrent with prior juvenile court disposition; 7-2.

State v. Hovland, 34 Wn.App. 830 (1983)
    For **speedy trial** purposes, start counting day after juvenile court enters order retaining jurisdiction; III.

State v. Tuffree, 35 Wn.App. 243 (1983)
    Colloquy to determine **competency** of a child witness performed in presence of jury is "bothersome, but ... not erroneous as a matter of law"; court cites with approval Stafford, *The Child as a Witness*, 37 Wash. L. Rev. 303 (1962).

State v. Holland, 98 Wn.2d 507 (1983)
    While written findings must be entered for a **decline** order, a court's oral findings may supplement inadequate written findings; statements made by a juvenile to a mental health professional prior to a decline hearing are privileged but privilege is waived if defendant takes the stand at trial; affirms *State v. Holland*, 30 Wn.App. 366 (1981); 9-0.

State v. Frazier, 99 Wn.2d 180 (1983)
    A juvenile may not plead guilty in juvenile court when a **decline** hearing is pending; 9-0.

State v. Sharon, 100 Wn.2d 230 (1983)
    Once juvenile court **declines** jurisdiction, juvenile court has lost jurisdiction for all subsequent offenses, RCW 13.40.020(10), *but see:* *State v. Mora*, 138 Wn.2d 43 (1999); *affirms* *State v. Sharon*, 33 Wn.App. 491 (1982); 9-0.

The Caseload Forecast Council is not liable for errors or omissions in the manual, for sentences that may be inappropriately calculated as a result of a practitioner's or court's reliance on the manual, or for any other written or verbal information related to adult or juvenile sentencing. The scoring sheets are intended to provide assistance in most cases but does not cover all permutations of the scoring rules. If you find any errors or omissions, we encourage you to report them to the Caseload Forecast Council.

SECTION 4: JUVENILE CASE LAW REVIEW: 2013

State v. Lawson, 37 Wn.App. 539 (1984)
Statutory defense to minor consuming alcohol, RCW 66.44.270, that defendant had permission to drink by his parents is an affirmative defense, not an element to be disproved by state; I.

State v. Fellers, 37 Wn.App. 613 (1984)
Juvenile court judge must enter written **findings** sufficiently specific to permit meaningful appellate review, RCW 13.40.130(4), JuCR 7.11(c), *State v. Witherspoon*, 60 Wn.App. 569 (1991), *State v. Peña*, 65 Wn.App. 711 (1992), *see: State v. Head*, 136 Wn.2d 619 (1998).

State v. Freeman, 38 Wn.App. 665 (1984)
A conflict in defense counsel's trial schedule is good cause for **continuance**, JuCR 7.8(d); CrR 3.3(f) requiring objection to trial date within ten days of trial setting applies to juvenile proceedings; I.

State v. Bushnell, 38 Wn.App. 809 (1984)
Defendant commits crime at 17 years, is charged as an adult at 19 years, Superior Court remands to juvenile court for trial, as defendant was on probation to age 21 for an unrelated offense; held: juvenile court has no jurisdiction to try a person who is more than 18 years old unless jurisdiction was extended in that case; III.

State v. Toomey, 38 Wn.App. 831 (1984)
Court may consider best interests of the public in deciding whether or not to **decline** jurisdiction, RCW 13.40.110(2), *State v. Furman*, 122 Wn.2d 440 (1993); II.

State v. Marshall, 39 Wn.App. 180 (1984)
Manslaughter 1° and 2° are not void for vagueness when applied to juveniles as definitions of reckless and negligence set standard of reasonable man "in the same situation", RCW 9A.08.010(1)(c), thus permitting court to view acts in terms of respondent's age; III.

State v. Steinbach, 101 Wn.2d 460 (1984)
Juvenile files alternative residential placement petition, RCW 13.32A.150, is placed by court in alternative residence; parent tells respondent she could not live at home, but could visit; ARP order does not order respondent out of home; held: no unlawful entry, thus no **burglary of parent's home** is possible, *but see: State v. Cantu*, 156 Wn.2d 819 (2006); reverses *State v. Steinbach*, 35 Wn.App. 473 (1983); *see: State v. Walsh*, 57 Wn.App. 488 (1990); *but see: State v. Jensen*, 57 Wn.App. 501 (1990); 5-4.

State v. McDowell, 102 Wn.2d 341 (1984)

SECTION 4: JUVENILE CASE LAW REVIEW: 2013

Juvenile accused of reckless endangerment rejects **diversion**, whereupon prosecutor files assault 2° for same incident; held: no presumption of vindictiveness or abuse of discretion, United States v. Goodwin, 73 L.Ed.2d 74 (1982), State v. Korum, 157 Wn.2d 614 (2006); 9-0.

State v. Sandomingo, 39 Wn.App. 709 (1985)
Defendant claimed he did not know how old he was, moves for remand to juvenile court; held: where there is reasonable basis for believing defendant to be adult and state has no means of verifying his claims, defendant has burden of proving his minority, State v. Mendoza-Lopez, 105 Wn.App. 382 (2001); II.

State v. Cirkovich, 41 Wn.App. 275 (1985)
Juvenile's commitment is stayed pending appeal, during which time he turns 18 years of age, argues that, in absence of a written order, juvenile court lacks jurisdiction upon appeal being affirmed, RCW 13.40.300(1)(c); held: stay pending appeal tolls age requirement and, if affirmed, court retains jurisdiction until offender's 21st birthday; I.

State v. Mershon, 43 Wn.App. 132 (1986)
State is barred by the double jeopardy clause from seeking revision from a commissioner's acquittal, RCW 2.24.050; II.

State v. Royster, 43 Wn.App. 613 (1986)
Where juvenile is being detained on new offense and also is being held on a prior commitment, 60-day rule applies, JuCR 7.8, as shorter time period only applies when defendant's pretrial detention is due solely to current charges, State v. Brown, 33 Wn.App. 843, 845-46 (1983), State v. Nelson, 26 Wn.App. 612, 616 (1980), State v. Worland, 20 Wn.App. 559, 564 (1978); I.

State v. Tracy M., 43 Wn.App. 888 (1986)
Power of prosecutor to divert a juvenile offender, RCW 13.40.070, does not violate separation of powers doctrine, due process or equal protection; III.

State v. Main, 46 Wn.App. 356 (1986)
Defendant is charged in juvenile court while on escape status, turns 18 before warrant is served, charges filed in Superior Court; held: because defendant was on escape status, "presumably" knew that warrant had been issued, authorities had little or no information concerning his whereabouts, then state made a good faith and diligent effort to arrest defendant, and delay was justified. State v. Perry 25, Wn.App. 621 (1980), distinguishing State v. Wirth, 39 Wn.App. 550 (1985); I.

State v. Hornaday, 105 Wn.2d 120 (1986)
Police lack probable cause to arrest a juvenile for the crime of minor consuming or possessing alcohol, RCW 66.44.270, where the only evidence is respondent's obvious intoxication and an odor of alcohol; presence of alcohol in the bloodstream is not possession or consumption, State v. A.T.P.-R., 132 Wn.App. 181 (2006), State v. Francisco, 148 Wn.App. 168,

SECTION 4: JUVENILE CASE LAW REVIEW: 2013

175-76 (2009), *but see: State v. Preston*, 66 Wn.App. 494 (1992), *State v. Dalton*, 72 Wn.App. 674 (1994), *State v. Fager*, 73 Wn.App. 617 (1994), *State v. Roth*, 131 Wn.App. 556, 563-66 (20060, RCW 10.31.100 (1987); 7-2.

State v. Day, 46 Wn.App. 882 (1987)
An available juvenile respondent must be arraigned within 14 days after information is filed; if the 14-day arraignment time plus the 60-day speedy trial time, JuCrR 7.8(b) is exceeded, charge must be dismissed, *State v. Chandler*, 143 Wn.2d 485 (2001); where juvenile keeps police, prosecutor or court advised of his address, but notice of arraignment is sent to wrong address, then **speedy arraignment** requirements may be violated, *see: State v. Hackett*, 122 Wn.2d 165 (1993), *State v. Hilderbrandt*, 109 Wn.App. 46 (2001); III.

State v. Curwood, 50 Wn.App. 228 (1987)
Where juvenile court has extended jurisdiction to a date beyond respondent's 18th birthday, and disposition occurs within the extended jurisdictional period, then state may retain custody over respondent during the full term of his confinement; I; *see also*: *State v. Forhan*, 59 Wn.App. 486 (1990).

State v. Chavez, 111 Wn.2d 548 (1988)
Local court rule permitting court to dismiss juvenile court case if there is more than 30-day delay between completion of police investigation and filing of information is valid, however trial court may only dismiss under rule if actual prejudice is established; 5-3.

State v. Adamski, 111 Wn.2d 574 (1988)
A mailed subpoena is a nullity, as it does not conform with JuCR 1.4, CR 45(c), CrR 4.8, and thus is not grounds for due diligence; a **continuance** beyond the expiration date, JuCR 7.8(b), to obtain a witness who was not properly served is an abuse of discretion, *State v. Hairychin*, 136 Wn.2d 862 (1998), *reversing State v. Adamski*, 49 Wn.App. 371 (1987); 5-3.

State v. Cooley, 53 Wn.App. 163 (1989)
Filing information in county where offense occurred amounts to "request" by prosecutor that charge be filed in county other than county where respondent resides, RCW 13.40.060(1); II.

State v. Merz, 54 Wn.App. 23 (1989)
A juvenile respondent's plea bargain with the prosecutor does not bind the probation counselor; *see*: *State v. Harris*, 57 Wn.2d 383 (1960); I.

State v. Espinoza, 112 Wn.2d 819 (1989)
A juvenile court commissioner is not disqualified by the filing of an affidavit of prejudice, since the ruling of a commissioner is subject to a de novo revision hearing, RCW 2.24.050, 13.04.021, *reversing State v. Espinoza*, 51 Wn.App. 719 (1988); 9-0.

State v. Poupart, 54 Wn.App. 440 (1989)

The Caseload Forecast Council is not liable for errors or omissions in the manual, for sentences that may be inappropriately calculated as a result of a practitioner's or court's reliance on the manual, or for any other written or verbal information related to adult or juvenile sentencing. The scoring sheets are intended to provide assistance in most cases but does not cover all permutations of the scoring rules. If you find any errors or omissions, we encourage you to report them to the Caseload Forecast Council.

SECTION 4: JUVENILE CASE LAW REVIEW: 2013

Probation counselors and caseworkers are not bound by a plea agreement and may make recommendations independent of the prosecutor, *see: State v. Harris*, 146 Wn.2d 339 (2002); I.

State v. Getty, 55 Wn.App. 152 (1989)
Police serve juvenile with municipal court citation but file it with county prosecutor in juvenile court; juvenile court judge orders state to obtain dismissal in municipal court (although citation never filed there), state fails to comply, trial court dismisses; held: municipal court lacked jurisdiction over juvenile, so no constitutional rights violation existed; no prejudice to respondent, thus trial court abused its discretion; I.

State v. Witherspoon, 60 Wn.App. 569 (1991)
Juvenile court fails to enter any written **findings** and conclusions following trial, JuCR 7.11(d), through oral argument on appeal; held: reversed and dismissed, as respondent's custody is prejudice plus permitting findings entered after appellant has framed issues in his brief has an appearance of unfairness, *State v. McGary*, 37 Wn.App. 856 (1984), *State v. Naranjo*, 83 Wn.App. 300 (1996), *see: State v. Commodore*, 38 Wn.App. 244 (1984), *State v. Fellers*, 37 Wn.App. 613 (1984), *State v. Charlie*, 62 Wn.App. 729 (1991), *State v. Bennett*, 62 Wn.App. 702 (1991), *State v. Royster*, 43 Wn.App. 613 (1986), *State v. Peña*, 65 Wn.App. 711 (1992), *but see: State v. Head*, 136 Wn.2d 619 (1998), *State v. Pray*, 96 Wn.App. 25, 30-31 (1999); II.

State v. Howe, 116 Wn.2d 466 (1991)
A parental order prohibiting minor child from entering parent's home is sufficient to revoke privilege for purposes of unlawful entry element of **burglary** where **parents** have provided some alternative means of assuring that the parents' statutory duty of care is met, *State v. Steinbach*, 101 Wn.2d 460 (1984), *see: State v. Cantu*, 156 Wn.2d 619 (2006); *affirms State v. Walsh*, 57 Wn.App. 488 (1990), *State v. Jensen*, 57 Wn.App. 501 (1990), reverses *State v. Howe*, 57 Wn.App. 63 (1990); 9-0; *see: State v. Woods*, 63 Wn.App. 588 (1991).

State v. Truong, 117 Wn.2d 63 (1991)
County ordinance which prohibits minors from appearing in a public place after having consumed alcohol unconstitutionally conflicts with RCW 70.96A.190, which preempts regulation of alcoholic beverage subject matter except, *inter alia*, for use of alcohol, since, once alcohol is consumed, the power to use it is at an end, *State v. Hornaday*, 105 Wn.2d 120 (1986); 7-2.

State v. Smith, 117 Wn.2d 263 (1991)
State may seek revision of any order or judgment entered by a juvenile court commissioner, RCW 2.24.050, 13.04.020(1), during which time speedy trial provisions are tolled, JuCR 7.8(d)(5), *see: State v. Lawley*, 32 Wn.App. 337 (1982), *State v. Hoffman*, 115 Wn.App. 91 (2003); 9-0.

State v. Charlie, 62 Wn.App. 729 (1991)
Following conviction by commissioner, respondent moves for revision, RCW 2.24.050,

SECTION 4: JUVENILE CASE LAW REVIEW: 2013

commissioner fails to enter findings; Superior Court judge remands to commissioner, who makes a verbal finding, from which respondent appeals; following submission of appellant's brief, commissioner enters written **findings**; held: commissioner must enter written findings and conclusions in cases that are appealed through revision, JuCR 7.11(c); Superior Court revision is *de novo*, and should not be remanded to commissioner; entry of written findings for appeal should have been by judge, not commissioner; filing of findings after respondent framed issues in brief, and errors committed throughout, compels reversal *c.f.*: State v. Bennett, 62 Wn.App. 702 (1991), State v. Royster, 43 Wn.App. 613 (1986), State v. McGary, 37 Wn.App. 856 (1984), State v. Fellers, 38 Wn.App. 613 (1984), State v. Harris, 66 Wn.App. 636 (1992), State v. Cowgill, 67 Wn.App. 239 (1992), *accord:* State v. Litts, 64 Wn.App. 831 (1992), *see:* State v. Peña, 65 Wn.App. 711 (1992), State v. Head, 136 Wn.2d 619 (1998), *but see:* State v. Pray, 96 Wn.App. 25, 30-31 (1999); I.

State v. Woods, 63 Wn.App. 588 (1991)
Mother arranges for son to live with another family, grants permission to enter home only when mother is present; defendant and son break door and enter home, act surprised that mother is home from work ill, run off; held: manner of entry supports sufficient evidence of unlawful entry; I.

State v. Austin, 65 Wn.App. 759 (1992)
Where trial court fails to enter finding regarding *mens rea* element, and where record supports missing element, then remand is remedy, State v. Royal, 122 Wn.2d 413 (1993), *but see:* State v. PeBa, 65 Wn.App. 711 (1992); double jeopardy clause precludes remand only where record is devoid of any evidence to support omitted finding; I, 2-1.

State v. Preston, 66 Wn.App. 494 (1992)
Odor of alcohol plus observing defendant dispose of beer bottles plus confession is sufficient to convict of minor consumption, RCW 66.44.270(2), State v. Walton, 67 Wn.App. 127, 131 (1992), State v. Little, 116 Wn.2d 488, 491 (1991), State v. Dalton, 72 Wn.App. 674 (1994), State v. Fager, 73 Wn.App. 617 (1994), *c.f.:* State v. A.T.P.-R., 132 Wn.App. 181 (2006), State v. Francisco, 148 Wn.App. 168, 175-76 (2009), which need not be committed in presence of officer for conviction in light of 1987 amendment to RCW 10.31.100(1), State v. Roth, 131 Wn.App. 556, 563-66 (2006), *distinguishing* State v. Hornaday, 105 Wn.2d 120 (1986); II.

State v. Decker, 68 Wn.App. 246 (1992)
Trial court may order predisposition psychological evaluation of respondent, State v. Escoto, 108 Wn.2d 1 (1987), State v. Jacobsen, 95 Wn.App. 967 (1999), and may preclude counsel from attending, *c.f.:* State v. P.B.T., 67 Wn.App. 292 (1992), State v. Diaz-Cardona, 123 Wn.App. 477 (2004); trial court has authority to grant use immunity absent prosecutor's motion, CrR 6.14; I.

State v. Webster, 69 Wn.App. 376 (1993)
Court must **seal** juvenile record if all conditions of RCW 13.50.050(11) are met; II.

SECTION 4: JUVENILE CASE LAW REVIEW: 2013

State v. Halstien, 122 Wn.2d 109 (1993)
Entering victim's home, taking vibrator and condoms, not taking valuable personal property is sufficient to establish burglary with a sexual motivation, RCW 13.40.135; juvenile sexual motivation statute is not vague or overbroad; *affirms* *State v. Halstien*, 65 Wn.App. 845 (1992); 8-0.

State v. Royal, 122 Wn.2d 413 (1993)
Where state fails to file **findings** of fact within 21 days of a notice of appeal, JuCR 7.11(d), dismissal is not a remedy unless petitioner shows prejudice resulting from late filing, *State v. Head*, 136 Wn.2d 619 (1998); prejudice includes additional incarceration; *see:* *State v. Bennett*, 62 Wn.App. 702 (1991), *State v. McGary*, 37 Wn.App. 856, 861 (1984), *State v. Cowgill*, 67 Wn.App. 239 (1992), *State v. Alvarez*, 128 Wn.2d 1 (1995), *State v. Naranjo*, 83 Wn.App. 300 (1996), *see:* *State v. Pray*, 96 Wn.App. 25, 30-31 (1999); 5-4.

State v. Wilcox, 71 Wn.App. 116 (1993)
Following an interlocutory stay, upon remand the juvenile time for trial rule does not start over with a new 60 days, but rather was tolled during the appellate review, applying CrR 3.3(g)(5) to JuCR 7.8, rather than the inconsistent CrR 3.3(d)(4); I.

State v. Dalton, 72 Wn.App. 674 (1994)
Evidence is sufficient to establish minor in possession of liquor, RCW 66.44.270(2), where officer observes defendant in house close to a keg and cups of beer, kegger in progress, signs of intoxication on defendant, smells of alcohol, *distinguishing* *State v. Hornaday*, 105 Wn.2d 120 (1986), *c.f.:* *State v. Roth*, 131 Wn.App. 556, 563-66 (2006), *State v. A.T.P.-R.*, 132 Wn.App. 181 (2006) *State v. Francisco*, 148 Wn.App. 168, 175-76 (2009); III.

State v. Schatmeier, 72 Wn.App. 711 (1994)
Following a DUI arrest, police advise 16 and 17-year-old suspects, *inter alia,* that any statement they make may be used against them in juvenile court unless declined; district court has exclusive jurisdiction in criminal traffic cases, RCW 13.04.030(5); held: while advice was inaccurate, the warnings were sufficient to apprise suspects of the right to remain silent and that anything they say could be used in court, thus suppression reversed, *Dutil v. State*, 93 Wn.2d 84, 90 (1980); III.

State v. Fager, 73 Wn.App. 617 (1994)
Odor of beer plus watery, bloodshot eyes, coated tongue plus beer bottles in vehicle is sufficient to convict of minor in possession, RCW 66.44.270, *State v. Preston*, 66 Wn.App. 494 (1992), *State v. Dalton*, 72 Wn.App. 674 (1994), *c.f.:* *State v. A.T.P.-R.*, 132 Wn.App. 181 (2006); where defendant testifies to consuming no beer but that he had taken cold medicine, and officer testifies on rebuttal that the odor was beer, not cold medicine, evidence is sufficient; III.

State v. Oreiro, 73 Wn.App. 868 (1994)

SECTION 4: JUVENILE CASE LAW REVIEW: 2013

Respondent is charged in juvenile court with six counts, requests three charges be continued pending decline hearing on other three; juvenile court declines, three continued charges are dismissed, then refiled in superior court; held: once juvenile court **declines** jurisdiction, it loses jurisdiction over challenged charges by dismissing them; delay in filing was due, in part, to defendant's request, thus no due process violation; II.

State v. Linares, 75 Wn.App. 404 (1994)
Statements obtained in violation of *Miranda* and RCW 13.40.140(10), while not admissible at trial, are admissible at a hearing to determine whether juvenile respondents are capable of committing the crimes charged; after-the-fact acknowledgment that a respondent understood that the conduct was wrong is insufficient, standing alone, to overcome a presumption of incapacity by clear and convincing evidence, *see: State v. K.R.L.*, 67 Wn.App. 721, 725 (1992), *State v. J.P.S.*, 135 Wn.2d 34 (1998), *State v. J.F.*, 87 Wn.App. 787 (1997); I.

State v. Bastas, 75 Wn.App. 882 (1994)
Counsel's motion to withdraw on appeal pursuant to *Anders v. California*, 18 L.Ed.2d 493 (1967), will be denied where the appeal concerns a motion for accelerated review from a manifest injustice disposition; I.

State v. W.W., 76 Wn.App. 754 (1995)
When respondent appeals both a manifest injustice sentence and conviction, appeal is bifurcated, RAP 18.13, and respondent should be released pending appeal upon completion of standard range disposition; JuCR 7.13 takes precedence over conflicting provisions of RCW 13.40.230, but JuCR violates equal protection clause by creating two classes of juvenile appellants without a rational basis; I.

State v. Alvarez, 128 Wn.2d 1 (1995)
Where evidence is sufficient but trial court's **findings** are not, proper remedy is remand, not dismissal, *State v. Souza*, 60 Wn.App. 534 (1991), *State v. Royal*, 122 Wn.2d 413 (1993), overruling *State v. PeBa*, 65 Wn.App. 711 (1992), *State v. BJS*, 72 Wn.App. 368 (1994); *affirms State v. Alvarez*, 74 Wn.App. 250 (1994), *see: State v. Naranjo*, 83 Wn.App. 300 (1996), *State v. Mewes*, 84 Wn.App. 620 (1997); 6-3.

State v. Werner, 129 Wn.2d 485 (1996)
Superior court judge may issue arrest warrant for a juvenile, *reversing State v. Werner*, 79 Wn.App. 872 (1995); 9-0.

In re Boot, 130 Wn.2d 553 (1996)
Statute mandating adult criminal court jurisdiction for certain juveniles charged with violent offenses, RCW 13.04.030(1)(e)(iv), without a **decline** hearing does not violate due process or equal protection clauses, *State v. Stackhouse*, 88 Wn.App. 963 (1997), *State v. Gilmer*, 96 Wn.App. 875, 880-83 (1999); 9-0.

State v. Parker, 81 Wn.App. 731 (1996)

The Caseload Forecast Council is not liable for errors or omissions in the manual, for sentences that may be inappropriately calculated as a result of a practitioner's or court's reliance on the manual, or for any other written or verbal information related to adult or juvenile sentencing. The scoring sheets are intended to provide assistance in most cases but does not cover all permutations of the scoring rules. If you find any errors or omissions, we encourage you to report them to the Caseload Forecast Council.

SECTION 4: JUVENILE CASE LAW REVIEW: 2013

Respondent is convicted of assault committed with sexual motivation, RCW 13.40.135, trial court does not enter oral or written **findings** of fact addressing special finding; held: because appellate courts may not weigh evidence or enter findings, special allegation must be dismissed, *State v. BJS*, 72 Wn.App. 368, 372-3 (1994), *State v. PeBa*, 65 Wn.App. 711, 715-6 (1992), *State v. Naranjo*, 83 Wn.App. 300 (1996), *but see: State v. Head*, 136 Wn.2d 619 (1998); III.

State v. Anderson, 83 Wn.App. 515 (1996)
At arrest, defendant gives birthdate to police establishing that she is 18, during *voir dire* defense discloses defendant is 17, trial proceeds, defendant is convicted; held: disclosure of age before jury is sworn is timely, *State v. Mendoza-Lopez*, 105 Wn.App. 382 (2001), distinguishing *Nelson v. Seattle Municipal Court*, 29 Wn.App. 7 (1981); because defendant is now an adult, Superior Court must hold a hearing to determine whether she should have been tried as a juvenile and, if so, defendant must be retried in adult court, *Dillenburg v. Maxwell*, 70 Wn.2d 331, 355-6 (1967), *Sheppard v. Rhay*, 73 Wn.2d 734 (1968), *Pers. Restraint of Dalluge*, 152 Wn.2d 772 (2004), if not, original conviction should be reinstated; I.

State v. E.C., 83 Wn.App. 523 (1996)
Juvenile court may dismiss with prejudice a case against an incompetent juvenile respondent in order to adequately respond to the needs of that offender as long as such dismissal poses no substantial danger to others; in general, RCW 10.77 should be followed for juveniles, although the Juvenile Justice Act takes precedence when a conflict arises; I.

State v. Nicholson, 84 Wn.App. 75 (1996)
With decline hearing pending, defendant turns 18, state obtains *ex parte* order of dismissal, juvenile court later determines state acted in bad faith and enters *nun pro tunc* order extending juvenile jurisdiction; held: juvenile court loses jurisdiction when defendant turns 18 unless juvenile court extends jurisdiction before that day, *State v. Calderon*, 102 Wn.2d 348, 352 (1984), *State v. Rosenbaum*, 56 Wn.App. 407 (1990), *but see: State v. Dion*, 160 Wn.2d 605 (2007); a *nunc pro tunc* order records some prior act of the court which was actually performed but not entered into the record, cannot correct something which was not done, *State v. Hendrickson*, 165 Wn.2d 473 (2009); II.

In re Weaver, 84 Wn.App. 290 (1996)
A juvenile acquitted by reason of insanity may not be committed pursuant to RCW 10.77, as a juvenile offense is not a felony, *In re Frederick*, 93 Wn.2d 28, 30 (1980); II.

State v. D.R., 84 Wn.App. 832 (1997)
Fourteen-year old is summoned to principal's office, told by plain clothed detective that he did not have to answer questions, but not advised of *Miranda* rights, questioned and makes inculpatory statement; held: considering respondent's youth, naturally coercive nature of school and principal's office environment, accusatory nature of the interrogation and fact that respondent was not told he was free to go, he was in custody, thus trial court erred in admitting statements absent *Miranda* warnings, as a 14-year old in respondent's position would have

SECTION 4: JUVENILE CASE LAW REVIEW: 2013

reasonably supposed his freedom of action was curtailed to a degree associated with formal arrest, *Berkemer v. McCarty*, 82 L.Ed.2d 317 (1984), *State v. Short*, 113 Wn.2d 35, 41 (1989), *State v. Sargent*, 111 Wn.2d 641, 649 (1988), *State v. Everybodytalksabout*, 161 Wn.2d 702 (2007), *but see: State v. S.J.W.*, 149 Wn.App. 912, 927-29 (2009), *aff'd, on other grounds*, 170 Wn.2d 92 (2010); III.

State v. E.D.W., 85 Wn.App. 601 (1997)
To establish **capacity** of an 11-year old who is presumed incapable of committing child molestation, state must prove respondent understood that touching private parts was done for the purpose of gratifying sexual desire of either party, RCW 9A.44.010(2), state has a greater burden when it has to prove a child appreciates the illegality of certain sexual acts, *State v. Linares*, 75 Wn.App. 404, 414 n.12 (1994), *see: State v. J.P.S.*, 85 Wn.App. 586 (1997)

State v. Murrin, 85 Wn.App. 754 (1997)
Respondent on community supervision commits new offense, prosecutor files modification petition, court modifies and sanctions respondent, prosecutor files information charging same new offense, trial court dismisses; held: where prosecutor seeks modification of community supervision for a new crime, RCW 13.40.070(3) directs that prosecutor may not file an information based on the same conduct, *State v. Tinh Quoc Tran*, 117 Wn.App. 126 (2003), *c.f.: State v. Whisenhunt*, 96 Wn.App. 18 (1999), *In re J.J.*, 96 Wn.App. 452 (1999), *State v. Zimmerman*, 130 Wn.App. 122 (2005); holding may not apply where modification is filed by probation officer at the direction of the court, at 759 n.17; I.

State v. J.D., 86 Wn.App. 501 (1997)
Bellingham curfew ordinance, BMC 10.62.030, violates juvenile's constitutional rights to freedom of movement and expression, and is vague; I.

State v. Wright, 88 Wn.App. 683 (1997)
Unlawful firearm possession statute, RCW 9.41.010, prohibits possession of a firearm by a juvenile previously convicted in juvenile court of a serious offense, *State v. Cheatham*, 80 Wn.App. 269 (1996), *State v. McKinley*, 84 Wn.App. 677 (1997); I.

State v. Kells, 134 Wn.2d 309 (1998)
Following guilty plea in adult court, declined juvenile retains right to appeal **decline** order, *State v. Pritchard*, 79 Wn.App. 14 (1995), state must demonstrate knowing, voluntary and intelligent waiver of right to appeal; 9-0.

State v. J.P.S., 135 Wn.2d 34 (1998)
To establish **capacity** of an 11-year old who is presumed incapable of committing rape, RCW 9A.04.050, state must prove that child knew the act was wrong, but not that the act was illegal or understand the legal consequences of the act, disapproving, in part, *State v. J.P.S.*, 85 Wn.App. 586 (1997); factors include (1) nature of crime, (2) age and maturity, (3) whether child showed a desire for secrecy, (4) whether child admonished victim not to tell, (5) prior conduct

SECTION 4: JUVENILE CASE LAW REVIEW: 2013

similar to that charged, (6) consequences that attached to the conduct, (7) acknowledgment that behavior was wrong and could lead to detention, State v. Linares, 75 Wn.App. 404 (1994), (8) expert testimony, and (9) testimony of acquaintances; developmentally disabled respondent's acknowledging his conduct was "bad" after repeated *Miranda* warnings, interrogation, being shunned by neighbors and classmates is insufficient to overcome presumption of incapacity by clear and convincing evidence, *see:* State v. E.D.W., 85 Wn.App. 601 (1997), State v. K.R.L., 67 Wn.App. 721, 725 (1992), State v. T.E.H., 91 Wn.App. 908 (1998); 9-0.

State v. S.E., 90 Wn.App. 886 (1998)
   Backyard patio is not a "public place," former RCW 66.04.010(23) [now RCW 66.04.010(27)], for purposes of **minor in possession of liquor**, RCW 66.44.270(2)(b); I.

State v. Detrick, 90 Wn.App. 939 (1998)
   Where one consolidated respondent files an affidavit of prejudice, it may be imputed to correspondents, LaMon v. Butler, 112 Wn.2d 193 (1989); where judge is disqualified, time for trial period may be extended, applying CrR 3.3(d)(6) to juvenile court, distinguishing State v. Sayers, 29 Wn.App. 128, 130 (1981), State v. Jacks, 25 Wn.App. 141, 145 (1980); I.

State v. Mora, 138 Wn.2d 43 (1999)
   Seventeen-year-old is charged in adult court with assault 2° pursuant to automatic decline statute, RCW 13.04.030(1)(e)(v), after which, pursuant to a plea agreement, court allows amendment to assault 3° and possession of firearm, which are not automatic decline offenses, defense motion to transfer to juvenile court is denied; held: nature of the charge dictates jurisdiction and, where the charge no longer comes within automatic decline statute, case must be remanded to juvenile court, *Pers. Restraint of Dalluge*, 152 Wn.2d 772 (2004), State v. Posey, 161 Wn.2d 638, 643-47 (2007), 174 Wn.2d 131 (2012), distinguishing State v. Sharon, 100 Wn.2d 230 (1983), *see also:* State v. Carpenter, 117 Wn.App. 673 (2003), *but see:* State v. Manro, 125 Wn.App. 165 (2005); 9-0.

State v. Whisenhunt, 96 Wn.App. 18, 20-22 (1999)
   Respondent, on special sex offender disposition alternative (SSODA), has inappropriate contact with females, at revocation hearing court finds he failed to make progress in treatment and is revoked, prosecutor subsequently charges respondent with child molestation based upon an incident considered at revocation hearing, defense seeks dismissal; held: while prosecutor may not charge a new crime that was the subject of a previous modification hearing, RCW 13.40.070(3), State v. Murrin, 85 Wn.App. 754 (1997), revocation of SSODA is not a modification of community supervision, thus statutory prohibition does not apply; revocation for failure to make progress in treatment, even if based in part upon a new offense, is not a revocation based upon the new offense; *see also:* State v. J.J., 96 Wn.App. 452 (1999), State v. Zimmerman, 130 Wn.App. 122 (2005); III.

State v. J.J., 96 Wn.App. 452 (1999)
   When a juvenile on a deferred disposition commits a new crime, state is not required to

SECTION 4: JUVENILE CASE LAW REVIEW: 2013

elect between revocation of deferred disposition and charging the new crime, RCW 13.40.070(3), *see: State v. Whisenhunt*, 96 Wn.App. 18 (1999), *State v. Zimmerman*, 130 Wn.App. 122 (2005), distinguishing *State v. Murrin*, 85 Wn.App. 754 (1997); I.

State v. Graves, 97 Wn.App. 55 (1999)
A juvenile charged with assaulting a parent may employ a claim of lawful force irrespective of the parent's right to use reasonable force for discipline; I.

State v. B.P.M., 97 Wn.App. 294 (1999)
Failure to hold a capacity hearing within 14 days, JuCR 7.6(e), is not jurisdictional, and dismissal is not warranted absent proof of prejudice; I.

State v. B.A.S., 103 Wn.App. 549 (2000)
Student in high school with closed campus policy is seen off-campus, is searched by attendance officer, drugs seized; held: while school authorities may search a student without a warrant if the search is justified at its inception and is reasonably related in scope to the circumstances that justified the interference in the first place, *New Jersey v. T.L.O.*, 83 L.Ed.2d 720 (1985), here there was no nexus between the violation (off-campus) and the search, thus evidence must be suppressed, *c.f.: State v. Slattery*, 56 Wn.App. 820 (1990); I.

State v. Chandler, 143 Wn.2d 485 (2001)
Respondent requests trial date within 60 days of proper date of arraignment, court sets trial outside 60 days, finding that because no judge sits in the county within the time period, a date outside the 60 days is permitted "in the due administration of justice," and because no prejudice was shown, JuCR 7.8(e)(3); held: JuCR 7.8(e)(3) permits a continuance in the due administration of justice, but not an original case setting beyond the 60-day rule, court could have obtained a visiting judge, judge *pro tempore*, court commissioner or, possibly, continued the case if all of those avenues were unavailable, but original setting outside the rule violates the rule, thus dismissed, *see: State v. Day*, 46 Wn.App. 882 (1987); 9-0.

State v. Gilman, 105 Wn.App. 366 (2001)
Where capacity determination is required, RCW 9A.04.050, a hearing must he held within 14 days of juvenile's first appearance, JuCR 7.6(e), which includes a detention hearing, even if charges are not filed; dismissal should be the remedy only if other lesser sanctions will not remedy prejudice to respondent; III.

State v. M.A., 106 Wn.App. 493 (2001)
Court may consider prior diversions and referrals in **decline hearing**, distinguishing *State v. Melton*, 63 Wn.App. 63, 72 (1991); I.

State v. Garcia, 107 Wn.App. 545 (2001)
Respondent using force against an officer in a juvenile facility must show that s/he was in actual, imminent danger of serious injury, *State v. Bradley*, 141 Wn.2d 731 (2000); II.

SECTION 4: JUVENILE CASE LAW REVIEW: 2013

State v. A.L.H., 116 Wn.App. 158 (2003)
    A juvenile accused of violating an At Risk Youth order, ch. 13.32A, RCW, may only be charged with civil contempt, RCW 7.21.030, 13.32A.250(2), *Interest of M.B.*, 101 Wn.App. 425, 443-44 (2000), *but see: Dependency of A.K.*, 162 Wn.2d 632 (2007), which must contain a purge clause, *Interest of Rebecca K.*, 101 Wn.App. 309 (2000); state may not file criminal contempt charge; II.

State v. Lown, 116 Wn.App. 402 (2003)
    When the superior court reviews a juvenile court commissioner's ruling, it must determine if the findings of fact are supported by substantial evidence, and reviews the conclusions of law *de novo*, RCW 2.24.050, *but see: State v. Wicker*, 105 Wn.App. 428 (2001); III.

State v. H.O., 119 Wn.App. 549, 552-56 (2003)
    Burden of proof for **decline** hearing is preponderance, *State v. Jacobson*, 33 Wn.App. 529 (1982), *Pers. Restraint of Hegney*, 138 Wn.App. 511, 528-31 (2007), *State v. Childress*, 169 Wn.App. 523 (2012), distinguishing *Apprendi v. New Jersey*, 147 L.Ed.2d 435 (2000); I.

State v. Ramer, 151 Wn.2d 106 (2004)
    Appellate review of a trial court **capacity** decision is one of substantial evidence, not *de novo*, *State v. J.P.S.*, 135 Wn.2d 34, 37 (1998); while actual knowledge of the legal consequences of a sex offense is not necessary, when a juvenile is charged with a sex crime, the state carries a greater burden of proving capacity, and must present a higher degree of proof that the child understood the illegality of the act, *State v. J.P.S., supra.* at 38; 9-0.

State v. Salavea, 151 Wn.2d 133 (2004)
    To invoke an automatic decline of jurisdiction, RCW 13.04.030(1)(e)(v), the age of the individual at the time of the proceedings controls, not the age at the time of the crime, *Sweet v. Porter*, 75 Wn.2d 869, 870 (1969), legislatively overruled, LAWS OF 2005, §1, RCW 13.04.030(1)(e)(v) (2005); affirms *State v. Salavea*, 115 Wn.App. 52 (2003); 9-0.

State v. R.J., 121 Wn.App. 215 (2004)
    Juvenile commits alcohol offense when he is 17, is adjudicated guilty at 18 years, court notifies Department of Licensing, RCW 66.44.365(1); held: juvenile's age on date of offense determines whether notification is required; I.

Pers. Restraint of Dalluge, 152 Wn.2d 772 (2004)
    Juvenile is charged as an adult with a serious violent offense resulting in automatic decline, RCW 13.04.030(1)(e)(v)(A), plea bargains to a less serious offense which, by law, requires a decline hearing, no party requests one, defendant is sentenced as an adult; held: superior court erred when it failed to remand to juvenile court for decline hearing after charge was amended, *State v. Mora*, 138 Wn.2d 43 (1999), *State v. Posey*, 161 Wn.2d 638, 643-47

SECTION 4: JUVENILE CASE LAW REVIEW: 2013

(2007), 174 Wn.2d 131 (2012), *but see:* *State v. Manro,* 125 Wn.App. 165 (2005); remedy is remand for a hearing on whether decline would have been appropriate and, if court finds it would not, defendant is entitled to a new trial in adult court, *Dillenburg v. Maxwell,* 70 Wn.2d 331, 354-56 (1967), *State v. Mendoza-Lopez,* 105 Wn.App. 382 (2001), *State v. Anderson,* 83 Wn.App. 515 (1996), *State v. Meridieth,* 144 Wn.App. 47 (2008); 6-3.

State v. K.N., 124 Wn.App. 875 (2004)

In minor in possession of alcohol case, juvenile court cannot take judicial notice, infer or presume age of respondent from the fact that the court is a juvenile court, nor is birth date on arraignment documents sufficient to establish age, *see:* *State v. Roth,* 131 Wn.App. 556 (2006), distinguishing *In re Welfare of Ward,* 22 Wn.App. 774 (1979); I.

State v. Sweeney, 125 Wn.App. 77 (2005)

A juvenile burglary conviction does not "wash" for purposes of serving as a predicate offense for an unlawful possession of a firearm 1° conviction, RCW 9.41.040(1)(a) even if it washes for purposes of the offender score; fact that at the time of the juvenile conviction it was not a crime to possess a firearm thereafter does not excuse to the crime enacted later and does not violate due process; III.

State v. J.R., 127 Wn.App. 293 (2005)

A 10 inch dagger is sufficient to establish the offense of possession of a dangerous weapon on school grounds, RCW 9.41.280, which includes all weapons described in RCW 9.41.250, not limited to RCW 9.41.250(1); I.

State v. Roth, 131 Wn.App. 556 (2006)

In minor in possession of alcohol case, RCW 66.44.270(2)(a), testimony that there were no adults at a party plus officer's issuing citation after checking respondent's license plus respondent's not disputing that he was under the age of 21 is sufficient to prove element that respondent is a minor even absent evidence of date of birth, distinguishing *State v. K.N.,* 124 Wn.App. 875 (2004); absent proof that respondent consumed alcohol, presence in a room with a refrigerator full of beer is insufficient to prove constructive possession, distinguishing *State v. Dalton,* 72 Wn.App. 674, 675-77 (1994); III.

State v. Dion, 131 Wn.App. 729 (2006)

Three days before she turned 18, juvenile is arrested, court finds probable cause, releases her and extends juvenile court jurisdiction, later state files information charging her as an adult, trial court dismisses; held: because no information was filed in juvenile court prior to defendant's 18th birthday, juvenile court lacked authority to extend jurisdiction, RCW 13.40.300; probable cause determination, *County of Riverside v. McLaughlin,* 114 L.Ed.2d 49 (1991), does not confer jurisdiction to extend, release of juvenile establishes that there was no proceeding pending; I.

State v. V.J., 132 Wn.App. 380 (2006)

Authority of court to enforce a disposition order is tolled when a warrant is outstanding,

SECTION 4: JUVENILE CASE LAW REVIEW: 2013

Spokane v. Marquette, 146 Wn.2d 124 (2002); I.

State v. Chavez, 134 Wn.App.657, 662-65 (2006)
    Juveniles are not entitled to a jury trial in juvenile court, *State v. J.H.,* 96 Wn.App.167 (1999), *State v. Schaaf,* 109 Wn.2d 1, 4 (1987), *McKeiver v. Pennsylvania,* 29 L.Ed.2d 647 (1971), *State v. Tai,* 127 Wn.App.733 (2005), *State v. Meade,* 129 Wn.App.918 (2005), RCW 13.04.021(2); II.

State v. Dion, 160 Wn.2d 605 (2007)
    Following arrest at detention review hearing, court finds probable cause, extends jurisdiction for six months beyond 18th birthday, sets information filing deadline for 72 hours later, state does not file charges by deadline, court vacates conditions and release respondent unconditionally, state charges her as an adult, trial court dismisses adult charge, state appeals; held: juvenile court may extend jurisdiction beyond juvenile's 18th birthday if proceedings are pending, RCW 13.40.300(1)(a), where charges are not filed proceedings are not pending thus trial court lacked authority to extend jurisdiction; affirms *State v. Dion,* 131 Wn.App. 729 (2006); 9-0.

State v. Posey, 161 Wn.2d 638, 643-47 (2007)
    Defendant is charged with assault 1°, automatically declined, RCW 13.04.030(1)(e)(v)(A), jury acquits but convicts of a lesser not specifically enumerated as an automatic decline offense, trial court sentences as an adult; held: any juvenile properly charged in adult court of an enumerated offense must be returned to juvenile court for a decline hearing or disposition as a juvenile if convicted of a non-enumerated offense, RCW 13.04.030(1)(e)(v)(E)(II), *State v. Mora,* 138 Wn.2d 43 (1999), *State v. Meridieth,* 144 Wn.App. 47 (2008), *State v. Posey,* 174 Wn.2d 131 (2012); reverses, in part, *State v. Posey,* 130 Wn.App. 262 (2005); 8-1.

State v. Ramirez, 140 Wn.App. 278 (2007)
    Automatic decline statute amendment, LAWS OF 2005, ch. 290, § 1, RCW 13.04.030(1)(e)(v), making automatic decline applicable when juvenile is 16 or 17 years old on the date the alleged offense is committed, legislatively overruling *State v. Salavea,* 151 Wn.2d 133 (2004), is not retroactive; II.

Pers. Restraint of Hegney, 138 Wn.App. 511 (2007)
    Evidence inadmissible at trial is admissible at a **decline** hearing, *In re Welfare of Harbert,* 85 Wn.2d 719 (1975); II.

State v. Chavez, 163 Wn.2d 262, 267-72 (2008)
    Juveniles are not entitled to a jury trial in juvenile court; affirms *State v. Chavez,* 134 Wn.App. 657 (2006); 6-3.

State v. Meridieth, 144 Wn.App. 47 (2008)

SECTION 4: JUVENILE CASE LAW REVIEW: 2013

Seventeen year old is charged with mandatory decline offenses, juvenile court enters automatic decline order absent probable cause that any of the offenses occurred after defendant turned 16, RCW 13.04.030(1)(e)(v) (2005); held: statute requires that there be probable cause that an automatic decline offense was committed after offender turned 16, thus automatic decline was faulty, remedy is to remand for a decline hearing and, if court declines then conviction stands, if court denies decline, then defendant is entitled to a new trial in adult court, as he has turned 18, *Pers. Restraint of Dalluge,* 152 Wn.2d 772 (2004); 2-1.

State v. Ramos, 152 Wn.App. 684, 690-93 (2009)
Fourteen year old may waive decline hearing, RCW 13.34.110(1) (1990), and pursuant to a plea bargain agree to transfer to adult court; III.

State v. Brown, 158 Wn.App. 49 (2010)
School resource officer observes respondent asleep in a car during school hours, observes a knife on the floor, removes respondent, respondent agrees to officer removing the knife, officer searches car finds guns; held: weapon in a car on campus is an emergency under the school search exception, *New Jersey v. T.L.O.,* 469 U.S. 325, 83 L.Ed.2d 720 (1985), *State v. Slatterty,* 56 Wn.App. 8209 (1990), justifying search without a warrant, search beyond seizing the knife was linked to the initial intrusion; III.

J.D.B. v. North Carolina, 564 U.S. ___, 180 L.Ed.2d 310 (2011)
In determining whether a juvenile is in custody requiring *Miranda* warnings prior to questioning, police and trial court must apply an objective standard, *i.e.*, would a reasonable person perceive that he or she is in custody, which includes consideration of the suspect's age, *c.f.: Yarborough v. Alvarado,* 541 U.S. 652, 158 L.Ed.2d 938 (2004); 5-4.

State v. Posey, 174 Wn.2d 131 (2012)
Respondent is charged with rape and assault 1°, is auto-declined because assault 1° is a serious violent offense, RCW 13.04.030 (2009), jury acquits of assault, is sentenced under SRA, Supreme Court reverses and remands to juvenile court for disposition, *State v. Posey,* 161 Wn.2d 638 (2007), before disposition on remand respondent turns 21, court treats defendant as an adult in superior court but imposes juvenile sentence range, respondent appeals claiming neither juvenile nor superior court had jurisdiction; held: superior court always retains jurisdiction over felony cases, CONST. art. IV, § 6, legislation cannot alter constitutional jurisdiction; 7-2.

State v. Miller, 165 Wn.App. 385 (2011)
Failure of police to advise a juvenile of the juvenile-specific language is not grounds for suppression, *State v. Prater,* 77 Wn.2d 526 (1970), *State v. Luoma,* 88 Wn.2d 28 (1977); III.

State v. Childress, 169 Wn.App. 523 (2012)
Decline standard is preponderance, not beyond a reasonable doubt, *State v. H.O.,* 119 Wn.App. 549, 552-56 (2003), respondent is not entitled to a jury determination of decline; I.

The Caseload Forecast Council is not liable for errors or omissions in the manual, for sentences that may be inappropriately calculated as a result of a practitioner's or court's reliance on the manual, or for any other written or verbal information related to adult or juvenile sentencing. The scoring sheets are intended to provide assistance in most cases but does not cover all permutations of the scoring rules. If you find any errors or omissions, we encourage you to report them to the Caseload Forecast Council.

SECTION 4: JUVENILE CASE LAW REVIEW: 2013

Delay in Filing

State v. Hodges, 28 Wn.App. 902 (1981)
    State delays three months before filing information in juvenile court, during which time defendant turned 18, whereupon case filed in Superior Court, which dismissed due to delay denying due process; held: *remanded* for evidentiary hearing to see if state can meet burden to justify delay; deliberate or negligent delay in filing violates due process; *see*: *State v. Lidge*, 49 Wn.App. 311 (1987); II.

State v. McAllaster, 31 Wn.App. 554 (1982)
    Trial court has discretion to dismiss an information for delay in referral to prosecutor, per King County LJuCR 7.14(b); I.

State v. Keller, 32 Wn.App. 135 (1982)
    Where court dismissed felony information for delay in referral, King County LJuCR 7.14(b), it is without prejudice and state may refile; I.

State v. Jacobson, 36 Wn.App. 446 (1983)
    March 6, juvenile commits burglary; March 26, commits robbery; April 13, juvenile court declines jurisdiction on robbery; April 15, defendant turns 18 years of age; thereafter, burglary charge filed in Superior Court; defendant moves to dismiss, CrR 8.3(b); held: defendant was not prejudiced by delay; I.

State v. Terrell, 38 Wn.App. 187 (1984)
    Trial court's decision not to dismiss, King County LJuCr 7.14(b), for delay in referral is within court's discretion where case was referred to prosecutor within two weeks but was returned to police for filing of a face sheet, referred back 28 days later; I.

State v. Calderon, 102 Wn.2d 348 (1984)
    Five months prior to respondent's 18th birthday, burglary is committed; due to delay in lab, fingerprints are not compared until after respondent turns 18, information filed in Superior Court; held: while delay beyond 18th birthday establishes prejudice, *State v. Hodges*, 28 Wn.App. 902 (1981), court must balance prejudice with reason for state's delay, *United States v. Lovasco*, 52 L.Ed.2d 752 (1977), *State v. Oppelt*, 172 Wn.2d 285 (2011); here, police needed prints to charge, lab backlog excused investigatory delay, *State v. Salavea*, 151 Wn.2d 133, 146-47 (2004), *see*: *State v. Lidge*, 111 Wn.2d 845 (1989), *State v. Brandt*, 99 Wn.App. 184 (2000); 9-0.

State v. Boseck, 45 Wn.App. 62 (1986)
Delay of 21 months in charging defendant, resulting in juvenile court losing jurisdiction, was justified as state was proceeding sequentially against numerous defendants to obtain each defendant's testimony, *State v. Calderon*, 102 Wn.2d 348 (1984); I.

State v. Robbers, 46 Wn.App. 558 (1987)

SECTION 4: JUVENILE CASE LAW REVIEW: 2013

Two-month delay in filing charges, resulting in juvenile court losing jurisdiction, does not mandate dismissal, *State v. Calderon*, 102 Wn.2d 348 (1984), where more arrests needed to be made in investigation, lab reports had not been received on some counts which were joined, it was not unreasonable to delay referral to police until sufficient evidence had been obtained for all counts; special procedures for juvenile suspects are not required; I.

State v. Anderson, 46 Wn.App. 565 (1987)
Prosecutor's established procedures for processing cases can justify delay in charging beyond respondent's 18th birthday; prosecutor need not expedite filing for a juvenile whose 18th birthday is imminent; *see*: *State v. Lidge*, 111 Wn.2d 845 (1989); I.

State v. Cantrell, 49 Wn.App. 917 (1987)
Juvenile court dismisses escape information for six-week delay in referral to court, King County LJuCR 7.14(b); held: state's justification for delay, obtaining evidence, is sufficient to establish no arbitrary action or governmental misconduct, CrR 8.3(b), *State v. Burri*, 87 Wn.2d 175 (1976), thus reversed; I.

State v. Alvin, 109 Wn.2d 602 (1987)
Police complete investigation into crime five weeks before defendant's 18th birthday but, due to vacation and training of detective, do not obtain criminal record or refer to prosecutor until after 18th birthday; held: police and prosecutor need not give special treatment to juvenile to assure juvenile court jurisdiction, *State v. Warner*, 125 Wn.2d 876, 891 (1995); sick leave, comp time, vacation and training courses are part of normal routine and are legitimate reasons for delay, *distinguishing State v. Calderon*, 102 Wn.2d 348 (1984); *accord*: *State v. Lidge*, 111 Wn.2d 845 (1989), *see: State v. Oppelt*, 172 Wn.2d 285 (2011); 9-0.

State v. Schifferl, 51 Wn.App. 268 (1988)
Where state negligently fails to process a case resulting in loss of juvenile court jurisdiction, the negligent delay will weigh against the state in balancing the reasons for the delay vs. prejudicial effect on defendant; the prejudice must be more than mere loss of jurisdiction; here, the negligence was less culpable than the "routine" delays in *State v. Alvin*, 109 Wn.2d 601 (1987), thus dismissal reversed, *see: State v. Gidley*, 79 Wn.App. 205 (1995), *State v. Brandt*, 99 Wn.App. 184 (2000), *but see: State v. Frazier*, 82 Wn.App. 576 (1996); I.

State v. Chavez, 111 Wn.2d 548 (1988)
Local court rule permitting court to dismiss juvenile court case if there is more than 30-day delay between completion of police investigation and filing of information is valid, however trial court may only dismiss under rule if actual prejudice is established; 5-3.

State v. Lidge, 111 Wn.2d 845 (1989)
Eight-day delay in filing charges in juvenile court due to a need for further investigation, resulting in loss of juvenile court jurisdiction as defendant turned 18, does not deprive defendant of due process, *State v. Salavea*, 151 Wn.2d 133, 146-47 (2004), where defense never inquired on cross-examination of prosecutor as to what investigation was necessary; the fact that one

SECTION 4: JUVENILE CASE LAW REVIEW: 2013

prosecutor filed charges against co-defendant yet other prosecutor delayed for further investigation does not establish negligence; reverses *State v. Lidge*, 49 Wn.App. 311 (1987); *see: State v. Frazier*, 82 Wn.App. 576 (1996), *State v. Brandt*, 99 Wn.App. 184 (2000), *see:* State v. Oppelt, 172 Wn.2d 285 (2011); 5-3.

State v. Dixon, 114 Wn.2d 857 (1990)
    Delay in filing due to sequential prosecution to get testimony of co-defendants will justify juvenile court losing jurisdiction; only intentional or negligent delay by prosecution will justify dismissal, *State v. Warner*, 125 Wn.2d 876, 889-91 (1995), *State v. Gidley*, 79 Wn.App. 205 (1995), *State v. Frazier*, 82 Wn.App. 576 (1991); appellate court cannot substitute judgment or weigh strength of prosecutor's case in determining whether delay was justified, *reversing State v. Dixon*, 55 Wn.App. 221 (1989); 9-0.

State v. Warner, 125 Wn.2d 876, 889-91 (1995)
    Juvenile sex offender, in state institution, while undergoing sex offender treatment, confesses to therapists to several offenses, authorities delay reporting offenses such that defendant turns 18 and is charged as an adult, seeks dismissal for delay; held: delay in reporting, even in violation of mandatory reporting provision's of RCW 26.44.030, does not establish negligence to justify dismissal *State v. Dixon*, 114 Wn.2d 857 (1990), as negligence *per se* has been largely abolished, RCW 5.40.050, and class of persons reporting statute was designed to protect was victims, not abusers; *see: State v. Frazier*, 82 Wn.App. 576 (1996); 9-0.

State v. Frazier, 82 Wn.App. 576 (1996)
    Negligent delay in filing charges, resulting in juvenile court losing jurisdiction, is grounds for dismissal where court finds no credible reason for state's delay, *State v. Dixon*, 114 Wn.2d 857 (1990), *State v. Lidge*, 111 Wn.2d 845, 848 (1989), *State v. Warner*, 125 Wn.2d 876, 890 (1995); where no justification is provided for the negligent delay, trial court need not balance the interests of the state and defendant, *State v. Warner, supra*, at 889; II.

State v. Hairychin, 136 Wn.2d 862 (1998)
    Prosecutor arranges for defense counsel to interview complainant, does not subpoena complainant who moves out of state, prosecutor obtains continuance beyond expiration date; held: a continuance may be granted if state's evidence is unavailable, prosecutor has exercised due diligence, and there are reasonable grounds to believe evidence will be available within reasonable time, JuCR 7.8(e)(2)(ii), due diligence requires proper issuance of subpoenas, *State v. Adamski*, 111 Wn.2d 574, 578 (1988), *State v. Duggins*, 121 Wn.2d 524, 525 (1993), *c.f.: State v. Bible*, 77 Wn.App. 470 (1995), thus continuance was improperly granted; *per curiam*.

State v. Brandt, 99 Wn.App. 184 (2000)
    Analysis of time period of delay halts with defendant's 18th birthday, since juvenile court loses jurisdiction at that point, after which defendant is not further prejudiced; defendant's confession to child molestation provides police with a lead to find victim, whose last name is unknown, police await contact from victim resulting in delay beyond defendant's 18th birthday, held: investigative delay was reasonable, within trial court's discretion, *State v. Gidley*, 79

SECTION 4: JUVENILE CASE LAW REVIEW: 2013

Wn.App. 205, 210 (1995), *State v. Lidge,* 111 Wn.2d 845, 850 (1989), *State v. Dixon,* 114 Wn.2d 857, 866 (1990); trial court may consider likelihood of decline, *State v. Schifferl,* 51 Wn.App. 268, 273 (1988); II.

State v. Francisco, 148 Wn.App. 168, 175-77 (2009)
Police find respondent passed out in driveway, strong odor of alcohol, incoherent, difficult to rouse, convicted of minor possession/consumption of liquor, RCW 66.44.270(2)(a); held: evidence of assimilation of alcohol is circumstantial evidence of prior possession and, when corroborated, may support a conviction, *State v. Dalton,* 72 Wn.App. 674 (1994), *State v. Preston,* 66 Wn.App. 494 (1992), *see: State v. Hornaday,* 105 Wn.2d 120, 126 (1986), but absent nearby alcohol containers or confession, evidence is insufficient that respondent exercised any dominion and control over alcohol; III.

SECTION 4: JUVENILE CASE LAW REVIEW: 2013

Dispositions

In re Trambitas, 96 Wn.2d 324 (1981)
    Juvenile respondents are entitled to credit for pretrial detention against the maximum term of confinement imposed under the standard range; 5-4.

State v. Chatham, 28 Wn.App. 580 (1981)
    Diversion unit may reject a referral as long as the rejection is based on standardized safeguards and the decision to reject is fair and reasoned; fact that rejection is not in writing does not deny defendant due process; I.

State v. Rice, 98 Wn.2d 384 (1982)
    Juveniles can be sentenced to more than maximum punishment for adults, *overruling, in part*, *State v. Rhodes*, 92 Wn.2d 755 (1979); 8-1.

State v. Smith, 33 Wn.App. 791 (1983)
    Standard for establishing restitution in a juvenile proceeding is "evidence sufficient to afford a reasonable basis for estimating the loss"; *see:* *State v. Fambrough*, 66 Wn.App. 223 (1992); only tangible damages, such as those for injury to or loss of property, are allowed, 79 ALR 3d 976 (1977); juvenile restitution provisions, RCW 13.40.020(17), 13.40.190, are not vague; I.

In re Hoffer, 34 Wn.App. 82 (1983)
    Juvenile court can commit to DSHS, extend jurisdiction to 21 and retain jurisdiction for purposes of enforcing restitution order; III.

State v. Bush, 34 Wn.App. 121 (1983)
    RCW 12.40.020(17) requires court to set restitution that is "easily ascertainable"; fact that restitution is disputed does not prohibit court from setting restitution where "sufficient evidence" exists; co-defendants who are ordered to pay different amounts do not have equal protection claim; I.

State v. Murphy, 35 Wn.App. 658 (1983)
    Manifest injustice finding is not limited to cases where defendant poses a clear threat of bodily harm; I.

State v. Elmore, 36 Wn.App. 38 (1983)
    Without a plea bargain, respondent pleads guilty, but is misinformed as to the standard range, seeks specific performance; held: no right to specific performance in the absence of a plea bargain that is breached; sole remedy is withdrawal of plea; II.

State v. Sargent, 36 Wn.App. 463 (1984)
    Crime victim penalty, RCW 7.68.010 *et seq.*, is mandatory in juvenile convictions; I.

The Caseload Forecast Council is not liable for errors or omissions in the manual, for sentences that may be inappropriately calculated as a result of a practitioner's or court's reliance on the manual, or for any other written or verbal information related to adult or juvenile sentencing. The scoring sheets are intended to provide assistance in most cases but does not cover all permutations of the scoring rules. If you find any errors or omissions, we encourage you to report them to the Caseload Forecast Council.

SECTION 4: JUVENILE CASE LAW REVIEW: 2013

State v. Adcock, 36 Wn.App. 699 (1984)
Failure of court to write in standard range in disposition order prior to imposing disposition is harmless error as long as respondent understands plea form; three offenses committed on one day count as three separate convictions for purposes of criminal history unless they are intimately related as part of a sequential plan; fact that there was no opportunity for reform or that respondent was sentenced on same day is not dispositive of issue of whether convictions are separate or from same course of conduct; I.

State v. Cook, 37 Wn.App. 269 (1984)
Juvenile respondent is constitutionally entitled to pre-trial detention credit against community service hours; I.

State v. Fellers, 37 Wn.App. 613 (1984)
At disposition hearing, respondent has the right to show he lacks ability to pay restitution, RCW 13.40.190(1); *see*: *State v. Commodore*, 38 Wn.App. 244 (1984), *reversing State v. Brown*, 30 Wn.App. 344 (1981); I.

State v. P., 37 Wn.App. 773 (1984)
Once a finding of manifest injustice is made, court has broad discretion to determine the proper sentence, *State v. E.J.H.*, 65 Wn.App. 771 (1992), but merely following the probation counselor's recommendation, without more, is a clearly excessive sentence since it cannot be justified by any reasonable review of the record; *but see:* *State v. B.E.W.*, 65 Wn.App. 370 (1992); III.

State v. Gutierrez, 37 Wn.App. 910 (1984)
Court finds manifest injustice and increases disposition based upon respondent's criminal history alone; last conviction was more than a year prior to disposition; held: trial court abused its discretion; here, respondent's criminal history alone does not support a finding that respondent is a clear danger to society beyond a reasonable doubt; *accord:* *State v. S.S.*, 67 Wn.App. 800 (1992); III.

State v. Martin, 102 Wn.2d 300 (1984)
Where respondent is detained for failure to complete community service hours, court need not reduce the community service obligation by eight hours per day of confinement, RCW 13.40.200(3)(b); reverses *State v. Martin*, 36 Wn.App. 1 (1983).

State v. McDowell, 102 Wn.2d 341 (1984)
Disposition may exceed that allowed in a diversion agreement, *distinguishing* RCW 13.40.160(3), unless defense proves actual vindictiveness; 9-0.

State v. Smith, 40 Wn.App. 477 (1985)

SECTION 4: JUVENILE CASE LAW REVIEW: 2013

In determining criminal history for disposition, each separate charge not arising out of the same course of conduct is a separate conviction even if respondent's disposition on each is contained in the same disposition order; I.

State v. WS, 40 Wn.App. 835 (1985)
Juvenile diversion may not categorically reject all prostitutes from acceptance into diversion, RCW 13.40.010(2)(g), *c.f.*: *State v. Pulfrey*, 120 Wn.App. 270 (2004); I.

State v. Ashley, 40 Wn.App. 877 (1985)
Defendant assaults and injures victim, later assaults victim, no injuries; defendant is charged and convicted only with second assault, restitution ordered for first assault; held: restitution may only be ordered for the crimes charged and proved at trial, RCW 13.40.190(1), *State v. Mark*, 36 Wn.App. 428 (1984); I.

State v. Malychewski, 41 Wn.App. 488 (1985)
Where juvenile is sentenced for two crimes, one of which qualifies him as a serious offender, RCW 13.40.020(1), respondent may be sentenced for both crimes within the range for serious offenders; II.

State v. Taylor, 42 Wn.App. 74 (1985)
To exceed standard range, state must prove beyond a reasonable doubt that juvenile would present a serious and clear danger to society if standard range were imposed; one need not be a "serious offender," RCW 13.30.020(1), to pose a serious danger to society; II.

State v. Cirkovich, 42 Wn.App. 403 (1985)
A serious offender or a juvenile sentenced to greater than 30 days may not thereafter have his sentence modified by the trial court; I.

State v. Calloway, 42 Wn.App. 420 (1985)
To determine criminal history, RCW 13.40.020(6)(a), "two or more charges arising out of the same course of conduct" means that there was no substantial change in the nature of the criminal objective; here, two burglaries committed in one hour to buy drugs did not arise from the same course of conduct; *but see*: *State v. Adcock*, 36 Wn.App. 699 (1984); II.

State v. Morse, 45 Wn.App. 197 (1986)
Restitution following juvenile court conviction of negligent driving may not include travel, telephone expenses or attorney fees, RCW 13.40.190(17); trial court need not consider comparative negligence in determining restitution amount; I.

State v. Huff, 45 Wn.App. 479 (1986)
In computing criminal history, prior convictions of reckless burning and burglary, committed at the same residence within a brief time span are not within the "same course of conduct," RCW 13.40.020(6)(a), as there was not an objectively discernible relationship between

SECTION 4: JUVENILE CASE LAW REVIEW: 2013

the crimes such that they arose from a single criminal objective, and one of the crimes did not merely facilitate the other, *State v. Adcock*, 36 Wn.App. 699 (1984), *State v. Calloway*, 42 Wn.App. 420 (1985), thus for purposes of disposition, the priors were distinct offenses; I.

In re Latson, 45 Wn.App. 716 (1986)
Recent extensive criminal history is a proper aggravating factor, RCW 13.40.150(3)(i)(iv) to permit a manifest injustice finding; II.

State v. Wall, 46 Wn.App. 218 (1986)
Respondent placed his hand on crotches of 14 and 17-year-old females, convicted of simple assault; trial court sentenced respondent as middle offender to detention, RCW 13.40.160(4), finding victims were particularly vulnerable, RCW 13.40.150(3)(i)(iii); held: to confine a juvenile middle offender beyond standard range without finding a manifest injustice, court must find an aggravating factor; to find victim particularly vulnerable, court must use same definition as under Sentencing Reform Act, RCW 9.94A.309, to include age, disability, thus *remanded* for resentencing; I.

State v. Quiroz, 107 Wn.2d 791 (1987)
A diversion agreement, RCW 13.40.080, may be used to enhance sentence in a subsequent proceeding where the agreement stated the crimes charged, the respondent was given written notice of his right to counsel; juvenile need not be notified of all of the constitutional rights which would apply if he were to plead guilty; 9-0.

State v. Brown, 47 Wn.App. 729 (1987)
RCW 13.40.181(2), limiting court to a disposition of not more than 300% of term imposed for the most serious offense, applies to offenses contained in a single information and not to all offenses heard at a single disposition hearing; *accord*: *State v. Dodd*, 56 Wn.App. 257 (1989); I.

State v. Escoto, 108 Wn.2d 1 (1987)
Juvenile court may order a psychological evaluation of respondent for use in disposition where the court permits counsel to be present at the evaluation and where the respondent is aware of his right to remain silent; *see*: *State v. Decker*, 68 Wn.App. 246 (1992), *State v. Jacobsen*, 95 Wn.App. 967 (1999), *State v. Diaz-Cardona*, 123 Wn.App. 477 (2004); 5-4.

State v. Perez, 49 Wn.App. 45 (1987)
At disposition where standard range calls for community supervision but state is seeking manifest injustice finding and commitment, there is a right to confront and cross-examine witnesses, *State v. Whittington*, 27 Wn.App. 422 (1980); where respondent is middle offender, and confinement is within standard range, court may consider hearsay reports at disposition; I.

State v. Curwood, 50 Wn.App. 228 (1987)
Where juvenile court has extended jurisdiction to a date beyond respondent's 18th

SECTION 4: JUVENILE CASE LAW REVIEW: 2013

birthday, and disposition occurs within the extended jurisdictional period, then state may retain custody over respondent during the full term of his confinement; I; *see also*: State v. Forhan, 59 Wn.App. 486 (1990).

State v. S.P., 110 Wn.2d 886 (1988)
At disposition hearing, juvenile has statutory right to confront author of a report that is relevant and material to the disposition if the author is reasonably available, RCW 13.40.151(1), *reversing* State v. S.P., 49 Wn.App. 45 (1986); 8-0.

State v. Bryant, 51 Wn.App. 258 (1988)
Court may confine for up to 30 days for violation of an order of community supervision, RCW 13.40.200(3)(a); III.

State v. Haaby, 51 Wn.App. 771 (1988)
Juvenile court may not enhance penalty by use of diversion agreements signed before respondent was 12 unless it rebuts the statutory presumption of incapacity, RCW 9A.04.050, *distinguishing* State v. Quiroz, 107 Wn.2d 791 (1987); III.

State v. Steward, 52 Wn.App. 413 (1988)
Respondent is convicted of taking a motor vehicle without permission, RCW 9A.56.070; juvenile court finds that respondent abandoned vehicle, which was stripped, orders restitution for damages; held: RCW 13.40.190 authorizes restitution as the damages resulted from the respondent's offense, *distinguishing* State v. Ashley, 40 Wn.App. 877 (1985); I.

State v. Yadon, 53 Wn.App. 489 (1989)
A minor/first offender may be sentenced to community supervision of up to one year; I.

State v. Horner, 53 Wn.App. 806 (1989)
The value of a victim's labor in making repairs to property damaged by respondent may be included in a restitution order, RCW 13.40.020(17); court may base restitution order upon an estimate of the cost a professional would have charged; I.

State v. Merz, 54 Wn.App. 23 (1989)
A juvenile respondent's plea bargain with the prosecutor does not bind the probation counselor; *see*: State v. Harris, 57 Wn.2d 383 (1960); I.

State v. Tauala, 54 Wn.App. 81 (1989)
Where the record supports an exceptional disposition (here, an aggravated assault), a probation counselor's recommendation that the standard range would provide sufficient treatment is not binding on the court, *distinguishing* State v. P., 37 Wn.App. 733 (1984); I.

State v. Barrett, 54 Wn.App. 178 (1989)
Juvenile passenger in stolen vehicle, convicted of taking and riding, RCW 9A.56.070,

SECTION 4: JUVENILE CASE LAW REVIEW: 2013

may be ordered to make restitution for damages to the vehicle pursuant to RCW 13.40.190(1); I.

State v. Poupart, 54 Wn.App. 440 (1989)
   Probation counselors and caseworkers are not bound by a plea agreement and may make recommendations independent of the prosecutor, *see: State v. Harris*, 146 Wn.2d 339 (2002); I.

State v. Miller, 54 Wn.App. 763 (1989)
   Juvenile offender may be sentenced to longer than an adult would receive for same crime under SRA; II.

State v. Anderson, 58 Wn.App. 107 (1990)
   The aggregate of consecutive terms imposed for two or more offenses in the same information shall not exceed 300% of the actual term imposed by the judge, not the most serious term which could be imposed, RCW 13.40.180(2); I.

State v. Richard, 58 Wn.App. 357 (1990)
   Where court does not expressly delegate to juvenile probation counselor authority to set a curfew, respondent's violation of curfew set by counselor is not a violation of the terms of community supervision, RCW 13.40.200, former RCW 13.40.020(3), *see also: State v. Clark*, 91 Wn.App. 581 (1998), *aff'd, on other grounds*, 139 Wn.2d 152 (1999); II.

State v. Payne, 58 Wn.App. 215 (1990)
   Inflicting serious bodily injury cannot be an aggravating factor justifying a manifest injustice for murder as it inheres in the crime charged; where victim dies instantly, then heinous, cruel or depraved manner is not an aggravating factor, *State v. Melton*, 63 Wn.App. 63 (1991); victim is not "particularly vulnerable" where she is shot in the back at home, off guard, *State v. Wall*, 46 Wn.App. 218 (1986); I.

State v. Radcliff, 58 Wn.App. 717 (1990)
   Written findings are not required for disposition hearings, JuCR 7.12; court is not limited to express statutory aggravating and mitigating factors in RCW 13.40.150, *State v. Strong*, 23 Wn.App. 789, 793 (1979); assaulting a staff member of a rehabilitation facility is an aggravating factor; I.

State v. Forhan, 59 Wn.App. 486 (1990)
   Where disposition is imposed prior to a respondent's 18th birthday, jurisdiction is automatically extended to allow for execution and enforcement of the disposition order, RCW 13.40.300(1)(c), *c.f.: State v. Curwood*, 50 Wn.App. 228 (1987), *State v. Dion*, 160 Wn.2d 605 (2007); I.

State v. Melton, 63 Wn.App. 63 (1991)
   Pending criminal charges is not aggravating factor to support manifest injustice finding; recent criminal history, previous failure to comply with disposition orders, need of long-term

The Caseload Forecast Council is not liable for errors or omissions in the manual, for sentences that may be inappropriately calculated as a result of a practitioner's or court's reliance on the manual, or for any other written or verbal information related to adult or juvenile sentencing. The scoring sheets are intended to provide assistance in most cases but does not cover all permutations of the scoring rules. If you find any errors or omissions, we encourage you to report them to the Caseload Forecast Council.

SECTION 4: JUVENILE CASE LAW REVIEW: 2013

residential treatment, danger to community are aggravating factors, State v. Tuala, 54 Wn.App. 81, 88 (1989), see: State v. Halstien, 122 Wn.2d 109 (1993); I.

State v. Bennett, 63 Wn.App. 530 (1991)
Juvenile on social security with representative payee is ordered to ask guardian for money to pay restitution; held: no abuse of discretion in ordering restitution and ordering respondent to ask payee for funds from social security checks; defendant has burden of establishing that she had proprietary interest in some of the property for which she is ordered to pay restitution, RCW 13.30.020(17); I.

State v. J.N., 64 Wn.App. 112 (1992)
In child rape 1°, finding of a high risk to reoffend based upon evidence of denial, projection of responsibility on victim, planning of offense, is sufficient to support manifest injustice, State v. S.H., 75 Wn.App. 1 (1994), State v. Jacobsen, 95 Wn.App. 967, 981-83 (1999), State v. Roberson, 118 Wn.App. 163 (2003); SRA cases on future dangerousness, e.g., State v. Pryor, 115 Wn.2d 445 (1990), State v. Barnes, 117 Wn.2d 701 (1991), do not apply to juvenile dispositions; I.

State v. B.E.W., 65 Wn.App. 370 (1992)
Where probation counselor recommends manifest injustice disposition, defense is on notice that one is possible; prosecutor need not seek manifest injustice and file supplemental information, *distinguishing* Specht v. Patterson, 18 L.Ed.2d 326 (1967), State v. Whittington, 27 Wn.App. 422 (1980).

State v. Bryant, 65 Wn.App. 547 (1992)
Judge makes oral findings, imposes exceptional sentence; after appeal filed, commissioner signs findings of fact; held: only judge who has heard evidence has authority to find facts, CR 63(b), CrR 6.11, thus remanded for entry of findings by disposition judge or for a new disposition hearing; I.

State v. Howell, 119 Wn.2d 513 (1992)
Special Sex Offender Disposition Alternative (SSODA), RCW 13.40.0357, Schedule D-1, option C and RCW 13.40.160(2), authorize trial court to impose up to 30 days confinement upon minor/first offender without manifest injustice finding; 9-0.

State v. E.J.H., 65 Wn.App. 771 (1992)
Written findings are not required to support manifest injustice finding, *see:* State v. Bevins, 85 Wn.App. 280 (1997); manifest injustice disposition is not clearly excessive where imposed for rehabilitation purposes and to remove respondent from society, *distinguishing* State v. P, 37 Wn.App. 773 (1984); I.

State v. Jackson, 65 Wn.App. 856 (1992)
Contribution to interlocal drug fund may not be ordered by juvenile court, *distinguishing*

SECTION 4: JUVENILE CASE LAW REVIEW: 2013

State v. Q.D., 102 Wn.2d 19, 29 (1984); I.

State v. Landrum, 66 Wn.App. 791 (1992)
Option B community service disposition is not appealable, RCW 13.40.160(2), 13.40.230; I.

State v. Weese, 67 Wn.App. 259 (1992)
Statute requiring juvenile court to notify Department of Licensing of minor in possession convictions for revocation of drivers licenses, RCW 13.40.265(1), 66.44.365(1), does not violate equal protection; II.

State v. P.B.T., 67 Wn.App. 292 (1992)
Abuse of trust is an aggravating factor where a scout leader sexually abuses a younger scout, as respondent was both in a position of trust as well as a position of authority, *State v. Marcum*, 61 Wn.App. 611, 614-5 (1991), and there is circumstantial evidence that perpetrator abused the position of trust to facilitate the crime, *State v. Brown*, 55 Wn.App. 738, 754 (1989), *State v. Stevens*, 58 Wn.App. 478, 500 (1990), *State v. Grewe*, 117 Wn.2d 211, 218 (1991), *distinguishing State v. Stuhr*, 58 Wn.App. 660, 662-3 (1991); *see also: State v. J.S.*, 70 Wn.App. 659 (1993); I.

State v. Foley, 67 Wn.App. 324 (1992)
Diversion agreement, RCW 13.40.080, supersedes conditions of release; I.

State v. S.S., 67 Wn.App. 800 (1992)
Court imposes manifest injustice disposition, relying in part upon social worker's written report, over objection, social worker being on vacation, state having made no effort to compel his attendance; held: confrontation clause did not bar admission of letter into evidence where the letter merely sought to add weight to identical recommendations of other professionals which defendant had the opportunity to rebut, *State v. Short*, 12 Wn.App. 125, 132 (1974), ER 1101(c)(3), *State v. Beard*, 39 Wn.App. 601, 607-8 (1985), *State v. S.P.*, 110 Wn.2d 886, 889 n. 1 (1988); *c.f.: State v. Whittington*, 27 Wn.App. 422, 428-9 (1980); a witness who prepares a written report for disposition is not reasonably available for cross-examination if that witness has, before becoming aware of the date of the hearing, scheduled a vacation which cannot easily and conveniently be rescheduled, RCW 13.40.150(1); trial court, in finding manifest injustice, should not merely adopt probation officer's list of aggravating factors; habitual truancy and prior inadequate punishment are not aggravating factors; court's finding that respondent is highly likely to reoffend if not treated beyond the sentence range is a basis for manifest injustice, *State v. Halstien*, 122 Wn.2d 109 (1993)), *distinguishing State v. Barnes*, 117 Wn.2d 701 (1991); violation of previous dispositions, escalating criminal activity, lack of parental ability to control child's criminal behavior are proper aggravating factors; I.

State v. Decker, 68 Wn.App. 246 (1992)
Trial court may order predisposition psychological evaluation of respondent, *State v.*

SECTION 4: JUVENILE CASE LAW REVIEW: 2013

Escoto, 108 Wn.2d 1 (1987), *State v. Jacobsen*, 95 Wn.App. 967, 981-83 (1999), and may preclude counsel from attending, *c.f.*: *State v. P.B.T.*, 67 Wn.App. 292 (1992), *State v. Diaz-Cardona*, 123 Wn.App. 477 (2004),; trial court has authority to grant use immunity absent prosecutor's motion, CrR 6.14; I.

In re A, B, C, D, E, 121 Wn.2d 80 (1993)
   Mandatory HIV testing for sex offenders, RCW 70.24.340(1)(a), applies to juveniles; 5-2.

State v. Ferreira, 69 Wn.App. 465 (1993)
   Where juvenile is an accomplice to a drive-by shooting at a house in which five people are present, the offense is not a "single act or omission," RCW 13.40.180(1), applying *State v. Dunaway*, 109 Wn.2d 207 (1987), SRA-same criminal conduct analysis to juvenile dispositions; *accord*: *State v. Contreras*, 124 Wn.2d 741 (1994); III.

State v. N.E., 70 Wn.App. 602 (1993)
   Long-term untreated substance abuse, lack of parental control, depression, ongoing prostitution, failure to remain in treatment present a high risk to reoffend and a danger to society, justifying manifest injustice, *State v. Bevins*, 85 Wn.App. 280 (1997), *see*: *State v. S.S.*, 67 Wn.App. 800 (1992), *c.f.*: *State v. Gutierrez*, 37 Wn.App. 910 (1984); where defense fails to argue the impact of mitigating factors, then trial judge need not expressly state that she has considered them; I.

State v. J.S., 70 Wn.App. 659 (1993)
   In child molestation of four-year old stepsister, denial by defendant is grounds for a manifest injustice finding where treatment is unavailable due to the denial, as treatment is a goal of the juvenile justice system, *State v. Jacobsen*, 95 Wn.App. 967, 981-83 (1999) *distinguishing State v. Vermillion*, 66 Wn.App. 332, 348 (1992); familial relationship is sufficient by itself to establish trust relationship for abuse of trust aggravating factor, *State v. Overvold*, 64 Wn.App. 440, 447 (1992), *State v. Hamby*, 69 Wn.App. 131, 132 (1993), *State v. Jacobsen, supra.*, at 980-81 (1999); extreme youth may be an aggravating factor even if victim's age is an element, *State v. Fisher*, 108 Wn.2d 419 (1987); I.

State v. Shawn P., 122 Wn.2d 553 (1993)
   Mandatory driving privilege revocation for minor in possession of alcohol or drug conviction of juveniles, RCW 13.40.265(1)(a) does not violate equal protection clause; *affirms State v. Preston*, 66 Wn.App. 494 (1992); 5-2.

State v. Hayden, 72 Wn.App. 27 (1993)
   Respondent-sex offender's community supervision conditions are modified to prohibit contact with juveniles when he moves to a home with young children, no evidence of a violation of previous conditions; held: court's authority to modify sex offender disposition can be implied from general structure of Juvenile Justice Act, *State v. T.E.C.*, 122 Wn.App. 9, 25-31 (2004); I.

The Caseload Forecast Council is not liable for errors or omissions in the manual, for sentences that may be inappropriately calculated as a result of a practitioner's or court's reliance on the manual, or for any other written or verbal information related to adult or juvenile sentencing. The scoring sheets are intended to provide assistance in most cases but does not cover all permutations of the scoring rules. If you find any errors or omissions, we encourage you to report them to the Caseload Forecast Council.

SECTION 4: JUVENILE CASE LAW REVIEW: 2013

State v. Bourgeois, 72 Wn.App. 650, 656-8 (1994)
  Juvenile court may impose a maximum term beyond offender's 21st birthday, although respondent must be released at 21 years of age; possible early release by Department of Juvenile Rehabilitation is not a basis for a manifest injustice finding, *State v. Fisher*, 108 Wn.2d 419 (1987), *State v. S.H.*, 75 Wn.App. 1 (1994), *State v. Roberson*, 118 Wn.App. 163, 164-65 (2003), *see: State v. Sledge*, 133 Wn.2d 828 (1997); in assault 1° case, gunshot wounds not atypical of injuries by firearms do not establish particularly egregious injuries to justify manifest injustice, *see: State v. Nordby*, 106 Wn.2d 514 (1986), *State v. George*, 67 Wn.App. 217, 222 (1992); I.

State v. Hefa, 73 Wn.App. 865 (1994)
  Restitution is ordered by juvenile court to burglary victim for lost wages to secure home; held: juvenile court may only order restitution for lost wages due to physical injury, RCW 13.40.020(21), *see: State v. Goodrich*, 47 Wn.App. 114 (1987); I.

State v. Derr, 74 Wn.App. 175 (1994)
  Crime victim's penalty assessment, RCW 7.68.035(7), must be imposed at disposition, but may immediately be modified to community service or a lesser figure; III.

State v. Michaelson, 124 Wn.2d 364 (1994)
  A juvenile's taking and riding diversion may not be forwarded to the Department of Licensing, as a diversion is not a conviction, and taking a motor vehicle without permission is a crime, not a violation of the vehicle operating laws, RCW 13.50.200; 9-0.

State v. Contreras, 124 Wn.2d 741 (1994)
  Unlawful imprisonment, custodial assault and escape, all committed in course of escaping from detention facility, are single act limiting disposition to 150% of most serious offense, RCW 13.40.180(1), *reversing State v. Contreras*, 71 Wn.App. 1 (1993); test for determining whether "same course of conduct" used in juvenile justice act and "same criminal conduct" under SRA is essentially the same, at 748, *State v. S.S.Y.*, 150 Wn.App. 325, 333-37 (2009), 170 Wn.2d 322 (2010); 9-0.

State v. S.H., 75 Wn.App. 1 (1994)
  Age and "some degree of size disparity" are inherent in rape of a child 1°, and are thus not aggravating factors absent extreme differences, *State v. Garibay*, 67 Wn.App. 773, 779 (1992); sleeping victim supports victim vulnerability, *State v. Hicks*, 61 Wn.App. 923, 931 (1991); forcible and maniacally obsessive manner of committing offense and high risk to offend are aggravating factors, *State v. T.E.H.*, 92 Wn.App. 908, 918 (1998); I.

State v. Acheson, 75 Wn.App. 151 (1994)
  Juvenile sex offender must comply with the Sex Offender Registration Act, RCW 9A.44.130, *see: State v. Heiskell*, 129 Wn.2d 113 (1996); registration requirements do not terminate at defendant's 21st birthday; II.

SECTION 4: JUVENILE CASE LAW REVIEW: 2013

State v. Bastas, 75 Wn.App. 882 (1994)
    Counsel's motion to withdraw on appeal pursuant to *Anders v. California*, 18 L.Ed.2d 493 (1967), will be denied where the appeal concerns a motion for accelerated review from a manifest injustice disposition; I.

State v. S.M.H., 76 Wn.App. 550 (1995)
    A juvenile convicted of burglary with sexual motivation, RCW 13.40.135, is not required to register as a sex offender, RCW 9A.44.130; I.

State v. May, 80 Wn.App. 711 (1996)
    Juvenile court's authority to revoke community supervision terminates when community supervision period expires, *State v. Y.I.*, 94 Wn.App. 919 (1999), *State v. J.O.*, 165 Wn.App. 570 (2011), unless a violation proceeding is then pending before the court, *see: State v. Todd*, 103 Wn.App. 783 (2000), *but see: State v. Tucker*, 171 Wn.2d 50 (2011); III.

State v. Heiskell, 129 Wn.2d 113 (1996)
    Juveniles must wait two years before first applying for waiver from **sex offender registration** requirement, RCW 9A.44.140(4), *see also: State v. Hooper*, 154 Wn.App. 428 (2010); reverses *State v. Heiskell*, 77 Wn.App. 943 (1995); 6-3.

State v. Ashbaker, 82 Wn.App. 630 (1996)
    Juvenile is entitled to credit for time spent in pretrial electronic home detention, *State v. Speaks*, 119 Wn.2d 204, 207-8 (1992), *see: State v. Dockens*, 156 Wn.App. 793 (2010); III.

State v. Mollichi, 132 Wn.2d 80 (1997)
    Juvenile court must determine restitution at disposition hearing, RCW 13.40.150(3)(f), unless waived by respondent, reversing *State v. Mollichi*, 81 Wn.App. 474 (1996); 9-0.

State v. J.W., 84 Wn.App. 808 (1997)
    Denial of sex offender disposition alternative (SSODA), RCW 13.40.160(5), is not appealable, *State v. Hays*, 55 Wn.App. 13 (1989); I.

State v. Kravchuk, 86 Wn.App. 276 (1997)
    Juvenile court may impose a fine for a traffic infraction, RCW 46.63.110(1), IRLJ 6.2, which is not an "offense" for purposes of a standard range disposition, RCW 13.40.020(19), -.020(27); I.

State v. Sledge, 133 Wn.2d 828 (1997)
    Juvenile court imposes exceptional sentence, stating that respondent should be held until he is 18 years old, calculating length to consider good-time release; held: absent a need for confinement for a specific treatment program requiring a set duration to successfully complete, court may not take into consideration the possibility of early release, *State v. Wakefield*, 130 Wn.2d 464, 478 (1996), *State v. Fisher*, 108 Wn.2d 419, 429 n.6 (1987), *State v. Bourgeois*, 72

SECTION 4: JUVENILE CASE LAW REVIEW: 2013

Wn.App. 650, 660 (1994), *State v. S.H.*, 75 Wn.App. 1, 15-16 (1994), *State v. Roberson*, 118 Wn.App. 151, 164-65 (2003), *but see*: *State v. Beaver*, 148 Wn.2d 338 (2002), reversing *State v. Sledge*, 83 Wn.App. 639 (1996); 9-0.

State v. Robertson, 88 Wn.App. 836, 847-9 (1997)
Malicious harassment, RCW 9A.36.080(1), and assault based upon same act is not a "single act" for purposes of the 150% rule, RCW 13.40.180(1), due to antimerger provision of malicious harassment, *State v. Lessley*, 118 Wn.2d 773, 781 (1992); I.

State v. Hartke, 89 Wn.App. 143 (1997)
Juvenile court's extending jurisdiction over juvenile sentenced in 1988 to collect **restitution** pursuant to RCW 13.40.190 which, as of 1994, allowed extension of jurisdiction over juveniles for restitution to age 28 did not violate *ex post facto* clause, as restitution is not punishment, RCW 13.40.010, *State v. Rice*, 98 Wn.2d 384, 391-4 (1982), even though punishment may be imposed later for failure to pay, *see*: *In re Marriage of Haugh*, 58 Wn.App. 1, 5-6 (1990), accord: *State v. Bennett*, 92 Wn.App. 637 (1998); III.

State v. M.L., 134 Wn.2d 657 (1997)
Ten-year-old pleads guilty to rape 1° and attempted rape 1°, prosecutor, defense and probation counselor recommend exceptional sentences, court sentences to ten times the longest recommended sentence, ordering confinement to age 21; held: sentence ten times as long as the longest sentence recommended is excessive when imposed upon a ten-year old boy, *c.f.*: *State v. Minor*, 133 Wn.App. 636, 645-47 (2006), *rev'd, on other grounds*, 162 Wn.2d 796 (2008), remanded for resentencing before a different judge; *per curiam*.

State v. Duncan, 90 Wn.App. 809 (1998)
Juvenile court judge states that he cannot consider good time in disposition, then imposes manifest injustice sentence to include sufficient time beyond respondent's 21st birthday to keep him in custody until 21 years of age, adopting juvenile rehabilitation board's recommendation which expressly considered good time; held: length of sentence did consider good time, which is an improper factor, *State v. Sledge*, 133 Wn.2d 828 (1997), *State v. Roberson*, 118 Wn.App. 151, 164-65 (2003), absent specific need for specific treatment program; III.

State v. Clark, 91 Wn.App. 581 (1998), *aff'd, on other grounds*, 139 Wn.2d 152 (1999)
Juvenile court judge may not suspend detention time absent express statutory authority, RCW 13.40.160; juvenile court may not delegate to a probation officer the authority to find a probation violation and place respondent in custody, *see*: *State v. Richard*, 58 Wn.App. 357 (1990); II.

State v. Edgley, 92 Wn.App. 478 (1998), *overruled, on other grounds, State v. Nolan*, 141 Wn.2d 620 (2000)
Court may impose consecutive 30-day sentences for each violation of separate community supervision orders, *State v. Veazie*, 123 a92 (2004), irrespective of whether

SECTION 4: JUVENILE CASE LAW REVIEW: 2013

underlying dispositions ran concurrently, *see: State v. Taplin*, 55 Wn.App. 668, 670 (1989), *State v. Barker*, 114 Wn.App. 504 (2002); II.

State v. Martin, 137 Wn.2d 149 (1999)
    Failure to hold disposition hearing within 14 or 21 days of adjudication, RCW 13.40.130(8), JuCR 7.12(a), is error, but is not grounds for dismissal absent proof of prejudice, *State v. Eugene W.*, 41 Wn.App. 758 (1985), *State v. Carlson*, 65 Wn.App. 153, 164-65 (1992), *see also: State v. Johnson*, 100 Wn.2d 607, 629-30 (1983), *overruled on other grounds, State v. Bergeron*, 105 Wn.2d 1 (1985); party may seek writ of mandamus to compel disposition, *State ex rel. Burgunder v. Superior Court*, 180 Wash. 311 (1935); 7-2.

State v. Tejada, 93 Wn.App. 907 (1999)
    Juvenile court has jurisdiction to collect **restitution** until the offender is 28 years old, RCW 13.40.190(1); III.

State v. Mora, 138 Wn.2d 43 (1999)
    Seventeen-year-old is charged in adult court with assault 2° pursuant to automatic decline statute, RCW 13.04.030(1)(e)(v), after which, pursuant to a plea agreement, court allows amendment to assault 3° and possession of firearm, which are not automatic decline offenses, defense motion to transfer to juvenile court is denied; held: nature of the charge dictates jurisdiction and, where the charge no longer comes within automatic decline statute, case must be remanded to juvenile court, *Pers. Restraint of Dalluge*, 152 Wn.2d 772 (2004), *State v. Posey*, 161 Wn.2d 638, 643-47 (2007), *State v. Posey*, 174 Wn.2d 131 (2012), distinguishing *State v. Sharon*, 100 Wn.2d 230 (1983), *see also: State v. Carpenter*, 117 Wn.App. 673 (2003), *but see: State v. Manro*, 125 Wn.App. 165 (2005);9-0.

State v. Evans, 97 Wn.App. 273 (1999)
    Where legislature sets standard range for a crime regardless of offender's criminal history, former RCW 13.40.0357, then lack of history is not a valid basis for manifest injustice disposition, *c.f.: State v. Lewis*, 114 Wn.App. 205 (2002); juvenile court may find a manifest injustice and impose a downward exceptional sentence where it finds that standard range is not needed to rehabilitate the offender or protect the public, *see: State v. M.L.*, 114 Wn.App. 358 (2002), and may consider a lack of criminal history; voluntary use of alcohol and drugs is not a mitigating factor; I.

State v. W.C.F., 97 Wn.App. 401 (1999)
    Upon finding violation of disposition, juvenile court may extend period of community supervision at a modification hearing beyond maximum statutory period without finding a manifest injustice, *In re Welfare of Hoffer*, 34 Wn.App. 82, 86-87 (1983), *State v. Martin*, 102 Wn.2d 300, 303 (1984); I.

State v. J.A.B., 98 Wn.App. 662 (2000)
    Probation counselor's statement of criminal history in predisposition report is sufficient

SECTION 4: JUVENILE CASE LAW REVIEW: 2013

evidence of history absent objection at disposition, *State v. Descoteaux,* 94 Wn.2d 31, 35-37 (1980), *State v. Thiefault,* 160 Wn.2d 409, 417 n.4 (2007), *c.f.: State v. Mendoza,* 165 Wn.2d 913 (2009), *Pers. Restraint of Adolph,* 170 Wn.2d 556, 565-71 (2010), distinguishing *State v. Ford,* 137 Wn.2d 472 (1999), *see: State v. Rivers,* 130 Wn.App. 689 (2005), *but see:* State v. Hunley, 161 Wn.App. 919, 927-32 (2011), *rev. granted,* 172 Wn.2d 1014 (2011); I.

State v. Ford, 99 Wn.App. 682 (2000)
    Compromise of misdemeanor statute, former RCW 10.22.010, is inapplicable in juvenile court, RCW 13.04.450, *see: State v. Norton,* 25 Wn.App. 377 (1980), *State v. Johnson,* 39 Wn.App. 295 (1984); I.

State v. T.C., 99 Wn.App. 701 (2000)
    In imposing a manifest injustice disposition, juvenile court may consider uncharged but admitted criminal conduct in support of a **high risk to reoffend** aggravating factor, *State v. J.N.,* 64 Wn.App. 112 (1992); I.

State v. L.W., 101 Wn.App. 595 (2000)
    Time spent pretrial in a group home pursuant to court order does not count as credit for time served even if restrictions are functionally equivalent to detention-type confinement; I.

State v. H.E.J., 102 Wn.2d 84 (2000)
    Respondent, convicted of a nonsex offense felony (indecent liberties), may be ordered to have a sexual deviancy evaluation and may be ordered to have no unsupervised contact with minors younger than himself; I.

State v. J.B., 102 Wn.App. 583 (2000)
    A suspended SSODA manifest injustice juvenile disposition cannot be appealed until it is revoked, *State v. Langland,* 42 Wn.App. 287, 292 (1985); I.

State v. D.H., 102 Wn.App. 620, 628-29 (2000)
    Respondent is convicted of one count of sexual exploitation of a minor, acquitted of another, court orders respondent to have no contact with complainant of acquitted count; held: juvenile court could reasonably find that prohibiting contact with complainant of acquitted count would facilitate respondent's rehabilitation, thus no abuse of discretion; I.

State v. Lopez, 105 Wn.App. 688 (2001)
    Trial court may not defer disposition, RCW 13.40.127, after trial, nor may a deferred disposition be granted pursuant to manifest injustice, *State v. Mohamoud,* 159 Wn.App. 753 (2011); III.

State v. J.A., 105 Wn.App. 879 (2001)
    During period of deferred disposition, RCW 13.40.127, respondent commits a new crime, juvenile court dismisses absent "full compliance," RCW 13.40.127(9), state appeals; held:

The Caseload Forecast Council is not liable for errors or omissions in the manual, for sentences that may be inappropriately calculated as a result of a practitioner's or court's reliance on the manual, or for any other written or verbal information related to adult or juvenile sentencing. The scoring sheets are intended to provide assistance in most cases but does not cover all permutations of the scoring rules. If you find any errors or omissions, we encourage you to report them to the Caseload Forecast Council.

SECTION 4: JUVENILE CASE LAW REVIEW: 2013

juvenile court has discretion to determine what constitutes lack of compliance and, upon finding no lack of compliance, then court may find full compliance and dismiss; I.

State v. A.K.B., 107 Wn.App. 209 (2001)
Where juvenile court defers disposition, RCW 13.40.127, and orders that it will set restitution during the deferral period but fails to do so, it may not set a restitution amount after the deferral period and, if other conditions are met, must dismiss; II.

State v. A.M., 109 Wn.App. 325 (2001)
Juvenile court must impose a victim penalty assessment "for each case or cause of action," RCW 7.68.035 (1)(b), see: *State v. Q.D.*, 102 Wn.2d. 19, 29 (1984); here, trial court "consolidated" three unrelated charges, brought under separate cause numbers, for disposition, but is still obliged to impose VPA for each; I.

State v. H.J., 111 Wn.App. 298 (2002)
Court sentences respondent to what it believes is a standard range sentence, state later moves to modify sentence on grounds that court erred as to length of community supervision, court imposes manifest injustice disposition over defense double jeopardy objection; held: except where a sentencing is more like a trial, as in death penalty, *Bullington v. Missouri*, 68 L.Ed.2d 270 (1981), or habitual criminal proceedings, *State v. Hennings*, 100 Wn.2d 379 (1983), double jeopardy clause does not bar the court from resentencing and finding manifest injustice, *State v. Strauss*, 119 Wn.2d 401, 410-12 (1992), at least where court rejects state's initial request for manifest injustice; I.

State v. Watson, 146 Wn.2d 947 (2002)
Juvenile court may not impose two deferred dispositions, RCW 13.40.127, for separate offenses, as once the first order is signed, respondent has a prior deferred disposition; affirms *State v. Watson*, 107 Wn.App. 540 (2001); 5-4.

State v. A.M.R., 147 Wn.2d 91 (2002)
Juvenile court must order restitution, including that owed insurers; affirms *State v. A.M.R.*, 108 Wn.App. 9 (2001); 9-0.

State v. Beaver, 148 Wn.2d 338 (2002)
Trial court finds manifest injustice, commits respondent to confinement until age 21 without possibility of early release; held: while only DSHS is authorized to set a release date, former RCW 13.40.210 (1994), *State v. Sledge*, 133 Wn.2d 828 (1997), *State v. S.H.*, 75 Wn.App. 1 (1994), *State v. Bourgeois*, 72 Wn.App. 650 (1994), it is the function of the juvenile court to set a minimum term, RCW 13.40.030, which may equal the maximum term; reverses *State v. Beaver*, 110 Wn.App. 519 (2002); 9-0.

State v. Lewis, 114 Wn.App. 205 (2002)
Escape 2° is amenable to manifest injustice disposition, *c.f.*: *State v. K.E. [Evans]*, 97

The Caseload Forecast Council is not liable for errors or omissions in the manual, for sentences that may be inappropriately calculated as a result of a practitioner's or court's reliance on the manual, or for any other written or verbal information related to adult or juvenile sentencing. The scoring sheets are intended to provide assistance in most cases but does not cover all permutations of the scoring rules. If you find any errors or omissions, we encourage you to report them to the Caseload Forecast Council.

SECTION 4: JUVENILE CASE LAW REVIEW: 2013

Wn.App. 273 (1999); III.

State v. M.L., 114 Wn.App. 358 (2002)
Juvenile court is not required to impose manifest injustice disposition downward when it finds that less time would adequately rehabilitate the offender, *c.f.: State v. K.E. [Evans]*, 97 Wn.App. 273 (1999); while court must consider on the record aggravating or mitigating circumstances, it need not impose a lesser disposition based upon them, RCW 13.40.150, *State v. Malychewski*, 41 Wn.App. 488, 489 (1985), *State v. N.E.*, 70 Wn.App. 602, 607 (1993); respondent may appeal a standard range disposition on grounds that juvenile court failed to apply correct legal standard and procedure, *State v. Mail*, 121 Wn.2d 707, 712 (1993); I.

State v. Barker, 114 Wn.App. 504 (2002)
Juvenile court may not impose more than 30 days for multiple probation violations of a single disposition order, RCW 13.40.200(3), distinguishing *State v. Edgley*, 92 Wn.App. 478 (1998), *overruled, on other grounds, State v. Nolan*, 141 Wn.2d 620 (2000); II.

State v. O'Brien, 115 Wn.App. 599 (2003)
Juvenile court has authority to issue no-contact order as part of disposition order; III.

State v. J.P., 149 Wn.2d 444 (2003)
Restitution for counseling may only be ordered for sex offenses in juvenile court, RCW 13.40.020(22), *see: State v. Landrum*, 66 Wn.App. 791 (1992), reversing *State v. J.P.*, 149 Wn.2d 444 (2003); 9-0.

State v. A.S., 116 Wn.App. 309 (2003)
Special Sex Offense Disposition Alternative, RCW 13.40.160(3), in not available for assault 4°, juvenile court may not suspend sentence, RCW 13.40.160(6); I.

State v. Lown, 116 Wn.App. 402, 408-11 (2003)
Respondent, on deferred disposition, RCW 13.40.127, is found to have used drugs, juvenile court reinstates deferred disposition; held: court is not obliged to revoke deferred disposition even if new crime is found, RCW 13.40.020(4); III.

State v. Crabtree, 116 Wn.App. 536 (2003)
Extreme youth, absence of effective treatment in institutions, good progress in community, underlying purposes of juvenile justice act, negative effect on community of institutionalizing 12 year old are all tenable grounds for manifest injustice downward; suspended sentence under Chemical Dependency Disposition Alternative, RCW 13.40.165, is proper where court enters disposition outside standard range; rehabilitation is a proper factor, distinguishing *State v. Bridges*, 104 Wn.App. 98 (2001); III.

State v. E.A.J., 116 Wn.App. 777, 789-94 (2003)

SECTION 4: JUVENILE CASE LAW REVIEW: 2013

Heinous, cruel or depraved aggravating factor, RCW 13.40.150(3)(h)(i)(ii), is not void for vagueness, *Walton v. Arizona,* 111 L.Ed.2d 511 (1990), *overruled, on other grounds, Ring v. Arizona,* 153 L.Ed.2d 556 (2002), *distinguishing* *Maynard v. Cartwright,* 100 L.Ed.2d 372 (1988) and *Godfrey v. Georgia,* 64 L.Ed.2d 398 (1980), *see:* *State v. Baldwin,* 150 Wn.2d 448, 457-61 (2003); I.

State v. Moro, 117 Wn.App. 913 (2003)
   Escalating pattern of criminal behavior justifies manifest injustice; as long as respondent is told at plea hearing that the court need not follow anyone's recommendation, then a *sua sponte* manifest injustice finding does not violate due process notice requirement, *but see:* *State v. Gutierrez,* 37 Wn.App. 910, 916 (1984), *State v. Falling,* 50 Wn.App. 47, 51-52 (1987); III.

State v. Haws, 118 Wn.App. 36 (2003)
   Court may consider the facts of an offense in deciding to deny a **deferred disposition**, RCW 13.40.127; II.

State v. T.E.C., 122 Wn.App. 9 (2004)
   Court imposes manifest injustice sentence upward, suspends it on condition of SSODA, RCW 13.40.160, directing that respondent be placed within secure treatment facility, five months later when no placement was obtained, revokes; held: following an evaluation, a "**moderate to high risk of reoffense**" is a proper aggravating factor, *see:* *State v. T.E.H.,* 91 Wn.App. 908, 917-18 (1998), *State v. T.C.,* 99 Wn.App. 701, 707 (2000), *State v. S.H.,* 75 Wn.App. 1, 7-8 (1994), *State v. Halstien,* 65 Wn.App. 845, 853 (1992), *aff'd,* 122 Wn.2d 109 (1993); **need for treatment** is a valid aggravating factor, *State v. S.H., supra.,* at 12, *State v. J.V.,* 132 Wn.App. 533, 541-42 (2006); court may impose a conditional SSODA subject to placement being available within a reasonable time, at 27, which may be revoked if placement is not found, distinguishing RCW 13.40.150(5); I.

State v. T.A.D., 122 Wn.App. 290 (2004)
   Juvenile convicted of shoplifting can be ordered to reimburse his father for paying the store a civil penalty, RCW 4.24.230(2); father's unsworn statement is admissible at a juvenile disposition hearing, *State v. Fambrough,* 66 Wn.App. 22, 227 (1992), ER 1101(c)(3); II.

State v. S.S., 122 Wn.App. 725 (2004)
   Statute requiring provision of DNA sample following conviction of a felony, RCW 43.43.754, does not constitute a search requiring a warrant, *State v. Olivas,* 122 Wn.2d 73 (1993), *State v. Surge,* 160 Wn.2d 65 (2007); WAC 446.75-060 authorizing cheek swab as opposed to blood draw is valid; I.

State v. Diaz-Cardona, 123 Wn.App. 477 (2004)
   Juvenile court may not require a juvenile who has pled guilty to participate in a sexual deviancy evaluation, even with a protective order, where the juvenile objects, *see:* *State v.*

SECTION 4: JUVENILE CASE LAW REVIEW: 2013

Decker, 68 Wn.App. 246 (1992), *State v. Jacobsen,* 95 Wn.App. 967 (1999), *State v. Escoto,* 108 Wn.2d 1, 6 (1987), *see: State v. N.B.,* 127 Wn.App. 776, 780-82 (2005), as it would violate respondent's privilege against self incrimination, RCW 13.40.180(8); I.

Redmond v. Bagby, 155 Wn.2d 59 (2005)
Statutes which mandate suspension of drivers' licenses following convictions for reckless driving, RCW 46.61.500, driving while license invalidated, RCW 46.20.342, vehicular homicide, RCW 46.61.520 and minor in possession of alcohol, RCW 66.44.270(2), do not violate due process, distinguishing *Redmond v. Moore,* 151 Wn.2d 664 (2004), due to a heightened government interest in highway safety and a decreased likelihood of erroneous deprivation; 7-2.

State v. Tai N., 127 Wn.App. 733 (2005)
Respondent is convicted of possession with intent to deliver 108 pounds of marijuana, receives manifest injustice sentence; held: quantity alone is not a basis to impose an exceptional sentence on a juvenile, distinguishing *State v. Hrycenko,* 85 Wn.App. 543, 548 (1997), since a juvenile court must find, beyond a reasonable doubt (clear and convincing equals beyond a reasonable doubt in this context), *State v. N.B.,* 127 Wn.App. 776 (2005), that the standard range for this offense and this respondent presents a danger to society, *State v. Rhodes,* 92 Wn.2d 755, 760 (1979), *overruled, on other grounds, State v. Baldwin,* 150 Wn.2d 448 (2003); juvenile court's imposition of manifest injustice to "send a message" is not a valid basis; I.

State v. N.B., 127 Wn.App. 776 (2005)
Following guilty plea, respondent submits to deviancy evaluation and admits to other sex offenses, court imposes manifest injustice; held: respondent's failure to invoke his Fifth Amendment privilege is a waiver, *State v. Jacobsen,* 95 Wn.App. 967, 973-75 (1999), *see: State v. Diaz-Cardona,* 123 Wn.App. 477 (2004); I.

State v. Meade, 129 Wn.App. 918 (2005)
Juvenile court must focus on offender's circumstances and consider numerous factors not relevant to adult sentencing, *State v. Tai N.,* 127 Wn.App. 733, 744 (2005); recent criminal history, failure to follow treatment programs, failure to comply with conditions of recent disposition or diversion order, offending while release pending, failure to follow probation, risk to reoffend are all aggravating factors justifying manifest injustice; respondent is not entitled to a jury trial on aggravating factors in juvenile court, *State v. Minor,* 133 Wn.App. 636, 647-48 (2006), *rev'd, on other grounds,* 162 Wn.2d 796 (2008), distinguishing *Blakely v. Washington,* 159 L.Ed.2d 403 (2004); proof of aggravating factors by clear and convincing evidence, RCW 13.40.160(2), is the equivalent of beyond a reasonable doubt, *State v. Rhodes,* 92 Wn.2d 755, 760 (1979), *overruled, on other grounds, State v. Baldwin,* 150 Wn.2d 448, 461 (2003); II.

State v. Zimmerman, 130 Wn.App. 122 (2005)
State files modification petition alleging new theft, withdraws it over objection and files new charge, defense motion to dismiss is denied; held: while state must elect between a modification based upon a new crime and a new charge, RCW 13.40.070(3), *State v. Tinh Quoc*

SECTION 4: JUVENILE CASE LAW REVIEW: 2013

Tran, 117 Wn.App. 126 (2003), *State v. Murrin,* 85 Wn.App. 754 (1997), respondent has no right to plead to a modification petition, state's initial decision to file a motion for a violation hearing does not bar it from withdrawing the allegation and separately prosecuting; III.

State v. Linssen, 131 Wn.App. 292 (2006)
When imposing a special sex offender disposition alternative (SSODA), RCW 13.40.160, trial court must impose a determinate sentence within the standard range and suspend it; III.

State v. J.V., 132 Wn.App. 533 (2006)
Respondent signs contract with state to enter treatment court, setting forth treatment conditions and agreement that court may impose sanctions including termination and sentence, upon revocation juvenile court imposes manifest injustice disposition; held: treatment court contract need not expressly advise respondent that minifest injustice disposition was a possibility as statutes provide notice that satisfies due process; need for treatment is a proper aggravating factor, *State v. S.H.,* 75 Wn.App. 1, 12 (1994); poor performance in treatment prior to revocation is a basis for manifest injustice disposition; where contract provides that what respondent says in treatment about drug and alcohol use cannot be used in court, it is error to use it for manifest injustice; failing to meet statutory mitigating factor of more than one year between current offense and a prior offense, RCW 13.40.150(3)(h)(v), cannot be considered an aggravating factor; I.

State v. R.L.D., 132 Wn.App. 699, 707-08 (2006)
Following filing of charge, juvenile probation counselor files notice of intent to seek manifest injustice, respondent pleads guilty to standard range recommendation by prosecutor, court imposes manifest injustice disposition; held: notice was sufficient, probation counselor was not obliged to include basis of manifest injustice in notice in juvenile court; II.

State v. G.A.H., 133 Wn.App. 567 (2006)
In a juvenile offender proceeding, court may not order DSHS to place respondent in foster care, as DSHS is not a party; I.

State v. C.D.C., 145 Wn.App. 621 (2008)
Maximum community supervision for assault 4° with sexual motivation is 12 months, as it is not a felony sex offense, RCW 9.94A.030; II.

State v. M.C., 148 Wn.App. 968 (2009)
Trial court may not impose victim penalty assessment, RCW 7.68.035(1)(b), as a condition of a deferred disposition, RCW 13.40.127, *see: State v. C.R.H.,* 107 Wn.App. 591 (2001); I.

State v. S.S.Y., 150 Wn.App. 325, 329-32 (2009), 170 Wn.2d 322 (2010)
Juvenile offenses of robbery and assault do not merge as legislature expressed its intent to punish the offenses separately, RCW 13.40.180, distinguishing *State v. Freeman,* 153 Wn.2d 765

SECTION 4: JUVENILE CASE LAW REVIEW: 2013

(2005); to apply 150% rule, disposition court must determine if offenses constitute same criminal conduct, *State v. Contreras*, 124 Wn.2d 741 (1994), and if one offense is an element of the other; II.

Graham v. Florida, 560 U.S. ___, 176 L.Ed.2d 825 (2010)
    Eighth Amendment precludes sentence of life without parole of a juvenile tried in adult court for a non-homicide offense, *Miller v. Alabama*, ___ U.S. ___, 183 L.Ed.2d 407 (2012); 6-3.

Pers. Restraint of Brady, 154 Wn.App. 189 (2010)
    In 1996 Juvenile Court enters restitution order, in 2007 court, by *ex parte* order, *State v. Hotrum*, 120 Wn.App. 681 (2004), extends jurisdiction for an additional ten years and imposes a $200 "extension fee;" held: because state waited more than ten years to apply for extension, judgments were unenforceable even though respondent had not turned 28 years old, RCW 13.40.190(1), -192, 6.17.020; extension of judgment fee, RCW 36.18.016(15), does not apply to juvenile court; generally, no right to counsel for post-conviction proceedings, *State v. Winston*, 105 Wn.App. 318, 321 (2001); III.

State v. Tucker, 171 Wn.App. 50 (2011)
    Before end of deferred disposition, probation officer files a report which recommends that revocation hearing be set if defendant doesn't prove payment of LFOs, after end of deferred disposition period prosecutor notes revocation hearing and court revokes; held: while a juvenile court maintains jurisdiction to enforce conditions if a violation proceeding is instituted before termination of the period of community custody, *State v. Todd*, 103 Wn.App. 783, 789-90 (2000), *see also: State v. J.O.*, 165 Wn.App. 570 (2011), report by probation officer did not seek current relief and state the basis for relief, CR 7(b), thus there was no timely written motion and court therefore lost jurisdiction when period of supervision expired; reverses, in part, *State v. N.S.T.*, 156 Wn.App. 444 (2010); 9-0.

State v. Mohamoud, 159 Wn.App. 753 (2011)
    Parties negotiate reduction of charge on condition defendant does not seek a deferred disposition, RCW 13.40.127, trial court *sua sponte* defers disposition, state appeals; held: statute which requires a motion for deferred disposition be made at least fourteen days before commencement of trial precludes a deferred disposition after a plea or trial where no timely motion was made, *State v. Lopez*, 105 Wn.App. 688 (2001); because statute requires parental consultation, consideration of benefit to community and respondent, absence of these findings precludes deferred disposition; juvenile court judge lacks authority to order deferred disposition on its own initiative; I.

State v. I.K.C., 160 Wn.App. 660 (2011)
    Juvenile court may not impose detention as a condition of a deferred disposition, RCW 13.40.127; II.

State v. J.O., 165 Wn.App. 570 (2011)

SECTION 4: JUVENILE CASE LAW REVIEW: 2013

Respondent receives deferred disposition on condition of pay restitution and provide DNA sample, RCW 43.43.754, before end of deferral period state files motion to revoke for failure to pay, court continues hearing beyond deferral period, at the hearing state withdraws motion to revoke as respondent would pay restitution that day, defense asks to strike DNA sample requirement, court later denies and orders respondent to supply DNA sample; held: court loses authority to enforce a condition of community supervision when a violation of the condition is not alleged by written motion prior to the end of the deferral period, *State v. Tucker*, 171 Wn.2d 50, 53 (2011), *State v. Y.I.*, 94 Wn.App. 919, 923-24 (1999), *State v. May*, 80 Wn.App. 711 (1996), even if condition is mandatory; here, state's motion to revoke filed within the deferral period did not allege failure to provide DNA sample, thus court lacked authority to order it after the deferral period; I.

Miller v. Alabama, ___ U.S. ___, 183 L.Ed.2d 407 (2012)
    Mandatory life without parole for defendants under 18 at the time of the offense violates Eighth Amendment, *Graham v. Florida*, 560 U.S. ___, 176 L.Ed.2d 825 (2010); 5-4.

State v. Villano, 166 Wn.App. 142 (2012)
    Order that a juvenile not possess "gang paraphernalia" is vague; III.

State v. D.P.G., 169 Wn.App. 396 (2012)
    Following imposition of **deferred disposition**, court shall not dismiss unless restitution is paid in full, RCW 13.40.127(9) (2009) [2012 amendment allows dismissal following good faith effort to pay restitution in full]; II.

State v. Sanchez, 169 Wn.App. 405 (2012)
    Following granting of special sex offender disposition alternative (SSODA), RCW 13.40.160, -.162 (2007), juvenile court must send evaluation to sheriff to establish risk assessment, RCW 4.24.550(6) (2008); I.

SECTION 5

JUVENILE REHABILITATION ADMINISTRATION SENTENCING WORKSHEET

Sentencing Worksheet Instructions

These instructions describe the use of the Juvenile Rehabilitation Administration's (JRA) Sentencing Worksheet DSHS 20-198.

Purpose

The Sentencing Worksheet is used to report information pertinent to the disposition of each juvenile admitted to JRA or those sentenced to community supervision through the Special Sex Offender Disposition Alternative (SSODA) or Option B (Chemical Dependency Disposition Alternative (CDDA)). The form serves as a worksheet for determining the minimum and maximum length of the standard range of confinement for each offense. The structure of the form conforms to and facilitates the application of the disposition standards developed by the Sentencing Guidelines Commission, as required by RCW 13.40.030.

A single disposition grid will establish standard ranges to be imposed, unless the court chooses Option B (CDDA) or Option C (Manifest Injustice).

If a Manifest Injustice is invoked or the 300% or 150% rule is in effect, the length of the actual sentence ordered by the court should be entered on the Sentencing Worksheet in lieu of the standard range.

Data from the Sentencing Worksheet will be processed and stored in the Juvenile Rehabilitation Administration's computer files in Olympia. For youths admitted to JRA the data will be used by JRA facilities for setting minimum and maximum release dates. Data about offenders assigned to the community through SSODA and Option B (CDDA) will be used to track offenders in those programs. Data extracted from the system will be used by JRA to study the impact of the implementation of the Juvenile Justice Act.

SECTION 5: JUVENILE JUSTICE AND REHABILITATION ADMINISTRATION – SENTENCING WORKSHEET INSTRUCTIONS

General Instructions

A JRA Sentencing Worksheet is completed for each juvenile admitted to the Juvenile Rehabilitation Administration and each juvenile sentenced to community supervision through either SSODA or Option B (suspended disposition).

The juvenile sentencing guidelines are subject to modification by the state legislature. It is the responsibility of the sentencing court to ensure that the appropriate standards are being used for a specific offender.

Questions regarding the use of the **Juvenile Disposition Guidelines Manual** should be referred to:

> Caseload Forecast Council
> P.O. Box 40962
> Olympia, WA 98504-0962
> (360) 664-9380

Questions regarding the use or completion of the **Juvenile Rehabilitation Administration's Sentencing Worksheet** should be referred to:

> Juvenile Rehabilitation Administration
> P.O. Box 45720
> Olympia, WA 98504-5720
> (360) 902-8085

Personnel designated by the juvenile court administrators are responsible for the accuracy of the information provided to JRA. Please read the detailed instructions on the following pages before completing the worksheet. If you have any questions regarding the worksheet or these instructions, please contact the JRA Information Services Manager.

For juveniles admitted to JRA, the court should place the white copy of the Sentencing Worksheet in the case file, send the yellow copy to JRA and retain the pink copy. The yellow copy of the worksheet should be sent to JRA, along with any other admittance documents, in time to <u>precede or coincide</u> with the juvenile's arrival.

For offenders sentenced to community supervision through SSODA or Option B (CDDA), the court should send a copy of the Sentencing Worksheet to the JRA regional office. The worksheet should be sent as soon as possible after the juvenile's disposition.

Up to three current offenses can be put on a worksheet. If there are more than four offenses, attach a second sheet.

If there are more than sixteen prior offenses, compute the total score of the additional prior offenses not listed and place it in the appropriate box.

The Caseload Forecast Council is not liable for errors or omissions in the manual, for sentences that may be inappropriately calculated as a result of a practitioner's or court's reliance on the manual, or for any other written or verbal information related to adult or juvenile sentencing. The scoring sheets are intended to provide assistance in most cases but does not cover all permutations of the scoring rules. If you find any errors or omissions, we encourage you to report them to the Caseload Forecast Council.

SECTION 5: JUVENILE JUSTICE AND REHABILITATION ADMINISTRATION – SENTENCING WORKSHEET INSTRUCTIONS

Supply of forms:

Requests for blank forms should be directed to your local JRA regional office.

Instructions for completing each item:

The following definitions and procedures are to be used for completing the individual items. (The numbers correspond to the numbers on the attached sample worksheet.)

SECTION 5: JUVENILE JUSTICE AND REHABILITATION ADMINISTRATION – SENTENCING WORKSHEET INSTRUCTIONS

Washington State Department of Social & Health Services

JUVENILE REHABILITATION ADMINISTRATION (JRA)
SENTENCING WORKSHEET

1. NAME (LAST, FIRST, MIDDLE INITIAL)
2. BIRTHDATE (MM/DD/YYYY)
3. SEX ☐ Male ☐ Female
4. RACE
5. HISPANIC ORIGIN
6. JRA NUMBER
7. DETENTION CREDIT DAYS
8. JUVIS NUMBER
9. NAME OF COUNTY COURT

A. CURRENT OFFENSE INFORMATION

10. Current offense number _____ of _____ total current offenses.
11. COURT ORDER NUMBER
12. SENTENCE START DATE (MM/DD/YYYY)
13. DISPOSITION DATE (MM/DD/YYYY)
14. ADJUDICATION DATE (MM/DD/YYYY)
15. OFFENSE DATE (MM/DD/YYYY)
16. JRA OFFENSE CODE
17. ANTICIPATORY TYPE ☐ Completed ☐ Attempted ☐ Conspiracy ☐ Solicitation
18. JRA OFFENSE CATEGORY
19. FINDING OF SEXUAL MOTIVATION ☐ Yes ☐ No
20. FINDING OF FIREARM ENHANCEMENT ☐ Yes ☐ No

21. TYPE OF PLACEMENT
☐ JRA Direct
☐ JRA SSODA Revoke
☐ JRA CDDA Revoke
☐ CDDA
☐ SSODA
☐ Suspended Disposition Alternative (SDA)
☐ JRA Suspended Disposition Alternative Revoked (JRA SDA Revoked)
☐ Mental Health Disposition Alternative (MHDA)
☐ JRA Mental Health Disposition Alternative Revoked (JRA MHDA Revoked)
☐ Disposition Alternative Community Commitment (DACC)

B. PRIOR OFFENSE INFORMATION

22. ADJUDICATION DATE (MM/DD/YYYY)	23. OFFENSE DATE (MM/DD/YYYY)	24. JRA OFFENSE CODE	25. ANTICIPATORY TYPE	26. CRIMINAL CLASS	27. PRIOR SCORE
			☐ COMPLETED ☐ CONSPIRACY ☐ ATTEMPTED ☐ SOLICITATION		
			☐ COMPLETED ☐ CONSPIRACY ☐ ATTEMPTED ☐ SOLICITATION		
			☐ COMPLETED ☐ CONSPIRACY ☐ ATTEMPTED ☐ SOLICITATION		
			☐ COMPLETED ☐ CONSPIRACY ☐ ATTEMPTED ☐ SOLICITATION		
			☐ COMPLETED ☐ CONSPIRACY ☐ ATTEMPTED ☐ SOLICITATION		
			☐ COMPLETED ☐ CONSPIRACY ☐ ATTEMPTED ☐ SOLICITATION		
			☐ COMPLETED ☐ CONSPIRACY ☐ ATTEMPTED ☐ SOLICITATION		
			☐ COMPLETED ☐ CONSPIRACY ☐ ATTEMPTED ☐ SOLICITATION		
			☐ COMPLETED ☐ CONSPIRACY ☐ ATTEMPTED ☐ SOLICITATION		
			☐ COMPLETED ☐ CONSPIRACY ☐ ATTEMPTED ☐ SOLICITATION		
			☐ COMPLETED ☐ CONSPIRACY ☐ ATTEMPTED ☐ SOLICITATION		
			☐ COMPLETED ☐ CONSPIRACY ☐ ATTEMPTED ☐ SOLICITATION		
			☐ COMPLETED ☐ CONSPIRACY ☐ ATTEMPTED ☐ SOLICITATION		
			☐ COMPLETED ☐ CONSPIRACY ☐ ATTEMPTED ☐ SOLICITATION		

C. SENTENCING INFORMATION

28. TOTAL PRIOR OFFENSE SCORE
29. SENTENCE ADJUSTMENT ☐ None (Standard Range) ☐ Manifest Injustice ☐ 150% Rule ☐ 300% Rule
30. THIS SENTENCE IS IN ☐ Days ☐ Weeks
31. TOTAL MINIMUM EXCLUDING FIREARM ENHANCEMENT
32. TOTAL MAXIMUM EXCLUDING FIREARM ENHANCEMENT
33. NAME OF PERSON COMPLETING THIS FORM FOR THE COURT
34. DATE COMPLETED (MM/DD/YYYY)
35. TELEPHONE NUMBER (INCLUDE AREA CODE)

DSHS 20-198 (REV. 07/2003)

SECTION 5: JUVENILE JUSTICE AND REHABILITATION ADMINISTRATION – SENTENCING WORKSHEET INSTRUCTIONS

SENTENCING WORKSHEET INSTRUCTIONS

1. **NAME:** Enter the youth's last name, first name, and middle initial as they appear on the court order.
2. **BIRTHDATE:** Enter the month, day, and year of the youth's birth. For example, enter 09/01/1986 for a youth born on September 1, 1986.
3. **SEX:** Check the box indicating whether the youth is male or female.
4. **RACE:** Using Appendix A of the Juvenile Disposition Manual, indicate the code for the youth's reported race.
5. **HISPANIC ORIGIN:** Using Appendix A of the Juvenile Disposition Manual, indicate the code for the youth's reported Hispanic origin.
6. **JRA NUMBER:** Enter the youth's JRA number for this youth if the youth has had a previous admission to a JRA facility. Leave blank if unknown.
7. **DETENTION CREDIT DAYS:** If the youth has detention credit, enter the days to be taken off the sentence. Detention credit is time in detention or jail prior to the court hearing at which an admittance to JRA is ordered and is listed on the court order. Any additional "pre-admission" detention credit, i.e., credit for time served after adjudication or disposition but prior to admission, will be determined separately by the JRA admitting agency.
8. **JUVIS NUMBER:** Enter the youth's JUVIS number.
9. **COUNTY COURT:** Enter the name of the Juvenile Court, e.g., Benton/Franklin, etc.

A. CURRENT OFFENSE INFORMATION

10. **CURRENT OFFENSE NUMBER:** Use one worksheet for each offense. Mark here which current offense this is and the total number of current offenses for this commitment. Staple all sheets together.
11. **COURT ORDER NUMBER:** Enter the court order number that has been assigned by the court for the sentence for this current offense.
12. **SENTENCE START DATE:** Enter the month, day, and year of the date that the youth's sentence actually began. This is the date that the "clock" technically began for youths committed to JRA.
13. **DISPOSITION DATE:** Enter the month, day, and year of the date of the court order establishing the youth's sentence for this offense.
14. **ADJUDICATION DATE:** Enter the date that the youth was found guilty for this current offense.
15. **OFFENSE DATE:** Enter the month, day, and year that the youth's current offense occurred, e.g. 07/15/2002.
16. **JRA OFFENSE CODE:** Enter the ten character JRA Offense Code from the JRA Code, Description, and Offense Category table in Section 2 of the Juvenile Disposition Manual. Use one sheet for each current offense.
17. **ANTICIPATORY TYPE:** Check one appropriate box to indicate whether the court charged the youth with completion, attempt, conspiracy, or solicitation of the crime.
18. **JUVENILE OFFENSE CATEGORY:** Enter the two character offense category from the JRA Code, Description, and Offense Category table in Section 2 of the Juvenile Disposition Manual. Seriousness is indicated by the offense category, an A+ offense being the most serious and E offense being the least serious. If the offense cannot be found in the Code, Description, and Offense Category table, use one of the generic codes at the end of the table to determine category. If the offense is a new one and expected to occur frequently, contact JRA in Olympia to determine if a new code can be assigned to the offense.
19. **FINDING OF SEXUAL MOTIVATION:** Check yes if the court order includes a finding of sexual motivation. Check no if there was no finding of sexual motivation in the court order.
20. **FINDING OF FIREARM ENHANCEMENT:** The court may apply an enhancement when an offender, or an accomplice, was armed with a firearm. The enhancement will apply to all felonies except those where the use of a firearm is an element of the offense definition (possession of a machine gun, possession of a stolen firearm, drive-by shooting, theft of a firearm, unlawful possession of a firearm 1 or 2, or use of a machine gun in a felony). The enhancement must be served consecutively to the base sentence. Check yes or no.
21. **TYPE OF PLACEMENT:** Indicate one type of placement for this current offense/sentence:
    JRA Direct: Check if the youth is being directly committed to JRA. JRA SSODA Revoke: Check if the youth is being committed to JRA because a SSODA sentence has been revoked.
    JRA CDDA Revoke: Check if the youth is being committed to JRA because a CDDA sentence has been revoked.
    CDDA: Check if the youth is being assigned to community supervision through the Chemical Dependency Disposition Alternative.
    SSODA: Check if the youth is being assigned to community supervision through the Special Sex Offender Disposition Alternative (SSODA).
    SDA: Check if youth is being assigned to community supervision through the suspended disposition alternative.
    JRA SDA Revoked: Check if the youth is being committed to JRA because a JRA SDA sentence has been revoked.
    MHDA: Check if the youth is being assigned to community supervision through the Mental Health Disposition Alternative.
    JRA MHDA Revoked: Check if the youth is being committed to JRA because a JRA MHDA sentence has been revoked.
    DACC: Check if youth is being assigned to community supervision through the Disposition Alternative Community Commitment.

B. PRIOR OFFENSE INFORMATION

22. **ADJUDICATION DATE:** Enter the date that the youth was adjudicated, i.e. found guilty, for this prior.
23. **OFFENSE DATE:** Enter the month, day, and year that the youth's prior offense occurred.
24. **JRA OFFENSE CODE:** Enter the JRA Offense Code from the JRA Code, Description, and Offense Category table in Section 2 of the Juvenile Disposition Manual.
25. **ANTICIPATORY TYPE:** Check the appropriate box to indicate whether the court charged the youth with completion, attempt, conspiracy, or solicitation of the offense.
26. **CRIMINAL CLASS:** Enter "A" if the offense was a Class A felony, "B" if it was a Class B felony, or "C" if it was a Class C felony. Enter "GM" if it was a gross misdemeanor, "M" if it was a misdemeanor, or "V" if it was a violation.
27. **PRIOR SCORE:** Each prior felony adjudication counts as one point. Each prior violation, misdemeanor, and gross misdemeanor adjudication counts as one-fourth point. Indicate the score for each prior offense.

C. SENTENCING INFORMATION

28. **PRIOR OFFENSE SCORE:** Add prior points and enter the total here. Fractional points are rounded down to the nearest whole number.
29. **SENTENCE ADJUSTMENT:** Check the appropriate box to indicate disposition:
    None (Standard Range): Check if there was no adjustment to the youth's standard range sentence.
    Manifest Injustice: Check if manifest injustice was invoked.
    150% Rule: Check if the 150% rule has been invoked, limiting the length of the youth's sentence. The 150% rule is intended to limit the amount of sanction (to 150% of the sanction for the most serious offense) that an offender may receive for offenses committed through a single act or omission.
    300% Rule: Check if the 300% rule has been invoked, limiting the length of the youth's sentence. The 300% rule has been invoked, limiting the amount of sanction (to 300% of the sanction for the most serious offense) that an offender may receive for multiple offenses which are disposed of during a court appearance. (See RCW 13.40.180 for an explanation.)
30. **DAYS OR WEEKS:** Check whether this sentence is listed in days or weeks.
31. **TOTAL MINIMUM SENTENCE EXCLUDING FIREARM ENHANCEMENT:** Indicate here the total of the minimum sentence.
32. **TOTAL MAXIMUM SENTENCE EXCLUDING FIREARM ENHANCEMENT:** Indicate here the total of the maximum sentence.
33. **PRINT NAME OF PERSON COMPLETING THIS FORM FOR THE COURT:** Print the name of the person completing this form.
34. **DATE COMPLETED PRIOR OFFENSE SCORE:** Add prior points and enter the total here. Fractional points are rounded down to the nearest whole number.
35. **TELEPHONE NUMBER:** Record the telephone number of the person who filled out this form

---

The Caseload Forecast Council is not liable for errors or omissions in the manual, for sentences that may be inappropriately calculated as a result of a practitioner's or court's reliance on the manual, or for any other written or verbal information related to adult or juvenile sentencing. The scoring sheets are intended to provide assistance in most cases but does not cover all permutations of the scoring rules. If you find any errors or omissions, we encourage you to report them to the Caseload Forecast Council.

SECTION 5: JUVENILE JUSTICE AND REHABILITATION ADMINISTRATION – SENTENCING WORKSHEET INSTRUCTIONS

JUVENILE OFFENDER SENTENCING GRID (OPTION A)

STANDARD RANGE

CURRENT OFFENSE CATEGORY	0	1	2	3	4 or more
A+	180 weeks to age 21 for all category A+ offenses				
A	103 - 129 weeks for all category A offenses				
A-	15 - 36 weeks Except 30 – 40 weeks for 15 to 17 year olds	52 - 65 weeks	80 - 100 weeks	103 - 129 weeks	103 - 129 weeks
B+	15 - 36 weeks	15 – 36 weeks	52 - 65 weeks	80 - 100 weeks	103 - 129 weeks
B	LS	LS	15 - 36 weeks	15 - 36 weeks	52 - 65 weeks
C+	LS	LS	LS	15 - 36 weeks	15 - 36 weeks
C	LS	LS	LS	LS	15 - 36 weeks
D+	LS	LS	LS	LS	LS
D	LS	LS	LS	LS	LS
E	LS	LS	LS	LS	LS

PRIOR ADJUDICATIONS

(4) The vertical axis of the grid is the current offense category. The current offense category is determined by the offense of adjudication.

(5) The horizontal axis of the grid is the number of the prior adjudications included in the juvenile's criminal history. Each prior felony adjudication counts as one point. Each prior violation, misdemeanor, and gross misdemeanor adjudication counts as ¼ point. Fractional points are rounded down.

(6) The standard range disposition for each offense is determined by the intersection of the column defined by the prior adjudications and the row defined by the current offense category.

(7) RCW 13.40.180 applies if the offenders is being sentenced for more than one offense.

(8) A current offense that is a violation is equivalent to an offense category of E. However, a disposition for a violation shall not include confinement.

LS = Local Sanctions: 0 - 30 days of confinement, and/or
　　　　　　　　　　0 - 12 months of community supervision, and/or
　　　　　　　　　　0 - 150 hours of community restitution, and/or
　　　　　　　　　　$0 - $500 fine.

The Caseload Forecast Council is not liable for errors or omissions in the manual, for sentences that may be inappropriately calculated as a result of a practitioner's or court's reliance on the manual, or for any other written or verbal information related to adult or juvenile sentencing. The scoring sheets are intended to provide assistance in most cases but does not cover all permutations of the scoring rules. If you find any errors or omissions, we encourage you to report them to the Caseload Forecast Council.

APPENDIX A

APPENDIX A:

RACE CODES

597	INDIAN-AMERICAN
600	ASIAN-INDIAN
604	CAMBODIAN
605	CHINESE
608	FILIPINO
611	JAPANESE
612	KOREAN
613	LAOTIAN
618	THAI
619	VIETNAMESE
653	HAWAIIAN
655	SAMOAN
660	GUAMANIAN
699	OTHER-ASIAN
799	OTHER RACE
800	WHITE
870	BLK-AFR-AMR
935	ESKIMO
941	ALEUT
999	UNREPORTED

HISPANIC ORIGIN CODES

709	YES, CUBAN
722	YES, MEXICAN-AMER
727	YES, PUERTO RICAN
799	YES, OTHER SPANISH
000	NOT REPORTED
999	NO

APPENDICE A - RACE, HISPANIC ORIGIN, AND COURT CODES

COURT CODE	COURT NAME
001	ADAMS
002	ASOTIN/GARFIELD
003	BENTON/FRANKLIN
004	CHELAN
005	CLALLAM
006	CLARK
007	COLUMBIA/WALLA WALLA
008	COWLITZ
009	DOUGLAS
026	PEND OR/STEVENS/FERRY
003	BENTON/FRANKLIN
002	ASOTIN/GARFIELD
013	GRANT
014	GRAYS HARBOR
015	ISLAND
016	JEFFERSON
017	KING
018	KITSAP
019	KITTITAS
020	KLICKITAT
021	LEWIS
022	LINCOLN
023	MASON
024	OKANOGAN
025	PACIFIC/WAHKIAKUM
026	PEND OR/STEVENS/FERRY
027	PIERCE
028	SAN JUAN
029	SKAGIT
030	SKAMANIA
031	SNOHOMISH
032	SPOKANE
026	PEND OR/STEVENS/FERRY
034	THURSTON
025	PACIFIC/WAHKIAKUM
007	COLUMBIA/WALLA WALLA
037	WHATCOM
038	WHITMAN
039	YAKIMA

The Caseload Forecast Council is not liable for errors or omissions in the manual, for sentences that may be inappropriately calculated as a result of a practitioner's or court's reliance on the manual, or for any other written or verbal information related to adult or juvenile sentencing. The scoring sheets are intended to provide assistance in most cases but does not cover all permutations of the scoring rules. If you find any errors or omissions, we encourage you to report them to the Caseload Forecast Council.

APPENDIX B

Note: Appendix B provides a list of JRA offenses code as a courtesy. These codes are used by JRA in its client tracking system. New codes are added as needed by JRA.

APPENDIX B: JRA OFFENSE CODES BY OFFENSE TITLE

OFFENSE TITLE	CATEGORY	RCW	JRA CODE
Aiming Or Discharging Firearms, Dangerous Weapons	D	9.41.230	DANWEAPAD
Aiming Or Discharging Firearms, Dangerous Weapons Attempted	E	9.41.230	DANWEAPAD
Aiming Or Discharging Firearms, Dangerous Weapons Conspiracy	E	9.41.230	DANWEAPAD
Aiming Or Discharging Firearms, Dangerous Weapons Solicitation	E	9.41.230	DANWEAPAD
Alien Possession Of Firearms	C	9.41.171	POSFIRARMA
Alien Possession Of Firearms Attempted	D	9.41.171	POSFIRARMA
Alien Possession Of Firearms Conspiracy	D	9.41.171	POSFIRARMA
Alien Possession Of Firearms Solicitation	D	9.41.171	POSFIRARMA
Alteration Of Identifying Marks On Firearm	E	9.41.140	FIRARMALT
Alteration Of Identifying Marks On Firearm Attempted	E	9.41.140	FIRARMALT
Alteration Of Identifying Marks On Firearm Conspiracy	E	9.41.140	FIRARMALT
Alteration Of Identifying Marks On Firearm Solicitation	E	9.41.140	FIRARMALT
Animal Cruelty 1	B	16.52.205	ANIMCRUEL1
Animal Cruelty 1 Attempt	D	16.52.205	ANIMCRUEL1
Animal Cruelty 1 Conspiracy	D	16.52.205	ANIMCRUEL1
Animal Cruelty 1 Solicitation	D	16.52.205	ANIMCRUEL1
Animal Cruelty 2	E	16.52.207	ANIMCRUEL2
Arson 1	A	9A.48.020	ARSON1
Arson 1 Attempt	B+	9A.48.020	ARSON1
Arson 1 Conspiracy	B+	9A.48.020	ARSON1
Arson 1 Solicitation	B+	9A.48.020	ARSON1
Arson 2	B	9A.48.030	ARSON2
Arson 2 Attempt	C	9A.48.030	ARSON2
Arson 2 Conspiracy	C	9A.48.030	ARSON2
Arson 2 Solicitation	C	9A.48.030	ARSON2
Assault 1	A	9A.36.011	ASSAULT1
Assault 1 Attempt	B+	9A.36.011	ASSAULT1

APPENDICE B – JRA OFFENSE CODES BY OFFENSE TITLE

OFFENSE TITLE	CATEGORY	RCW	JRA CODE
Assault 1 Conspiracy	B+	9A.36.011	ASSAULT1
Assault 1 Solicitation	B+	9A.36.011	ASSAULT1
Assault 2	B+	9A.36.021	ASSAULT2
Assault 2 Accomplice	B+	9A.36.021	ASSAULT2AC
Assault 2 Accomplice Attempted	C+	9A.36.021	ASSAULT2AC
Assault 2 Accomplice Conspiracy	C+	9A.36.021	ASSAULT2AC
Assault 2 Accomplice Solicitation	C+	9A.36.021	ASSAULT2AC
Assault 2 Attempt	C+	9A.36.021	ASSAULT2
Assault 2 Conspiracy	C+	9A.36.021	ASSAULT2
Assault 2 Solicitation	C+	9A.36.021	ASSAULT2
Assault 2 With Sexual Motivation	A	9A.36.021	ASSAULT2SM
Assault 2 With Sexual Motivation Attempt	B+	9A.36.021	ASSAULT2SM
Assault 2 With Sexual Motivation Conspiracy	B+	9A.36.021	ASSAULT2SM
Assault 2 With Sexual Motivation Solicitation	B+	9A.36.021	ASSAULT2SM
Assault 3	C+	9A.36.031	ASSAULT3
Assault 3 Attempt	D+	9A.36.031	ASSAULT3
Assault 3 Conspiracy	D+	9A.36.031	ASSAULT3
Assault 3 Solicitation	D+	9A.36.031	ASSAULT3
Assault 4	D+	9A.36.041	ASSAULT4
Assault 4 Attempt	E	9A.36.041	ASSAULT4
Assault 4 Conspiracy	E	9A.36.041	ASSAULT4
Assault 4 Solicitation	E	9A.36.041	ASSAULT4
Assault By Watercraft	B	79A.60.060	ASSAULTWC
Assault By Watercraft Attempt	C	79A.60.060	ASSAULTWC
Assault By Watercraft Conspiracy	C	79A.60.060	ASSAULTWC
Assault By Watercraft Solicitation	C	79A.60.060	ASSAULTWC
Assault Of Child 1	A	9A.36.120	ASSAULTCH1
Assault Of Child 1 Attempt	B	9A.36.120	ASSAULTCH1
Assault Of Child 1 Conspiracy	B	9A.36.120	ASSAULTCH1
Assault Of Child 1 Solicitation	B	9A.36.120	ASSAULTCH1
Assault Of Child 2	B	9A.36.130	ASSAULTCH2
Assault Of Child 2 Attempt	C	9A.36.130	ASSAULTCH2
Assault Of Child 2 Conspiracy	C	9A.36.130	ASSAULTCH2
Assault Of Child 2 Solicitation	C	9A.36.130	ASSAULTCH2
Attempting To Elude A Police Vehicle	C	46.61.024	ELUDEPV

The Caseload Forecast Council is not liable for errors or omissions in the manual, for sentences that may be inappropriately calculated as a result of a practitioner's or court's reliance on the manual, or for any other written or verbal information related to adult or juvenile sentencing. The scoring sheets are intended to provide assistance in most cases but does not cover all permutations of the scoring rules. If you find any errors or omissions, we encourage you to report them to the Caseload Forecast Council.

APPENDICE B – JRA OFFENSE CODES BY OFFENSE TITLE

OFFENSE TITLE	CATEGORY	RCW	JRA CODE
Attempting To Elude A Police Vehicle Attempt	D	46.61.024	ELUDEPV
Attempting To Elude A Police Vehicle Conspiracy	D	46.61.024	ELUDEPV
Attempting To Elude A Police Vehicle Solicitation	D	46.61.024	ELUDEPV
Bomb Threat	B	9.61.160	BOMBTHREAT
Bomb Threat Attempt	C	9.61.160	BOMBTHREAT
Bomb Threat Conspiracy	C	9.61.160	BOMBTHREAT
Bomb Threat Solicitation	C	9.61.160	BOMBTHREAT
Burg Tools (Possession Of) Attempt	E	9A.52.020	BURGTOOLS
Burg Tools (Possession Of) Conspiracy	E	9A.52.020	BURGTOOLS
Burg Tools (Possession Of) Solicitation	E	9A.52.020	BURGTOOLS
Burglary 1	B+	9A.52.020	BURG1
Burglary 1 Attempt	C+	9A.52.020	BURG1
Burglary 1 Conspiracy	C+	9A.52.020	BURG1
Burglary 1 Solicitation	C+	9A.52.020	BURG1
Burglary 2	B	9A.52.030	BURG2
Burglary 2 Attempt	C	9A.52.030	BURG2
Burglary 2 Conspiracy	C	9A.52.030	BURG2
Burglary 2 Solicitation	C	9A.52.030	BURG2
Burglary Tools (Possession Of)	D	9A.52.020	BURGTOOLS
Carry Weapon To School	D	9.41.280	CARWEAPSCH
Carry Weapon To School Attempt	E	9.41.280	CARWEAPSCH
Carry Weapon To School Conspiracy	E	9.41.280	CARWEAPSCH
Carry Weapon To School Solicitation	E	9.41.280	CARWEAPSCH
Child Molestation 1	A-	9A.44.083	CHILDMOL1
Child Molestation 1 Attempt	B+	9A.44.083	CHILDMOL1
Child Molestation 1 Conspiracy	B+	9A.44.083	CHILDMOL1
Child Molestation 1 Solicitation	B+	9A.44.083	CHILDMOL1
Child Molestation 2	B	9A.44.086	CHILDMOL2
Child Molestation 2 Attempt (Post 5/11/98)	C+	9A.44.086	CHILDMOL2
Child Molestation 2 Conspiracy	C+	9A.44.086	CHILDMOL2
Child Molestation 2 Solicitation	C+	9A.44.086	CHILDMOL2
Child Molestation 3	C	9A.44.089	CHILDMOL3
Child Molestation 3 Attempted	D	9A.44.089	CHILDMOL3
Child Molestation 3 Conspiracy	D	9A.44.089	CHILDMOL3
Child Molestation 3 Solicitation	D	9A.44.089	CHILDMOL3

The Caseload Forecast Council is not liable for errors or omissions in the manual, for sentences that may be inappropriately calculated as a result of a practitioner's or court's reliance on the manual, or for any other written or verbal information related to adult or juvenile sentencing. The scoring sheets are intended to provide assistance in most cases but does not cover all permutations of the scoring rules. If you find any errors or omissions, we encourage you to report them to the Caseload Forecast Council.

APPENDICE B – JRA OFFENSE CODES BY OFFENSE TITLE

OFFENSE TITLE	CATEGORY	RCW	JRA CODE
Coercion	D+	9A.36.070	COERCION
Coercion Attempt	E	9A.36.070	COERCION
Coercion Conspiracy	E	9A.36.070	COERCION
Coercion Solicitation	E	9A.36.070	COERCION
Commercial Sexual Abuse Of A Minor	B	9.68A.100	SEXABUSEMI
Commercial Sexual Abuse Of A Minor Attempted	C	9.68A.100	SEXABUSEMI
Commercial Sexual Abuse Of A Minor Conspiracy	C	9.68A.100	SEXABUSEMI
Commercial Sexual Abuse Of A Minor Solicitation	C	9.68A.100	SEXABUSEMI
Commit Crime With Firearms	C+	94.10.25	CRIMEARMS
Commit Crime With Firearms Attempt	D+	94.10.25	CRIMEARMS
Communicating With A Minor For Immoral Purpose	D	9.68A.091	COMMINOR
Communicating With A Minor For Immoral Purpose - Subsequent Sex Offense	C	9.68A.090	COMMINORSS
Communicating With A Minor For Immoral Purpose - Subsequent Sex Offense Attempt	D	9.68A.090	COMMINORSS
Communicating With A Minor For Immoral Purpose - Subsequent Sex Offense Conspiracy	D	9.68A.090	COMMINORSS
Communicating With A Minor For Immoral Purpose - Subsequent Sex Offense Solicitation	D	9.68A.090	COMMINORSS
Communicating With A Minor For Immoral Purpose Attempt	E	9.68A.091	COMMINOR
Communicating With A Minor For Immoral Purpose Conspiracy	E	9.68A.091	COMMINOR
Communicating With A Minor For Immoral Purpose Solicitation	E	9.68A.091	COMMINOR
Contempt	E	7.21	CONTEMPT
Controlled Substances Homicide	B	69.50.415	HOMICIDECS
Controlled Substances Homicide Attempt	C	69.50.415	HOMICIDECS
Controlled Substances Homicide Conspiracy	C	69.50.415	HOMICIDECS
Controlled Substances Homicide Solicitation	C	69.50.415	HOMICIDECS
Criminal Contempt	E	9.23.010	CRIMCONT
Criminal Impersonation 1	C	9A.60.040	IMPERSON1
Criminal Impersonation 1 Attempt	D	9A.60.040	IMPERSON1
Criminal Impersonation 1 Conspiracy	D	9A.60.040	IMPERSON1
Criminal Impersonation 1 Solicitation	D	9A.60.040	IMPERSON1
Criminal Impersonation 2	D	9A.60.045	IMPERSON2
Criminal Impersonation 2 Attempt	E	9A.60.045	IMPERSON2
Criminal Impersonation 2 Conspiracy	E	9A.60.045	IMPERSON2
Criminal Impersonation 2 Solicitation	E	9A.60.045	IMPERSON2
Criminal Trespass 1	D	9A.52.070	CRIMTRES1

The Caseload Forecast Council is not liable for errors or omissions in the manual, for sentences that may be inappropriately calculated as a result of a practitioner's or court's reliance on the manual, or for any other written or verbal information related to adult or juvenile sentencing. The scoring sheets are intended to provide assistance in most cases but does not cover all permutations of the scoring rules. If you find any errors or omissions, we encourage you to report them to the Caseload Forecast Council.

APPENDICE B – JRA OFFENSE CODES BY OFFENSE TITLE

OFFENSE TITLE	CATEGORY	RCW	JRA CODE
Criminal Trespass 1 Attempt	E	9A.52.070	CRIMTRES1
Criminal Trespass 1 Conspiracy	E	9A.52.070	CRIMTRES1
Criminal Trespass 1 Solicitation	E	9A.52.070	CRIMTRES1
Criminal Trespass 2	E	9A.52.080	CRIMTRES2
Criminal Trespass 2 Attempt	E	9A.52.080	CRIMTRES2
Criminal Trespass 2 Conspiracy	E	9A.52.080	CRIMTRES2
Criminal Trespass 2 Solicitation	E	9A.52.080	CRIMTRES2
Custodial Assault	C+	9A.36.100	CUSASSAULT
Custodial Assault Attempt	D+	9A.36.100	CUSASSAULT
Custodial Assault Conspiracy	D+	9A.36.100	CUSASSAULT
Custodial Assault Solicitation	D+	9A.36.100	CUSASSAULT
Custodial Interference	E	9A.40.050	CUSINTER
Custodial Interference 1	C	9A.40.060	CUSINTER1
Custodial Interference 1 Attempt	D	9A.40.060	CUSINTER1
Custodial Interference 1 Conspiracy	D	9A.40.060	CUSINTER1
Custodial Interference 1 Solicitation	D	9A.40.060	CUSINTER1
Custodial Interference 2	D	9A.40.070	CUSINTER2
Custodial Interference 2 Attempt	D	9A.40.070	CUSINTER2
Custodial Interference 2 Conspiracy	D	9A.40.070	CUSINTER2
Custodial Interference 2 Solicitation	D	9A.40.070	CUSINTER2
Custodial Interference 2 Subsequent	C	9A.40.070	CUSINTER2S
Custodial Interference 2 Subsequent Attempt	D	9A.40.070	CUSINTER2S
Custodial Interference 2 Subsequent Conspiracy	D	9A.40.070	CUSINTER2S
Custodial Interference 2 subsequent Solicitation	D	9A.40.070	CUSINTER2S
Dealing In Depictions Of Minor Engaged In Sexually Explicit Conduct 1	B	9.68A.050	DELCHPORN1
Dealing In Depictions Of Minor Engaged In Sexually Explicit Conduct 1 Attempt	C	9.68A.050	DELCHPORN1
Dealing In Depictions Of Minor Engaged In Sexually Explicit Conduct 1 Conspiracy	C	9.68A.050	DELCHPORN1
Dealing In Depictions Of Minor Engaged In Sexually Explicit Conduct 1 Solicitation	C	9.68A.050	DELCHPORN1
Dealing In Depictions Of Minor Engaged In Sexually Explicit Conduct 2	C	9.68A.050	DELCHPORN2
Dealing In Depictions Of Minor Engaged In Sexually Explicit Conduct 2 Attempt	D	9.68A.050	DELCHPORN2
Dealing In Depictions Of Minor Engaged In Sexually Explicit Conduct 2 Conspiracy	D	9.68A.050	DELCHPORN2

The Caseload Forecast Council is not liable for errors or omissions in the manual, for sentences that may be inappropriately calculated as a result of a practitioner's or court's reliance on the manual, or for any other written or verbal information related to adult or juvenile sentencing. The scoring sheets are intended to provide assistance in most cases but does not cover all permutations of the scoring rules. If you find any errors or omissions, we encourage you to report them to the Caseload Forecast Council.

APPENDICE B – JRA OFFENSE CODES BY OFFENSE TITLE

OFFENSE TITLE	CATEGORY	RCW	JRA CODE
Dealing In Depictions Of Minor Engaged In Sexually Explicit Conduct 2 Solicitation	D	9.68A.050	DELCHPORN2
Diagnostic Only	X	9973	DIAGNOSTIC
Disorderly Conduct	E	9A.84.030	DISCONDUCT
Disorderly Conduct Attempt	E	9A.84.030	DISCONDUCT
Disorderly Conduct Conspiracy	E	9A.84.030	DISCONDUCT
Disorderly Conduct Solicitation	E	9A.84.030	DISCONDUCT
Disturbing School, School Activities Or Meetings	E	28A.635.030	DISTRBSCHL
Drive By Shooting	B+	9A.36.045	DBSHOOTING
Drive By Shooting Attempt	C+	9A.36.045	DBSHOOTING
Drive By Shooting Conspiracy	C+	9A.36.045	DBSHOOTING
Drive By Shooting Solicitation	C+	9A.36.045	DBSHOOTING
Driving Under Influence	D	46.61.502	DUI
Driving Under Influence Attempt	E	46.61.502	DUI
Driving Under Influence Conspiracy	E	46.61.502	DUI
Driving Under Influence Solicitation	E	46.61.502	DUI
Driving While License Invalidated	D	46.20.342	DWIL
Driving While License Invalidated 2	D	46.20.342	DWIL2
Driving While License Invalidated 3	E	46.20.342	DWIL3
Driving Without A License	E	46.20.005	DWOL
Drug Paraphernalia	E	69.50.412	DRUGPARA
Elude A Police Vehicle	C	46.61.024	ELUDEPV
Elude A Police Vehicle Attempt	D	46.61.024	ELUDEPV
Elude A Police Vehicle Conspiracy	D	46.61.024	ELUDEPV
Elude A Police Vehicle Solicitation	D	46.61.024	ELUDEPV
Escape 1	C	9A.76.110	ESCAPE1
Escape 1 Attempt	C	9A.76.110	ESCAPE1
Escape 1 Conspiracy	C	9A.76.110	ESCAPE1
Escape 1 Solicitation	C	9A.76.110	ESCAPE1
Escape 2	C	9A.76.120	ESCAPE2
Escape 2 Attempt	C	9A.76.120	ESCAPE2
Escape 2 Conspiracy	C	9A.76.120	ESCAPE2
Escape 2 Solicitation	C	9A.76.120	ESCAPE2
Escape 3	D	9A.76.130	ESCAPE3
Escape 3 Attempt	E	9A.76.130	ESCAPE3
Escape 3 Conspiracy	E	9A.76.130	ESCAPE3

The Caseload Forecast Council is not liable for errors or omissions in the manual, for sentences that may be inappropriately calculated as a result of a practitioner's or court's reliance on the manual, or for any other written or verbal information related to adult or juvenile sentencing. The scoring sheets are intended to provide assistance in most cases but does not cover all permutations of the scoring rules. If you find any errors or omissions, we encourage you to report them to the Caseload Forecast Council.

APPENDICE B – JRA OFFENSE CODES BY OFFENSE TITLE

OFFENSE TITLE	CATEGORY	RCW	JRA CODE
Escape 3 Solicitation	E	9A.76.130	ESCAPE3
Extortion 1 Attempt	C+	9A.56.120	EXTORTION1
Extortion 1 Conspiracy	C+	9A.56.120	EXTORTION1
Extortion 1 Solicitation	C+	9A.56.120	EXTORTION1
Extortion 2	C+	9A.56.130	EXTORTION2
Extortion 2 Attempt	D+	9A.56.130	EXTORTION2
Extortion 2 Conspiracy	D+	9A.56.130	EXTORTION2
Extortion 2 Solicitation	D+	9A.56.130	EXTORTION2
Extortion1	B+	9A.56.120	EXTORTION1
Fail To Register As A Kidnapper	C	9A.44.132	FAILREGK
Fail To Register As A Kidnapper Attempt	D	9A.44.132	FAILREGK
Fail To Register As A Kidnapper Conspiracy	D	9A.44.132	FAILREGK
Fail To Register As A Kidnapper Solicitation	D	9A.44.132	FAILREGK
Fail To Register As A Sex Offender	C	9A.44.130	FAILREGS
Fail To Register As A Sex Offender Attempt	D	9A.44.130	FAILREGS
Fail To Register As A Sex Offender Conspiracy	D	9A.44.130	FAILREGS
Fail To Register As A Sex Offender Solicitation	D	9A.44.130	FAILREGS
Failure To Disperse	E	9A.56.130	FAILDISP
False Reporting	D	9A.84.040	FALSEREP
False Reporting Attempt	E	9A.84.040	FALSEREP
False Reporting Conspiracy	E	9A.84.040	FALSEREP
False Reporting Solicitation	E	9A.84.040	FALSEREP
Forgery	C	9A.60.020	FORGERY
Forgery Attempt	D	9A.60.020	FORGERY
Forgery Conspiracy	D	9A.60.020	FORGERY
Forgery Solicitation	D	9A.60.020	FORGERY
Fraudulently Obtaining Controlled Substance	C	96.50.403	FRAUDOBTCS
Game, Traffic, Tobacco And Other Violations	V	9972	VIOLATION
Harassment - 1st Time	D	9A.46.020	HARASS
Harassment - 1st Time Attempt	E	9A.46.020	HARASS
Harassment - 1st Time Conspiracy	E	9A.46.020	HARASS
Harassment - 1st Time Solicitation	E	9A.46.020	HARASS
Harassment - 1st Time With Threat To Kill	C	9A.46.020	HARASSTHRT
Harassment - Because Of Race, Color, Religion, Ancestry, National Origin, Gender, Sexual Orientation, Mental, Physical, Or Sensory Handicap	C	9A.36.080	HARASSMAL

The Caseload Forecast Council is not liable for errors or omissions in the manual, for sentences that may be inappropriately calculated as a result of a practitioner's or court's reliance on the manual, or for any other written or verbal information related to adult or juvenile sentencing. The scoring sheets are intended to provide assistance in most cases but does not cover all permutations of the scoring rules. If you find any errors or omissions, we encourage you to report them to the Caseload Forecast Council.

APPENDICE B – JRA OFFENSE CODES BY OFFENSE TITLE

OFFENSE TITLE	CATEGORY	RCW	JRA CODE
Harassment - Because Of Race, Color, Religion, Ancestry, National Origin, Gender, Sexual Orientation, Mental, Physical, Or Sensory Handicap - Conspiracy	D	9A.36.080	HARASSMAL
Harassment - Because Of Race, Color, Religion, Ancestry, National Origin, Gender, Sexual Orientation, Mental, Physical, Or Sensory Handicap - Solicitation	D	9A.36.080	HARASSMAL
Harassment - Because Of Race, Color, Religion, Ancestry, National Origin, Gender, Sexual Orientation, Mental, Physical, Or Sensory Handicap -Attempt	D	9A.36.080	HARASSMAL
Harassment (Repeat)	C	9A.46.020	HARASSREP
Harassment (Repeat) Attempt	D	9A.46.020	HARASSREP
Harassment (Repeat) Conspiracy	D	9A.46.020	HARASSREP
Harassment (Repeat) Solicitation	D	9A.46.020	HARASSREP
Hit and Run Attended	D	46.52.022	HITRUNAT
Hit and Run Attended Attempt	E	46.52.022	HITRUNAT
Hit and Run Attended Conspiracy	E	46.52.022	HITRUNAT
Hit and Run Attended Solicitation	E	46.52.022	HITRUNAT
Hit and Run Death	D	46.52.022	HITRUNDE
Hit and Run Death Attempt	E	46.52.022	HITRUNDE
Hit and Run Death Conspiracy	E	46.52.022	HITRUNDE
Hit and Run Death Solicitation	E	46.52.022	HITRUNDE
Hit and Run Injury	C	46.52.021	HITRUNIN
Hit and Run Injury Attempt	D	46.52.021	HITRUNIN
Hit and Run Injury Conspiracy	D	46.52.021	HITRUNIN
Hit and Run Injury Solicitation	D	46.52.021	HITRUNIN
Hit and Run Unattended	E	46.52.010	HITRUNUN
Homicide By Watercraft, By Disregard For The Safety Of Others	A	79A.60.050	HOMICIDEWD
Homicide By Watercraft, By Disregard For The Safety Of Others Attempt	B	79A.60.050	HOMICIDEWD
Homicide By Watercraft, By Disregard For The Safety Of Others Conspiracy	B	79A.60.050	HOMICIDEWD
Homicide By Watercraft, By Disregard For The Safety Of Others Solicitation	B	79A.60.050	HOMICIDEWD
Homicide By Watercraft, Operating Any Vessel In A Reckless Manner	A	79A.60.050	HOMICIDEWR
Homicide By Watercraft, Operating Any Vessel In A Reckless Manner Attempt	B	79A.60.050	HOMICIDEWR
Homicide By Watercraft, Operating Any Vessel In A Reckless Manner Conspiracy	B	79A.60.050	HOMICIDEWR

The Caseload Forecast Council is not liable for errors or omissions in the manual, for sentences that may be inappropriately calculated as a result of a practitioner's or court's reliance on the manual, or for any other written or verbal information related to adult or juvenile sentencing. The scoring sheets are intended to provide assistance in most cases but does not cover all permutations of the scoring rules. If you find any errors or omissions, we encourage you to report them to the Caseload Forecast Council.

APPENDICE B – JRA OFFENSE CODES BY OFFENSE TITLE

OFFENSE TITLE	CATEGORY	RCW	JRA CODE
Homicide By Watercraft, Operating Any Vessel In A Reckless Manner Solicitation	B	79A.60.050	HOMICIDEWR
Homicide By Watercraft, While Under The Influence Of Intoxicating Liquor Or Any Drug	A	79A.60.050	HOMICIDEWI
Homicide By Watercraft, While Under The Influence Of Intoxicating Liquor Or Any Drug Attempt	B	79A.60.050	HOMICIDEWI
Homicide By Watercraft, While Under The Influence Of Intoxicating Liquor Or Any Drug Conspiracy	B	79A.60.050	HOMICIDEWI
Homicide By Watercraft, While Under The Influence Of Intoxicating Liquor Or Any Drug Solicitation	B	79A.60.050	HOMICIDEWI
Identity Theft 1	C	9.35.020	IDENTITY1
Identity Theft 1 Attempt	D	9.35.020	IDENTITY1
Identity Theft 1 Conspiracy	D	9.35.020	IDENTITY1
Identity Theft 1 Solicitation	D	9.35.020	IDENTITY1
Identity Theft 2	D	9.35.020	IDENTITY2
Identity Theft 2 Attempt	E	9.35.020	IDENTITY2
Identity Theft 2 Conspiracy	E	9.35.020	IDENTITY2
Identity Theft 2 Solicitation	E	9.35.020	IDENTITY2
Incest 1	B	9A.64.020	INCEST1
Incest 1 Attempt	C	9A.64.020	INCEST1
Incest 1 Conspiracy	C	9A.64.020	INCEST1
Incest 1 Solicitation	C	9A.64.020	INCEST1
Incest 2	C	9A.64.020	INCEST2
Incest 2 Attempt	D	9A.64.020	INCEST2
Incest 2 Conspiracy	D	9A.64.020	INCEST2
Incest 2 Solicitation	D	9A.64.020	INCEST2
Indecent Exposure (Victim <14)	D+	9A.88.010	INDEXP
Indecent Exposure (Victim <14) Attempt	E	9A.88.010	INDEXP<14
Indecent Exposure (Victim <14) Conspiracy	E	9A.88.010	INDEXP<14
Indecent Exposure (Victim <14) Repeat	C	9A.88.010	INDEXP<14R
Indecent Exposure (Victim <14) Solicitation	E	9A.88.010	INDEXP<14
Indecent Exposure (Victim 14+)	E	9A.88.010	INDEXP14+
Indecent Exposure (Victim 14+) Repeat	C	9A.88.010	INDEXP14+R
Indecent Liberties With Forcible Compulsion	B+	9A.44.100	INDLIBFC
Indecent Liberties With Forcible Compulsion Attempt	C+	9A.44.100	INDLIBFC
Indecent Liberties With Forcible Compulsion Conspiracy	C+	9A.44.100	INDLIBFC
Indecent Liberties With Forcible Compulsion Solicitation	C+	9A.44.100	INDLIBFC

The Caseload Forecast Council is not liable for errors or omissions in the manual, for sentences that may be inappropriately calculated as a result of a practitioner's or court's reliance on the manual, or for any other written or verbal information related to adult or juvenile sentencing. The scoring sheets are intended to provide assistance in most cases but does not cover all permutations of the scoring rules. If you find any errors or omissions, we encourage you to report them to the Caseload Forecast Council.

APPENDICE B – JRA OFFENSE CODES BY OFFENSE TITLE

OFFENSE TITLE	CATEGORY	RCW	JRA CODE
Indecent Liberties Without Forcible Compulsion	B+	9A.44.100	INDLIB
Indecent Liberties Without Forcible Compulsion Attempt	C+	9A.44.100	INDLIB
Indecent Liberties Without Forcible Compulsion Conspiracy	C+	9A.44.100	INDLIB
Indecent Liberties Without Forcible Compulsion Solicitation	C+	9A.44.100	INDLIBWOC
Interfering With The Reporting Of Domestic Violence	D	9A.36.150	DVREPINTER
Interfering With The Reporting Of Domestic Violence Attempted	E	9A.36.150	DVREPINTER
Interfering With The Reporting Of Domestic Violence Conspiracy	E	9A.36.150	DVREPINTER
Interfering With The Reporting Of Domestic Violence Solicitation	E	9A.36.150	DVREPINTER
Intimidating A Public Servant	B+	9A.76.180	INTPUBSERV
Intimidating A Public Servant Attempt	C+	9A.76.180	INTPUBSERV
Intimidating A Public Servant Conspiracy	C+	9A.76.180	INTPUBSERV
Intimidating A Public Servant Solicitation	C+	9A.76.180	INTPUBSERV
Intimidating Another Person By Use Of A Weapon	D	9.41.270	INTWWEAPON
Intimidating Another Person By Use Of A Weapon Attempt	E	9.41.270	INTWWEAPON
Intimidating Another Person By Use Of A Weapon Conspiracy	E	9.41.270	INTWWEAPON
Intimidating Another Person By Use Of A Weapon Solicitation	E	9.41.270	INTWWEAPON
Intimidating Witness	B+	9A.72.110	INTWITNESS
Intimidating Witness Attempt	C+	9A.72.110	INTWITNESS
Intimidating Witness Conspiracy	C+	9A.72.110	INTWITNESS
Intimidating Witness Solicitation	C+	9A.72.110	INTWITNESS
Introducing Contraband 1	B	9A.76.140	INTCONT1
Introducing Contraband 1 Attempt	C	9A.76.140	INTCONT1
Introducing Contraband 1 Conspiracy	C	9A.76.140	INTCONT1
Introducing Contraband 1 Solicitation	C	9A.76.140	INTCONT1
Introducing Contraband 2	C	9A.76.150	INTCONT2
Introducing Contraband 2 Attempt	D	9A.76.150	INTCONT2
Introducing Contraband 2 Conspiracy	D	9A.76.150	INTCONT2
Introducing Contraband 2 Solicitation	D	9A.76.150	INTCONT2
Introducing Contraband 3	E	9A.76.160	INTCONT3
Kidnap 1	A	9A.40.020	KIDNAP1
Kidnap 1 Attempt	B+	9A.40.020	KIDNAP1
Kidnap 1 Conspiracy	B+	9A.40.020	KIDNAP1
Kidnap 1 Solicitation	B+	9A.40.020	KIDNAP1
Kidnap 2	B+	9A.40.030	KIDNAP2

The Caseload Forecast Council is not liable for errors or omissions in the manual, for sentences that may be inappropriately calculated as a result of a practitioner's or court's reliance on the manual, or for any other written or verbal information related to adult or juvenile sentencing. The scoring sheets are intended to provide assistance in most cases but does not cover all permutations of the scoring rules. If you find any errors or omissions, we encourage you to report them to the Caseload Forecast Council.

APPENDICE B – JRA OFFENSE CODES BY OFFENSE TITLE

OFFENSE TITLE	CATEGORY	RCW	JRA CODE
Kidnap 2 Attempt	C+	9A.40.030	KIDNAP2
Kidnap 2 Conspiracy	C+	9A.40.030	KIDNAP2
Kidnap 2 Solicitation	C+	9A.40.030	KIDNAP2
Legend Drug With Intent To Deliver	C+	69.41.030.	LEGDRUGSAL
Legend Drug With Intent to Deliver Attempt	D+	69.41.030.	LEGDRUGSAL
Legend Drug With Intent to Deliver Conspiracy	D+	69.41.030	LEGDRUGSAL
Legend Drug With Intent to Deliver Solicitation	D+	69.41.030	LEGDRUGSAL
License Required To Manufacture, Purchase, Sell, Use, Possess, Transport, Or Store Explosives	C	70.74.022	EXPLLICREQ
License Required To Manufacture, Purchase, Sell, Use, Possess, Transport, Or Store Explosives Attempted	D	70.74.022	EXPLLICREQ
License Required To Manufacture, Purchase, Sell, Use, Possess, Transport, Or Store Explosives Conspiracy	D	70.74.022	EXPLLICREQ
License Required To Manufacture, Purchase, Sell, Use, Possess, Transport, Or Store Explosives Solicitation	D	70.74.022	EXPLLICREQ
Maintain A Dwelling Or Place For Controlled Substance	C	69.50.402	MDCONTSUB
Making False Or Misleading Statement To A Public Servant Attempted	E	9A.76.175	FALSESTATE
Making False Or Misleading Statement To A Public Servant Conspiracy	E	9A.76.175	FALSESTATE
Making False Or Misleading Statement To A Public Servant Solicitation	E	9A.76.175	FALSESTATE
Making False Or Misleading Statements To A Public Servant	D	9A.76.175	FALSESTATE
Malicious Mischief 1	B	9A.48.070	MALMIS1
Malicious Mischief 1 Attempt	C	9A.48.070	MALMIS1
Malicious Mischief 1 Conspiracy	C	9A.48.070	MALMIS1
Malicious Mischief 1 Solicitation	C	9A.48.070	MALMIS1
Malicious Mischief 2	C	9A.48.080	MALMIS2
Malicious Mischief 2 Attempt	D	9A.48.080	MALMIS2
Malicious Mischief 2 Conspiracy	D	9A.48.080	MALMIS2
Malicious Mischief 2 Solicitation	D	9A.48.080	MALMIS2
Malicious Mischief 3	D	9A.48.090	MALMIS3
Malicious Mischief 3 (<$50 is Class E)	D	9A.48.090	MALMIS3<50
Malicious Mischief 3 Attempt	E	9A.48.090	MALMIS3
Malicious Mischief 3 Conspiracy	E	9A.48.090	MALMIS3
Malicious Mischief 3 Solicitation	E	9A.48.090	MALMIS3
Manslaughter 1	B+	9A.32.060	MANSL1
Manslaughter 1 Attempt	C+	9A.32.060	MANSL1

The Caseload Forecast Council is not liable for errors or omissions in the manual, for sentences that may be inappropriately calculated as a result of a practitioner's or court's reliance on the manual, or for any other written or verbal information related to adult or juvenile sentencing. The scoring sheets are intended to provide assistance in most cases but does not cover all permutations of the scoring rules. If you find any errors or omissions, we encourage you to report them to the Caseload Forecast Council.

APPENDICE B – JRA OFFENSE CODES BY OFFENSE TITLE

OFFENSE TITLE	CATEGORY	RCW	JRA CODE
Manslaughter 1 Conspiracy	C+	9A.32.060	MANSL1
Manslaughter 1 Solicitation	C+	9A.32.060	MANSL1
Manslaughter 2	C+	9A.32.070	MANSL2
Manslaughter 2 Attempt	D+	9A.32.070	MANSL2
Manslaughter 2 Conspiracy	D+	9A.32.070	MANSL2
Manslaughter 2 Solicitation	D+	9A.32.070	MANSL2
Multiple Detention	V	9990000	MULTDET
Murder 1	A+	9A.32.030	MURDER1
Murder 1 Attempt	A	9A.32.030	MURDER1
Murder 1 Conspiracy	A	9A.32.030	MURDER1
Murder 1 Solicitation	A	9A.32.030	MURDER1
Murder 2	A+	9A.32.050	MURDER2
Murder 2 Attempt	B+	9A.32.050	MURDER2
Murder 2 Conspiracy	B+	9A.32.050	MURDER2
Murder 2 Solicitation	B+	9A.32.050	MURDER2
Negligent Homicide-Vehicular	B+	46.61.520	VEHHOMICID
Negligent Homicide-Vehicular Attempt	C+	46.61.520	VEHHOMICID
Negligent Homicide-Vehicular Conspiracy	C+	46.61.520	VEHHOMICID
Negligent Homicide-Vehicular Solicitation	C+	46.61.520	VEHHOMICID
Obscene Phone Calls	E	9.61.230	OBSCENEPC
Obstructing A Public Servant	D	9A.76.020	OBSPUBSERV
Obstructing A Public Servant Attempt	E	9A.76.020	OBSPUBSERV
Obstructing A Public Servant Conspiracy	E	9A.76.020	OBSPUBSERV
Obstructing A Public Servant Solicitation	E	9A.76.020	OBSPUBSERV
Obstructing Law Enforcement Officer	D	9A.76.020	OBSLAWOFF
Obstructing Law Enforcement Officer Attempt	E	9A.76.020	OBSLAWOFF
Obstructing Law Enforcement Officer Conspiracy	E	9A.76.020	OBSLAWOFF
Obstructing Law Enforcement Officer Solicitation	E	9A.76.020	OBSLAWOFF
Obtain Legend Drug	C	69.41.030	OBTLEGDRUG
Obtain Legend Drug Attempt	D	69.41.030	OBTLEGDRUG
Obtain Legend Drug Conspiracy	D	69.41.030	OBTLEGDRUG
Obtain Legend Drug Solicitation	D	69.41.030	OBTLEGDRUG
Offering And Agreeing (Prostitution)	E	9A.32.050	O&APROST
Organized Retail Theft 2	C	9A.56.350	THEFT2ORG
Other A Offense	A	13.40.030	OTHERAOFF

The Caseload Forecast Council is not liable for errors or omissions in the manual, for sentences that may be inappropriately calculated as a result of a practitioner's or court's reliance on the manual, or for any other written or verbal information related to adult or juvenile sentencing. The scoring sheets are intended to provide assistance in most cases but does not cover all permutations of the scoring rules. If you find any errors or omissions, we encourage you to report them to the Caseload Forecast Council.

APPENDICE B – JRA OFFENSE CODES BY OFFENSE TITLE

OFFENSE TITLE	CATEGORY	RCW	JRA CODE
Other A Offense Attempt	B+	13.40.030	OTHERAOFF
Other A Offense Conspiracy	B+	13.40.030	OTHERAOFF
Other A Offense Solicitation	B+	13.40.030	OTHERAOFF
Other B Offense	B	13.40.030	OTHERBOFF
Other B Offense Attempt	C	13.40.030	OTHERBOFF
Other B Offense Conspiracy	C	13.40.030	OTHERBOFF
Other B Offense Solicitation	C	13.40.030	OTHERBOFF
Other B+ Offense	B+	9A.20.010	OTHERB+OFF
Other B+ Offense Attempt	C+	9A.20.010	OTHERB+OFF
Other B+ Offense Conspiracy	C+	9A.20.010	OTHERB+OFF
Other B+ Offense Solicitation	C+	9A.20.010	OTHERB+OFF
Other C Offense	C	9A.20.010	OTHERCOFF
Other C Offense Attempt	D	9A.20.010	OTHERCOFF
Other C Offense Conspiracy	D	9A.20.010	OTHERCOFF
Other C Offense Solicitation	D	9A.20.010	OTHERCOFF
Other C+ Offense	C+	9A.20.010	OTHERC+OFF
Other C+ Offense Attempt	D+	9A.20.010	OTHERC+OFF
Other C+ Offense Conspiracy	D+	9A.20.010	OTHERC+OFF
Other C+ Offense Solicitation	D+	9A.20.010	OTHERC+OFF
Other D+ Offense	D+	13.40.030	OTHERD+OFF
Other D+ Offense Attempt	E	13.40.030	OTHERD+OFF
Other D+ Offense Conspiracy	E	13.40.030	OTHERD+OFF
Other D+ Offense Solicitation	E	13.40.030	OTHERD+OFF
Other Offense Equivalent To Adult Gross Misdemeanor	D	13.40.030	OTHERDOFF
Other Offense Equivalent To Adult Gross Misdemeanor Attempt	E	13.40.030	OTHERDOFF
Other Offense Equivalent To Adult Gross Misdemeanor Conspiracy	E	13.40.030	OTHERDOFF
Other Offense Equivalent To Adult Gross Misdemeanor Solicitation	E	13.40.030	OTHERDOFF
Other Offense Equivalent To Adult Misdemeanor	E	13.40.030	OTHEREOFF
Patronizing A Prostitute	E	9A.88.110	PATPROSTI
Patronizing A Prostitute Attempted	E	9A.88.110	PATPROSTI
Patronizing A Prostitute Conspiracy	E	9A.88.110	PATPROSTI
Patronizing A Prostitute Solicitation	E	9A.88.110	PATPROSTI
Possession Of A Firearm 1	B	9.41.040(1)(a)	PFIREARM1
Possession Of A Firearm 1 Attempt	C	9.41.040(1)(a)	PFIREARM1

The Caseload Forecast Council is not liable for errors or omissions in the manual, for sentences that may be inappropriately calculated as a result of a practitioner's or court's reliance on the manual, or for any other written or verbal information related to adult or juvenile sentencing. The scoring sheets are intended to provide assistance in most cases but does not cover all permutations of the scoring rules. If you find any errors or omissions, we encourage you to report them to the Caseload Forecast Council.

APPENDICE B – JRA OFFENSE CODES BY OFFENSE TITLE

OFFENSE TITLE	CATEGORY	RCW	JRA CODE
Possession Of A Firearm 1 Conspiracy	C	9.41.040(1)(a)	PFIREARM1
Possession Of A Firearm 1 Solicitation	C	9.41.040(1)(a)	PFIREARM1
Possession Of A Firearm 2	C	9.41.040(1)(b)	PFIREARM2
Possession Of A Firearm 2 Attempt	D	9.41.040(1)(b)	PFIREARM2
Possession Of A Firearm 2 Conspiracy	D	9.41.040(1)(b)	PFIREARM2
Possession Of A Firearm 2 Solicitation	D	9.41.040(1)(b)	PFIREARM2
Possession Of A Firearm By Minor (<18 Years)	C	9.41.040	PFIREARMM
Possession Of A Firearm By Minor (<18 Years) Attempt	D	9.41.040	PFIREARMM
Possession Of A Firearm By Minor (<18 Years) Conspiracy	D	9.41.040	PFIREARMM
Possession Of A Firearm By Minor (<18 Years) Solicitation	D	9.41.040	PFIREARMM
Possession Of A Stolen Vehicle	B	9A.56.068	POSSTOLVEH
Possession Of A Stolen Vehicle Attempted	C	9A.56.068	POSSTOLVEH
Possession Of A Stolen Vehicle Attempted Conspiracy	C	9A.56.068	POSSTOLVEH
Possession Of A Stolen Vehicle Solicitation	C	9A.56.068	POSSTOLVEH
Possession Of Controlled Substance	C	69.50.401(d)	POSCONTSUB
Possession Of Dangerous Weapon	D+	9.41.250	POSDANGW
Possession Of Dangerous Weapon At School	D	9.41.280	POSDANGWAS
Possession Of Dangerous Weapon At School Attempt	E	9.41.280	POSDANGWAS
Possession Of Dangerous Weapon At School Conspiracy	E	9.41.280	POSDANGWAS
Possession Of Dangerous Weapon At School Solicitation	E	9.41.280	POSDANGWAS
Possession Of Dangerous Weapon Attempt	E	9.41.250	POSDANGW
Possession Of Dangerous Weapon Conspiracy	E	9.41.250	POSDANGW
Possession Of Dangerous Weapon Solicitation	E	9.41.250	POSDANGW
Possession Of Depictions Of Minor Engaged In Sexually Explicit Conduct	C	9.68A.070	POSCHPORN2
Possession Of Depictions Of Minor Engaged In Sexually Explicit Conduct 1	B	9.68A.070	POSCHPORN1
Possession Of Depictions Of Minor Engaged In Sexually Explicit Conduct 1 Attempt	C	9.68A.070	POSCHPORN1
Possession Of Depictions Of Minor Engaged In Sexually Explicit Conduct 1 Conspiracy	C	9.68A.070	POSCHPORN1
Possession Of Depictions Of Minor Engaged In Sexually Explicit Conduct 1 Solicitation	C	9.68A.070	POSCHPORN1
Possession Of Depictions Of Minor Engaged In Sexually Explicit Conduct Attempt	D	9.68A.070	POSCHPORN2
Possession Of Depictions Of Minor Engaged In Sexually Explicit Conduct Conspiracy	D	9.68A.070	POSCHPORN2

The Caseload Forecast Council is not liable for errors or omissions in the manual, for sentences that may be inappropriately calculated as a result of a practitioner's or court's reliance on the manual, or for any other written or verbal information related to adult or juvenile sentencing. The scoring sheets are intended to provide assistance in most cases but does not cover all permutations of the scoring rules. If you find any errors or omissions, we encourage you to report them to the Caseload Forecast Council.

APPENDICE B – JRA OFFENSE CODES BY OFFENSE TITLE

OFFENSE TITLE	CATEGORY	RCW	JRA CODE
Possession Of Depictions Of Minor Engaged In Sexually Explicit Conduct Solicitation	D	9.68A.070	POSCHPORN2
Possession Of Explosive Devices	A	70.74.180	POSEXPDEV
Possession Of Explosive Devices Attempt	B+	70.74.180	POSEXPDEV
Possession Of Explosive Devices Conspiracy	B+	70.74.180	POSEXPDEV
Possession Of Explosive Devices Solicitation	B+	70.74.180	POSEXPDEV
Possession Of Illegal Fireworks	E	70.77.255	POSILLFWKS
Possession Of Incendiary Conspiracy	B+	9.40.120	POSINCEND
Possession Of Incendiary Device	A	9.40.120	POSINCEND
Possession Of Incendiary Device Attempt	B+	940120	POSINCEND
Possession Of Incendiary Solicitation	B+	9.40.120	POSINCEND
Possession Of Legend Drug	E	69.41.030	POSLEGDRUG
Possession Of Machine Gun Or Short-Barreled Shotgun Or Rifle	C	9.41.190	POSMACHGUN
Possession Of Machine Gun Or Short-Barreled Shotgun Or Rifle Attempt	D	9.41.190	POSMACHGUN
Possession Of Machine Gun Or Short-Barreled Shotgun Or Rifle Conspiracy	D	9.41.190	POSMACHGUN
Possession Of Machine Gun Or Short-Barreled Shotgun Or Rifle Solicitation	D	9.41.190	POSMACHGUN
Possession Of Marijuana <40 Grams	E	69.50.401	POSPOT<40
Possession Of Stolen Firearm	B	9.41.040	PSFIREARM
Possession Of Stolen Firearm Attempt	C	9.41.040	PSFIREARM
Possession Of Stolen Firearm Conspiracy	C	9.41.040	PSFIREARM
Possession Of Stolen Firearm Solicitation	C	9.41.040	PSFIREARM
Possession Of Stolen Property 1	B	9A.56.150	PSP1
Possession Of Stolen Property 1 Attempt	C	9A.56.150	PSP1
Possession Of Stolen Property 1 Conspiracy	C	9A.56.150	PSP1
Possession Of Stolen Property 1 Solicitation	C	9A.56.150	PSP1
Possession Of Stolen Property 2	C	9A.56.160	PSP2
Possession Of Stolen Property 2 Attempt	D	9A.56.160	PSP2
Possession Of Stolen Property 2 Conspiracy	D	9A.56.160	PSP2
Possession Of Stolen Property 2 Solicitation	D	9A.56.160	PSP2
Possession Of Stolen Property 3	D	9A.56.170	PSP3
Possession Of Stolen Property 3 Attempt	E	9A.56.170	PSP3
Possession Of Stolen Property 3 Conspiracy	E	9A.56.170	PSP3
Possession Of Stolen Property 3 Solicitation	E	9A.56.170	PSP3
Possession Of Weapons By Prisoner County Facility	C	9.94.040	POSWEAPONC

The Caseload Forecast Council is not liable for errors or omissions in the manual, for sentences that may be inappropriately calculated as a result of a practitioner's or court's reliance on the manual, or for any other written or verbal information related to adult or juvenile sentencing. The scoring sheets are intended to provide assistance in most cases but does not cover all permutations of the scoring rules. If you find any errors or omissions, we encourage you to report them to the Caseload Forecast Council.

APPENDICE B – JRA OFFENSE CODES BY OFFENSE TITLE

OFFENSE TITLE	CATEGORY	RCW	JRA CODE
Possession Of Weapons By Prisoner County Facility Attempted	D	9.94.040	POSWEAPON
Possession Of Weapons By Prisoner County Facility Conspiracy	D	9.94.040	POSWEAPON
Possession Of Weapons By Prisoner County Facility Solicitation	D	9.94.040	POSWEAPON
Possession Of Weapons By Prisoner State Facility	B	9.94.040	POSWEAPONB
Possession Of Weapons By Prisoner State Facility Attempted	C	9.94.040	POSWEAPONS
Possession Of Weapons By Prisoner State Facility Conspiracy	C	9.94.040	POSWEAPONS
Possession Of Weapons By Prisoner State Facility Solicitation	C	9.94.040	POSWEAPONS
Possession/Consumption Of Alcohol	E	66.44.270	POSOFALCOH
Promote Suicide	C+	9A.36.060	PROSUICIDE
Promote Suicide Attempt	D+	9A.36.060	PROSUICIDE
Promote Suicide Conspiracy	D+	9A.36.060	PROSUICIDE
Promote Suicide Solicitation	D+	9A.36.060	PROSUICIDE
Promoting Commercial Sexual Abuse Of A Minor	A	9.68A.101	PRSEXABSMI
Promoting Commercial Sexual Abuse Of A Minor Attempted	B	9.68A.101	PRSEXABSMI
Promoting Commercial Sexual Abuse Of A Minor Conspiracy	B	9.68A.101	PRSEXABSMI
Promoting Commercial Sexual Abuse Of A Minor Solicitation	B	9.68A.101	PRSEXABSMI
Promoting Prostitution 1	B+	9A.88.070	PROPROST1
Promoting Prostitution 1 Attempt	C+	9A.88.070	PROPROST1
Promoting Prostitution 1 Conspiracy	C+	9A.88.070	PROPROST1
Promoting Prostitution 1 Solicitation	C+	9A.88.070	PROPROST1
Promoting Prostitution 2	C+	9A.88.080	PROPROST2
Promoting Prostitution 2 Attempt	D+	9A.88.080	PROPROST2
Promoting Prostitution 2 Conspiracy	D+	9A.88.080	PROPROST2
Promoting Prostitution 2 Solicitation	D+	9A.88.080	PROPROST2
Rape 1	A	9A.44.040	RAPE1
Rape 1 Attempt	B+	9A.44.040	RAPE1
Rape 1 Conspiracy	B+	9A.44.040	RAPE1
Rape 1 Solicitation	B+	9A.44.040	RAPE1
Rape 2	A-	9A.44.050	RAPE2
Rape 2 Attempt	B+	9A.44.050	RAPE2
Rape 2 Conspiracy	B+	9A.44.050	RAPE2
Rape 2 Solicitation	B+	9A.44.050	RAPE2
Rape 3	C+	9A.44.060	RAPE3
Rape 3 Attempt	D+	9A.44.060	RAPE3

The Caseload Forecast Council is not liable for errors or omissions in the manual, for sentences that may be inappropriately calculated as a result of a practitioner's or court's reliance on the manual, or for any other written or verbal information related to adult or juvenile sentencing. The scoring sheets are intended to provide assistance in most cases but does not cover all permutations of the scoring rules. If you find any errors or omissions, we encourage you to report them to the Caseload Forecast Council.

APPENDICE B – JRA OFFENSE CODES BY OFFENSE TITLE

OFFENSE TITLE	CATEGORY	RCW	JRA CODE
Rape 3 Conspiracy	D+	9A.44.060	RAPE3
Rape 3 Solicitation	D+	9A.44.060	RAPE3
Rape Of A Child 1	A-	9A.44.073	RAPECHILD1
Rape Of A Child 1 Attempt	B+	9A.44.073	RAPECHILD1
Rape Of A Child 1 Conspiracy	B+	9A.44.073	RAPECHILD1
Rape Of A Child 1 Solicitation	B+	9A.44.073	RAPECHILD1
Rape Of A Child 2	B+	9A.44.076	RAPECHILD2
Rape Of A Child 2 Attempt	C+	9A.44.076	RAPECHILD2
Rape Of A Child 2 Conspiracy	C+	9A.44.076	RAPECHILD2
Rape Of A Child 2 Solicitation	C+	9A.44.076	RAPECHILC2
Rape Of A Child 3	C	9A.44.079	RAPECHILD3
Rape Of A Child 3 Attempt	D	9A.44.079	RAPECHILD3
Rape Of A Child 3 Conspiracy	D	9A.44.079	RAPECHILD3
Rape Of A Child 3 Solicitation	D	9A.44.079	RAPECHILD3
Reckless Burning 1	C	9A.48.040	RECKBURN1
Reckless Burning 1 Attempt	D	9A.48.040	RECKBURN1
Reckless Burning 1 Conspiracy	D	9A.48.040	RECKBURN1
Reckless Burning 1 Solicitation	D	9A.48.040	RECKBURN1
Reckless Burning 2	D	9A.48.050	RECKBURN2
Reckless Burning 2 Attempt	E	9A.48.050	RECKBURN2
Reckless Burning 2 Conspiracy	E	9A.48.050	RECKBURN2
Reckless Burning 2 Solicitation	E	9A.48.050	RECKBURN2
Reckless Driving	E	46.61.500	RECKDRIV
Reckless Endangerment	D+	9A.36.050	RECKEND
Reckless Endangerment 1	B	9A.36.050	RECKEND1
Reckless Endangerment 1 Attempt	C	9A.36.050	RECKEND1
Reckless Endangerment 2	D+	9A.36.050	RECKEND2
Reckless Endangerment 2 Attempt	E	9A.36.050	RECKEND2
Reckless Endangerment Attempt	E	9A.36.050	RECKEND
Reckless Endangerment Conspiracy	E	9A.36.050	RECKEND
Reckless Endangerment Solicitation	E	9A.36.050	RECKEND
Refusing To Leave Public Property	D	28A.635.020	REFLEAVE
Rendering Criminal Assistance 1	C	9A.76.070	RENDCRIM
Rendering Criminal Assistance 1 Attempt	D	9A.76.070	RENDCRIM
Rendering Criminal Assistance 1 Conspiracy	D	9A.76.070	RENDCRIM

The Caseload Forecast Council is not liable for errors or omissions in the manual, for sentences that may be inappropriately calculated as a result of a practitioner's or court's reliance on the manual, or for any other written or verbal information related to adult or juvenile sentencing. The scoring sheets are intended to provide assistance in most cases but does not cover all permutations of the scoring rules. If you find any errors or omissions, we encourage you to report them to the Caseload Forecast Council.

APPENDICE B – JRA OFFENSE CODES BY OFFENSE TITLE

OFFENSE TITLE	CATEGORY	RCW	JRA CODE
Rendering Criminal Assistance 1 Solicitation	D	9A.76.070	RENDCRIM
Residential Burglary	B	9A.52.025	BURGRES
Residential Burglary Attempt	C	9A.52.025	BURGRES
Residential Burglary Conspiracy	C	9A.52.025	BURGRES
Residential Burglary Solicitation	C	9A.52.025	BURGRES
Resisting Arrest	E	9A.76.040	RESARREST
Retail Theft With Extenuating Circumstances 1	B	9A.56.360	THEFT1RET
Retail Theft With Extenuating Circumstances 1 Attempted	C	9A.56.360	THEFT1RET
Retail Theft With Extenuating Circumstances 1 Conspiracy	C	9A.56.360	THEFT1RET
Retail Theft With Extenuating Circumstances 1 Solicitation	C	9A.56.360	THEFT1RET
Retail Theft With Extenuating Circumstances 2	C	9A.56.360	THEFT2RET
Retail Theft With Extenuating Circumstances 2 Attempted	D	9A.56.360	THEFT2RET
Retail Theft With Extenuating Circumstances 2 Conspiracy	D	9A.56.360	THEFT2RET
Retail Theft With Extenuating Circumstances 2 Solicitation	D	9A.56.360	THEFT2RET
Retail Theft With Extenuating Circumstances 3	C	9A.56.360	THEFT3RET
Retail Theft With Extenuating Circumstances 3 Attempted	D	9A.56.360	THEFT3RET
Retail Theft With Extenuating Circumstances 3 Conspiracy	D	9A.56.360	THEFT3RET
Retail Theft With Extenuating Circumstances 3 Solicitation	D	9A.56.360	THEFT3RET
Riot With Weapon	C+	9A.84.010	RIOTWWEAP
Riot With Weapon Attempt	D+	9A.84.010	RIOTWWEAP
Riot With Weapon Conspiracy	D+	9A.84.010	RIOTWWEAP
Riot With Weapon Solicitation	D+	9A.84.010	RIOTWWEAP
Riot Without Weapon	D+	9A.84.010	RIOTWOWEAP
Riot Without Weapon Attempt	E	9A.84.010	RIOTWOWEAP
Riot Without Weapon Conspiracy	E	9A.84.010	RIOTWOWEAP
Riot Without Weapon Solicitation	E	9A.84.010	RIOTWOWEAP
Robbery 1	A	9A.56.200	ROBBERY1
Robbery 1 Accomplice	A	9A.08.020	ROB1ACC
Robbery 1 Attempt	B+	9A.56.200	ROBBERY1
Robbery 1 Conspiracy	B+	9A.56.200	ROBBERY1
Robbery 1 Solicitation	B+	9A.56.200	ROBBERY1
Robbery 2	B+	9A.56.210	ROBBERY2
Robbery 2 Attempt	C+	9A.56.210	ROBBERY2
Robbery 2 Conspiracy	C+	9A.56.210	ROBBERY2
Robbery 2 Solicitation	C+	9A.56.210	ROBBERY2

The Caseload Forecast Council is not liable for errors or omissions in the manual, for sentences that may be inappropriately calculated as a result of a practitioner's or court's reliance on the manual, or for any other written or verbal information related to adult or juvenile sentencing. The scoring sheets are intended to provide assistance in most cases but does not cover all permutations of the scoring rules. If you find any errors or omissions, we encourage you to report them to the Caseload Forecast Council.

APPENDICE B – JRA OFFENSE CODES BY OFFENSE TITLE

OFFENSE TITLE	CATEGORY	RCW	JRA CODE
Sale Of Controlled Substance For Profit	C+	69.50.410	SALECONSUB
Sending, Bringing Into State Depictions Of Minor Engaged In Sexually Explicit Conduct 1	B	9.68A.060	SBCHPORN1
Sending, Bringing Into State Depictions Of Minor Engaged In Sexually Explicit Conduct 1 Attempt	C	9.68A.060	SBCHPORN1
Sending, Bringing Into State Depictions Of Minor Engaged In Sexually Explicit Conduct 1 Conspiracy	C	9.68A.060	SBCHPORN1
Sending, Bringing Into State Depictions Of Minor Engaged In Sexually Explicit Conduct 1 Solicitation	C	9.68A.060	SBCHPORN1
Sending, Bringing Into State Depictions Of Minor Engaged In Sexually Explicit Conduct 2	C	9.68A.060	SBCHPORN2
Sending, Bringing Into State Depictions Of Minor Engaged In Sexually Explicit Conduct 2 Attempt	D	9.68A.060	SBCHPORN2
Sending, Bringing Into State Depictions Of Minor Engaged In Sexually Explicit Conduct 2 Conspiracy	D	9.68A.060	SBCHPORN2
Sending, Bringing Into State Depictions Of Minor Engaged In Sexually Explicit Conduct 2 Solicitation	D	9.68A.060	SBCHPORN2
Sentence Rescinded	X	9975	SENRESCIND
Sentence Reversed And Remanded	X		SENTREVERS
Sex Offender Parole Revoke	V	9A.44.130	SOPARREV
Sexual Exploitation Of Minor	B	9.68A.040	SEXEXPLMNR
Sexual Exploitation Of Minor Attempt	C	9.68A.040	SEXEXPLMNR
Sexual Exploitation Of Minor Conspiracy	C	9.68A.040	SEXEXPLMNR
Sexual Exploitation Of Minor Solicitation	C	9.68A.040	SEXEXPLMNR
Sexual Violation Of Human Remains	C	9A.44.105	SEXVIOLREM
Sexual Violation Of Human Remains Attempt	D	9A.44.105	SEXVIOLREM
Sexual Violation Of Human Remains Conspiracy	D	9A.44.105	SEXVIOLREM
Sexual Violation Of Human Remains Solicitation	D	9A.44.105	SEXVIOLREM
Stalking (1st Time)	D	9A.46.110	STALK
Stalking (1st Time) Attempt	E	9A.46.110	STALK
Stalking (1st Time) Conspiracy	E	9A.46.110	STALK
Stalking (1st Time) Solicitation	E	9A.46.110	STALK
Stalking (Repeat)	C	9A.46.110	STALKREP
Stalking (Repeat) Attempt	D	9A.46.110	STALKREP
Stalking (Repeat) Conspiracy	D	9A.46.110	STALKREP
Stalking (Repeat) Solicitation	D	9A.46.110	STALKREP
Taking Motor Vehicle Without Permission 1	B	9A.56.070	TAMVWOOP1
Taking Motor Vehicle Without Permission 1 Attempt	C	9A.56.070	TAMVWOOP1

The Caseload Forecast Council is not liable for errors or omissions in the manual, for sentences that may be inappropriately calculated as a result of a practitioner's or court's reliance on the manual, or for any other written or verbal information related to adult or juvenile sentencing. The scoring sheets are intended to provide assistance in most cases but does not cover all permutations of the scoring rules. If you find any errors or omissions, we encourage you to report them to the Caseload Forecast Council.

APPENDICE B – JRA OFFENSE CODES BY OFFENSE TITLE

OFFENSE TITLE	CATEGORY	RCW	JRA CODE
Taking Motor Vehicle Without Permission 1 Conspiracy	C	9A.56.070	TAMVWOOP1
Taking Motor Vehicle Without Permission 1 Solicitation	C	9A.56.070	TAMVWOOP1
Taking Motor Vehicle Without Permission 2	C	9A.56.075	TAMVWOOP2
Taking Motor Vehicle Without Permission 2 Attempt	D	9A.56.075	TAMVWOOP2
Taking Motor Vehicle Without Permission 2 Conspiracy	D	9A.56.075	TAMVWOOP2
Taking Motor Vehicle Without Permission 2 Solicitation	D	9A.56.075	TAMVWOOP2
Tampering With A Witness	C	9A.72.120	TAMPWITN
Tampering With A Witness Attempt	D	9A.72.120	TAMPWITN
Tampering With A Witness Conspiracy	D	9A.72.120	TAMPWITN
Tampering With A Witness Solicitation	D	9A.72.120	TAMPWITN
Tampering With Fire Alarm Apparatus	E	9.40.100	TAMPFIREAL
Theft 1	B	9A.56.030	THEFT1
Theft 1 Attempt	C	9A.56.030	THEFT1
Theft 1 Conspiracy	C	9A.56.030	THEFT1
Theft 1 Solicitation	C	9A.56.030	THEFT1
Theft 2	C	9A.56.040	THEFT2
Theft 2 Attempt	D	9A.56.040	THEFT2
Theft 2 Conspiracy	D	9A.56.040	THEFT2
Theft 2 Solicitation	D	9A.56.040	THEFT2
Theft 3	D	9A.56.050	THEFT3
Theft 3 Attempt	E	9A.56.050	THEFT3
Theft 3 Conspiracy	E	9A.56.050	THEFT3
Theft 3 Solicitation	E	9A.56.050	THEFT3
Theft Of A Motor Vehicle	B	9A.56.030	THEFTVEH
Theft Of A Motor Vehicle Attempted	C	9A.56.065	THEFTVEH
Theft Of A Motor Vehicle Conspiracy	C	9A.56.065	THEFTVEH
Theft Of A Motor Vehicle Solicitation	C	9A.56.065	THEFTVEH
Theft Of Firearm	B	9A.56.300	THEFTFIREA
Theft Of Firearm Attempt	C	9A.56.300	THEFTFIREA
Theft Of Firearm Conspiracy	C	9A.56.300	THEFTFIREA
Theft Of Firearm Solicitation	C	9A.56.300	THEFTFIREA
Theft Of Livestock	B	9A.56.080	THEFTLIVES
Theft Of Livestock Attempt	C	9A.56.080	THEFTLIVES
Theft Of Livestock Conspiracy	C	9A.56.080	THEFTLIVES
Theft Of Livestock Solicitation	C	9A.56.080	THEFTLIVES

The Caseload Forecast Council is not liable for errors or omissions in the manual, for sentences that may be inappropriately calculated as a result of a practitioner's or court's reliance on the manual, or for any other written or verbal information related to adult or juvenile sentencing. The scoring sheets are intended to provide assistance in most cases but does not cover all permutations of the scoring rules. If you find any errors or omissions, we encourage you to report them to the Caseload Forecast Council.

APPENDICE B – JRA OFFENSE CODES BY OFFENSE TITLE

OFFENSE TITLE	CATEGORY	RCW	JRA CODE
Theft Of Stolen Firearm	B	9A.56.300	THEFTSTFIR
Theft Of Stolen Firearm Attempt	C	9A.56.300	THEFTSTFIR
Theft Of Stolen Firearm Conspiracy	C	9A.56.300	THEFTSTFIR
Theft Of Stolen Firearm Solicitation	C	9A.56.300	THEFTSTFIR
Trafficking (Human) 2	A	9A.40.100	TRAFFIKNG2
Trafficking (Human) 2 Attempt	B	9A.40.100	TRAFFIKNG2
Trafficking (Human) 2 Conspiracy	B	9A.40.100	TRAFFIKNG2
Trafficking (Human) 2 Solicitation	B	9A.40.100	TRAFFIKNG2
Trafficking In Stolen Property	B	9A.82.050	TRAFSTPROP
Trafficking In Stolen Property 1	B	9A82050	TRAFSTPRO1
Trafficking In Stolen Property 1 Attempt	C	9A82050	TRAFSTPRO1
Trafficking In Stolen Property 1 Conspiracy	C	9A82050	TRAFSTPRO1
Trafficking In Stolen Property 1 Solicitation	C	9A82050	TRAFSTPRO1
Trafficking In Stolen Property 2	C	9A82055	TRAFSTPRO2
Trafficking In Stolen Property 2 Attempt	D	9A82055	TRAFSTPRO2
Trafficking In Stolen Property 2 Conspiracy	D	9A82055	TRAFSTPRO2
Trafficking In Stolen Property 2 Solicitation	D	9A82055	TRAFSTPRO2
Trafficking In Stolen Property Attempt	C	9A.82.050	TRAFSTPROP
Trafficking In Stolen Property Conspiracy	C	9A.82.050	TRAFSTPROP
Trafficking In Stolen Property Solicitation	C	9A.82.050	TRAFSTPROP
Unknown Offense	X	9999998	UNKNOWNOFF
Unlawful Imprisonment	C+	9A.40.040	UNLAWIMPRI
Unlawful Imprisonment Attempt	D+	9A.40.040	UNLAWIMPRI
Unlawful Imprisonment Conspiracy	D+	9A.40.040	UNLAWIMPRI
Unlawful Imprisonment Solicitation	D+	9A.40.040	UNLAWIMPRI
Unlawful Inhalation	E	9.47A.020	UNLAWINHAL
Vehicle Homicide NV	B+	46.61.520	VEHHOMICNV
Vehicle Homicide NV Attempt	C+	46.61.520	VEHHOMICNV
Vehicle Homicide NV Conspiracy	C+	46.61.520	VEHHOMICNV
Vehicle Homicide NV Solicitation	C+	46.61.520	VEHHOMICNV
Vehicle Prowling 1	C	9A.52.095	VEHPROWL1
Vehicle Prowling 1 Attempt	D	9A.52.095	VEHPROWL1
Vehicle Prowling 1 Conspiracy	D	9A.52.095	VEHPROWL1
Vehicle Prowling 1 Solicitation	D	9A.52.095	VEHPROWL1
Vehicle Prowling 2	D	9A.52.100	VEHPROWL2

The Caseload Forecast Council is not liable for errors or omissions in the manual, for sentences that may be inappropriately calculated as a result of a practitioner's or court's reliance on the manual, or for any other written or verbal information related to adult or juvenile sentencing. The scoring sheets are intended to provide assistance in most cases but does not cover all permutations of the scoring rules. If you find any errors or omissions, we encourage you to report them to the Caseload Forecast Council.

APPENDICE B – JRA OFFENSE CODES BY OFFENSE TITLE

OFFENSE TITLE	CATEGORY	RCW	JRA CODE
Vehicle Prowling 2 Attempt	E	9A.52.100	VEHPROWL2
Vehicle Prowling 2 Conspiracy	E	9A.52.100	VEHPROWL2
Vehicle Prowling 2 Solicitation	E	9A.52.100	VEHPROWL2
Vehicular Assault	C	46.61.522	VEHASSAULT
Vehicular Assault Attempt	D	46.61.522	VEHASSAULT
Vehicular Assault Conspiracy	D	46.61.522	VEHASSAULT
Vehicular Assault Solicitation	D	46.61.522	VEHASSAULT
Vehicular Homicide	B+	46.61.520	VEHHOMICID
Vehicular Homicide Attempt	C+	46.61.520	VEHHOMICID
Vehicular Homicide Conspiracy	C+	46.61.520	VEHHOMICID
Vehicular Homicide Not Violent (Must Be On Court Order)	B+	46.61.520	VEHHOMICNV
Vehicular Homicide Not Violent Attempt	C+	46.61.520	VEHHOMICNV
Vehicular Homicide Not Violent Conspiracy	C+	46.61.520	VEHHOMICNV
Vehicular Homicide Not Violent Solicitation	C+	46.61.520	VEHHOMICNV
Vehicular Homicide Solicitation	C+	46.61.520	VEHHOMICID
Violation Of Court Order	V	9980	VIOLCO
Violation Of Sexual Assault Protection Order	V	7.9	VIOLSEXAO
Violation Of SSODA	V	9979	VIOLSSODA
Violation Of Uniform Controlled Substances Act- Narcotic, Methamphetamine Or Flunitrazepam Sale Attempted	B+	69.50.401(a)	SALENARC
Violation Of Uniform Controlled Substances Act- Narcotic, Methamphetamine Or Flunitrazepam Sale Conspiracy	B+	69.50.401(a)	SALENARC
Violation Of Uniform Controlled Substances Act- Narcotic, Methamphetamine Or Flunitrazepam Sale Solicitation	B+	69.50.401(a)	SALENARC
Violation Of Uniform Controlled Substances Act-Narcotic Counterfeit Substance	C	69.50.401	COUNTNNARC
Violation Of Uniform Controlled Substances Act--Narcotic, Methamphetamine Or Flunitrazepam Sale	B+	69.50.401(a)	SALENARC
Violation Of Uniform Controlled Substances Act-Narcotic, Methamphetamine, Or Flunitrazepam Counterfeit Substance	B	69.50.401	COUNTNARC
Violation Of Uniform Controlled Substances Act--Narcotic, Methamphetamine, Or Flunitrazepam Counterfeit Substance	B	69.50.401(c)	COUNTNARC
Violation Of Uniform Controlled Substances Act--Narcotic, Methamphetamine, Or Flunitrazepam Poss With Intent To Deliver	B+	69.50.401(a)	POSS INT D
Violation Of Uniform Controlled Substances Act-Narcotic, Methamphetamine, Or Flunitrazepam Sale	B+	69.50.401	SALENARC
Violation Of Uniform Controlled Substances Act--Nonnarcotic Counterfeit Substance Attempt	D	69.50.401(d)	COUNTNNARC

The Caseload Forecast Council is not liable for errors or omissions in the manual, for sentences that may be inappropriately calculated as a result of a practitioner's or court's reliance on the manual, or for any other written or verbal information related to adult or juvenile sentencing. The scoring sheets are intended to provide assistance in most cases but does not cover all permutations of the scoring rules. If you find any errors or omissions, we encourage you to report them to the Caseload Forecast Council.

2013 Washington State Juvenile Dispositions Guidelines Manual   Rev. 20140301

APPENDICE B – JRA OFFENSE CODES BY OFFENSE TITLE

OFFENSE TITLE	CATEGORY	RCW	JRA CODE
Violation Of Uniform Controlled Substances Act--Nonnarcotic Counterfeit Substance Conspiracy	D	69.50.401(d)	COUNTNNARC
Violation Of Uniform Controlled Substances Act--Nonnarcotic Counterfeit Substance Solicitation	D	69.50.401(d)	COUNTNNARC
Violation Of Uniform Controlled Substances Act-Non-Narcotic Sale	C	69.50.401	SALENNARC
Violation Of Uniform Controlled Substances Act-Possession Of A Controlled Substance	C	69.50.401(f)	POSCONTSUB
Violation Of Uniform Controlled Substances Act-Possession Of A Controlled Substance Attempt	C	69.50.403	POSCONTSUB
Violation Of Uniform Controlled Substances Act-Possession Of A Controlled Substance Conspiracy	C	69.50.403	POSCONTSUB
Violation Of Uniform Controlled Substances Act-Possession Of A Controlled Substance Solicitation	C	69.50.403	POSCONTSUB
Violation Of Uniform Controlled Substances Act-Sale Of Substitute Substance	C	69.50.401(e)	SALESUBSUB
Voyeurism	C	9A.44.155	VOYEURISM
Voyeurism Attempt	D	9A.44.155	VOYEURISM
Voyeurism Conspiracy	D	9A.44.115	VOYEURISM
Voyeurism Solicitation	D	9A.44.115	VOYEURISM
Weapon Without A Permit	E	9.41.050	WEAPONWOP
Weapons Apparently Capable Of Producing Bodily Harm	D	9.41.270	WEAPONCBH
Weapons Apparently Capable Of Producing Bodily Harm Attempted	E	9.41.270	WEAPONCBH
Weapons Apparently Capable Of Producing Bodily Harm Conspiracy	E	9.41.270	WEAPONCBH
Weapons Apparently Capable Of Producing Bodily Harm Solicitation	E	9.41.270	WEAPONCBH

The Caseload Forecast Council is not liable for errors or omissions in the manual, for sentences that may be inappropriately calculated as a result of a practitioner's or court's reliance on the manual, or for any other written or verbal information related to adult or juvenile sentencing. The scoring sheets are intended to provide assistance in most cases but does not cover all permutations of the scoring rules. If you find any errors or omissions, we encourage you to report them to the Caseload Forecast Council.

APPENDIX C

Note: Appendix C provides a list of JRA offenses code as a courtesy. These codes are used by JRA in its client tracking system. New codes are added as needed by JRA.

APPENDIX C: JRA OFFENSE CODES BY OFFENSE CATEGORY

Offense	Level	Statute	Code
LEVEL A+			
Murder 1	A+	9A.32.030	MURDER1
Murder 2	A+	9A.32.050	MURDER2
LEVEL A			
Arson 1	A	9A.48.020	ARSON1
Assault 1	A	9A.36.011	ASSAULT1
Assault 2 With Sexual Motivation	A	9A.36.021	ASSAULT2SM
Assault Of Child 1	A	9A.36.120	ASSAULTCH1
Homicide By Watercraft, By Disregard For The Safety Of Others	A	79A.60.050	HOMICIDEWD
Homicide By Watercraft, Operating Any Vessel In A Reckless Manner	A	79A.60.050	HOMICIDEWR
Homicide By Watercraft, While Under The Influence Of Intoxicating Liquor Or Any Drug	A	79A.60.050	HOMICIDEWI
Kidnap 1	A	9A.40.020	KIDNAP1
Murder 1 Attempt	A	9A.32.030	MURDER1
Murder 1 Conspiracy	A	9A.32.030	MURDER1
Murder 1 Solicitation	A	9A.32.030	MURDER1
Other A Offense	A	13.40.030	OTHERAOFF
Possession Of Explosive Devices	A	70.74.180	POSEXPDEV
Possession Of Incendiary Device	A	9.40.120	POSINCEND
Promoting Commercial Sexual Abuse Of A Minor	A	9.68A.101	PRSEXABSMI
Rape 1	A	9A.44.040	RAPE1
Robbery 1	A	9A.56.200	ROBBERY1
Robbery 1 Accomplice	A	9A.08.020	ROB1ACC
Trafficking (Human) 2	A	9A.40.100	TRAFFIKNG2
LEVEL A-			
Child Molestation 1	A-	9A.44.083	CHILDMOL1
Rape 2	A-	9A.44.050	RAPE2
Rape Of A Child 1	A-	9A.44.073	RAPECHILD1
LEVEL B+			
Arson 1 Attempt	B+	9A.48.020	ARSON1
Arson 1 Conspiracy	B+	9A.48.020	ARSON1
Arson 1 Solicitation	B+	9A.48.020	ARSON1
Assault 1 Attempt	B+	9A.36.011	ASSAULT1
Assault 1 Conspiracy	B+	9A.36.011	ASSAULT1
Assault 1 Solicitation	B+	9A.36.011	ASSAULT1

APPENDICE C – JRA OFFENSE CODES BY OFFENSE CATEGORY

OFFENSE TITLE	CATEGORY	RCW	JRA CODE
Assault 2	B+	9A.36.021	ASSAULT2
Assault 2 Accomplice	B+	9A.36.021	ASSAULT2AC
Assault 2 With Sexual Motivation Attempt	B+	9A.36.021	ASSAULT2SM
Assault 2 With Sexual Motivation Conspiracy	B+	9A.36.021	ASSAULT2SM
Assault 2 With Sexual Motivation Solicitation	B+	9A.36.021	ASSAULT2SM
Burglary 1	B+	9A.52.020	BURG1
Child Molestation 1 Attempt	B+	9A.44.083	CHILDMOL1
Child Molestation 1 Conspiracy	B+	9A.44.083	CHILDMOL1
Child Molestation 1 Solicitation	B+	9A.44.083	CHILDMOL1
Drive By Shooting	B+	9A.36.045	DBSHOOTING
Extortion1	B+	9A.56.120	EXTORTION1
Indecent Liberties With Forcible Compulsion	B+	9A.44.100	INDLIBFC
Indecent Liberties Without Forcible Compulsion	B+	9A.44.100	INDLIB
Intimidating A Public Servant	B+	9A.76.180	INTPUBSERV
Intimidating Witness	B+	9A.72.110	INTWITNESS
Kidnap 1 Attempt	B+	9A.40.020	KIDNAP1
Kidnap 1 Conspiracy	B+	9A.40.020	KIDNAP1
Kidnap 1 Solicitation	B+	9A.40.020	KIDNAP1
Kidnap 2	B+	9A.40.030	KIDNAP2
Manslaughter 1	B+	9A.32.060	MANSL1
Murder 2 Attempt	B+	9A.32.050	MURDER2
Murder 2 Conspiracy	B+	9A.32.050	MURDER2
Murder 2 Solicitation	B+	9A.32.050	MURDER2
Negligent Homicide-Vehicular	B+	46.61.520	VEHHOMICID
Other A Offense Attempt	B+	13.40.030	OTHERAOFF
Other A Offense Conspiracy	B+	13.40.030	OTHERAOFF
Other A Offense Solicitation	B+	13.40.030	OTHERAOFF
Other B+ Offense	B+	9A.20.010	OTHERB+OFF
Possession Of Explosive Devices Attempt	B+	70.74.180	POSEXPDEV
Possession Of Explosive Devices Conspiracy	B+	70.74.180	POSEXPDEV
Possession Of Explosive Devices Solicitation	B+	70.74.180	POSEXPDEV
Possession Of Incendiary Conspiracy	B+	9.40.120	POSINCEND
Possession Of Incendiary Device Attempt	B+	940120	POSINCEND
Possession Of Incendiary Solicitation	B+	9.40.120	POSINCEND
Promoting Prostitution 1	B+	9A.88.070	PROPROST1
Rape 1 Attempt	B+	9A.44.040	RAPE1

The Caseload Forecast Council is not liable for errors or omissions in the manual, for sentences that may be inappropriately calculated as a result of a practitioner's or court's reliance on the manual, or for any other written or verbal information related to adult or juvenile sentencing. The scoring sheets are intended to provide assistance in most cases but does not cover all permutations of the scoring rules. If you find any errors or omissions, we encourage you to report them to the Caseload Forecast Council.

APPENDICE C – JRA OFFENSE CODES BY OFFENSE CATEGORY

OFFENSE TITLE	CATEGORY	RCW	JRA CODE
Rape 1 Conspiracy	B+	9A.44.040	RAPE1
Rape 1 Solicitation	B+	9A.44.040	RAPE1
Rape 2 Attempt	B+	9A.44.050	RAPE2
Rape 2 Conspiracy	B+	9A.44.050	RAPE2
Rape 2 Solicitation	B+	9A.44.050	RAPE2
Rape Of A Child 1 Attempt	B+	9A.44.073	RAPECHILD1
Rape Of A Child 1 Conspiracy	B+	9A.44.073	RAPECHILD1
Rape Of A Child 1 Solicitation	B+	9A.44.073	RAPECHILD1
Rape Of A Child 2	B+	9A.44.076	RAPECHILD2
Robbery 1 Attempt	B+	9A.56.200	ROBBERY1
Robbery 1 Conspiracy	B+	9A.56.200	ROBBERY1
Robbery 1 Solicitation	B+	9A.56.200	ROBBERY1
Robbery 2	B+	9A.56.210	ROBBERY2
Vehicle Homicide NV	B+	46.61.520	VEHHOMICNV
Vehicular Homicide	B+	46.61.520	VEHHOMICID
Vehicular Homicide Not Violent (Must Be On Court Order)	B+	46.61.520	VEHHOMICNV
Violation Of Uniform Controlled Substances Act- Narcotic, Methamphetamine Or Flunitrazepam Sale Attempted	B+	69.50.401(a)	SALENARC
Violation Of Uniform Controlled Substances Act- Narcotic, Methamphetamine Or Flunitrazepam Sale Conspiracy	B+	69.50.401(a)	SALENARC
Violation Of Uniform Controlled Substances Act- Narcotic, Methamphetamine Or Flunitrazepam Sale Solicitation	B+	69.50.401(a)	SALENARC
Violation Of Uniform Controlled Substances Act--Narcotic, Methamphetamine Or Flunitrazepam Sale	B+	69.50.401(a)	SALENARC
Violation Of Uniform Controlled Substances Act--Narcotic, Methamphetamine, Or Flunitrazepam Poss With Intent To Deliver	B+	69.50.401(a)	POSS INT D
Violation Of Uniform Controlled Substances Act-Narcotic, Methamphetamine, Or Flunitrazepam Sale	B+	69.50.401	SALENARC
LEVEL B			
Animal Cruelty 1	B	16.52.205	ANIMCRUEL1
Arson 2	B	9A.48.030	ARSON2
Assault By Watercraft	B	79A.60.060	ASSAULTWC
Assault Of Child 1 Attempt	B	9A.36.120	ASSAULTCH1
Assault Of Child 1 Conspiracy	B	9A.36.120	ASSAULTCH1
Assault Of Child 1 Solicitation	B	9A.36.120	ASSAULTCH1
Assault Of Child 2	B	9A.36.130	ASSAULTCH2
Bomb Threat	B	9.61.160	BOMBTHREAT

The Caseload Forecast Council is not liable for errors or omissions in the manual, for sentences that may be inappropriately calculated as a result of a practitioner's or court's reliance on the manual, or for any other written or verbal information related to adult or juvenile sentencing. The scoring sheets are intended to provide assistance in most cases but does not cover all permutations of the scoring rules. If you find any errors or omissions, we encourage you to report them to the Caseload Forecast Council.

APPENDICE C – JRA OFFENSE CODES BY OFFENSE CATEGORY

OFFENSE TITLE	CATEGORY	RCW	JRA CODE
Burglary 2	B	9A.52.030	BURG2
Child Molestation 2	B	9A.44.086	CHILDMOL2
Commercial Sexual Abuse Of A Minor	B	9.68A.100	SEXABUSEMI
Controlled Substances Homicide	B	69.50.415	HOMICIDECS
Dealing In Depictions Of Minor Engaged In Sexually Explicit Conduct 1	B	9.68A.050	DELCHPORN1
Homicide By Watercraft, By Disregard For The Safety Of Others Attempt	B	79A.60.050	HOMICIDEWD
Homicide By Watercraft, By Disregard For The Safety Of Others Conspiracy	B	79A.60.050	HOMICIDEWD
Homicide By Watercraft, By Disregard For The Safety Of Others Solicitation	B	79A.60.050	HOMICIDEWD
Homicide By Watercraft, Operating Any Vessel In A Reckless Manner Attempt	B	79A.60.050	HOMICIDEWR
Homicide By Watercraft, Operating Any Vessel In A Reckless Manner Conspiracy	B	79A.60.050	HOMICIDEWR
Homicide By Watercraft, Operating Any Vessel In A Reckless Manner Solicitation	B	79A.60.050	HOMICIDEWR
Homicide By Watercraft, While Under The Influence Of Intoxicating Liquor Or Any Drug Attempt	B	79A.60.050	HOMICIDEWI
Homicide By Watercraft, While Under The Influence Of Intoxicating Liquor Or Any Drug Conspiracy	B	79A.60.050	HOMICIDEWI
Homicide By Watercraft, While Under The Influence Of Intoxicating Liquor Or Any Drug Solicitation	B	79A.60.050	HOMICIDEWI
Incest 1	B	9A.64.020	INCEST1
Introducing Contraband 1	B	9A.76.140	INTCONT1
Malicious Mischief 1	B	9A.48.070	MALMIS1
Other B Offense	B	13.40.030	OTHERBOFF
Possession Of A Firearm 1	B	9.41.040(1)(a)	PFIREARM1
Possession Of A Stolen Vehicle	B	9A.56.068	POSSTOLVEH
Possession Of Depictions Of Minor Engaged In Sexually Explicit Conduct 1	B	9.68A.070	POSCHPORN1
Possession Of Stolen Firearm	B	9.41.040	PSFIREARM
Possession Of Stolen Property 1	B	9A.56.150	PSP1
Possession Of Weapons By Prisoner State Facility	B	9.94.040	POSWEAPONB
Promoting Commercial Sexual Abuse Of A Minor Attempted	B	9.68A.101	PRSEXABSMI
Promoting Commercial Sexual Abuse Of A Minor Conspiracy	B	9.68A.101	PRSEXABSMI
Promoting Commercial Sexual Abuse Of A Minor Solicitation	B	9.68A.101	PRSEXABSMI
Reckless Endangerment 1	B	9A.36.050	RECKEND1
Residential Burglary	B	9A.52.025	BURGRES

The Caseload Forecast Council is not liable for errors or omissions in the manual, for sentences that may be inappropriately calculated as a result of a practitioner's or court's reliance on the manual, or for any other written or verbal information related to adult or juvenile sentencing. The scoring sheets are intended to provide assistance in most cases but does not cover all permutations of the scoring rules. If you find any errors or omissions, we encourage you to report them to the Caseload Forecast Council.

APPENDICE C – JRA OFFENSE CODES BY OFFENSE CATEGORY

OFFENSE TITLE	CATEGORY	RCW	JRA CODE
Retail Theft With Extenuating Circumstances 1	B	9A.56.360	THEFT1RET
Sending, Bringing Into State Depictions Of Minor Engaged In Sexually Explicit Conduct 1	B	9.68A.060	SBCHPORN1
Sexual Exploitation Of Minor	B	9.68A.040	SEXEXPLMNR
Taking Motor Vehicle Without Permission 1	B	9A.56.070	TAMVWOOP1
Theft 1	B	9A.56.030	THEFT1
Theft Of A Motor Vehicle	B	9A.56.030	THEFTVEH
Theft Of Firearm	B	9A.56.300	THEFTFIREA
Theft Of Livestock	B	9A.56.080	THEFTLIVES
Theft Of Stolen Firearm	B	9A.56.300	THEFTSTFIR
Trafficking (Human) 2 Attempt	B	9A.40.100	TRAFFIKNG2
Trafficking (Human) 2 Conspiracy	B	9A.40.100	TRAFFIKNG2
Trafficking (Human) 2 Solicitation	B	9A.40.100	TRAFFIKNG2
Trafficking In Stolen Property	B	9A.82.050	TRAFSTPROP
Trafficking In Stolen Property 1	B	9A82050	TRAFSTPRO1
Violation Of Uniform Controlled Substances Act-Narcotic, Methamphetamine, Or Flunitrazepam Counterfeit Substance	B	69.50.401	COUNTNARC
Violation Of Uniform Controlled Substances Act--Narcotic, Methamphetamine, Or Flunitrazepam Counterfeit Substance	B	69.50.401(c)	COUNTNARC
LEVEL C+			
Assault 2 Accomplice Attempted	C+	9A.36.021	ASSAULT2AC
Assault 2 Accomplice Conspiracy	C+	9A.36.021	ASSAULT2AC
Assault 2 Accomplice Solicitation	C+	9A.36.021	ASSAULT2AC
Assault 2 Attempt	C+	9A.36.021	ASSAULT2
Assault 2 Conspiracy	C+	9A.36.021	ASSAULT2
Assault 2 Solicitation	C+	9A.36.021	ASSAULT2
Assault 3	C+	9A.36.031	ASSAULT3
Burglary 1 Attempt	C+	9A.52.020	BURG1
Burglary 1 Conspiracy	C+	9A.52.020	BURG1
Burglary 1 Solicitation	C+	9A.52.020	BURG1
Child Molestation 2 Attempt (Post 5/11/98)	C+	9A.44.086	CHILDMOL2
Child Molestation 2 Conspiracy	C+	9A.44.086	CHILDMOL2
Child Molestation 2 Solicitation	C+	9A.44.086	CHILDMOL2
Commit Crime With Firearms	C+	94.10.25	CRIMEARMS
Custodial Assault	C+	9A.36.100	CUSASSAULT
Drive By Shooting Attempt	C+	9A.36.045	DBSHOOTING
Drive By Shooting Conspiracy	C+	9A.36.045	DBSHOOTING

The Caseload Forecast Council is not liable for errors or omissions in the manual, for sentences that may be inappropriately calculated as a result of a practitioner's or court's reliance on the manual, or for any other written or verbal information related to adult or juvenile sentencing. The scoring sheets are intended to provide assistance in most cases but does not cover all permutations of the scoring rules. If you find any errors or omissions, we encourage you to report them to the Caseload Forecast Council.

APPENDICE C – JRA OFFENSE CODES BY OFFENSE CATEGORY

OFFENSE TITLE	CATEGORY	RCW	JRA CODE
Drive By Shooting Solicitation	C+	9A.36.045	DBSHOOTING
Extortion 1 Attempt	C+	9A.56.120	EXTORTION1
Extortion 1 Conspiracy	C+	9A.56.120	EXTORTION1
Extortion 1 Solicitation	C+	9A.56.120	EXTORTION1
Extortion 2	C+	9A.56.130	EXTORTION2
Indecent Liberties With Forcible Compulsion Attempt	C+	9A.44.100	INDLIBFC
Indecent Liberties With Forcible Compulsion Conspiracy	C+	9A.44.100	INDLIBFC
Indecent Liberties With Forcible Compulsion Solicitation	C+	9A.44.100	INDLIBFC
Indecent Liberties Without Forcible Compulsion Attempt	C+	9A.44.100	INDLIB
Indecent Liberties Without Forcible Compulsion Conspiracy	C+	9A.44.100	INDLIB
Indecent Liberties Without Forcible Compulsion Solicitation	C+	9A.44.100	INDLIBWOC
Intimidating A Public Servant Attempt	C+	9A.76.180	INTPUBSERV
Intimidating A Public Servant Conspiracy	C+	9A.76.180	INTPUBSERV
Intimidating A Public Servant Solicitation	C+	9A.76.180	INTPUBSERV
Intimidating Witness Attempt	C+	9A.72.110	INTWITNESS
Intimidating Witness Conspiracy	C+	9A.72.110	INTWITNESS
Intimidating Witness Solicitation	C+	9A.72.110	INTWITNESS
Kidnap 2 Attempt	C+	9A.40.030	KIDNAP2
Kidnap 2 Conspiracy	C+	9A.40.030	KIDNAP2
Kidnap 2 Solicitation	C+	9A.40.030	KIDNAP2
Legend Drug With Intent To Deliver	C+	69.41.030.	LEGDRUGSAL
Manslaughter 1 Attempt	C+	9A.32.060	MANSL1
Manslaughter 1 Conspiracy	C+	9A.32.060	MANSL1
Manslaughter 1 Solicitation	C+	9A.32.060	MANSL1
Manslaughter 2	C+	9A.32.070	MANSL2
Negligent Homicide-Vehicular Attempt	C+	46.61.520	VEHHOMICID
Negligent Homicide-Vehicular Conspiracy	C+	46.61.520	VEHHOMICID
Negligent Homicide-Vehicular Solicitation	C+	46.61.520	VEHHOMICID
Other B+ Offense Attempt	C+	9A.20.010	OTHERB+OFF
Other B+ Offense Conspiracy	C+	9A.20.010	OTHERB+OFF
Other B+ Offense Solicitation	C+	9A.20.010	OTHERB+OFF
Other C+ Offense	C+	9A.20.010	OTHERC+OFF
Promote Suicide	C+	9A.36.060	PROSUICIDE
Promoting Prostitution 1 Attempt	C+	9A.88.070	PROPROST1
Promoting Prostitution 1 Conspiracy	C+	9A.88.070	PROPROST1
Promoting Prostitution 1 Solicitation	C+	9A.88.070	PROPROST1

The Caseload Forecast Council is not liable for errors or omissions in the manual, for sentences that may be inappropriately calculated as a result of a practitioner's or court's reliance on the manual, or for any other written or verbal information related to adult or juvenile sentencing. The scoring sheets are intended to provide assistance in most cases but does not cover all permutations of the scoring rules. If you find any errors or omissions, we encourage you to report them to the Caseload Forecast Council.

APPENDICE C – JRA OFFENSE CODES BY OFFENSE CATEGORY

OFFENSE TITLE	CATEGORY	RCW	JRA CODE
Promoting Prostitution 2	C+	9A.88.080	PROPROST2
Rape 3	C+	9A.44.060	RAPE3
Rape Of A Child 2 Attempt	C+	9A.44.076	RAPECHILD2
Rape Of A Child 2 Conspiracy	C+	9A.44.076	RAPECHILD2
Rape Of A Child 2 Solicitation	C+	9A.44.076	RAPECHILC2
Riot With Weapon	C+	9A.84.010	RIOTWWEAP
Robbery 2 Attempt	C+	9A.56.210	ROBBERY2
Robbery 2 Conspiracy	C+	9A.56.210	ROBBERY2
Robbery 2 Solicitation	C+	9A.56.210	ROBBERY2
Sale Of Controlled Substance For Profit	C+	69.50.410	SALECONSUB
Unlawful Imprisonment	C+	9A.40.040	UNLAWIMPRI
Vehicle Homicide NV Attempt	C+	46.61.520	VEHHOMICNV
Vehicle Homicide NV Conspiracy	C+	46.61.520	VEHHOMICNV
Vehicle Homicide NV Solicitation	C+	46.61.520	VEHHOMICNV
Vehicular Homicide Attempt	C+	46.61.520	VEHHOMICID
Vehicular Homicide Conspiracy	C+	46.61.520	VEHHOMICID
Vehicular Homicide Not Violent Attempt	C+	46.61.520	VEHHOMICNV
Vehicular Homicide Not Violent Conspiracy	C+	46.61.520	VEHHOMICNV
Vehicular Homicide Not Violent Solicitation	C+	46.61.520	VEHHOMICNV
Vehicular Homicide Solicitation	C+	46.61.520	VEHHOMICID
LEVEL C			
Alien Possession Of Firearms	C	9.41.171	POSFIRARMA
Arson 2 Attempt	C	9A.48.030	ARSON2
Arson 2 Conspiracy	C	9A.48.030	ARSON2
Arson 2 Solicitation	C	9A.48.030	ARSON2
Assault By Watercraft Attempt	C	79A.60.060	ASSAULTWC
Assault By Watercraft Conspiracy	C	79A.60.060	ASSAULTWC
Assault By Watercraft Solicitation	C	79A.60.060	ASSAULTWC
Assault Of Child 2 Attempt	C	9A.36.130	ASSAULTCH2
Assault Of Child 2 Conspiracy	C	9A.36.130	ASSAULTCH2
Assault Of Child 2 Solicitation	C	9A.36.130	ASSAULTCH2
Attempting To Elude A Police Vehicle	C	46.61.024	ELUDEPV
Bomb Threat Attempt	C	9.61.160	BOMBTHREAT
Bomb Threat Conspiracy	C	9.61.160	BOMBTHREAT
Bomb Threat Solicitation	C	9.61.160	BOMBTHREAT
Burglary 2 Attempt	C	9A.52.030	BURG2

The Caseload Forecast Council is not liable for errors or omissions in the manual, for sentences that may be inappropriately calculated as a result of a practitioner's or court's reliance on the manual, or for any other written or verbal information related to adult or juvenile sentencing. The scoring sheets are intended to provide assistance in most cases but does not cover all permutations of the scoring rules. If you find any errors or omissions, we encourage you to report them to the Caseload Forecast Council.

APPENDICE C – JRA OFFENSE CODES BY OFFENSE CATEGORY

OFFENSE TITLE	CATEGORY	RCW	JRA CODE
Burglary 2 Conspiracy	C	9A.52.030	BURG2
Burglary 2 Solicitation	C	9A.52.030	BURG2
Child Molestation 3	C	9A.44.089	CHILDMOL3
Commercial Sexual Abuse Of A Minor Attempted	C	9.68A.100	SEXABUSEMI
Commercial Sexual Abuse Of A Minor Conspiracy	C	9.68A.100	SEXABUSEMI
Commercial Sexual Abuse Of A Minor Solicitation	C	9.68A.100	SEXABUSEMI
Communicating With A Minor For Immoral Purpose - Subsequent Sex Offense	C	9.68A.090	COMMINORSS
Controlled Substances Homicide Attempt	C	69.50.415	HOMICIDECS
Controlled Substances Homicide Conspiracy	C	69.50.415	HOMICIDECS
Controlled Substances Homicide Solicitation	C	69.50.415	HOMICIDECS
Criminal Impersonation 1	C	9A.60.040	IMPERSON1
Custodial Interference 1	C	9A.40.060	CUSINTER1
Custodial Interference 2 Subsequent	C	9A.40.070	CUSINTER2S
Dealing In Depictions Of Minor Engaged In Sexually Explicit Conduct 1 Attempt	C	9.68A.050	DELCHPORN1
Dealing In Depictions Of Minor Engaged In Sexually Explicit Conduct 1 Conspiracy	C	9.68A.050	DELCHPORN1
Dealing In Depictions Of Minor Engaged In Sexually Explicit Conduct 1 Solicitation	C	9.68A.050	DELCHPORN1
Dealing In Depictions Of Minor Engaged In Sexually Explicit Conduct 2	C	9.68A.050	DELCHPORN2
Elude A Police Vehicle	C	46.61.024	ELUDEPV
Escape 1	C	9A.76.110	ESCAPE1
Escape 1 Attempt	C	9A.76.110	ESCAPE1
Escape 1 Conspiracy	C	9A.76.110	ESCAPE1
Escape 1 Solicitation	C	9A.76.110	ESCAPE1
Escape 2	C	9A.76.120	ESCAPE2
Escape 2 Attempt	C	9A.76.120	ESCAPE2
Escape 2 Conspiracy	C	9A.76.120	ESCAPE2
Escape 2 Solicitation	C	9A.76.120	ESCAPE2
Fail To Register As A Kidnapper	C	9A.44.132	FAILREGK
Fail To Register As A Sex Offender	C	9A.44.130	FAILREGS
Forgery	C	9A.60.020	FORGERY
Fraudulently Obtaining Controlled Substance	C	96.50.403	FRAUDOBTCS
Harassment - 1st Time With Threat To Kill	C	9A.46.020	HARASSTHRT

The Caseload Forecast Council is not liable for errors or omissions in the manual, for sentences that may be inappropriately calculated as a result of a practitioner's or court's reliance on the manual, or for any other written or verbal information related to adult or juvenile sentencing. The scoring sheets are intended to provide assistance in most cases but does not cover all permutations of the scoring rules. If you find any errors or omissions, we encourage you to report them to the Caseload Forecast Council.

APPENDICE C – JRA OFFENSE CODES BY OFFENSE CATEGORY

OFFENSE TITLE	CATEGORY	RCW	JRA CODE
Harassment - Because Of Race, Color, Religion, Ancestry, National Origin, Gender, Sexual Orientation, Mental, Physical, Or Sensory Handicap	C	9A.36.080	HARASSMAL
Harassment (Repeat)	C	9A.46.020	HARASSREP
Hit and Run Injury	C	46.52.021	HITRUNIN
Identity Theft 1	C	9.35.020	IDENTITY1
Incest 1 Attempt	C	9A.64.020	INCEST1
Incest 1 Conspiracy	C	9A.64.020	INCEST1
Incest 1 Solicitation	C	9A.64.020	INCEST1
Incest 2	C	9A.64.020	INCEST2
Indecent Exposure (Victim <14) Repeat	C	9A.88.010	INDEXP<14R
Indecent Exposure (Victim 14+) Repeat	C	9A.88.010	INDEXP14+R
Introducing Contraband 1 Attempt	C	9A.76.140	INTCONT1
Introducing Contraband 1 Conspiracy	C	9A.76.140	INTCONT1
Introducing Contraband 1 Solicitation	C	9A.76.140	INTCONT1
Introducing Contraband 2	C	9A.76.150	INTCONT2
License Required To Manufacture, Purchase, Sell, Use, Possess, Transport, Or Store Explosives	C	70.74.022	EXPLLICREQ
Maintain A Dwelling Or Place For Controlled Substance	C	69.50.402	MDCONTSUB
Malicious Mischief 1 Attempt	C	9A.48.070	MALMIS1
Malicious Mischief 1 Conspiracy	C	9A.48.070	MALMIS1
Malicious Mischief 1 Solicitation	C	9A.48.070	MALMIS1
Malicious Mischief 2	C	9A.48.080	MALMIS2
Obtain Legend Drug	C	69.41.030	OBTLEGDRUG
Organized Retail Theft 2	C	9A.56.350	THEFT2ORG
Other B Offense Attempt	C	13.40.030	OTHERBOFF
Other B Offense Conspiracy	C	13.40.030	OTHERBOFF
Other B Offense Solicitation	C	13.40.030	OTHERBOFF
Other C Offense	C	9A.20.010	OTHERCOFF
Possession Of A Firearm 1 Attempt	C	9.41.040(1)(a)	PFIREARM1
Possession Of A Firearm 1 Conspiracy	C	9.41.040(1)(a)	PFIREARM1
Possession Of A Firearm 1 Solicitation	C	9.41.040(1)(a)	PFIREARM1
Possession Of A Firearm 2	C	9.41.040(1)(b)	PFIREARM2
Possession Of A Firearm By Minor (<18 Years)	C	9.41.040	PFIREARMM
Possession Of A Stolen Vehicle Attempted	C	9A.56.068	POSSTOLVEH
Possession Of A Stolen Vehicle Attempted Conspiracy	C	9A.56.068	POSSTOLVEH
Possession Of A Stolen Vehicle Solicitation	C	9A.56.068	POSSTOLVEH

The Caseload Forecast Council is not liable for errors or omissions in the manual, for sentences that may be inappropriately calculated as a result of a practitioner's or court's reliance on the manual, or for any other written or verbal information related to adult or juvenile sentencing. The scoring sheets are intended to provide assistance in most cases but does not cover all permutations of the scoring rules. If you find any errors or omissions, we encourage you to report them to the Caseload Forecast Council.

APPENDICE C – JRA OFFENSE CODES BY OFFENSE CATEGORY

OFFENSE TITLE	CATEGORY	RCW	JRA CODE
Possession Of Controlled Substance	C	69.50.401(d)	POSCONTSUB
Possession Of Depictions Of Minor Engaged In Sexually Explicit Conduct	C	9.68A.070	POSCHPORN2
Possession Of Depictions Of Minor Engaged In Sexually Explicit Conduct 1 Attempt	C	9.68A.070	POSCHPORN1
Possession Of Depictions Of Minor Engaged In Sexually Explicit Conduct 1 Conspiracy	C	9.68A.070	POSCHPORN1
Possession Of Depictions Of Minor Engaged In Sexually Explicit Conduct 1 Solicitation	C	9.68A.070	POSCHPORN1
Possession Of Machine Gun Or Short-Barreled Shotgun Or Rifle	C	9.41.190	POSMACHGUN
Possession Of Stolen Firearm Attempt	C	9.41.040	PSFIREARM
Possession Of Stolen Firearm Conspiracy	C	9.41.040	PSFIREARM
Possession Of Stolen Firearm Solicitation	C	9.41.040	PSFIREARM
Possession Of Stolen Property 1 Attempt	C	9A.56.150	PSP1
Possession Of Stolen Property 1 Conspiracy	C	9A.56.150	PSP1
Possession Of Stolen Property 1 Solicitation	C	9A.56.150	PSP1
Possession Of Stolen Property 2	C	9A.56.160	PSP2
Possession Of Weapons By Prisoner County Facility	C	9.94.040	POSWEAPONC
Possession Of Weapons By Prisoner State Facility Attempted	C	9.94.040	POSWEAPONS
Possession Of Weapons By Prisoner State Facility Conspiracy	C	9.94.040	POSWEAPONS
Possession Of Weapons By Prisoner State Facility Solicitation	C	9.94.040	POSWEAPONS
Rape Of A Child 3	C	9A.44.079	RAPECHILD3
Reckless Burning 1	C	9A.48.040	RECKBURN1
Reckless Endangerment 1 Attempt	C	9A.36.050	RECKEND1
Rendering Criminal Assistance 1	C	9A.76.070	RENDCRIM
Residential Burglary Attempt	C	9A.52.025	BURGRES
Residential Burglary Conspiracy	C	9A.52.025	BURGRES
Residential Burglary Solicitation	C	9A.52.025	BURGRES
Retail Theft With Extenuating Circumstances 1 Attempted	C	9A.56.360	THEFT1RET
Retail Theft With Extenuating Circumstances 1 Conspiracy	C	9A.56.360	THEFT1RET
Retail Theft With Extenuating Circumstances 1 Solicitation	C	9A.56.360	THEFT1RET
Retail Theft With Extenuating Circumstances 2	C	9A.56.360	THEFT2RET
Retail Theft With Extenuating Circumstances 3	C	9A.56.360	THEFT3RET
Sending, Bringing Into State Depictions Of Minor Engaged In Sexually Explicit Conduct 1 Attempt	C	9.68A.060	SBCHPORN1
Sending, Bringing Into State Depictions Of Minor Engaged In Sexually Explicit Conduct 1 Conspiracy	C	9.68A.060	SBCHPORN1

The Caseload Forecast Council is not liable for errors or omissions in the manual, for sentences that may be inappropriately calculated as a result of a practitioner's or court's reliance on the manual, or for any other written or verbal information related to adult or juvenile sentencing. The scoring sheets are intended to provide assistance in most cases but does not cover all permutations of the scoring rules. If you find any errors or omissions, we encourage you to report them to the Caseload Forecast Council.

APPENDICE C – JRA OFFENSE CODES BY OFFENSE CATEGORY

OFFENSE TITLE	CATEGORY	RCW	JRA CODE
Sending, Bringing Into State Depictions Of Minor Engaged In Sexually Explicit Conduct 1 Solicitation	C	9.68A.060	SBCHPORN1
Sending, Bringing Into State Depictions Of Minor Engaged In Sexually Explicit Conduct 2	C	9.68A.060	SBCHPORN2
Sexual Exploitation Of Minor Attempt	C	9.68A.040	SEXEXPLMNR
Sexual Exploitation Of Minor Conspiracy	C	9.68A.040	SEXEXPLMNR
Sexual Exploitation Of Minor Solicitation	C	9.68A.040	SEXEXPLMNR
Sexual Violation Of Human Remains	C	9A.44.105	SEXVIOLREM
Stalking (Repeat)	C	9A.46.110	STALKREP
Taking Motor Vehicle Without Permission 1 Attempt	C	9A.56.070	TAMVWOOP1
Taking Motor Vehicle Without Permission 1 Conspiracy	C	9A.56.070	TAMVWOOP1
Taking Motor Vehicle Without Permission 1 Solicitation	C	9A.56.070	TAMVWOOP1
Taking Motor Vehicle Without Permission 2	C	9A.56.075	TAMVWOOP2
Tampering With A Witness	C	9A.72.120	TAMPWITN
Theft 1 Attempt	C	9A.56.030	THEFT1
Theft 1 Conspiracy	C	9A.56.030	THEFT1
Theft 1 Solicitation	C	9A.56.030	THEFT1
Theft 2	C	9A.56.040	THEFT2
Theft Of A Motor Vehicle Attempted	C	9A.56.065	THEFTVEH
Theft Of A Motor Vehicle Conspiracy	C	9A.56.065	THEFTVEH
Theft Of A Motor Vehicle Solicitation	C	9A.56.065	THEFTVEH
Theft Of Firearm Attempt	C	9A.56.300	THEFTFIREA
Theft Of Firearm Conspiracy	C	9A.56.300	THEFTFIREA
Theft Of Firearm Solicitation	C	9A.56.300	THEFTFIREA
Theft Of Livestock Attempt	C	9A.56.080	THEFTLIVES
Theft Of Livestock Conspiracy	C	9A.56.080	THEFTLIVES
Theft Of Livestock Solicitation	C	9A.56.080	THEFTLIVES
Theft Of Stolen Firearm Attempt	C	9A.56.300	THEFTSTFIR
Theft Of Stolen Firearm Conspiracy	C	9A.56.300	THEFTSTFIR
Theft Of Stolen Firearm Solicitation	C	9A.56.300	THEFTSTFIR
Trafficking In Stolen Property 1 Attempt	C	9A82050	TRAFSTPRO1
Trafficking In Stolen Property 1 Conspiracy	C	9A82050	TRAFSTPRO1
Trafficking In Stolen Property 1 Solicitation	C	9A82050	TRAFSTPRO1
Trafficking In Stolen Property 2	C	9A82055	TRAFSTPRO2
Trafficking In Stolen Property Attempt	C	9A.82.050	TRAFSTPROP
Trafficking In Stolen Property Conspiracy	C	9A.82.050	TRAFSTPROP
Trafficking In Stolen Property Solicitation	C	9A.82.050	TRAFSTPROP

The Caseload Forecast Council is not liable for errors or omissions in the manual, for sentences that may be inappropriately calculated as a result of a practitioner's or court's reliance on the manual, or for any other written or verbal information related to adult or juvenile sentencing. The scoring sheets are intended to provide assistance in most cases but does not cover all permutations of the scoring rules. If you find any errors or omissions, we encourage you to report them to the Caseload Forecast Council.

APPENDICE C – JRA OFFENSE CODES BY OFFENSE CATEGORY

OFFENSE TITLE	CATEGORY	RCW	JRA CODE
Vehicle Prowling 1	C	9A.52.095	VEHPROWL1
Vehicular Assault	C	46.61.522	VEHASSAULT
Violation Of Uniform Controlled Substances Act-Narcotic Counterfeit Substance	C	69.50.401	COUNTNNARC
Violation Of Uniform Controlled Substances Act-Non-Narcotic Sale	C	69.50.401	SALENNARC
Violation Of Uniform Controlled Substances Act-Possession Of A Controlled Substance	C	69.50.401(f)	POSCONTSUB
Violation Of Uniform Controlled Substances Act-Possession Of A Controlled Substance Attempt	C	69.50.403	POSCONTSUB
Violation Of Uniform Controlled Substances Act-Possession Of A Controlled Substance Conspiracy	C	69.50.403	POSCONTSUB
Violation Of Uniform Controlled Substances Act-Possession Of A Controlled Substance Solicitation	C	69.50.403	POSCONTSUB
Violation Of Uniform Controlled Substances Act-Sale Of Substitute Substance	C	69.50.401(e)	SALESUBSUB
Voyeurism	C	9A.44.155	VOYEURISM
LEVEL D+			
Assault 3 Attempt	D+	9A.36.031	ASSAULT3
Assault 3 Conspiracy	D+	9A.36.031	ASSAULT3
Assault 3 Solicitation	D+	9A.36.031	ASSAULT3
Assault 4	D+	9A.36.041	ASSAULT4
Coercion	D+	9A.36.070	COERCION
Commit Crime With Firearms Attempt	D+	94.10.25	CRIMEARMS
Custodial Assault Attempt	D+	9A.36.100	CUSASSAULT
Custodial Assault Conspiracy	D+	9A.36.100	CUSASSAULT
Custodial Assault Solicitation	D+	9A.36.100	CUSASSAULT
Extortion 2 Attempt	D+	9A.56.130	EXTORTION2
Extortion 2 Conspiracy	D+	9A.56.130	EXTORTION2
Extortion 2 Solicitation	D+	9A.56.130	EXTORTION2
Indecent Exposure (Victim <14)	D+	9A.88.010	INDEXP
Legend Drug With Intent to Deliver Attempt	D+	69.41.030.	LEGDRUGSAL
Legend Drug With Intent to Deliver Conspiracy	D+	69.41.030	LEGDRUGSAL
Legend Drug With Intent to Deliver Solicitation	D+	69.41.030	LEGDRUGSAL
Manslaughter 2 Attempt	D+	9A.32.070	MANSL2
Manslaughter 2 Conspiracy	D+	9A.32.070	MANSL2
Manslaughter 2 Solicitation	D+	9A.32.070	MANSL2
Other C+ Offense Attempt	D+	9A.20.010	OTHERC+OFF

The Caseload Forecast Council is not liable for errors or omissions in the manual, for sentences that may be inappropriately calculated as a result of a practitioner's or court's reliance on the manual, or for any other written or verbal information related to adult or juvenile sentencing. The scoring sheets are intended to provide assistance in most cases but does not cover all permutations of the scoring rules. If you find any errors or omissions, we encourage you to report them to the Caseload Forecast Council.

APPENDICE C – JRA OFFENSE CODES BY OFFENSE CATEGORY

OFFENSE TITLE	CATEGORY	RCW	JRA CODE
Other C+ Offense Conspiracy	D+	9A.20.010	OTHERC+OFF
Other C+ Offense Solicitation	D+	9A.20.010	OTHERC+OFF
Other D+ Offense	D+	13.40.030	OTHERD+OFF
Possession Of Dangerous Weapon	D+	9.41.250	POSDANGW
Promote Suicide Attempt	D+	9A.36.060	PROSUICIDE
Promote Suicide Conspiracy	D+	9A.36.060	PROSUICIDE
Promote Suicide Solicitation	D+	9A.36.060	PROSUICIDE
Promoting Prostitution 2 Attempt	D+	9A.88.080	PROPROST2
Promoting Prostitution 2 Conspiracy	D+	9A.88.080	PROPROST2
Promoting Prostitution 2 Solicitation	D+	9A.88.080	PROPROST2
Rape 3 Attempt	D+	9A.44.060	RAPE3
Rape 3 Conspiracy	D+	9A.44.060	RAPE3
Rape 3 Solicitation	D+	9A.44.060	RAPE3
Reckless Endangerment	D+	9A.36.050	RECKEND
Reckless Endangerment 2	D+	9A.36.050	RECKEND2
Riot With Weapon Attempt	D+	9A.84.010	RIOTWWEAP
Riot With Weapon Conspiracy	D+	9A.84.010	RIOTWWEAP
Riot With Weapon Solicitation	D+	9A.84.010	RIOTWWEAP
Riot Without Weapon	D+	9A.84.010	RIOTWOWEAP
Unlawful Imprisonment Attempt	D+	9A.40.040	UNLAWIMPRI
Unlawful Imprisonment Conspiracy	D+	9A.40.040	UNLAWIMPRI
Unlawful Imprisonment Solicitation	D+	9A.40.040	UNLAWIMPRI
LEVEL D			
Aiming Or Discharging Firearms, Dangerous Weapons	D	9.41.230	DANWEAPAD
Alien Possession Of Firearms Attempted	D	9.41.171	POSFIRARMA
Alien Possession Of Firearms Conspiracy	D	9.41.171	POSFIRARMA
Alien Possession Of Firearms Solicitation	D	9.41.171	POSFIRARMA
Animal Cruelty 1 Attempt	D	16.52.205	ANIMCRUEL1
Animal Cruelty 1 Conspiracy	D	16.52.205	ANIMCRUEL1
Animal Cruelty 1 Solicitation	D	16.52.205	ANIMCRUEL1
Attempting To Elude A Police Vehicle Attempt	D	46.61.024	ELUDEPV
Attempting To Elude A Police Vehicle Conspiracy	D	46.61.024	ELUDEPV
Attempting To Elude A Police Vehicle Solicitation	D	46.61.024	ELUDEPV
Burglary Tools (Possession Of)	D	9A.52.020	BURGTOOLS
Carry Weapon To School	D	9.41.280	CARWEAPSCH
Child Molestation 3 Attempted	D	9A.44.089	CHILDMOL3

The Caseload Forecast Council is not liable for errors or omissions in the manual, for sentences that may be inappropriately calculated as a result of a practitioner's or court's reliance on the manual, or for any other written or verbal information related to adult or juvenile sentencing. The scoring sheets are intended to provide assistance in most cases but does not cover all permutations of the scoring rules. If you find any errors or omissions, we encourage you to report them to the Caseload Forecast Council.

APPENDICE C – JRA OFFENSE CODES BY OFFENSE CATEGORY

OFFENSE TITLE	CATEGORY	RCW	JRA CODE
Child Molestation 3 Conspiracy	D	9A.44.089	CHILDMOL3
Child Molestation 3 Solicitation	D	9A.44.089	CHILDMOL3
Communicating With A Minor For Immoral Purpose	D	9.68A.091	COMMINOR
Communicating With A Minor For Immoral Purpose - Subsequent Sex Offense Attempt	D	9.68A.090	COMMINORSS
Communicating With A Minor For Immoral Purpose - Subsequent Sex Offense Conspiracy	D	9.68A.090	COMMINORSS
Communicating With A Minor For Immoral Purpose - Subsequent Sex Offense Solicitation	D	9.68A.090	COMMINORSS
Criminal Impersonation 1 Attempt	D	9A.60.040	IMPERSON1
Criminal Impersonation 1 Conspiracy	D	9A.60.040	IMPERSON1
Criminal Impersonation 1 Solicitation	D	9A.60.040	IMPERSON1
Criminal Impersonation 2	D	9A.60.045	IMPERSON2
Criminal Trespass 1	D	9A.52.070	CRIMTRES1
Custodial Interference 1 Attempt	D	9A.40.060	CUSINTER1
Custodial Interference 1 Conspiracy	D	9A.40.060	CUSINTER1
Custodial Interference 1 Solicitation	D	9A.40.060	CUSINTER1
Custodial Interference 2	D	9A.40.070	CUSINTER2
Custodial Interference 2 Attempt	D	9A.40.070	CUSINTER2
Custodial Interference 2 Conspiracy	D	9A.40.070	CUSINTER2
Custodial Interference 2 Solicitation	D	9A.40.070	CUSINTER2
Custodial Interference 2 Subsequent Attempt	D	9A.40.070	CUSINTER2S
Custodial Interference 2 Subsequent Conspiracy	D	9A.40.070	CUSINTER2S
Custodial Interference 2 subsequent Solicitation	D	9A.40.070	CUSINTER2S
Dealing In Depictions Of Minor Engaged In Sexually Explicit Conduct 2 Attempt	D	9.68A.050	DELCHPORN2
Dealing In Depictions Of Minor Engaged In Sexually Explicit Conduct 2 Conspiracy	D	9.68A.050	DELCHPORN2
Dealing In Depictions Of Minor Engaged In Sexually Explicit Conduct 2 Solicitation	D	9.68A.050	DELCHPORN2
Driving Under Influence	D	46.61.502	DUI
Driving While License Invalidated	D	46.20.342	DWIL
Driving While License Invalidated 2	D	46.20.342	DWIL2
Elude A Police Vehicle Attempt	D	46.61.024	ELUDEPV
Elude A Police Vehicle Conspiracy	D	46.61.024	ELUDEPV
Elude A Police Vehicle Solicitation	D	46.61.024	ELUDEPV
Escape 3	D	9A.76.130	ESCAPE3
Fail To Register As A Kidnapper Attempt	D	9A.44.132	FAILREGK

The Caseload Forecast Council is not liable for errors or omissions in the manual, for sentences that may be inappropriately calculated as a result of a practitioner's or court's reliance on the manual, or for any other written or verbal information related to adult or juvenile sentencing. The scoring sheets are intended to provide assistance in most cases but does not cover all permutations of the scoring rules. If you find any errors or omissions, we encourage you to report them to the Caseload Forecast Council.

APPENDICE C – JRA OFFENSE CODES BY OFFENSE CATEGORY

OFFENSE TITLE	CATEGORY	RCW	JRA CODE
Fail To Register As A Kidnapper Conspiracy	D	9A.44.132	FAILREGK
Fail To Register As A Kidnapper Solicitation	D	9A.44.132	FAILREGK
Fail To Register As A Sex Offender Attempt	D	9A.44.130	FAILREGS
Fail To Register As A Sex Offender Conspiracy	D	9A.44.130	FAILREGS
Fail To Register As A Sex Offender Solicitation	D	9A.44.130	FAILREGS
False Reporting	D	9A.84.040	FALSEREP
Forgery Attempt	D	9A.60.020	FORGERY
Forgery Conspiracy	D	9A.60.020	FORGERY
Forgery Solicitation	D	9A.60.020	FORGERY
Harassment - 1st Time	D	9A.46.020	HARASS
Harassment - Because Of Race, Color, Religion, Ancestry, National Origin, Gender, Sexual Orientation, Mental, Physical, Or Sensory Handicap - Conspiracy	D	9A.36.080	HARASSMAL
Harassment - Because Of Race, Color, Religion, Ancestry, National Origin, Gender, Sexual Orientation, Mental, Physical, Or Sensory Handicap - Solicitation	D	9A.36.080	HARASSMAL
Harassment - Because Of Race, Color, Religion, Ancestry, National Origin, Gender, Sexual Orientation, Mental, Physical, Or Sensory Handicap -Attempt	D	9A.36.080	HARASSMAL
Harassment (Repeat) Attempt	D	9A.46.020	HARASSREP
Harassment (Repeat) Conspiracy	D	9A.46.020	HARASSREP
Harassment (Repeat) Solicitation	D	9A.46.020	HARASSREP
Hit and Run Attended	D	46.52.022	HITRUNAT
Hit and Run Death	D	46.52.022	HITRUNDE
Hit and Run Injury Attempt	D	46.52.021	HITRUNIN
Hit and Run Injury Conspiracy	D	46.52.021	HITRUNIN
Hit and Run Injury Solicitation	D	46.52.021	HITRUNIN
Identity Theft 1 Attempt	D	9.35.020	IDENTITY1
Identity Theft 1 Conspiracy	D	9.35.020	IDENTITY1
Identity Theft 1 Solicitation	D	9.35.020	IDENTITY1
Identity Theft 2	D	9.35.020	IDENTITY2
Incest 2 Attempt	D	9A.64.020	INCEST2
Incest 2 Conspiracy	D	9A.64.020	INCEST2
Incest 2 Solicitation	D	9A.64.020	INCEST2
Interfering With The Reporting Of Domestic Violence	D	9A.36.150	DVREPINTER
Intimidating Another Person By Use Of A Weapon	D	9.41.270	INTWWEAPON
Introducing Contraband 2 Attempt	D	9A.76.150	INTCONT2
Introducing Contraband 2 Conspiracy	D	9A.76.150	INTCONT2

The Caseload Forecast Council is not liable for errors or omissions in the manual, for sentences that may be inappropriately calculated as a result of a practitioner's or court's reliance on the manual, or for any other written or verbal information related to adult or juvenile sentencing. The scoring sheets are intended to provide assistance in most cases but does not cover all permutations of the scoring rules. If you find any errors or omissions, we encourage you to report them to the Caseload Forecast Council.

APPENDICE C – JRA OFFENSE CODES BY OFFENSE CATEGORY

OFFENSE TITLE	CATEGORY	RCW	JRA CODE
Introducing Contraband 2 Solicitation	D	9A.76.150	INTCONT2
License Required To Manufacture, Purchase, Sell, Use, Possess, Transport, Or Store Explosives Attempted	D	70.74.022	EXPLLICREQ
License Required To Manufacture, Purchase, Sell, Use, Possess, Transport, Or Store Explosives Conspiracy	D	70.74.022	EXPLLICREQ
License Required To Manufacture, Purchase, Sell, Use, Possess, Transport, Or Store Explosives Solicitation	D	70.74.022	EXPLLICREQ
Making False Or Misleading Statements To A Public Servant	D	9A.76.175	FALSESTATE
Malicious Mischief 2 Attempt	D	9A.48.080	MALMIS2
Malicious Mischief 2 Conspiracy	D	9A.48.080	MALMIS2
Malicious Mischief 2 Solicitation	D	9A.48.080	MALMIS2
Malicious Mischief 3	D	9A.48.090	MALMIS3
Malicious Mischief 3 (<$50 is Class E)	D	9A.48.090	MALMIS3<50
Obstructing A Public Servant	D	9A.76.020	OBSPUBSERV
Obstructing Law Enforcement Officer	D	9A.76.020	OBSLAWOFF
Obtain Legend Drug Attempt	D	69.41.030	OBTLEGDRUG
Obtain Legend Drug Conspiracy	D	69.41.030	OBTLEGDRUG
Obtain Legend Drug Solicitation	D	69.41.030	OBTLEGDRUG
Other C Offense Attempt	D	9A.20.010	OTHERCOFF
Other C Offense Conspiracy	D	9A.20.010	OTHERCOFF
Other C Offense Solicitation	D	9A.20.010	OTHERCOFF
Other Offense Equivalent To Adult Gross Misdemeanor	D	13.40.030	OTHERDOFF
Possession Of A Firearm 2 Attempt	D	9.41.040(1)(b)	PFIREARM2
Possession Of A Firearm 2 Conspiracy	D	9.41.040(1)(b)	PFIREARM2
Possession Of A Firearm 2 Solicitation	D	9.41.040(1)(b)	PFIREARM2
Possession Of A Firearm By Minor (<18 Years) Attempt	D	9.41.040	PFIREARMM
Possession Of A Firearm By Minor (<18 Years) Conspiracy	D	9.41.040	PFIREARMM
Possession Of A Firearm By Minor (<18 Years) Solicitation	D	9.41.040	PFIREARMM
Possession Of Dangerous Weapon At School	D	9.41.280	POSDANGWAS
Possession Of Depictions Of Minor Engaged In Sexually Explicit Conduct Attempt	D	9.68A.070	POSCHPORN2
Possession Of Depictions Of Minor Engaged In Sexually Explicit Conduct Conspiracy	D	9.68A.070	POSCHPORN2
Possession Of Depictions Of Minor Engaged In Sexually Explicit Conduct Solicitation	D	9.68A.070	POSCHPORN2
Possession Of Machine Gun Or Short-Barreled Shotgun Or Rifle Attempt	D	9.41.190	POSMACHGUN
Possession Of Machine Gun Or Short-Barreled Shotgun Or Rifle Conspiracy	D	9.41.190	POSMACHGUN

The Caseload Forecast Council is not liable for errors or omissions in the manual, for sentences that may be inappropriately calculated as a result of a practitioner's or court's reliance on the manual, or for any other written or verbal information related to adult or juvenile sentencing. The scoring sheets are intended to provide assistance in most cases but does not cover all permutations of the scoring rules. If you find any errors or omissions, we encourage you to report them to the Caseload Forecast Council.

APPENDICE C – JRA OFFENSE CODES BY OFFENSE CATEGORY

OFFENSE TITLE	CATEGORY	RCW	JRA CODE
Possession Of Machine Gun Or Short-Barreled Shotgun Or Rifle Solicitation	D	9.41.190	POSMACHGUN
Possession Of Stolen Property 2 Attempt	D	9A.56.160	PSP2
Possession Of Stolen Property 2 Conspiracy	D	9A.56.160	PSP2
Possession Of Stolen Property 2 Solicitation	D	9A.56.160	PSP2
Possession Of Stolen Property 3	D	9A.56.170	PSP3
Possession Of Weapons By Prisoner County Facility Attempted	D	9.94.040	POSWEAPON
Possession Of Weapons By Prisoner County Facility Conspiracy	D	9.94.040	POSWEAPON
Possession Of Weapons By Prisoner County Facility Solicitation	D	9.94.040	POSWEAPON
Rape Of A Child 3 Attempt	D	9A.44.079	RAPECHILD3
Rape Of A Child 3 Conspiracy	D	9A.44.079	RAPECHILD3
Rape Of A Child 3 Solicitation	D	9A.44.079	RAPECHILD3
Reckless Burning 1 Attempt	D	9A.48.040	RECKBURN1
Reckless Burning 1 Conspiracy	D	9A.48.040	RECKBURN1
Reckless Burning 1 Solicitation	D	9A.48.040	RECKBURN1
Reckless Burning 2	D	9A.48.050	RECKBURN2
Refusing To Leave Public Property	D	28A.635.020	REFLEAVE
Rendering Criminal Assistance 1 Attempt	D	9A.76.070	RENDCRIM
Rendering Criminal Assistance 1 Conspiracy	D	9A.76.070	RENDCRIM
Rendering Criminal Assistance 1 Solicitation	D	9A.76.070	RENDCRIM
Retail Theft With Extenuating Circumstances 2 Attempted	D	9A.56.360	THEFT2RET
Retail Theft With Extenuating Circumstances 2 Conspiracy	D	9A.56.360	THEFT2RET
Retail Theft With Extenuating Circumstances 2 Solicitation	D	9A.56.360	THEFT2RET
Retail Theft With Extenuating Circumstances 3 Attempted	D	9A.56.360	THEFT3RET
Retail Theft With Extenuating Circumstances 3 Conspiracy	D	9A.56.360	THEFT3RET
Retail Theft With Extenuating Circumstances 3 Solicitation	D	9A.56.360	THEFT3RET
Sending, Bringing Into State Depictions Of Minor Engaged In Sexually Explicit Conduct 2 Attempt	D	9.68A.060	SBCHPORN2
Sending, Bringing Into State Depictions Of Minor Engaged In Sexually Explicit Conduct 2 Conspiracy	D	9.68A.060	SBCHPORN2
Sending, Bringing Into State Depictions Of Minor Engaged In Sexually Explicit Conduct 2 Solicitation	D	9.68A.060	SBCHPORN2
Sexual Violation Of Human Remains Attempt	D	9A.44.105	SEXVIOLREM
Sexual Violation Of Human Remains Conspiracy	D	9A.44.105	SEXVIOLREM
Sexual Violation Of Human Remains Solicitation	D	9A.44.105	SEXVIOLREM
Stalking (1st Time)	D	9A.46.110	STALK

The Caseload Forecast Council is not liable for errors or omissions in the manual, for sentences that may be inappropriately calculated as a result of a practitioner's or court's reliance on the manual, or for any other written or verbal information related to adult or juvenile sentencing. The scoring sheets are intended to provide assistance in most cases but does not cover all permutations of the scoring rules. If you find any errors or omissions, we encourage you to report them to the Caseload Forecast Council.

APPENDICE C – JRA OFFENSE CODES BY OFFENSE CATEGORY

OFFENSE TITLE	CATEGORY	RCW	JRA CODE
Stalking (Repeat) Attempt	D	9A.46.110	STALKREP
Stalking (Repeat) Conspiracy	D	9A.46.110	STALKREP
Stalking (Repeat) Solicitation	D	9A.46.110	STALKREP
Taking Motor Vehicle Without Permission 2 Attempt	D	9A.56.075	TAMVWOOP2
Taking Motor Vehicle Without Permission 2 Conspiracy	D	9A.56.075	TAMVWOOP2
Taking Motor Vehicle Without Permission 2 Solicitation	D	9A.56.075	TAMVWOOP2
Tampering With A Witness Attempt	D	9A.72.120	TAMPWITN
Tampering With A Witness Conspiracy	D	9A.72.120	TAMPWITN
Tampering With A Witness Solicitation	D	9A.72.120	TAMPWITN
Theft 2 Attempt	D	9A.56.040	THEFT2
Theft 2 Conspiracy	D	9A.56.040	THEFT2
Theft 2 Solicitation	D	9A.56.040	THEFT2
Theft 3	D	9A.56.050	THEFT3
Trafficking In Stolen Property 2 Attempt	D	9A82055	TRAFSTPRO2
Trafficking In Stolen Property 2 Conspiracy	D	9A82055	TRAFSTPRO2
Trafficking In Stolen Property 2 Solicitation	D	9A82055	TRAFSTPRO2
Vehicle Prowling 1 Attempt	D	9A.52.095	VEHPROWL1
Vehicle Prowling 1 Conspiracy	D	9A.52.095	VEHPROWL1
Vehicle Prowling 1 Solicitation	D	9A.52.095	VEHPROWL1
Vehicle Prowling 2	D	9A.52.100	VEHPROWL2
Vehicular Assault Attempt	D	46.61.522	VEHASSAULT
Vehicular Assault Conspiracy	D	46.61.522	VEHASSAULT
Vehicular Assault Solicitation	D	46.61.522	VEHASSAULT
Violation Of Uniform Controlled Substances Act--Nonnarcotic Counterfeit Substance Attempt	D	69.50.401(d)	COUNTNNARC
Violation Of Uniform Controlled Substances Act--Nonnarcotic Counterfeit Substance Conspiracy	D	69.50.401(d)	COUNTNNARC
Violation Of Uniform Controlled Substances Act--Nonnarcotic Counterfeit Substance Solicitation	D	69.50.401(d)	COUNTNNARC
Voyeurism Attempt	D	9A.44.155	VOYEURISM
Voyeurism Conspiracy	D	9A.44.115	VOYEURISM
Voyeurism Solicitation	D	9A.44.115	VOYEURISM
Weapons Apparently Capable Of Producing Bodily Harm	D	9.41.270	WEAPONCBH
LEVEL E			
Aiming Or Discharging Firearms, Dangerous Weapons Attempted	E	9.41.230	DANWEAPAD
Aiming Or Discharging Firearms, Dangerous Weapons Conspiracy	E	9.41.230	DANWEAPAD

The Caseload Forecast Council is not liable for errors or omissions in the manual, for sentences that may be inappropriately calculated as a result of a practitioner's or court's reliance on the manual, or for any other written or verbal information related to adult or juvenile sentencing. The scoring sheets are intended to provide assistance in most cases but does not cover all permutations of the scoring rules. If you find any errors or omissions, we encourage you to report them to the Caseload Forecast Council.

APPENDICE C – JRA OFFENSE CODES BY OFFENSE CATEGORY

OFFENSE TITLE	CATEGORY	RCW	JRA CODE
Aiming Or Discharging Firearms, Dangerous Weapons Solicitation	E	9.41.230	DANWEAPAD
Alteration Of Identifying Marks On Firearm	E	9.41.140	FIRARMALT
Alteration Of Identifying Marks On Firearm Attempted	E	9.41.140	FIRARMALT
Alteration Of Identifying Marks On Firearm Conspiracy	E	9.41.140	FIRARMALT
Alteration Of Identifying Marks On Firearm Solicitation	E	9.41.140	FIRARMALT
Animal Cruelty 2	E	16.52.207	ANIMCRUEL2
Assault 4 Attempt	E	9A.36.041	ASSAULT4
Assault 4 Conspiracy	E	9A.36.041	ASSAULT4
Assault 4 Solicitation	E	9A.36.041	ASSAULT4
Burg Tools (Possession Of) Attempt	E	9A.52.020	BURGTOOLS
Burg Tools (Possession Of) Conspiracy	E	9A.52.020	BURGTOOLS
Burg Tools (Possession Of) Solicitation	E	9A.52.020	BURGTOOLS
Carry Weapon To School Attempt	E	9.41.280	CARWEAPSCH
Carry Weapon To School Conspiracy	E	9.41.280	CARWEAPSCH
Carry Weapon To School Solicitation	E	9.41.280	CARWEAPSCH
Coercion Attempt	E	9A.36.070	COERCION
Coercion Conspiracy	E	9A.36.070	COERCION
Coercion Solicitation	E	9A.36.070	COERCION
Communicating With A Minor For Immoral Purpose Attempt	E	9.68A.091	COMMINOR
Communicating With A Minor For Immoral Purpose Conspiracy	E	9.68A.091	COMMINOR
Communicating With A Minor For Immoral Purpose Solicitation	E	9.68A.091	COMMINOR
Contempt	E	7.21	CONTEMPT
Criminal Contempt	E	9.23.010	CRIMCONT
Criminal Impersonation 2 Attempt	E	9A.60.045	IMPERSON2
Criminal Impersonation 2 Conspiracy	E	9A.60.045	IMPERSON2
Criminal Impersonation 2 Solicitation	E	9A.60.045	IMPERSON2
Criminal Trespass 1 Attempt	E	9A.52.070	CRIMTRES1
Criminal Trespass 1 Conspiracy	E	9A.52.070	CRIMTRES1
Criminal Trespass 1 Solicitation	E	9A.52.070	CRIMTRES1
Criminal Trespass 2	E	9A.52.080	CRIMTRES2
Criminal Trespass 2 Attempt	E	9A.52.080	CRIMTRES2
Criminal Trespass 2 Conspiracy	E	9A.52.080	CRIMTRES2
Criminal Trespass 2 Solicitation	E	9A.52.080	CRIMTRES2
Custodial Interference	E	9A.40.050	CUSINTER

The Caseload Forecast Council is not liable for errors or omissions in the manual, for sentences that may be inappropriately calculated as a result of a practitioner's or court's reliance on the manual, or for any other written or verbal information related to adult or juvenile sentencing. The scoring sheets are intended to provide assistance in most cases but does not cover all permutations of the scoring rules. If you find any errors or omissions, we encourage you to report them to the Caseload Forecast Council.

APPENDICE C – JRA OFFENSE CODES BY OFFENSE CATEGORY

OFFENSE TITLE	CATEGORY	RCW	JRA CODE
Disorderly Conduct	E	9A.84.030	DISCONDUCT
Disorderly Conduct Attempt	E	9A.84.030	DISCONDUCT
Disorderly Conduct Conspiracy	E	9A.84.030	DISCONDUCT
Disorderly Conduct Solicitation	E	9A.84.030	DISCONDUCT
Disturbing School, School Activities Or Meetings	E	28A.635.030	DISTRBSCHL
Driving Under Influence Attempt	E	46.61.502	DUI
Driving Under Influence Conspiracy	E	46.61.502	DUI
Driving Under Influence Solicitation	E	46.61.502	DUI
Driving While License Invalidated 3	E	46.20.342	DWIL3
Driving Without A License	E	46.20.005	DWOL
Drug Paraphernalia	E	69.50.412	DRUGPARA
Escape 3 Attempt	E	9A.76.130	ESCAPE3
Escape 3 Conspiracy	E	9A.76.130	ESCAPE3
Escape 3 Solicitation	E	9A.76.130	ESCAPE3
Failure To Disperse	E	9A.56.130	FAILDISP
False Reporting Attempt	E	9A.84.040	FALSEREP
False Reporting Conspiracy	E	9A.84.040	FALSEREP
False Reporting Solicitation	E	9A.84.040	FALSEREP
Harassment - 1st Time Attempt	E	9A.46.020	HARASS
Harassment - 1st Time Conspiracy	E	9A.46.020	HARASS
Harassment - 1st Time Solicitation	E	9A.46.020	HARASS
Hit and Run Attended Attempt	E	46.52.022	HITRUNAT
Hit and Run Attended Conspiracy	E	46.52.022	HITRUNAT
Hit and Run Attended Solicitation	E	46.52.022	HITRUNAT
Hit and Run Death Attempt	E	46.52.022	HITRUNDE
Hit and Run Death Conspiracy	E	46.52.022	HITRUNDE
Hit and Run Death Solicitation	E	46.52.022	HITRUNDE
Hit and Run Unattended	E	46.52.010	HITRUNUN
Identity Theft 2 Attempt	E	9.35.020	IDENTITY2
Identity Theft 2 Conspiracy	E	9.35.020	IDENTITY2
Identity Theft 2 Solicitation	E	9.35.020	IDENTITY2
Indecent Exposure (Victim <14) Attempt	E	9A.88.010	INDEXP<14
Indecent Exposure (Victim <14) Conspiracy	E	9A.88.010	INDEXP<14
Indecent Exposure (Victim <14) Solicitation	E	9A.88.010	INDEXP<14
Indecent Exposure (Victim 14+)	E	9A.88.010	INDEXP14+
Interfering With The Reporting Of Domestic Violence Attempted	E	9A.36.150	DVREPINTER

The Caseload Forecast Council is not liable for errors or omissions in the manual, for sentences that may be inappropriately calculated as a result of a practitioner's or court's reliance on the manual, or for any other written or verbal information related to adult or juvenile sentencing. The scoring sheets are intended to provide assistance in most cases but does not cover all permutations of the scoring rules. If you find any errors or omissions, we encourage you to report them to the Caseload Forecast Council.

APPENDICE C – JRA OFFENSE CODES BY OFFENSE CATEGORY

OFFENSE TITLE	CATEGORY	RCW	JRA CODE
Interfering With The Reporting Of Domestic Violence Conspiracy	E	9A.36.150	DVREPINTER
Interfering With The Reporting Of Domestic Violence Solicitation	E	9A.36.150	DVREPINTER
Intimidating Another Person By Use Of A Weapon Attempt	E	9.41.270	INTWWEAPON
Intimidating Another Person By Use Of A Weapon Conspiracy	E	9.41.270	INTWWEAPON
Intimidating Another Person By Use Of A Weapon Solicitation	E	9.41.270	INTWWEAPON
Introducing Contraband 3	E	9A.76.160	INTCONT3
Making False Or Misleading Statement To A Public Servant Attempted	E	9A.76.175	FALSESTATE
Making False Or Misleading Statement To A Public Servant Conspiracy	E	9A.76.175	FALSESTATE
Making False Or Misleading Statement To A Public Servant Solicitation	E	9A.76.175	FALSESTATE
Malicious Mischief 3 Attempt	E	9A.48.090	MALMIS3
Malicious Mischief 3 Conspiracy	E	9A.48.090	MALMIS3
Malicious Mischief 3 Solicitation	E	9A.48.090	MALMIS3
Obscene Phone Calls	E	9.61.230	OBSCENEPC
Obstructing A Public Servant Attempt	E	9A.76.020	OBSPUBSERV
Obstructing A Public Servant Conspiracy	E	9A.76.020	OBSPUBSERV
Obstructing A Public Servant Solicitation	E	9A.76.020	OBSPUBSERV
Obstructing Law Enforcement Officer Attempt	E	9A.76.020	OBSLAWOFF
Obstructing Law Enforcement Officer Conspiracy	E	9A.76.020	OBSLAWOFF
Obstructing Law Enforcement Officer Solicitation	E	9A.76.020	OBSLAWOFF
Offering And Agreeing (Prostitution)	E	9A.32.050	O&APROST
Other D+ Offense Attempt	E	13.40.030	OTHERD+OFF
Other D+ Offense Conspiracy	E	13.40.030	OTHERD+OFF
Other D+ Offense Solicitation	E	13.40.030	OTHERD+OFF
Other Offense Equivalent To Adult Gross Misdemeanor Attempt	E	13.40.030	OTHERDOFF
Other Offense Equivalent To Adult Gross Misdemeanor Conspiracy	E	13.40.030	OTHERDOFF
Other Offense Equivalent To Adult Gross Misdemeanor Solicitation	E	13.40.030	OTHERDOFF
Other Offense Equivalent To Adult Misdemeanor	E	13.40.030	OTHEREOFF
Patronizing A Prostitute	E	9A.88.110	PATPROSTI
Patronizing A Prostitute Attempted	E	9A.88.110	PATPROSTI
Patronizing A Prostitute Conspiracy	E	9A.88.110	PATPROSTI
Patronizing A Prostitute Solicitation	E	9A.88.110	PATPROSTI

The Caseload Forecast Council is not liable for errors or omissions in the manual, for sentences that may be inappropriately calculated as a result of a practitioner's or court's reliance on the manual, or for any other written or verbal information related to adult or juvenile sentencing. The scoring sheets are intended to provide assistance in most cases but does not cover all permutations of the scoring rules. If you find any errors or omissions, we encourage you to report them to the Caseload Forecast Council.

APPENDICE C – JRA OFFENSE CODES BY OFFENSE CATEGORY

OFFENSE TITLE	CATEGORY	RCW	JRA CODE
Possession Of Dangerous Weapon At School Attempt	E	9.41.280	POSDANGWAS
Possession Of Dangerous Weapon At School Conspiracy	E	9.41.280	POSDANGWAS
Possession Of Dangerous Weapon At School Solicitation	E	9.41.280	POSDANGWAS
Possession Of Dangerous Weapon Attempt	E	9.41.250	POSDANGW
Possession Of Dangerous Weapon Conspiracy	E	9.41.250	POSDANGW
Possession Of Dangerous Weapon Solicitation	E	9.41.250	POSDANGW
Possession Of Illegal Fireworks	E	70.77.255	POSILLFWKS
Possession Of Legend Drug	E	69.41.030	POSLEGDRUG
Possession Of Marijuana <40 Grams	E	69.50.401	POSPOT<40
Possession Of Stolen Property 3 Attempt	E	9A.56.170	PSP3
Possession Of Stolen Property 3 Conspiracy	E	9A.56.170	PSP3
Possession Of Stolen Property 3 Solicitation	E	9A.56.170	PSP3
Possession/Consumption Of Alcohol	E	66.44.270	POSOFALCOH
Reckless Burning 2 Attempt	E	9A.48.050	RECKBURN2
Reckless Burning 2 Conspiracy	E	9A.48.050	RECKBURN2
Reckless Burning 2 Solicitation	E	9A.48.050	RECKBURN2
Reckless Driving	E	46.61.500	RECKDRIV
Reckless Endangerment 2 Attempt	E	9A.36.050	RECKEND2
Reckless Endangerment Attempt	E	9A.36.050	RECKEND
Reckless Endangerment Conspiracy	E	9A.36.050	RECKEND
Reckless Endangerment Solicitation	E	9A.36.050	RECKEND
Resisting Arrest	E	9A.76.040	RESARREST
Riot Without Weapon Attempt	E	9A.84.010	RIOTWOWEAP
Riot Without Weapon Conspiracy	E	9A.84.010	RIOTWOWEAP
Riot Without Weapon Solicitation	E	9A.84.010	RIOTWOWEAP
Stalking (1st Time) Attempt	E	9A.46.110	STALK
Stalking (1st Time) Conspiracy	E	9A.46.110	STALK
Stalking (1st Time) Solicitation	E	9A.46.110	STALK
Tampering With Fire Alarm Apparatus	E	9.40.100	TAMPFIREAL
Theft 3 Attempt	E	9A.56.050	THEFT3
Theft 3 Conspiracy	E	9A.56.050	THEFT3
Theft 3 Solicitation	E	9A.56.050	THEFT3
Unlawful Inhalation	E	9.47A.020	UNLAWINHAL
Vehicle Prowling 2 Attempt	E	9A.52.100	VEHPROWL2
Vehicle Prowling 2 Conspiracy	E	9A.52.100	VEHPROWL2
Vehicle Prowling 2 Solicitation	E	9A.52.100	VEHPROWL2

The Caseload Forecast Council is not liable for errors or omissions in the manual, for sentences that may be inappropriately calculated as a result of a practitioner's or court's reliance on the manual, or for any other written or verbal information related to adult or juvenile sentencing. The scoring sheets are intended to provide assistance in most cases but does not cover all permutations of the scoring rules. If you find any errors or omissions, we encourage you to report them to the Caseload Forecast Council.

APPENDICE C – JRA OFFENSE CODES BY OFFENSE CATEGORY

OFFENSE TITLE	CATEGORY	RCW	JRA CODE
Weapon Without A Permit	E	9.41.050	WEAPONWOP
Weapons Apparently Capable Of Producing Bodily Harm Attempted	E	9.41.270	WEAPONCBH
Weapons Apparently Capable Of Producing Bodily Harm Conspiracy	E	9.41.270	WEAPONCBH
Weapons Apparently Capable Of Producing Bodily Harm Solicitation	E	9.41.270	WEAPONCBH
LEVEL V			
Game, Traffic, Tobacco And Other Violations	V	9972	VIOLATION
Multiple Detention	V	9990000	MULTDET
Sex Offender Parole Revoke	V	9A.44.130	SOPARREV
Violation Of Court Order	V	9980	VIOLCO
Violation Of Sexual Assault Protection Order	V	7.9	VIOLSEXAO
Violation Of SSODA	V	9979	VIOLSSODA
LEVEL X			
Diagnostic Only	X	9973	DIAGNOSTIC
Sentence Rescinded	X	9975	SENRESCIND
Sentence Reversed And Remanded	X		SENTREVERS
Unknown Offense	X	9999998	UNKNOWNOFF

The Caseload Forecast Council is not liable for errors or omissions in the manual, for sentences that may be inappropriately calculated as a result of a practitioner's or court's reliance on the manual, or for any other written or verbal information related to adult or juvenile sentencing. The scoring sheets are intended to provide assistance in most cases but does not cover all permutations of the scoring rules. If you find any errors or omissions, we encourage you to report them to the Caseload Forecast Council.

APPENDIX D

APPENDIX D: Beyond Juvenile Court: Long-Term Impact of a Juvenile Record*

What Defense Attorneys Need to Know About Collateral and Other Non-confinement Consequences of Juvenile Adjudications

Washington Defender Association

110 Prefontaine Pl. S., Suite 610
Seattle, WA 98104
(206) 623-4321

www.defensenet.org
WDA@defensenet.org

*Reprinted with permission of the Washington Defender Association

NOTE: This publication was produced by the Washington Defenders Association and updated in 2013. It is used with permission of the association. The association is solely responsible for the content.

APPENDIX D: Beyond Juvenile Court: Long-Term Impact of a Juvenile Record. Washington Defenders Association

Acknowledgements

Beyond Juvenile Court: Long-Term Impacts of a Juvenile Record was written by Kim Ambrose, WDA resource attorney, with Alison Millikan. Stacy Chen and Christie Hedman, director of WDA, edited the manual, and Sarah Yatsko formatted and supervised its production. This manual was updated in 2013 by Jessica Erickson, Travis Stearns and George Yeanakkis.

The following persons contributed in the compilation of this booklet and deserve recognition:

Hong Tran, *Staff Attorney*, Northwest Justice Project
Ann Benson, *Director*, WDA Immigration Project
Jonathan Moore, *Immigration Resource Specialist*, WDA Immigration Project
Mark Dalton, *Administrator*, Department of Social and Health Services
Sascha Sprinkle, WDA Technical Assistance

The Caseload Forecast Council is not liable for errors or omissions in the manual, for sentences that may be inappropriately calculated as a result of a practitioner's or court's reliance on the manual, or for any other written or verbal information related to adult or juvenile sentencing. The scoring sheets are intended to provide assistance in most cases but does not cover all permutations of the scoring rules. If you find any errors or omissions, we encourage you to report them to the Caseload Forecast Council.

APPENDIX D: Beyond Juvenile Court: Long-Term Impact of a Juvenile Record.
Washington Defenders Association

Beyond Juvenile Court:
What Defense Attorneys Need to Know About
Collateral and Other Non-confinement Consequences
of Juvenile Adjudications

I don't know why I did it, I don't know why I enjoyed it, and I don't know why I'll do it again.
 -- Bart Simpson, from *The Simpsons*

Who should use this Booklet?

The information in this booklet is intended for use by public defense attorneys, their juvenile clients, and their clients' parents in Washington State. It is not comprehensive. It is meant as a starting point for defenders and juveniles to understand the hidden penalties that may occur after juvenile court adjudications and can follow juveniles into adulthood. Juvenile respondents and their parents should understand the potential civil and other consequences of an adjudication and always should consult with an attorney before they plead guilty in juvenile court.

This booklet is also for other criminal justice professionals, social service providers, community members or anyone who is concerned about the vast array of non-incarcerative penalties that follow juveniles with criminal adjudications or convictions.

For a more detailed discussion of consequences of convictions in Washington, see *Beyond the Conviction: What Defense Attorneys in Washington State Need to Know About Collateral and Other Non-Confinement Consequences of Criminal Convictions*, available to WDA members and on-line at www.defensenet.org.

Is a Juvenile Adjudication a "Conviction"?

Although it may depend on the context, for the most part under Washington law the answer is **"no."** Since 1961, the Basic Juvenile Court Act has provided that "an order of the court adjudging a child delinquent . . . shall in no case be deemed conviction of a crime."[68] However, in 2010 the Act was amended to state that an adjudication has the same meaning as "conviction" only for the purposes of sentencing under RCW 9.94A (the Sentencing Reform Act).[69] Similarly, the Sentencing Reform Act ("SRA") was also amended in 1997 to define "criminal history" as including both convictions and juvenile adjudications.[70]

There are two important contexts where juvenile adjudications are treated as convictions:

---

[68] RCW 13.04.240.
[69] RCW 13.04.011(1).
[70] RCW 9.94A.030(11).

The Caseload Forecast Council is not liable for errors or omissions in the manual, for sentences that may be inappropriately calculated as a result of a practitioner's or court's reliance on the manual, or for any other written or verbal information related to adult or juvenile sentencing. The scoring sheets are intended to provide assistance in most cases but does not cover all permutations of the scoring rules. If you find any errors or omissions, we encourage you to report them to the Caseload Forecast Council.

**APPENDIX D: Beyond Juvenile Court: Long-Term Impact of a Juvenile Record.
Washington Defenders Association**

(1) Public access to juvenile criminal history;[71] and
(2) Adult sentencing under the SRA.[72]

Public Access to Juvenile Criminal History: No matter what you call it, conviction or adjudication, a juvenile's criminal history is accessible to the public through public court records and the Washington State Patrol database.[73] See Section II, *Criminal History Records*. When responding to criminal background checks, the Washington State Patrol reports all adult and juvenile convictions without distinction.

Effect of Juvenile Adjudications on Adult Sentencing: For adult felony offenses committed on or after June 13, 2002, juvenile felony adjudications will be included in calculating an adult's offender score for purposes of sentencing under the SRA.[74] In other words, juvenile adjudications "count" for purposes of adult sentencing and will increase an adult's offender score which can result in a longer sentence.

Juvenile Criminal History Records

Criminal history, which is easily accessible to the general public, includes juvenile adjudications that were committed in Washington after 1977. **While juvenile criminal history does not "go away" when a person turns 18, access to these records is greatly reduced once the juvenile turns twenty-one and even more restricted at twenty-three. No consumer reporting agency may make a consumer report containing any juvenile records, as defined in RCW 13.50.010(1)(c), when the subject of those records is twenty-one or older.**[75] Criminal history record information is maintained centrally in Washington State through the Washington State Patrol Identification and Criminal History Section, 3000 Pacific Avenue, PO Box 42633, Olympia, Washington 98504-2633, (360) 705-5100. The Washington State Patrol may disseminate conviction records without restriction.[76]

Access to Juvenile Records: Juvenile adjudication and arrest information is available to the public at the courthouse, the Washington State Patrol, and via the internet. For a small fee, anyone -- employers, landlords, potential love interests, etc. -- may access any individual's juvenile and adult criminal conviction records, arrests under one year old, and pending charges through the Washington State Patrol website, https://watch.wsp.wa.gov.[77] The public can also access juvenile arrest records that are less than one year old, even if they have not led to a

---

[71] RCW 13.50.050.
[72] RCW 9.94A.525.
[73] RCW 13.50.050.
[74] *State v. Varga*, 151 Wash.2d 179, 198, 86 P.3d 139 (2004); RCW 9.94A.525; see also, *In re Carrier*, 173 Wash.2d 791 (2012) (washed out adjudications may also score).
[75] *See* RCW 19.182.040(1)(f); *see also* RCW 13.50.050.
[76] RCW 10.97.050.
[77] RCW 10.97.050.

The Caseload Forecast Council is not liable for errors or omissions in the manual, for sentences that may be inappropriately calculated as a result of a practitioner's or court's reliance on the manual, or for any other written or verbal information related to adult or juvenile sentencing. The scoring sheets are intended to provide assistance in most cases but does not cover all permutations of the scoring rules. If you find any errors or omissions, we encourage you to report them to the Caseload Forecast Council.

APPENDIX D: Beyond Juvenile Court: Long-Term Impact of a Juvenile Record.
Washington Defenders Association

juvenile adjudication.[78] More complete criminal history records, including juvenile non-conviction data (dismissals, findings of not guilty et al.) are also available to the public at superior court clerk's offices and through the Washington State Courts Judicial Information System ("JIS") on-line service, accessible at http://www.courts.wa.gov/jis/. Certain agencies have free access to criminal history information, e.g., criminal justice agencies and the Department of Social and Human Services (DSHS), while others may subscribe to the on-line service for a fee.[79] **Juvenile criminal records are available to the public unless and until they are sealed by a court order.[80] Beginning in 2011, no consumer reporting agency may make a consumer report containing any juvenile records, as defined in RCW 13.50.010(1)(c), when the subject of those records is twenty-one or older.[81]**

Correcting Juvenile Records: Requests to correct juvenile criminal history records held by a "juvenile justice care agency"[82] may be submitted by filing a motion in the juvenile court where the adjudication was entered.[83] Forms from the Washington State Courts website can be found at http://www.courts.wa.gov/forms/?fa=forms.contribute&formID=45 or by calling the Administrative Office of the Courts at (360) 705-5328.[84]

Vacating, Sealing and Destroying Juvenile Records:

> **To vacate** means "to annul, set aside, cancel or rescind; to render an act void."[85] Juvenile adjudications may be **vacated** only after completion of a deferred disposition or after prevailing on appeal or through other post-conviction relief.[86] Vacated juvenile adjudications are still accessible to the public and must be **sealed** in order to remove them from public view.

> **Sealing** a court record means to hide it from the public's view, but the record still exists.[87] Certain adjudications (described below) may be sealed by filing a Motion to Seal with the juvenile court that entered the adjudication.[88] If the court grants the Motion to Seal, any agency receiving a request for the juvenile's record must reply that the record is

---

[78] RCW 10.97.050.
[79] RCW 10.97.050; RCW 10.97.100; RCW 43.43.838.
[80] RCW 13.50.050.
[81] See RCW 19.182.040(1). See also RCW 13.50.050, amended by ESSB 6561, Chapter 150, Sec. 2(2), 2010 Washington Laws, signed by Governor March 22, 2010.
[82] RCW 10.97.050.
[83] RCW 43.43.730; RCW 10.97.080.
[84] RCW 13.50.010(6).
[85] State v. Noel, 5 P.3d 747, 749, 101 Wn. App. 623 (2000), quoting Black's Law Dictionary at 1548 (6th ed.1990).
[86] Id.
[87] "To seal means to protect from examination by the public or unauthorized court personnel." A record can be completely or partially sealed. The existence of a sealed file, unless statutorily protected, is still viewable by the public, but is "limited to the case number, names of the parties, the notation 'case sealed,' the case type in civil cases and the cause of the action or charge in criminal cases." 2 Wash. Prac., Rules Practice GR 15 (6th ed.).
[88] RCW 13.50.050(11). See also http://www.courts.wa.gov/forms/?fa=forms.contribute&formID=45.

The Caseload Forecast Council is not liable for errors or omissions in the manual, for sentences that may be inappropriately calculated as a result of a practitioner's or court's reliance on the manual, or for any other written or verbal information related to adult or juvenile sentencing. The scoring sheets are intended to provide assistance in most cases but does not cover all permutations of the scoring rules. If you find any errors or omissions, we encourage you to report them to the Caseload Forecast Council.

APPENDIX D: Beyond Juvenile Court: Long-Term Impact of a Juvenile Record.
Washington Defenders Association

confidential, and may not give out any information about its existence or nonexistence. The subject of the sealed record may respond that they have never been convicted on job, housing or other applications.[14] Subsequent juvenile adjudications or adult convictions will result in "unsealing" a previously sealed juvenile adjudication.[15]

Juvenile data is accessible similar to adult data; however, the rules for sealing/vacating and destroying are different.[89] A juvenile conviction may be sealed if the following criteria are met:[90]
- The order is a deferred disposition vacated under WA St 13.40.127(9), the juvenile is age eighteen or older, and the full restitution has been paid; or
- There must be no proceeding pending seeking conviction for a juvenile or criminal offense; there must be no proceeding pending seeking a diversion program agreement, and:
  - **Sex Offenses**: Rape 1, Rape 2 and Indecent Liberties with actual forcible compulsion may not be sealed. All other sex offenses are eligible to be sealed by meeting the following requirements if the person is no longer required to register as a sex offender;
  - **A Felonies**: the juvenile must be crime-free for **5 years** from the last date of release from confinement and full restitution has been paid;
  - **B and C Felonies**: the juvenile must be crime-free for **2 years** from the last date of release from confinement;
  - **Misdemeanors and Gross Misdemeanors**: the juvenile must be crime-free for **2 years** from the last date of release from confinement and full restitution has been paid.
- Unless the offender receives a full and unconditional pardon, in which case the proceedings will be treated as if they had never occurred.
- For full information on how these rules changed, contact WDA technical assistance staff.

Destruction or Deletion of juvenile court records is only possible for **non-conviction data**[91] and **diversions**.[92] This is also referred to as expungement.

> **Diversion records** may be destroyed if either of the following criteria are met:
> - The person is **18 years** or older and
>   - **2 years** have elapsed since completion of the diversion agreement or counsel and release; and
>   - The criminal history includes only one referral for a diversion, no prior convictions/adjudications and no subsequent arrests or charges; and
>   - There is no restitution owing in the case.[93]

---

[89] RCW 13.50.50.
[90] RCW 13.50.050(12).
[91] RCW 10.97.060 (2005); WAC 446-16-025.
[92] RCW 10.97.060 (2005); WAC 446-16-025 (2005); RCW 13.50.050(17).
[93] RCW 13.50.050(17).

The Caseload Forecast Council is not liable for errors or omissions in the manual, for sentences that may be inappropriately calculated as a result of a practitioner's or court's reliance on the manual, or for any other written or verbal information related to adult or juvenile sentencing. The scoring sheets are intended to provide assistance in most cases but does not cover all permutations of the scoring rules. If you find any errors or omissions, we encourage you to report them to the Caseload Forecast Council.

APPENDIX D: Beyond Juvenile Court: Long-Term Impact of a Juvenile Record.
Washington Defenders Association

-or-
- The person is 23 years or older and
    - has completed the diversion agreement and has no pending criminal charges; and
    - criminal history includes only referrals for diversion (may be more than one).[94]

Courts are permitted to "routinely destroy" juvenile records where the juvenile is 23 years or older or the juvenile is 18 years or older **and** he or she only has 1 diversion agreement **and** 2 years have passed since that agreement was completed.[95] If a person is adjudicated of a new juvenile offense or convicted of a crime, the sealing order is nullified and the public may again access the court record.[96] When a juvenile record is sealed "the proceedings in the case shall be treated as if they never occurred, and the subject of the records may reply accordingly to any inquiry about the events, records of which are sealed."[97]

Favorable dispositions (e.g., acquittals and dismissals, but not dismissals after a successful period of probation, suspension or deferral of sentence) may be **deleted** from a person's criminal history record information **2 years** after entry of the disposition favorable to the defendant.[98]

Arrest information not leading to adjudication may be deleted **3 years** after the date of arrest or issuance of citation or warrant.[99]

Federal juvenile adjudications: Records relating to federal juvenile adjudications are not released to the public and specifically are prohibited from release "when the request for information is related to an application for employment, license, bonding, or any civil right or privilege."[100] Federal juvenile adjudications may only be released to law enforcement, courts, treatment programs, the victim of the crime, and to agencies considering the person for employment that directly affects national security.[101]

NOTE: At the time of this writing, the FBI does not remove sealed Washington juvenile records from their database because they are not "expunged" under Washington law. (Washington law does not have a procedure for "expungement.") The FBI receives juvenile adjudication and arrest information from the Washington State Patrol. The FBI does not release records directly to the public; however, federal agencies and law enforcement have access to FBI records.

---

[94] RCW 13.50.050(22).
[95] *Id.*
[96] RCW 13.50.050.
[97] RCW 13.50.050(14).
[98] RCW 10.97.060.
[99] *Id.*
[100] 18 U.S.C. § 5038(a)(2005).
[101] *Id.*

The Caseload Forecast Council is not liable for errors or omissions in the manual, for sentences that may be inappropriately calculated as a result of a practitioner's or court's reliance on the manual, or for any other written or verbal information related to adult or juvenile sentencing. The scoring sheets are intended to provide assistance in most cases but does not cover all permutations of the scoring rules. If you find any errors or omissions, we encourage you to report them to the Caseload Forecast Council.

APPENDIX D: Beyond Juvenile Court: Long-Term Impact of a Juvenile Record.
Washington Defenders Association

Unfortunately, because the Washington Administrative Office of the Courts displays juvenile criminal history online and continues to sell court records to private companies that specialize in records searching, a record that has been officially sealed may be discoverable through any number of private companies.[102]

> **PRACTICE TIP:** Remind your clients that juvenile adjudications will **not** go away when they turn 18. Always go over criminal history with clients and remind them of the importance of sealing and destroying records as soon as they are eligible. Point them to the self-help resources found below.

> **PRACTICE TIP:** Remind clients that sealing juvenile records will not reinstate their ability to possess a firearm. This requires a separate motion and order. See Section IX, *Right to Possess Firearms*.

RESOURCES: Good self-help resources are available:

"Sealing Juvenile Court Records in Washington State," from www.washingtonlawhelp.org at http://www.washingtonlawhelp.org/documents/4603414902EN.pdf?stateabbrev=/WA/ (June 2010)

"A Guide to Sealing and Destroying Court Records, Vacating Convictions, and Deleting Criminal History Records" from the Washington Courts website at http://www.courts.wa.gov/newsinfo/index.cfm?fa=newsinfo.displayContent&theFile=content/guideToCrimHistoryRecords (September 2012).

Immigration

A juvenile adjudication and disposition will not generally trigger removal (a.k.a. deportation) or inadmissibility for non-citizens, because under the federal immigration laws juvenile dispositions are not considered convictions. However, several circuit courts have held that an offense committed before an alleged offender's 18th birthday can serve as a basis for removal if the alleged offender is tried as an adult.[103] In 2010, the United States Supreme Court ruled in *Padilla v. Kentucky*, 599 U.S. 356 (2010) that an attorney representing a non-citizen *adult* client has an affirmative duty to inform the client of the immigration consequences of a guilty plea.[104] The mere omission of incorrect information is not enough to insulate an attorney from an ineffective

---

[102] Testimony at Washington State House Judiciary Committee Hearing, June 8, 2010, found at the TVW website http://www.tvw.org/media/mediaplayer.cfm?evid=2010060031B&TYPE=V&CFID=13028&CFTOKEN=10017140&bhcp=1, last visited on August 26, 2013.
[103] *Matter of Ramirez-Rivero*, 18 I. & N. Dec. 135 (B.I.A. 1981); *Matter of Devison*, 22 I. & N. Dec. 1362 (B.I.A. 2000).
[104] *Padilla v. Kentucky*, 559 U.S. 356, 130 S.Ct. 1473, 176 L.Ed.2d 284 (2010).

The Caseload Forecast Council is not liable for errors or omissions in the manual, for sentences that may be inappropriately calculated as a result of a practitioner's or court's reliance on the manual, or for any other written or verbal information related to adult or juvenile sentencing. The scoring sheets are intended to provide assistance in most cases but does not cover all permutations of the scoring rules. If you find any errors or omissions, we encourage you to report them to the Caseload Forecast Council.

APPENDIX D: Beyond Juvenile Court: Long-Term Impact of a Juvenile Record.
Washington Defenders Association

assistance of counsel claim.[105] Failure to properly advise your client of the immigration consequences of the disposition may violate the clients' Sixth Amendment right to effective assistance of counsel.[106] Nevertheless, there still may be immigration consequences. Determining these consequences can be challenging and complex. This opinion was affirmed by the Washington State Supreme Court in *State v. Sandoval*, 249 P.3d 1015, 171 Wash.2d 163 (Wash. 2011).

Determine the Juvenile's Immigration Status: If a juvenile respondent was not born in the United States and is not otherwise a U.S. citizen, the first step is determining the juvenile's *immigration status*. The immigration consequences of a juvenile adjudication will depend on the juvenile's immigration status—whether the non-citizen juvenile respondent is living in the United States legally (e.g., as a permanent resident with a "green card") or whether the juvenile respondent is living in the United States without legal immigration status (i.e., undocumented).

Non-citizen Juvenile Respondents Residing in U.S. Legally: If a non-citizen juvenile is legally residing in the United States (e.g., has lawful permanent residence), a juvenile adjudication will not automatically trigger removal proceedings as an adult conviction might.[107] Nevertheless, not all of the criminal provisions under immigration law require convictions, and a juvenile disposition will be sufficient to trigger deportation/removal under those provisions. For example, a juvenile disposition for the offense of delivery of a controlled substance will likely fall under the INA's "reason to believe" provision that the non-citizen is a drug trafficker.[108] Additionally, a finding by a juvenile court that the youth has violated a domestic violence restraining, protective, or no contact order can trigger deportation under INA's "violation of a family protective order" ground.[109]

Additionally, for those juveniles who are in the U.S. legally but have not yet obtained permanent legal residence (a green card) or citizenship, the Department of Homeland Security can and will consider juvenile dispositions in making the decision whether to grant their applications.[110] Since these decisions are discretionary it is difficult to predict with any certainty the affect of juvenile dispositions.

Juvenile Respondents Residing in the U.S. Illegally: Juveniles residing in this country who are undocumented (here "illegally") may be put into removal/deportation proceedings at any time regardless of their criminal history. If an undocumented juvenile is placed into removal proceedings he or she may still be able to remain in the country legally if eligible for some type

---

[105] *Id.* at 366.
[106] *Id.*
[107] See, e.g., *Matter of Devison*, 22 I. & N. Dec. 1362 (B.I.A. 2000).
[108] 8 USC § 1182(a)(2)(C)(2013).
[109] 8 USC § 1227(a)(2)(E)(ii)(2008).
[110] *See* INA § 103(a)(1) (2010).

The Caseload Forecast Council is not liable for errors or omissions in the manual, for sentences that may be inappropriately calculated as a result of a practitioner's or court's reliance on the manual, or for any other written or verbal information related to adult or juvenile sentencing. The scoring sheets are intended to provide assistance in most cases but does not cover all permutations of the scoring rules. If you find any errors or omissions, we encourage you to report them to the Caseload Forecast Council.

APPENDIX D: Beyond Juvenile Court: Long-Term Impact of a Juvenile Record.
Washington Defenders Association

of immigration relief such as Asylum[111] or Special Immigrant Juvenile Status.[112] However, non-citizens do not have a right to counsel in removal proceedings and indigent clients are rarely represented and/or made aware of possible avenues of relief. A juvenile adjudication will not automatically bar admissibility under immigration laws as an adult conviction might but it can and will be considered by DHS and Immigration Courts for discretionary determinations such as requests for relief from removal and applications for permanent legal residence.

Whether or not juveniles are put into removal proceedings depends largely on whether DHS acting through Immigration and Customs Enforcement ("ICE") finds them and wants to remove them. The Juvenile Rehabilitation Administration ("JRA") and some juvenile detention facilities report juveniles who are foreign nationals and in their custody to ICE.[113] JRA's policy requires foreign nationals to stay in the institution through the duration of their disposition and makes them ineligible for authorized leave or community placement until "(1) The youth is placed in ICE custody; (2) ICE informs JRA in writing that they have no interest in the youth or does not respond within 90 days of sending the 'Notice of Foreign National Incarceration'…; or (3) the youth reaches his/her release date."[114]

Drug Abuse or Drug Addiction: Drug abuse and drug addiction are both grounds of inadmissibility[115] and deportability.[116] Since these provisions do not require a conviction they may be applied against a non-citizen juvenile. It is important to be aware of this consequence when considering entering pleas or dispositions for purposes of Juvenile Drug or Juvenile Treatment Courts.

The following resources are available on the WDA website at www.defensenet.org:

- *Immigration and Washington State Criminal Law*, by Ann Benson, Director and Jonathan Moore, Immigration Resource Specialist of the Washington Defender Association's Immigration Project (2005) *available at* http://www.defensenet.org/resources/publications-1/immigration-and-washington-criminal-law/Immigration%20Crimes%20FINAL%2001-06-09.pdf; and

- For information about Special Immigrant Juvenile Status see www.defensenet.org and the Immigrant Legal Resource Center website at www.ilrc.org.

> **PRACTICE TIP:** For technical assistance, WDA members should call or e-mail the Washington Defender Association Immigration Project at (206)726-3332 or complete the online form found at: http://www.defensenet.org/immigration-project/immigration.

---

[111] 8 USC § 1158 (2009).
[112] 8 USC 1101(a)(27)(J)(iii) (2013).
[113] JRA Bulletin 38, § 38-400(1)(2)(2007) (interpreting RCW 10.70.140 to apply to juveniles as well as adults and therefore require reporting the juvenile to ICE).
[114] JRA Bulletin 38, § 38-400 (6)(2010).
[115] 8 USC § 1182(a)(1)(A)(iv)(2013).
[116] 8 USC § 1227(a)(2)(B)(ii)(2008).

The Caseload Forecast Council is not liable for errors or omissions in the manual, for sentences that may be inappropriately calculated as a result of a practitioner's or court's reliance on the manual, or for any other written or verbal information related to adult or juvenile sentencing. The scoring sheets are intended to provide assistance in most cases but does not cover all permutations of the scoring rules. If you find any errors or omissions, we encourage you to report them to the Caseload Forecast Council.

APPENDIX D: Beyond Juvenile Court: Long-Term Impact of a Juvenile Record.
Washington Defenders Association

Legal Financial Obligations (LFOs)

Juvenile respondents are required to pay legal financial obligations similar to adult defendants. These legal financial obligations include restitution,[117] fines, crime victim penalty assessments,[118] court costs, and court appointed attorneys fees and costs of defense.[119] One difference between adult and juvenile legal financial obligations is that interest does not accrue on juvenile obligations; however, collection fees may be assessed.[120] **Legal financial obligations imposed on juveniles do not "go away" when the juvenile becomes an adult.**

Restitution is the money owed by the respondent to the victim for damages for injury or loss of property. Restitution must be "easily ascertainable"[121] and a "foreseeable consequence" of the crime committed.[122] Restitution must be ordered and cannot be waived, reduced or converted, with only one exception: restitution ordered to an insurance company may be reduced or waived if the respondent can show that he or she could not reasonably acquire the means to pay the insurance company over a ten-year period.[123] All co-respondents are liable for restitution jointly and severally.[124] Restitution may be enforced for 10 years after the respondent's 18th birthday and then jurisdiction to enforce restitution may be extended an additional 10 years.[125]

Fines may be ordered by the court pursuant to the juvenile offender sentencing standards.[126] Fines may be converted into "community restitution" (which is similar to community service hours) if, due to a change in circumstances after the fine has been ordered, the juvenile cannot pay, unless the monetary penalty is the crime victim penalty assessment, which cannot be converted, waived, or otherwise modified, except for schedule of payment.[127] Fines may be extended in the same manner as restitution, and may be enforced up to 20 years after the respondent's 18th birthday.[128]

Victim penalty assessments cannot be waived and must be ordered in every juvenile disposition, regardless of whether there is a "victim."[129] Like other financial obligations, victim penalty assessments can be enforced for a total of 20 years after the respondent's 18th birthday.[130]

---

[117] RCW 13.40.020(25).
[118] RCW 7.68.035(1)(b).
[119] RCW 13.40.145.
[120] Unlike the 12% interest rate assessed on adult legal financial obligations, See RCW 10.82.090, RCW 4.56.110, the Juvenile Justice Act, RCW 13.40, does not provide for interest on legal financial obligations. Collection fees may be imposed. See e.g., King County Code 4.71.160 (Ord. 13995 § 2, 2000).
[121] RCW 13.40.020(25).
[122] State v. Hiett, 154 Wn.2d 560, 572, 115 P.3d 274 (2005).
[123] RCW 13.40.190(1).
[124] RCW 13.40.190(1)(f).
[125] RCW 13.40.192.
[126] RCW 13.40.0357.
[127] RCW 13.40.200(4).
[128] RCW 13.40.192.
[129] RCW 7.68.035(1)(b); RCW 13.40.200(4).
[130] RCW 13.40.192; RCW 13.40.198.

The Caseload Forecast Council is not liable for errors or omissions in the manual, for sentences that may be inappropriately calculated as a result of a practitioner's or court's reliance on the manual, or for any other written or verbal information related to adult or juvenile sentencing. The scoring sheets are intended to provide assistance in most cases but does not cover all permutations of the scoring rules. If you find any errors or omissions, we encourage you to report them to the Caseload Forecast Council.

APPENDIX D: Beyond Juvenile Court: Long-Term Impact of a Juvenile Record. Washington Defenders Association

Court-appointed attorneys' fees and costs of appeal may be ordered against a juvenile, a parent or another person legally obligated to support the juvenile if the state prevails on an appeal of a juvenile disposition, if the court finds an ability to pay.[131] This obligation is enforceable for 10 years after the respondent's 18th birthday or 10 years from the date the juvenile court jurisdiction expires.[132]

> **PRACTICE TIP:** Remind clients that **every** juvenile adjudication will carry some financial obligation, i.e., the victim penalty assessment, and these obligations may remain enforceable for 20 years.

> **PRACTICE TIP:** Ask the court to reduce or waive restitution to insurance companies where it is clear that your client will not have the earning potential in the next ten years to pay the restitution.

> **PRACTICE TIP:** Where there are multiple co-respondents jointly and severally liable, advise your client that the court will not "refund" a co-respondent that pays more than his or her share. If a co-respondent makes a restitution payment to the court after one or more of the co-respondents have already paid off the total obligation, the court will return the payment to that co-respondent. Co-respondents who pay off the total restitution obligation have only civil recourse against their non-paying co-respondents.

Driving

A juvenile's ability to keep or obtain a driver's license will be affected by adjudications for offenses related to drugs, alcohol, firearms and driving. The juvenile court is required to notify the Department of Licensing ("DOL") when juveniles are adjudicated of certain offenses or when they enter into diversion agreements for certain offenses.[133]

Minors in Possession of Alcohol, Drugs or Firearms: A juvenile adjudicated of Minor in Possession of Alcohol ("MIP");[134] possession, sale or use of controlled substances ("VUCSA")[135] illegal possession, sale or use of prescription drugs[136] or imitation controlled substances;[137] or possession of a firearm[138] will have his or her right to drive revoked for a period of 1 year or until the juvenile turns 17 (whichever is longer) for a first offense.[139] For a second offense the revocation is for two years or until the juvenile is 18 (whichever is longer). The

---

[131] RCW 13.40.145.
[132] *Id.*
[133] RCW 13.40.265.
[134] RCW 66.44.365.
[135] RCW 69.50.420.
[136] RCW 69.41.065.
[137] RCW 69.52.070.
[138] RCW 13.40.265; RCW 9.41.040(5).
[139] RCW 13.40.265(1)(c).

The Caseload Forecast Council is not liable for errors or omissions in the manual, for sentences that may be inappropriately calculated as a result of a practitioner's or court's reliance on the manual, or for any other written or verbal information related to adult or juvenile sentencing. The scoring sheets are intended to provide assistance in most cases but does not cover all permutations of the scoring rules. If you find any errors or omissions, we encourage you to report them to the Caseload Forecast Council.

APPENDIX D: Beyond Juvenile Court: Long-Term Impact of a Juvenile Record.
Washington Defenders Association

revocation periods for multiple MIP's are treated consecutively but they cannot last beyond a juvenile's 21st birthday.[140]

For both adults and juveniles alike, there are consequences for DUI's and driving with a "lack of physical control." The consequences depend on whether or not this is a first offense, the level of intoxication or impaired ability[141], and the resulting offense.[142]

Reinstatement: A juvenile convicted of their first offense involving drugs, alcohol or a firearm can petition the court for reinstatement ninety days after the date the juvenile turns 16 or ninety days after the incident date (whichever was later).[143] If it is the second offense then the juvenile cannot petition until they are seventeen or until one year has passed (whichever is longer).[144] Where a juvenile's license has been suspended because of consecutive MIP revocations the license is automatically reinstated when a juvenile turns 21.[145]

Other Offenses Involving Motor Vehicles: For all juveniles who are driving during the offense, adjudications for the following crimes require suspension, revocation or disqualification of driving privileges for varying time periods depending upon whether it is the first or subsequent offense:

- Taking a Motor Vehicle (drivers only) and any felony involving a motor vehicle (1 year revocation);[146]
- Vehicular Assault (1 year revocation);[147]
- Vehicular Homicide (2 year revocation);[148]
- Racing or Reckless Driving (potential 1 year revocation);[149]
- Hit and Run Attended (potential 1 year);[150]
- DWLS/R 1st or 2nd degree;[151]
- Attempting to Elude;[152]
- Unattended Child in Running Vehicle;[153]
- Reckless Endangerment in a Construction Zone (60+ day suspension).[154]

---

[140] *Id.*
[141] *See* RCW 46.61.5055 for penalty schedule driving under the influence of alcohol.
[142] *See* RCW 46.61.502 (DUI); RCW 46.61.504 (Physical Control).
[143] RCW 13.40.265(1)(c).
[144] *Id.*
[145] RCW 46.20.265.
[146] RCW 46.20.285.
[147] RCW 46.20.285(2).
[148] RCW 46.20.285(1).
[149] RCW 46.61.500, RCW 46.61.530, RCW 46.20.285.
[150] RCW 46.20.285(5), RCW 46.52.020.
[151] RCW 46.20.342.
[152] RCW 46.61.024.
[153] RCW 46.61.685.
[154] RCW 46.61.527(5).

The Caseload Forecast Council is not liable for errors or omissions in the manual, for sentences that may be inappropriately calculated as a result of a practitioner's or court's reliance on the manual, or for any other written or verbal information related to adult or juvenile sentencing. The scoring sheets are intended to provide assistance in most cases but does not cover all permutations of the scoring rules. If you find any errors or omissions, we encourage you to report them to the Caseload Forecast Council.

**APPENDIX D: Beyond Juvenile Court: Long-Term Impact of a Juvenile Record.
Washington Defenders Association**

Juveniles convicted of these offenses may not petition DOL for early reinstatement.[155]

Diversion Agreements: Juveniles entering into diversion agreements for drug or alcohol offenses will have their licenses suspended or revoked by the Department of Licensing ("DOL") similar to if they were adjudicated guilty in court.[156]

- **Counsel and Release Agreements:** Under certain circumstances, a diversion unit is permitted to "counsel and release" a juvenile rather than enter into a diversion agreement.[157] Counsel and release agreements are not sent to the DOL and so do not affect a juveniles' ability to drive.[158]

- **Reinstatement After Diversion:** DOL will reinstate a juvenile's driving privileges upon receiving notice of completion of a diversion agreement; however, not before 90 days after their 16th birthday or 90 days after they entered into the diversion agreement, whichever is longer, if it was their first offense.[159] If it is their second or subsequent offense, DOL will not reinstate the juvenile's driving privileges until their 17th birthday or 1 year after they entered the diversion agreement, whichever is longer.[160]

Intermediate Licenses for 16 and 17 Year Olds: New drivers under the age of 18 must obtain an "intermediate license."[161] A juvenile will not be eligible for the intermediate license if he or she has received any traffic violations for the previous six months or been adjudicated for any offenses related to alcohol or drugs during the time the applicant had an instruction permit.[162] An MIP or other driving offense will affect an intermediate license in the same way as a standard license.

Driving Without a License or Driving While Suspended or Revoked: It is a misdemeanor to drive without a valid driver's license if the person's license has been suspended or revoked or if the person is not carrying valid identifying documentation.[163] Otherwise, driving without a valid driver's license is an infraction.[164]

Anyone over the age of 13 driving without a valid license can have their license revoked or suspended by the DOL for the same amount of time that a licensed driver would.[165] A juvenile

---

[155] There is no statute that allows for reinstatement for these offenses.
[156] RCW 13.40.265(2).
[157] RCW 13.40.080(14).
[158] *Id.*
[159] RCW 13.40.265(1)(c).
[160] *Id.*
[161] RCW 46.20.075.
[162] RCW 46.20.075(e)-(f).
[163] RCW 46.20.005.
[164] *Id.*
[165] RCW 46.20.317.

The Caseload Forecast Council is not liable for errors or omissions in the manual, for sentences that may be inappropriately calculated as a result of a practitioner's or court's reliance on the manual, or for any other written or verbal information related to adult or juvenile sentencing. The scoring sheets are intended to provide assistance in most cases but does not cover all permutations of the scoring rules. If you find any errors or omissions, we encourage you to report them to the Caseload Forecast Council.

APPENDIX D: Beyond Juvenile Court: Long-Term Impact of a Juvenile Record.
Washington Defenders Association

caught driving with a suspended or revoked driver's license or privilege faces several possible consequences ranging from additional revocation, to imprisonment and fines, depending on the status of the driving privilege.[166]

Temporary Restricted Licenses: Under certain circumstances, a juvenile whose driver's license has been revoked or suspended as a result of criminal adjudications may obtain a "temporary restricted license" by demonstrating that driving a vehicle is necessary to go to school, work, medical appointments, or for other reasons enumerated by statute.[167]

Insurance Rates: Most juveniles who drive are covered by their parents' or guardian's insurance policy. The cost of insurance depends on multiple variables including the kind of car, the residence location, the car the parents' or legal guardians' drive, the juvenile's driving record and whether the guardian owns or rents their house. The result of having an adjudication that has been reported to DOL could increase insurance costs.

> **PRACTICE TIP:** The laws regarding license suspension, revocation and reinstatement are complex. For specific questions, review RCW 46.20 and WAC 308-104, contact DOL Customer Service at (360) 902-3900, or e-mail drivers@dol.wa.gov or consult the DOL website: http://www.dol.wa.gov/ds.

> **PRACTICE TIP:** Parents concerned about their insurance rates should consult directly with their insurance companies to assess whether their child's diversion or adjudication will affect their policy.

School Issues

School Notification: After any arrest or decision to arrest, the police or prosecuting attorney **may give to a school** any information "pertaining to the investigation, diversion, and prosecution of a juvenile attending the school," including any incident reports.[168]

Adjudication of the following offenses **requires notification to the principal** of the school where the juvenile attends:[169]

- a violent offense as defined in RCW 9.94A.030;
- a sex offense as defined in RCW 9.94A.030;
- inhaling toxic fumes under chapter 9.47A RCW;
- a controlled substance violation under chapter 69.50 RCW;

---

[166] RCW 46.20.342.
[167] RCW 46.20.391.
[168] RCW 13.50.050(7).
[169] RCW 13.04.155(1).

The Caseload Forecast Council is not liable for errors or omissions in the manual, for sentences that may be inappropriately calculated as a result of a practitioner's or court's reliance on the manual, or for any other written or verbal information related to adult or juvenile sentencing. The scoring sheets are intended to provide assistance in most cases but does not cover all permutations of the scoring rules. If you find any errors or omissions, we encourage you to report them to the Caseload Forecast Council.

APPENDIX D: Beyond Juvenile Court: Long-Term Impact of a Juvenile Record. Washington Defenders Association

- a liquor violation under RCW 66.44.270; and
- any crime under RCW's 9.41 (Firearms), 9A.36 (Assault), 9A.40 (Kidnapping), 9A.46 (Harassment), and 9A.48 (Arson).

The principal must give information received pursuant to the above notification to the student's teachers, persons who supervise the student and anyone else the principal deems necessary for security purposes.[170]

Discipline, Suspension or Expulsion: All juveniles in Washington have a constitutional right to education. Nevertheless, a student may be disciplined, suspended or expelled from school for violating school rules as defined by the school district.[171] Suspension or expulsion from school may result from criminal or non-criminal misconduct.[172] For the offenses listed above which require school notification (violent offenses, sex offenses, etc.) the principal is required to "consider" imposing a long-term suspension or expulsion.[173]

- **Firearms:** A **mandatory one year expulsion** will be imposed on a student who is "determined to have" carried a firearm onto, or to have possessed a firearm on, public elementary or secondary school premises, public school-provided transportation, or areas of facilities while being used exclusively by public schools.[174]

- **Crimes Against Teachers and Other Students:** By statute, if a juvenile commits assault, kidnapping, harassment or arson directed toward a teacher, that student cannot be assigned to that teacher's classroom again.[175] If a juvenile commits any of those offenses against another student, the juvenile may be removed from the classroom of the victim for the duration of their school attendance.[176] Commission of any of those offenses is grounds for suspension or expulsion.[177]

- **Gang Activity:** A student enrolled in a public school may be suspended or expelled if the student is a member of a gang and knowingly engages in "gang activity" on school grounds.[178] A student found to have committed the offense of "criminal gang intimidation"[179] must also be considered for long-term suspension or expulsion where there have been two or more violations in three years.[180]

---

[170] RCW 13.04.155(2).
[171] RCW 28A.600.010-RCW 28A.600.040.
[172] Id.
[173] RCW 28A.600.020(5).
[174] RCW 28A.600.420, RCW 28A.600.010.
[175] RCW 28A.600.460(2).
[176] RCW 28A.600.460(3).
[177] Id.
[178] RCW 28A.600.455.
[179] RCW 9A.46.120.
[180] RCW 9A.46.120.

The Caseload Forecast Council is not liable for errors or omissions in the manual, for sentences that may be inappropriately calculated as a result of a practitioner's or court's reliance on the manual, or for any other written or verbal information related to adult or juvenile sentencing. The scoring sheets are intended to provide assistance in most cases but does not cover all permutations of the scoring rules. If you find any errors or omissions, we encourage you to report them to the Caseload Forecast Council.

APPENDIX D: Beyond Juvenile Court: Long-Term Impact of a Juvenile Record. Washington Defenders Association

Sports Eligibility: Eligibility to participate in school athletic programs in Washington is governed by the rules of the Washington Interscholastic Activities Association (WIAA), individual school districts and individual schools.

- **Drugs:** Student athletes found to have violated the laws of prescription drugs (RCW 69.41) or controlled substances (RCW 69.50), either by the illegal possession, use or sale, will be immediately ineligible for participation in an interscholastic sports program pursuant to WIAA rules.[181] The ineligibility continues for the remainder of the year for the first violation, unless the student accesses a community or school assistance program.[182] In order to be eligible the following year, the student must meet with a "sports eligibility board." A second violation requires ineligibility for 1 calendar year and a third violation results in permanent ineligibility.[183] School Districts and schools may have their own eligibility policies that are not inconsistent with the WIAA rules.[184]

- **Other Criminal Activity:** WIAA rules do not specifically address other criminal activity; however, the rules do require eligible athletes to meet academic and attendance requirements. School districts generally have codes of conduct which, if violated, may preclude sports eligibility. For example, school districts may have ineligibility rules regarding the possession or use of alcohol or unsportsmanlike conduct.[185]

Applying to College

College and University Admissions: Some Washington colleges use an applicant's criminal history to inform their admissions decisions.[186] However, a student's criminal history may influence his or her ability to complete a practicum in fields that have restrictions on participation. For example, early childhood education, teaching and health care practicums are limited to students who are not legally banned from having contact with people from vulnerable

---

[181] WAC 392-183A-015.
[182] WIAA Policy 18.26.2.
[183] Id.
[184] See e.g., Seattle Public Schools Athletic/Activity Substance Use Policy, http://www.seattleschools.org/modules/groups/homepagefiles/cms/1583136/File/Forms/Athletics/Handbook.pdf (2009). Under Seattle School District policy, a student caught selling or distributing any quantity of illegal drugs, counterfeit drugs or controlled substances will be excluded from athletic participation for 1 calendar year and law enforcement will be contacted. A student caught in possession, use, distribution, transmittal, or under the influence of any drug or counterfeit drugs will be immediately excluded from the sports team for 20% of the contests, but not practice. If the student and parents do not agree to participate in assessment and approved substance abuse education, the student will be excluded from participation in athletic events for one calendar year.
[185] See e.g., Tacoma School District Regulation 2151R, http://www.tacoma.k12.wa.us/calendar/Calendar%20PDFs/2010-11RRR.pdf.
[186] For example, certain schools at University of Washington require a criminal background check. See, e.g., http://www.tacoma.washington.edu/enrollmentservices/admissions/docs/nur_bsn_app_kit.pdf. However, community colleges generally do not. See, e.g., http://www.seattlecentral.edu/admissions/admissApplication.pdf.

The Caseload Forecast Council is not liable for errors or omissions in the manual, for sentences that may be inappropriately calculated as a result of a practitioner's or court's reliance on the manual, or for any other written or verbal information related to adult or juvenile sentencing. The scoring sheets are intended to provide assistance in most cases but does not cover all permutations of the scoring rules. If you find any errors or omissions, we encourage you to report them to the Caseload Forecast Council.

APPENDIX D: Beyond Juvenile Court: Long-Term Impact of a Juvenile Record.
Washington Defenders Association

populations and require criminal background checks for participation.[187] See also Section XII, *Employment*.

The "**Common Application**" used by many **private schools** around the country **does not ask** about prior convictions/adjudications. However it requires a teacher evaluation and school report, which may disclose conviction/adjudication information. In Washington, each private college or university treats an applicant's criminal history differently. Some ask the applicant about his or her criminal history directly, others do not ask the student but expect the information to come from teachers and/or counselors.[188]

Eligibility for the Washington State Needs Grant is not affected by juvenile criminal history and is determined through the Federal Application for Financial Student Aid (FAFSA) application, which excludes juvenile arrests and adjudications from being considered.[189]

Federal Student Loans

Juveniles convicted of drug offenses do not fall under the Higher Education Act's ban on federal financial aid.[190]

Until 2006, a person convicted **as an adult** of **any drug offense** including possession of marijuana was not eligible for any federal higher education grant, loan, or work study assistance for various time periods. Only those convicted of a drug offense while receiving federal student aid are now suspended from receiving federal student aid.[191] If a student is not convicted while enrolled there should be no suspension of financial aid.

Additionally, a person may not claim the tax benefits of the Hope Scholarship Credit for an academic period if he or she "has been convicted of a Federal or State felony offense consisting of the possession or distribution of a controlled substance before the end of the taxable year with or within" which the academic period ends.[192]

---

[187] RCW 43.43.842.
[188] For example, Gonzaga and Seattle Pacific University ask about a student's criminal history on their applications. The University of Puget Sound and Whitman College do not ask applicants about criminal history but will consider it if it is revealed through recommendations or other sources.
[189] RCW 28B.92.080 (2010); WAC 250-20-011 (2010); 20 U.S.C. § 1091(r)(2); FAFSA Student Aid Eligibility Worksheet available online at https://studentaid.ed.gov/sites/default/files/2012-13-student-aid-eligibility-drug-worksheet.pdf, last visited on August 29, 2013.
[190] 34 C.F.R.§668.40 (a)(2).
[191] *See* Federal benefits found under 20 U.S.C. §1070 *et seq.* and 42 U.S.C. §2751 *et seq.*; Higher Education Act, 20 U.S.C. §1091(r)(1); Deficit Reduction Act of 2005, Pub. L. No. 171, §8021, 120 Stat. 4.
[192] 26 U.S.C. § 25A(b)(2)(D).

The Caseload Forecast Council is not liable for errors or omissions in the manual, for sentences that may be inappropriately calculated as a result of a practitioner's or court's reliance on the manual, or for any other written or verbal information related to adult or juvenile sentencing. The scoring sheets are intended to provide assistance in most cases but does not cover all permutations of the scoring rules. If you find any errors or omissions, we encourage you to report them to the Caseload Forecast Council.

APPENDIX D: Beyond Juvenile Court: Long-Term Impact of a Juvenile Record.
Washington Defenders Association

The student may receive a **waiver** if the student successfully completes an approved drug rehabilitation program.[193]

Right to Possess Firearms

Possession of Firearms Generally Prohibited for Minors: A person under 18 years old may not lawfully own or be in possession of a gun in Washington except under statutorily limited circumstances.[194] Federal law also has restrictions on gun ownership by persons under 21[195] and prohibits possession of firearms by fugitives, drug addicts, illegal aliens, persons dishonorably discharged from the military and persons subject to domestic violence protection orders.[196]

Revocation of the Right to Possess Firearms: The following crimes, upon adjudication, a finding of not-guilty by reason of insanity, or a dismissal after a period of deferral, will take away a juvenile's right to possess firearms **even after they turn 18**, until their right is restored by a court of record:

- any felony;
- the following crimes of domestic violence:
    - assault in the fourth degree;
    - coercion;
    - stalking;
    - reckless endangerment;
    - criminal trespass in the first degree;
    - violation of the provisions of a protection order or no-contact order restraining the person or excluding the person from a residence.

Possessing a firearm after the right has been revoked is a felony.[197]

Reinstatement: In Washington, an adult or juvenile who is prohibited from possessing a firearm because of a criminal adjudication may petition the court for reinstatement of this right under the following circumstances:[198]

- The person has not been convicted of a sex offense or a Class A felony; and

---

[193] 20 U.S.C. § 1091(r)(2).
[194] RCW 9.41.040(2)(a)(iii); RCW 9.41.042. Some permissible circumstances include, among others: at an authorized shooting range, hunting with a valid license, on his or her parent's property with parental consent, or as a member of the armed forces.
[195] 18 U.S.C. § 922(x)(2010).
[196] 18 U.S.C. § 922(g)(2010).
[197] RCW 9.41.040(3).
[198] *Id., See also State v. Mihali*,152 Wn.App. 879, 218 P.3d 922 (2009).

The Caseload Forecast Council is not liable for errors or omissions in the manual, for sentences that may be inappropriately calculated as a result of a practitioner's or court's reliance on the manual, or for any other written or verbal information related to adult or juvenile sentencing. The scoring sheets are intended to provide assistance in most cases but does not cover all permutations of the scoring rules. If you find any errors or omissions, we encourage you to report them to the Caseload Forecast Council.

APPENDIX D: Beyond Juvenile Court: Long-Term Impact of a Juvenile Record.
Washington Defenders Association

- **Felony offense:** after **5 years** crime free if the individual has no prior felony convictions/adjudications that prohibit the possession of a firearm counted as part of his or her offender score;
- **Non-felony offense:** after **3 years** crime free, if the individual has no prior felony convictions/ adjudications that prohibit the possession of a firearm counted as part of the offender score and the individual has completed all conditions of the sentence.

Class A felons and sex offenders can only reinstate their rights to possess firearms in Washington by **obtaining a pardon, annulment, or a certificate of rehabilitation** (which is not available for Washington convictions[199]). These are also the only means available for reinstating firearm rights before the requisite time periods have expired.[200]

Federal Law: Persons convicted of felonies or DV misdemeanors are also prohibited from possessing firearms under federal law.[201] Whether a juvenile adjudication is a "conviction" for purposes of the federal law of unlawful possession of a firearm is determined by the state law where the person was "convicted."[202] Although there are no federal decisions specifically addressing this issue, state juvenile adjudications in Washington have been found to be "convictions" for purposes of Washington's law prohibiting felons from possessing firearms.[203] Ambiguities still may exist; however, there are statutes and cases that weigh in favor of a Washington state juvenile adjudication being considered a conviction for federal firearms prohibitions.[204] *See also* Section I, *Is a Juvenile Adjudication a "Conviction"?* Conversely, a federal juvenile adjudication will not remove the right to possess a firearm under federal law because under the Federal Juvenile Delinquency Act, a juvenile is not "convicted" but "adjudicated."[205]

Reinstatement under Washington law of firearm rights lost pursuant to a Washington state juvenile adjudication should prevent prosecution under federal law.[206]

> **PRACTICE TIP:** Juvenile clients with felony or domestic violence adjudications should be reminded that they cannot legally possess a firearm even after they turn 18 unless a court grants them the right. It is not automatic. Sealing juvenile records will not reinstate the right. A hunting license may be issued to persons whose right to possess a gun has been revoked, but this will not protect them from criminal liability. Also, the right will need to be restored to obtain any employment that requires possession or use of a firearm.

[199] *State v. Masangkay*, 121 Wash. App. 904, 91 P.3d 140 (Div. 1 2004), *petition for review granted*, 153 Wash.2d 1017, 108 P.3d 1226, March 1, 2005.
[200] *Id.*
[201] 18 U.S.C. § 922(g).
[202] 18 U.S.C. § 921(a)(20).
[203] *See, e.g., State v. Wright*, 88 Wash. App. 683, 946 P.2d 792 (1997), *State v. McKinley*, 84 Wash. App. 677, 929 P.2d 1145 (1997).
[204] RCW 9.94A.030(11); RCW 13.04.011(1); *See In the Matter of JUVENILES A, B, C, D, E*, 121 Wash.2d 80, 847 P.2d 455 (1993)(holding juveniles found to have committed sex offenses must submit to HIV testing under RCW 70.24.340(1)(a) and finding "Numerous other statutes, including sections of the Sentencing Reform Act of 1981, RCW 9.94A, and the Juvenile Justice Act of 1977, RCW 13.40, use 'convicted' to reference both adult and juvenile offenders."); *But see U.S. v. Walters*, 359 F.3d 340 (4th Cir. 2004)(Virginia law finding a juvenile delinquent was not a "conviction" for purposes of the federal firearms statute).
[205] 18. U.S.C. § 5031-5042 (2005); *U.S. v. Walters*, 359 F.3d at 343.
[206] 18 U.S.C. § 921(a)(20)(2010).

The Caseload Forecast Council is not liable for errors or omissions in the manual, for sentences that may be inappropriately calculated as a result of a practitioner's or court's reliance on the manual, or for any other written or verbal information related to adult or juvenile sentencing. The scoring sheets are intended to provide assistance in most cases but does not cover all permutations of the scoring rules. If you find any errors or omissions, we encourage you to report them to the Caseload Forecast Council.

APPENDIX D: Beyond Juvenile Court: Long-Term Impact of a Juvenile Record.
Washington Defenders Association

Voting and Jury Service

Voting: Juvenile adjudications do not result in the loss of the right to vote.[207] Adult felony convictions will prohibit persons from voting until their civil rights have been restored.[208]

Jury Service: Juvenile adjudications should not affect a person's ability to serve on a jury. Like voting, only adult felons who have had their civil rights restored may serve on juries.[209]

Military Service

All branches of the military are required to do criminal background checks on applicants, which include juvenile criminal histories (citations, arrests and adjudications).[210] An applicant's **full and complete criminal history** must be given to the Armed Forces, including disclosure of convictions/adjudications that have been expunged or sealed.[211]

A juvenile felony adjudication will generally preclude military service; however, each branch has the discretion to make exceptions by granting **waivers.**[212] According to the Department of Defense, "The waiver procedure is not automatic and approval is based on each individual case, including consideration of the individual's adjustment to civilian life."[213]

---

[207] RCW 29A.08.520 (requires the clerk of the court to forward notice of felony "convictions" of "defendants" to the county auditor or custodian of voting records.) Although some ambiguity may exist with respect to juvenile felonies and voting since the definition of "adjudication" and "conviction" have become more interchangeable after amendments to RCW 13.40 and RCW 9.94 in the mid-1990's, juvenile adjudications cannot remove civil rights which have not attached and where there is no statutory provision for restoration of civil rights following such adjudications.

[208] RCW 29A.08.520.

[209] RCW 2.36.070.

[210] 32 C.F.R. § 96.3.

[211] 32 CFR § 571.1 (Army regulations).

[212] 10 U.S.C. §504, 32 C.F.R. §96.1 *et seq* (2005). The standards for waivers can be complex and variable. The following information is current as of 6/2005. Current information should be obtained directly from a recruiter. The **Army** requires a waiver for applicants with (1) six or more minor traffic offenses (where the fine was $250 or more per offense); (2) three or more minor non-traffic offenses; (3) two or more misdemeanors; or (4) one or more felonies. See AR 601-210 Chapter 4. The **Air Force** divides offenses into five different categories based on seriousness and requires waivers based on the category, the number of adjudications and the time frame in which the offenses were committed. *See* "Air Education and Training Command Instruction 36-200," *Air Force Recruiting*. The **Marines** divide criminal offenses into one of six categories. In general, a waiver is required for: five to nine minor traffic offenses; two to five more serious traffic offenses; two or more Class 1 minor non-traffic offenses; two to nine Class 2 minor non-traffic offenses; two to five serious offenses; or one felony. Individuals with ten or more minor traffic offenses, six or more serious traffic offenses, ten or more Class 2 minor non-traffic offenses, six or more serious non-traffic offenses, or more than one felony are not eligible for a waiver. *See* Marine Corps Order (MCO) P1100.72.B, *Military Personnel Procurement Manual, Volume 2, Enlisted Procurement*. The **Navy** divides criminal offenses into four categories. Applicants with six or more minor traffic violations, three or more Minor Non-Traffic Violations/Minor Misdemeanors, one or more Non-Minor Misdemeanors, or one or more felonies, require a waiver. *See* "Comnavcruitcominst 1130.8F," *Navy Enlisted Recruiting Program*.

[213] DOD Directive 1304.26 *Qualification Standards for Enlistment, Appointment and Induction* (September 20, 2005, incorporating change, September 20, 2011).

The Caseload Forecast Council is not liable for errors or omissions in the manual, for sentences that may be inappropriately calculated as a result of a practitioner's or court's reliance on the manual, or for any other written or verbal information related to adult or juvenile sentencing. The scoring sheets are intended to provide assistance in most cases but does not cover all permutations of the scoring rules. If you find any errors or omissions, we encourage you to report them to the Caseload Forecast Council.

APPENDIX D: Beyond Juvenile Court: Long-Term Impact of a Juvenile Record.
Washington Defenders Association

Even sealed juvenile adjudications may require a waiver.[214]

Other Barriers to Enlistment: The Armed Forces will test applicants for **drug and alcohol use and dependency**. Anyone found to be dependent on drugs or alcohol will be denied entrance.[215] Also, **ineligibility to possess a firearm** as a result of a conviction may preclude service until the right has been restored.[216] See Section IX, *Right to Possess Firearms*.

> **PRACTICE TIP:** Juvenile clients considering military service should contact a local recruiter to determine whether convictions/adjudications will preclude service or can be waived.

Employment

Juvenile adjudications, like adult convictions, can result in ineligibility for a variety jobs and occupational licenses in Washington State. Although the Restoration of Employment Rights Act, RCW 9.96A, prohibits government entities from denying employment or occupational licenses to persons *solely* based on their felony convictions, there are numerous exceptions to this general rule.[217] Unless they have been sealed, juvenile adjudications are accessible to employers through the Washington State Patrol, the courts, and private companies that collect information from public databases. See Section II, *Juvenile Criminal History Records*.

Background Checks Required: Criminal background checks are required for all persons and organizations who are licensed to **provide services to children or vulnerable adults.**[218] For people applying for licenses to provide child care, foster care or care for persons with developmental disabilities, DSHS must do background checks on all household members 16 years and older who are not already foster children.[219] **School districts and their contractors** who have employees who will have regular unsupervised access to children are also required to do criminal background checks on their employees.[220] Juvenile adjudications will be disclosed just like adult convictions on criminal background checks. See Section II, *Juvenile Criminal History Records*.

---

[214] 32 CFR § 571.3 (2005)(Army enlistment and waiver criteria).
[215] 10 U.S.C. § 978 (c)(1) (2005) (This section can be waived by the president during a time of war).
[216] "Former juvenile offender, who had pleaded guilty to second degree robbery and served sentence in juvenile detention facility, requested 'certificate of rehabilitation' less than three years after his release, to reinstate his right to possess firearms so that he could join the Marines." *State v. Masangkay*, 121 Wash. App. 904, 91 P.3d 140 (Div. 1, 2004) *petition for review granted*, 153 Wash.2d 1017, 108 P.3d 1228 (March 1, 2005).
[217] RCW 9.96A.020.
[218] RCW 43.43.834.
[219] WAC 388-06-0110.
[220] RCW 28A.400.303.

The Caseload Forecast Council is not liable for errors or omissions in the manual, for sentences that may be inappropriately calculated as a result of a practitioner's or court's reliance on the manual, or for any other written or verbal information related to adult or juvenile sentencing. The scoring sheets are intended to provide assistance in most cases but does not cover all permutations of the scoring rules. If you find any errors or omissions, we encourage you to report them to the Caseload Forecast Council.

**APPENDIX D: Beyond Juvenile Court: Long-Term Impact of a Juvenile Record.
Washington Defenders Association**

Nursing Homes, Childcare, etc.: "**Crime against children or other persons**"[221] will prohibit persons from working in **nursing homes, adult family homes, boarding homes, and child care facilities**.[222] This includes, among other offenses, assault in the fourth degree. "**Crimes relating to financial exploitation**,"[223] including theft in the third degree, will also make a person ineligible to work with vulnerable adults, e.g., in nursing homes. The time limits for ineligibility for such jobs may vary depending on the crime committed.

Persons who have **felony convictions for crimes against children, "spousal abuse," and violent crimes** will be permanently prohibited from contracting with or being licensed by DSHS to provide any type of care to children or individuals with a developmental disability.[224] Convictions for **assault or sex offenses not included in the permanent bar, any felony drug conviction or any other felony** will disqualify individuals from licensing, contracting, certification, or from having unsupervised access to children or to individuals with a developmental disability for 5 years.[225]

Schools: Crimes against children will disqualify persons from being school employees, contractors with schools or school bus drivers.[226] Volunteers may also be disqualified because of criminal history. Certified school employees, e.g., teachers, are also required to have "good moral character" which means no convictions in the last ten years, including motor vehicle violations, which "would materially and substantially impair the individual's worthiness and ability to serve as a professional within the public and private schools of the state."[227]

Professional Licenses: Many jobs require a person to be licensed by the Washington State Department of Licensing. Examples include, among others, massage therapists, midwives, chiropractors, cosmetologists, nursing assistants, dental assistants, and mental health counselors.[228] Some jobs also require licensing by specific boards, such as the optometry board and board of pharmacy.[229] Juvenile adjudications can interfere with a person's ability to obtain these licenses from the Department of Licensing. Violating drug laws is specifically listed as "unprofessional conduct" to be considered in licensing determinations.[230]

---

[221] RCW 43.43.830(7).
[222] RCW 43.43.842; WAC 388-97-1800 (nursing homes); WAC 388-76-10161 (adult family homes); WAC 388-06-0170 (access to children).
[223] RCW 43.43.830(9).
[224] WAC 388-06-0170.
[225] WAC 388-06-0180.
[226] RCW 28A.400.320 (2005) (school employees); RCW 28A.400.330 (school contractors); WAC 392-144-101 (school bus drivers).
[227] WAC 180-86-013.
[228] RCW 18.130.040.
[229] Id.
[230] RCW 18.130.180.

The Caseload Forecast Council is not liable for errors or omissions in the manual, for sentences that may be inappropriately calculated as a result of a practitioner's or court's reliance on the manual, or for any other written or verbal information related to adult or juvenile sentencing. The scoring sheets are intended to provide assistance in most cases but does not cover all permutations of the scoring rules. If you find any errors or omissions, we encourage you to report them to the Caseload Forecast Council.

APPENDIX D: Beyond Juvenile Court: Long-Term Impact of a Juvenile Record.
Washington Defenders Association

Federal Laws Affecting Employment Opportunities:[231] Federal law prohibits financial institutions from employing a person who has been convicted of a crime of dishonesty, breach of trust, or money unless he or she has received written consent from the Federal Deposit Insurance Corporation (FDIC).[232] For purposes of this law, pre-trial diversion or similar programs are considered to be convictions. Federal law also bars certain classes of felons from the following jobs:

- working in the insurance industry without having received permission from an insurance regulatory official;[233]
- holding any of several positions in a union or other organization that manages an employee benefit plan;[234]
- providing healthcare services for which they will receive payment from Medicare;[235]
- working for the generic drug industry;[236]
- providing prisoner transportation;[237] and
- employment in airport security.[238]

Other Jobs Affected: Other examples of jobs that are affected by certain types of convictions include (this list does not purport to include all jobs impacted by criminal history):

- Law enforcement;[239]
- Tow truck operators contracting with Washington State Patrol;[240]
- Washington State Patrol assistance van drivers;[241]
- JRA employment or volunteer positions.[242]

Jobs Requiring a Driver's License or Ability to Possess a Firearm: Since many jobs require the ability to drive, the penalty of losing a driver's license (see Section V, Driving) may prohibit some individuals from future employment, at least for a period of time.[243] Similarly, the consequence of losing the right to possess a firearm will naturally disqualify people from certain

---

[231] The federal laws in this section do not specifically address juvenile adjudications; however, definitions of "conviction" may be broad enough to include Washington juvenile adjudications. Specific statutes should be consulted.
[232] 12 U.S.C. § 1829.
[233] 18 U.S.C. § 1033(e).
[234] 29 U.S.C. § 504.
[235] 42 U.S.C. § 1320a-7.
[236] 21 U.S.C. § 335a.
[237] 42 U.S.C. § 13726b.
[238] 49 U.S.C. § 44935; 49 U.S.C. § 44936.
[239] *See* WAC 139-05-220 (2005).
[240] WAC 204-91A-060.
[241] WAC 204-93-040.
[242] RCW 72.05.440.
[243] *But see* RCW 46.20.391 (2013) (occupational driver's licenses).

The Caseload Forecast Council is not liable for errors or omissions in the manual, for sentences that may be inappropriately calculated as a result of a practitioner's or court's reliance on the manual, or for any other written or verbal information related to adult or juvenile sentencing. The scoring sheets are intended to provide assistance in most cases but does not cover all permutations of the scoring rules. If you find any errors or omissions, we encourage you to report them to the Caseload Forecast Council.

APPENDIX D: Beyond Juvenile Court: Long-Term Impact of a Juvenile Record. Washington Defenders Association

types of employment that require the ability to possess (e.g., security guards, federal park rangers, etc.).

Employment Discrimination:

Permissible Pre-employment Inquiries: Although some states ban the practice, in Washington employers and occupational licensing authorities are permitted to ask job applicants about and consider arrests not leading to conviction.[244] However, there is some limit. Because statistical studies regarding arrests have shown a disparate impact on racial minorities, it is an **unfair practice to ask about arrests older than 10 years** and inquiries must include whether the charges are still pending, have been dismissed or led to conviction of a crime involving behavior that would adversely affect job performance.[245] Certain organizations, such as law enforcement, state agencies and organizations that have direct responsibility for the supervision, care, or treatment of children, mentally ill persons, developmentally disabled persons, or other vulnerable adults are exempt from these restrictions.[246]

Similarly, for inquiries concerning **convictions** to be considered "fair" under Washington's discrimination law they must concern **convictions less than ten years old (from the date of release from prison) and relating reasonably to the job duties.**[247] Certain agencies and organizations, e.g., schools and DSHS, are exempt from this requirement.

> **PRACTICE TIP:** Remind juvenile clients that unsealed juvenile criminal history will be accessible to employers, even after the juvenile turns 18, and should be disclosed on employment applications. **The only way to remove juvenile criminal history from public view is by obtaining an order sealing the records in the court where the juvenile disposition occurred.**

Housing

Residential Screening: Both public and private housing landlords may look at an individual's criminal history, including juvenile criminal history, before or during their tenancy.[248] A juvenile's criminal history can discredit their entire household from housing. Many landlords rely on tenant screening services, which get their information from public records.[249] If a public housing authority wants to terminate a tenant's lease based on information from their criminal

---

[244] WAC 162-12-140(3)(b).
[245] Id.
[246] Id.
[247] RCW 49.60 et seq.; WAC 162-12-140(3) (2005).
[248] See Generally, 24 CFR § 966.4 (2010).
[249] Examples include First Advantage Corporation at www.fadv.com and Tenant Screening Services at www.tenantscreening.com.

The Caseload Forecast Council is not liable for errors or omissions in the manual, for sentences that may be inappropriately calculated as a result of a practitioner's or court's reliance on the manual, or for any other written or verbal information related to adult or juvenile sentencing. The scoring sheets are intended to provide assistance in most cases but does not cover all permutations of the scoring rules. If you find any errors or omissions, we encourage you to report them to the Caseload Forecast Council.

APPENDIX D: Beyond Juvenile Court: Long-Term Impact of a Juvenile Record.
Washington Defenders Association

history they must first notify the tenant and allow the tenant to dispute the accuracy or relevance of the record.[250]

Private Housing: In Washington, landlords are permitted to screen and deny housing to individuals based on criminal history.[251] A private landlord is not permitted to deny housing for discriminatory reasons, e.g., solely because of past drug addiction.[252] But **a private landlord may deny housing based on conviction for the manufacture or distribution of a controlled substance**[253] or **a reasonable belief that an applicant is currently engaged in illegal drug use.**[254] Also a tenant who is aware of a subtenant, sublessee, resident or anyone else engaging in drug, criminal or gang activity at the rental premise may be evicted from private residential property.[255]

The statutes governing **eviction** from residential property[256] allow landlords to evict a person who has been **arrested** for assault occurring on the premises or unlawful use of a firearm or other deadly weapon on the premises.[257] A landlord also may evict a tenant for engaging in **gang or drug related activity** or allowing another to engage in such activity on the premises.[258] Different laws apply to **mobile home parks** and allow for eviction for criminal activity that threatens the health, safety or welfare of the tenants.[259]

Public Housing: Federal law regulates admission and eviction from housing programs funded through the U.S. Department of Housing and Urban Development ("HUD"). There are different types of HUD programs[260] generally administered through local Public Housing Authorities ("PHAs") like the Seattle Housing Authority. Different housing providers receiving the same HUD funding may have different admission and eviction requirements; however, HUD requires landlords to deny housing for certain crimes. **For federal housing laws, juvenile adjudications will be treated as convictions.**[261]

---

[250] 24 CFR § 966.4 (2010).
[251] The United States Fair Housing Act does not include criminal history as a protected class. 42 U.S.C. § 3604.
[252] 24 C.F.R. § 100.201(a)(2).
[253] RCW 59.18.130(6).
[254] *Id.*
[255] RCW 59.18.130.
[256] RCW 59.16 *et seq.* (Unlawful Detainer Statute), RCW 59.18 *et seq.* (Residential Landlord-Tenant Act).
[257] RCW 59.18.130(8).
[258] RCW 59.18.130(6) and (9).
[259] RCW 59.20 *et seq.* (Mobile Home Landlord-Tenant Act).
[260] 42 U.S.C. § 1437n (2005), 24 CFR 966.4(i)(A) (2005).
[261] 42 U.S.C. 1437 (f)(d)(1)(B)(iii) and other related statutes do not limit the language solely to convictions, rather stating that "[t]he owner may terminate the tenancy for criminal activity by a household member... if the owner determines that the household member has committed the criminal activity, regardless of whether the household member has been arrested or convicted for such activity." http://www.seattlehousing.org/landlords/pdf/project/Tenancy_Addendum.pdf.

The Caseload Forecast Council is not liable for errors or omissions in the manual, for sentences that may be inappropriately calculated as a result of a practitioner's or court's reliance on the manual, or for any other written or verbal information related to adult or juvenile sentencing. The scoring sheets are intended to provide assistance in most cases but does not cover all permutations of the scoring rules. If you find any errors or omissions, we encourage you to report them to the Caseload Forecast Council.

APPENDIX D: Beyond Juvenile Court: Long-Term Impact of a Juvenile Record.
Washington Defenders Association

Mandatory Lifetime Bans on Admission:

- Households which include a registered sex offender, adult or juvenile;[262] and
- Households where a member has been convicted, as an adult or juvenile, of manufacturing or otherwise producing methamphetamine on the premises of a federally assisted housing program.[263]

Other Mandatory Bans on Admission:

- **3 year** ban from the date of eviction against any household which includes an individual who was evicted from federal assisted housing for drug related activity, unless the housing provider determines that the evicted household member has successfully completed a supervised drug rehabilitation program approved by the PHA or the circumstances leading to the eviction no longer exist (for example, the criminal household member has died or is imprisoned).[264]
- Households which include a member, adult or juvenile, who the housing provider determines **is currently engaged in illegal use of a controlled substance** or who the housing provider has a reasonable belief that the household member's **pattern of illegal drug use may threaten the health safety or right to peaceful enjoyment of the premises** by other residents. For the latter, the housing provider may consider the household member's rehabilitation as evidenced by completing or participating in treatment.[265]

Discretionary Bans on Admission:

A HUD housing provider *may* exclude any household which includes a member currently engaging in, or has engaged in during a reasonable time before the admissions decision any drug-related or violent criminal activity or other criminal activity which would adversely affect the health, safety, or right to peaceful enjoyment of the premises by other residents, the owner, or public housing agency employees.[266]

Discretionary Evictions:[267] **Drug related criminal activity by juvenile household members, "on or off" the premises of a public housing project** *may* result in the entire family being evicted since family members may be evicted for the drug related activity of other household

---

[262] Quality Housing and Work Responsibility Act of 1998 (QHWRA) § 578, 112 Stat. 2461, P.L. 105-276; *see also* 66 Fed. Reg. 28,776 (May 24, 2001).
[263] 42 U.S.C. § 1437n(f).
[264] 42 U.S.C. § 13661, 24 CFR § 982.553.
[265] 42 U.S.C. § 13661(c).
[266] *Id.*
[267] 24 CFR § 5.851.

The Caseload Forecast Council is not liable for errors or omissions in the manual, for sentences that may be inappropriately calculated as a result of a practitioner's or court's reliance on the manual, or for any other written or verbal information related to adult or juvenile sentencing. The scoring sheets are intended to provide assistance in most cases but does not cover all permutations of the scoring rules. If you find any errors or omissions, we encourage you to report them to the Caseload Forecast Council.

APPENDIX D: Beyond Juvenile Court: Long-Term Impact of a Juvenile Record.
Washington Defenders Association

members or guests.[268] There may be an "innocent tenant" defense under Washington law[269] or some municipal codes. For other HUD funded projects, **drug related criminal activity "on or near" the premises** or **any criminal activity that threatens the health, safety, or right to peaceful enjoyment** of residents living in the immediate vicinity may result in eviction.[270] **Illegal drug use or a pattern of illegal drug use or alcohol abuse** that interferes with the health, safety or right to peaceful enjoyment of the premises may result in eviction, although evidence of rehabilitation may be considered.[271]

Fleeing felons (people with felony warrants) and probation or parole violators may also be evicted from federally funded housing.[272]

> **PRACTICE TIP:** Ask your client whether he or she lives in government subsidized housing and advise the client that a criminal adjudication could result in the loss of their family's housing and also impact their ability to get into government funded housing, especially HUD funded housing, in the future.

> **PRACTICE TIP:** Since so many evictions are discretionary, rehabilitation efforts are helpful. Evidence that the offender is participating or has participated in a treatment program can be used to negotiate with the housing authority.

> **PRACTICE TIP:** If your client's family is involved in an eviction proceeding, contact a housing specialist through the Northwest Justice Project in your region at www.nwjustice.org.

Public Benefits

Temporary Assistance for Needy Families (TANF): TANF provides cash benefits and food assistance to families who have at least one minor child residing at home, or to an individual who is pregnant.[273] Each family receives cash assistance and food stamps according to a calculation based on income and number of eligible family members.[274]

Although state and federal law previously banned both adult and juvenile drug felons from receiving cash assistance under TANF[275], **neither juvenile nor adult felony drug convictions**

---

[268] 42 U.S.C. 1437d(l)(6).
[269] RCW 59.18.130(6).
[270] 42 U.S.C. § 1437f(d)(1)(B)(iii).
[271] 42 U.S.C. § 13662.
[272] 42 U.S.C. § 1437f(d)(1)(B)(v).
[273] 42 U.S.C. § 608(a)(1). A "dependent child" is someone under 18 (unless a court order for support exists), not married, self-supporting, or a member of the armed forces. RCW 74.20A.
[274] 21 U.S.C. § 862a. *See also* WAC 388-408-0015 for who is eligible in a household to receive TANF in Washington.
[275] 21 USC §862(b), *see also* 21 USC §862(d)(1).

The Caseload Forecast Council is not liable for errors or omissions in the manual, for sentences that may be inappropriately calculated as a result of a practitioner's or court's reliance on the manual, or for any other written or verbal information related to adult or juvenile sentencing. The scoring sheets are intended to provide assistance in most cases but does not cover all permutations of the scoring rules. If you find any errors or omissions, we encourage you to report them to the Caseload Forecast Council.

APPENDIX D: Beyond Juvenile Court: Long-Term Impact of a Juvenile Record.
Washington Defenders Association

affect TANF eligibility in Washington State.[276] **Food stamps** are also no longer affected by drug convictions.[277]

Detention/Institution Time and TANF: If a juvenile is detained for longer than 90 days, the family will not receive TANF assistance for them.[278] Treatment in a substance abuse facility does not trigger ineligibility and is treated as a "temporary absence" unless for more than one hundred and eighty days.[279] If the caretaker fails to report the child's absence within five calendar days from when the caretaker first learns that the child will be absent for more than 90 days, they will be ineligible for cash benefits for one calendar month.[280]

Fleeing Felons: Juveniles with outstanding felony warrants or outstanding warrants issued as a result of parole or probation violations are ineligible to receive cash or food assistance.[281]

Social Security Income: Many juveniles qualify for SSI and receive it through a representative payee. Juvenile adjudications will not affect a juvenile's eligibility to receive these federal benefits.[282]

Traveling to Canada

Canadian border officials at the Washington border have the ability to run criminal history checks and may deny entry to individuals based on "inadmissible" criminal history; however, juvenile adjudications should not bar entry to Canada. Under Canadian law, a foreign national may be inadmissible to Canada for, among other reasons, "committing an act outside Canada that is an offence in the place where it was committed and that, if committed in Canada, would constitute an indictable offence under an Act of Parliament."[283] Inadmissibility under this provision excludes offenses under the "Young Offenders Act,"[284] which is the equivalent of the Juvenile Justice Act. Therefore, **juvenile adjudications should not bar a person's entrance into Canada.**

---

[276] RCW 74.08.025(4); 21 U.S.C. 862a(a).
[277] RCW 74.08.025.
[278] RCW 74.08.025
[279] WAC 388-454-0015.
[280] WAC 388-454-0015(5), WAC 388-418-0007(6).
[281] WAC 388-442-0010(2). Fleeing felons are ineligible for all of the above (TANF, food assistance, SFA). A fleeing felon is a person who is fleeing to avoid prosecution, custody or confinement for a crime or an attempt to commit a crime.
[282] See 42 U.S.C. 1320a-7.
[283] Immigrant and Refugee Protection Act [Canada], 36(2)(c).
[284] Immigration and Refugee Protection Act [Canada], 36(3)(e). The "Young Offenders Act" is the Canadian statute dealing with juveniles.

The Caseload Forecast Council is not liable for errors or omissions in the manual, for sentences that may be inappropriately calculated as a result of a practitioner's or court's reliance on the manual, or for any other written or verbal information related to adult or juvenile sentencing. The scoring sheets are intended to provide assistance in most cases but does not cover all permutations of the scoring rules. If you find any errors or omissions, we encourage you to report them to the Caseload Forecast Council.

APPENDIX D: Beyond Juvenile Court: Long-Term Impact of a Juvenile Record.
Washington Defenders Association

Other Countries:

The U.S. Department of State lists "Foreign Entry Requirements" on their website, http://travel.state.gov/visa/americans1.html. The information is provided from foreign embassies and, as of October 2004, only Canada listed a criminal record as something that could affect entry. Current entry requirements should be obtained directly from consular offices of the countries to be visited.

Juvenile Sex Offenses

In Washington, **juveniles convicted of sex offenses or kidnapping offenses as juveniles are subject to the same sex offender and kidnapping registration and notification requirements as adults.**[285] They are required to register as sex offenders for sex offenses committed in Washington or in another state.[286] Knowingly failing to register or failing to notify the sheriff of a changed name or changed residence is a crime.[287] **The duty to register for a juvenile sex offense does not "go away" when the person becomes an adult.**

End of the Duty to Register as a Sex Offender:

- Offenders required to register for a sex offense or kidnapping offense who have committed a class A felony at the age of 15 or older may, after five years after release from confinement, petition the court to be relieved of the duty to register.
- Juveniles who committed a class A sex or kidnapping offenses at age 14 years or younger and juveniles who have committed a non-class A sex or kidnapping offense may petition the court to be relieved from the duty to register two years after being released from confinement.
- Creates a uniform burden of proof for individuals who petition the court for relief from the duty to register as a sex offender for offenses committed as a juvenile.
- Allows records for most juvenile sex offenses to be sealed where a person convicted of a juvenile sex offense has been relieved of the duty to register and the person has complied with all other statutory requirements.
- Requires case-by-case risk assessments of sex offenders being released from confinement and those accepted for supervision from another state under the Interstate Corrections Compact.

Effect of the Duty to Register: Sex offender registration will result in various levels of community notification depending upon the person's risk level and the discretion of the county

---

[285] RCW 9A.44.130; RCW 13.40.217 (2005) authorizes the release of information to law enforcement agencies and to a website, regarding juveniles adjudicated of sex offenses. RCW 4.24.550 governs the release of information to a website.
[286] *Id.*
[287] RCW 9A.44.132.

The Caseload Forecast Council is not liable for errors or omissions in the manual, for sentences that may be inappropriately calculated as a result of a practitioner's or court's reliance on the manual, or for any other written or verbal information related to adult or juvenile sentencing. The scoring sheets are intended to provide assistance in most cases but does not cover all permutations of the scoring rules. If you find any errors or omissions, we encourage you to report them to the Caseload Forecast Council.

APPENDIX D: Beyond Juvenile Court: Long-Term Impact of a Juvenile Record.
Washington Defenders Association

sheriff. The law **requires** some level of notification/public disclosure of sex offender information and **permits** other disclosure at the discretion of the county sheriff.[288]

Risk Levels: All juveniles convicted of sex or kidnapping offenses are assigned a risk level of I, II or III by the Department of Social and Health Services, through the Juvenile Rehabilitation Administration ("JRA"). Levels I, II and III indicate a low, moderate or high risk of re-offense in the community at large.[289]

Once a juvenile is released to the community, the sheriff of the county where the juvenile resides must assign a risk level after considering the level assigned by JRA. If the sheriff makes a decision to change the offender's risk level, the sheriff must give notice to JRA with reasons for the change in classification. Notice of the change must also be given to the Washington Association of Sheriff and Police Chiefs (WASPC).[290] There are no statutory criteria for determining when a risk level should be changed by the county sheriff and no statutory procedures for an offender to request a change in risk classification.

Notification: For any juvenile convicted of a sex, violent or stalking offense, no later than 30 days prior to discharge, parole, release, leave or transfer to a community residential facility, JRA must send written notice to:

- The chief of police of the city where the juvenile will reside;
- The sheriff of the county where the juvenile will reside;
- The public or private school board of the district where the juvenile will attend or last attended school;
- The victim, if the victim requested notice in writing;
- Any witnesses who testified against the juvenile, if the witnesses requested notice in writing;
- Any person specified in writing by the prosecuting attorney.[291]

Notices to law enforcement must include at a minimum, the identity and criminal history behavior of the offender and the department's risk level classification.[292]

For **Level III** sex offenders, the county sheriff where the offender is registered must publish notice in at least one "legal newspaper with general circulation in the area of the sex offender's registered address or location."[293] The sheriff **may** also provide notice to the public at large

---

[288] RCW 9A.44.140.
[289] RCW 13.40.217(3).
[290] RCW 4.24.550(10).
[291] RCW 13.40.215.
[292] RCW 13.40.217.
[293] RCW 4.24.550(4).

The Caseload Forecast Council is not liable for errors or omissions in the manual, for sentences that may be inappropriately calculated as a result of a practitioner's or court's reliance on the manual, or for any other written or verbal information related to adult or juvenile sentencing. The scoring sheets are intended to provide assistance in most cases but does not cover all permutations of the scoring rules. If you find any errors or omissions, we encourage you to report them to the Caseload Forecast Council.

APPENDIX D: Beyond Juvenile Court: Long-Term Impact of a Juvenile Record. Washington Defenders Association

through community notification meetings, fliers, etc.[294] For sex offenders classified as **Level I and II**, the sheriff must disclose "relevant" information to "other appropriate law enforcement agencies" and **may** disclose information upon request to the victim, witnesses or neighbors of the offender.[295] For **Level II** offenders, the sheriff **may** also disclose information to, among others, public and private schools, day care centers, public libraries, and organizations serving women, children and vulnerable adults that are near where the offender will reside or will be regularly found.[296]

Sex Offender Websites

- **State Website:** Since 2004, WASPC maintains a searchable statewide sex offender website, which includes juvenile sex offenders, *The Washington State Sex Offender Information Center*.[297] The website posts the following information about Level II and III registered adult and juvenile sex offenders:
    - Photograph;[298]
    - Identifying information;
    - Conviction/adjudication information – without detail (no date of offense, nature of crime, or age of victim);
    - Address within a block, e.g., "85XX N. 100th St.[299]

- **County Websites:** At the time of this writing, some county sheriffs in Washington continue to maintain sex offender websites pursuant to RCW 4.24.550(4) while others are phasing them out. A list of all of the counties websites may be accessed through the WASPC website.[300] Individual counties vary in the amount of information they provide on their sex offender websites, for example, some counties describe the offenders offense in detail, some counties list names of Level I sex offenders, etc.

<u>**School Attendance and Notification:**</u> A juvenile who is found guilty of a sex offense will not be allowed to attend the school attended by the victim or their siblings.[301] If a juvenile is enrolled in school and convicted of a sex offense, the court must notify the principal of the student's school of the disposition of the case, after first notifying the parent or legal guardian that the notification will be made.[302] The principal shall then notify all of the student's teachers

---

[294] RCW 4.24.550(3).
[295] Id.
[296] Id.
[297] RCW 4.24.550(5).
[298] Whereas Washington is one of the more liberal states regarding displaying juvenile photos, federal law prohibits pictures and names from being given to the public unless the juvenile is prosecuted as if an adult under 18 U.S.C. § 5038(e) (2005).
[299] RCW 4.24.550(5).
[300] http://www.waspc.org/.
[301] RCW 13.40.160(3)(b)(ix).
[302] RCW 13.04.155.

The Caseload Forecast Council is not liable for errors or omissions in the manual, for sentences that may be inappropriately calculated as a result of a practitioner's or court's reliance on the manual, or for any other written or verbal information related to adult or juvenile sentencing. The scoring sheets are intended to provide assistance in most cases but does not cover all permutations of the scoring rules. If you find any errors or omissions, we encourage you to report them to the Caseload Forecast Council.

APPENDIX D: Beyond Juvenile Court: Long-Term Impact of a Juvenile Record. Washington Defenders Association

and anyone who supervises the student or "for security purposes" should be aware of the student's criminal record.[303] (NOTE: This requirement applies to students who are enrolled in school at the time of disposition—which many detained juveniles are not.)

Juvenile sex offenders who are admitted to or employed by **a public or private institution of higher education** must notify the sheriff of their county of their intent to attend the institution or begin employment within ten days of enrolling/acceptance or by the first business day after arriving at the institution, whichever is earlier.[304]

Juveniles required to register as sex offenders must notify the sheriff of their county of their intent to attend **any public or private school** within 10 days of enrolling or prior to arriving at the school, whichever is earlier. The sheriff is then required to notify the principal of the school.[305] The principal is required to notify all of the student's teachers and any others who supervise the juvenile or "for security purposes" should be aware of the juvenile's record, if the juvenile sex offender is classified as risk Level II or III. For Level I offenders, the principal must provide information only to school personnel who "for security purposes should be aware of the student's record."[306]

Foster Children

Juveniles in the state's custody as foster children, i.e., dependent children, may face additional consequences related to criminal adjudications. A foster child's criminal history may affect where that child may be placed, for example, whether they will be placed in a foster home or in a group home. Dependent children who are charged with sex offenses may be considered "sexually aggressive youth" requiring specialized placement even if not convicted of a sex offense.[307]

> **PRACTICE TIP:** If a juvenile client is dependent, coordinate representation with the client's dependency attorney. A dependency attorney may have useful information about the client, the client's family and services available to the client. If no dependency attorney has been appointed, have your client request appointment of counsel in the dependency proceeding pursuant to RCW 13.34.100(6).

Parental Responsibility

Civil Liability for Shoplifters: In the case of a minor who shoplifts, a parent or legal guardian is liable for the cost of the stolen goods (not more than $500), penalties between $100-$200,

---

[303] *Id.*
[304] RCW 9A.44.130(1)(b).
[305] RCW 9A.44.130(4)(a).
[306] RCW 9A.44.130(1)(c)(d)(i)(A).
[307] RCW 74.13.075.

The Caseload Forecast Council is not liable for errors or omissions in the manual, for sentences that may be inappropriately calculated as a result of a practitioner's or court's reliance on the manual, or for any other written or verbal information related to adult or juvenile sentencing. The scoring sheets are intended to provide assistance in most cases but does not cover all permutations of the scoring rules. If you find any errors or omissions, we encourage you to report them to the Caseload Forecast Council.

APPENDIX D: Beyond Juvenile Court: Long-Term Impact of a Juvenile Record.
Washington Defenders Association

attorney's fees and court costs of the victim.[308] The minor, however, can be liable for restitution to parents for paying the penalty.[309]

Civil Liability for Malicious Mischief: Parents are liable in civil damages up to $5000 for their minor child's malicious destruction of property or malicious injury to a person if the child is living with them. This does not limit civil damages that might arise from the parents' own negligence.[310]

Attorney's Fees: The court may order parents, legal guardians or juveniles to pay, as they are able, for the costs of publicly funded counsel after a juvenile disposition, modification, or after the state prevails on an appeal.[311]

Costs of Incarceration: The court may order the parent or legal custodian to pay in whole or in part for the costs of "support, treatment, and confinement of the child."[312]

Diversion Costs: Parents or legal guardians must pay, as they are able, for the cost of diversion services.[313]

> *There can be no keener revelation of a society's soul than the way in which it treats its children.*
> — Nelson Mandela

---

[308] RCW 4.24.230(2).
[309] *State v. T.A.D.*, 122 Wash. App. 290, 95 P.3d 775 (Div.1 2004).
[310] RCW 4.24.190.
[311] RCW 13.40.145.
[312] RCW 13.40.220.
[313] RCW 13.40.085.

The Caseload Forecast Council is not liable for errors or omissions in the manual, for sentences that may be inappropriately calculated as a result of a practitioner's or court's reliance on the manual, or for any other written or verbal information related to adult or juvenile sentencing. The scoring sheets are intended to provide assistance in most cases but does not cover all permutations of the scoring rules. If you find any errors or omissions, we encourage you to report them to the Caseload Forecast Council.

APPENDIX E

APPENDIX E: Juvenile Disposition Summary - Fiscal Year 2013

Washington State
Caseload Forecast Council
January 2014

The Caseload Forecast Council (CFC)[314] received 7,685 juvenile dispositions rendered by Washington State juvenile courts in fiscal year 2013.

Washington State Juvenile Sentencing Guidelines

The Washington State juvenile code mandates a system of presumptive sentencing guidelines for juvenile offenders.

The presumptive standard range for an offense[315] is a function of the offender's age, the seriousness of the current offense (Current Offense Category) and criminal history (Prior Adjudications Score).

Although the level of presumptive sanction increases with age, offense seriousness and prior adjudication score, the increase is not linear (see Figure 1).

Generally, current offense seriousness outweighs prior adjudication score. Age is only a factor for first time offense category "A-" offenders.

Courts also have the option of using several sentencing alternatives to the standard range.

Current Offense Category

While the juvenile system utilizes adult crime statutes, individual offenses are assigned a more differentiated juvenile "current offense category" (with + and – added to differentiate within a class) for sentencing purposes. While juvenile offense categories generally parallel adult felony classes (i.e., Class B felonies are typically B+, B, or B- category offenses), that is not universally the case.

Prior Adjudication Score

The seriousness of criminal history is summarized by the "prior adjudication score." Prior felony adjudications count as one point each and misdemeanors and gross misdemeanors count as ¼ point. The prior adjudication score is the sum of the points for all prior adjudicated offenses, with fractions rounded down.

Standard Range: Local Sanctions vs. Confinement to JRA

The juvenile sentencing guidelines specify two types of presumptive penalties: a <u>standard range</u> of confinement under the supervision of the state Juvenile Rehabilitation Administration (JRA) for more than thirty

---

[314] Juvenile courts are required by statute (RCW 13.50.010(8)) to report all dispositions to the Caseload Forecast Council.
[315] Washington's juvenile code, while paralleling the adult criminal justice system in most respects, retains traditional juvenile court terminology where juvenile offenders are "adjudicated" rather than "convicted" of "offenses" rather than "crimes." This report uses the juvenile and adult terms interchangeably, recognizing that in some cases absolute accuracy is subordinated to readability.

APPENDIX E – STATISTICAL SUMMARY OF WASHINGTON STATE FY2013 JUVENILE DISPOSITIONS

days or a local sanction administered at the county level.

"Standard ranges" exceed 30 days include a minimum and a maximum term, and are served in a JRA facility. JRA has the limited discretion to set a release date between the minimum and maximum. Offenders do not earn a sentence reduction for "good behavior."

Figure 1. Option A - Juvenile Offender Sentencing Grid Standard Range (RCW 13.40.0357)

Current Offense Category	Standard Range Sanction				
A+	180 weeks to age 21 for all category A+ offenses				
A	103-129 weeks for all category A offenses				
A-	15-36 wks[a]	52-65 weeks	80-100 weeks	103-129 weeks	103-129 weeks
B+	15-36 weeks	15-36 weeks	52-65 weeks	80-100 weeks	103-129 weeks
B	Local Sanctions	Local Sanctions	15-36 weeks	15-36 weeks	52-65 weeks
C+	Local Sanctions	Local Sanctions	Local Sanctions	15-36 weeks	15-36 weeks
C	Local Sanctions	Local Sanctions	Local Sanctions	Local Sanctions	15-36 weeks
D+	Local Sanctions	Local Sanctions	Local Sanctions	Local Sanctions	Local Sanctions
D	Local Sanctions	Local Sanctions	Local Sanctions	Local Sanctions	Local Sanctions
E	Local Sanctions	Local Sanctions	Local Sanctions	Local Sanctions	Local Sanctions
Prior Adjudication Score[b]	0	1	2	3	4 or more

Note: Local sanctions may include up to 30 days confinement.

[a] Except 30-40 weeks for 15 to 17 year olds.

[b] Prior felony adjudications count as one point each and misdemeanors and gross misdemeanors count as ¼ point. The prior adjudication score is the sum of the points for all prior adjudications, with fractions rounded down.

"Local sanctions" are supervised by county probation departments. Courts sentencing an offender to a local sanction have the discretion to select from a menu of options including confinement, home monitoring, community supervision, fines, community service and work crews.

The presumptive sanction for category "B+" or higher offenses (class A felonies and some violent class B felonies) is a standard range of confinement in a JRA facility.

Less serious offenses, the equivalent of B and C felonies, carry a presumption of a standard range of confinement or a local sanction, depending on the offense category and prior adjudication score.

Misdemeanors or gross misdemeanors carry a presumptive local sanction.

Figure 2. Juvenile Dispositions by Prior Adjudication Score[316]

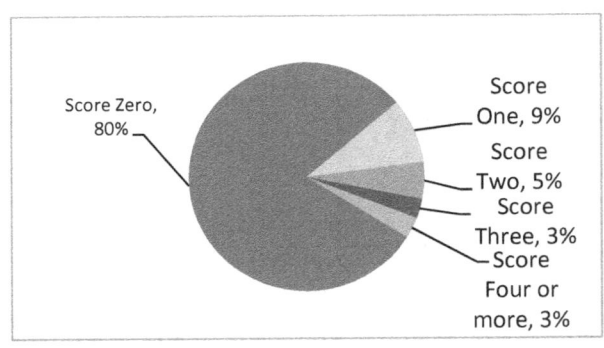

[316] Fractions are rounded down meaning a score 1.75 is reported as a score of 1.

The Caseload Forecast Council is not liable for errors or omissions in the manual, for sentences that may be inappropriately calculated as a result of a practitioner's or court's reliance on the manual, or for any other written or verbal information related to adult or juvenile sentencing. The scoring sheets are intended to provide assistance in most cases but does not cover all permutations of the scoring rules. If you find any errors or omissions, we encourage you to report them to the Caseload Forecast Council.

APPENDIX E – STATISTICAL SUMMARY OF WASHINGTON STATE FY2013 JUVENILE DISPOSITIONS

FY2013 Juvenile Court Dispositions

Most juvenile offenders sentenced in FY2013 had little or no criminal history. Over three quarters (80.0%) of those sentenced were first time offenders with no prior adjudications. Another 9.1% had a prior adjudication score of one. Only 10.9% had prior adjudication scores of 2 or more (Figure 2).

Demographics
Table 1. Demographics

Gender*	Number	Percentage
Male	5,872	76.41%
Female	1,774	23.08%
Race/Ethnicity**		
African American	1,243	16.17%
Asian/Pacific Islander	211	2.75%
Caucasian	4,019	52.30%
Hispanic***	1,657	21.56%
Native American	369	4.80%
Age Range		
Under 10 years old	2	0.03%
10 years old	12	0.16%
11 years old	31	0.40%
12 years old	255	3.32%
13 years old	610	7.94%
14 years old	1,186	15.43%
15 years old	1,706	22.20%
16 years old	2,031	26.43%
17 and above	1,852	24.10%

*Gender was missing on 39 dispositions (.5%).
**Race/Ethnicity was missing on 186 dispositions (2.4%).
***Hispanic is treated as a "race" category.

Table 1 shows the dispositions distribution by gender, age, and race/ethnicity. Most offenders sentenced in FY2013 were male (76%) and a majority, Caucasian (52%). The least common racial group was Asian/Pacific Islander (3%).

Most offenders cluster toward the upper end of the 14-17 year old age bracket. The single most common age at disposition was 16.

Race/Ethnicity: Dispositions v. State Population

Minorities are typically disproportionately over-represented in juvenile offender populations. One common method of measuring disproportionality is to construct a ratio of the percentage of a given race/ethnicity in a target population to the percentage in the general population. If the percentages are the same, the ratio or "coefficient of disproportionality," is 1.0. If the percentage is greater in the target population (e. g., juvenile offenders) than in the state population, the ratio will be greater than 1.0 indicating over-representation." Likewise, a ratio less than 1.0 indicates an "under-representation." The magnitude of the ratio indicates the degree of disproportionality.

Table 2 presents the race/ethnicity breakdown of the FY2013 juvenile dispositions compared to the 2010 census state population.

The last column presents the coefficients of disproportionality. For example, the coefficient of disproportionality for African American offenders is 4.5. In other words, the proportion of African Americans sentenced (16.2%) was 4.5 times the proportion in the general population (3.6%). In contrast, the

APPENDIX E – STATISTICAL SUMMARY OF WASHINGTON STATE FY2013 JUVENILE DISPOSITIONS

coefficient for Caucasians is 0.7, which means the proportion of juvenile dispositions involving Caucasians is less than the proportion of Caucasians in the state population. Asian/Pacific Islanders are the most "under-represented" racial group in the offender population with a coefficient of disproportionality of 0.3.

Table 2. Racial/Ethnic Disproportionality

Race/ Ethnicity**	% FY2013 Juvenile Dispositions	% FY2010 Washington State	Coefficient of Disproportionality
African American	16.2%	3.6%	4.5
Asian/Pacific Islander	2.7%	8.0%	0.3
Caucasian	52.3%	75.4%	0.7
Hispanic***	21.6%	11.7%	1.8
Native American	4.8%	1.4%	3.5
Total	100.0%	100.0%	
(N)	7,499	6,484,272	
**Race/Ethnicity was missing on 186 dispositions (2.4%).			
***Hispanic is treated as a "race" category.			

Note: state population is taken from the Office of Financial Management (Census 2010)

County

As would be expected, most juvenile dispositions occur in the more populated counties in the state.

Table 3 shows the number of juvenile dispositions by county. King County had the highest number of dispositions (1,073 or 14.0%), followed by Clark County (759 or 9.9%), and Pierce County (753 or 9.8%).

Together, these 3 counties (King, Clark and Pierce) accounted for a third of all dispositions in the state. In contrast, 20 of 39 counties had less than 100 dispositions each and 5 of the smallest counties had less than a 10 dispositions.

Table 3. Juvenile Dispositions by County

County	Number	Percentage
Adams	27	0.4%
Asotin	66	0.9%
Benton	500	6.5%
Chelan	141	1.8%
Clallam	125	1.6%
Clark	759	9.9%
Columbia	14	0.2%
Cowlitz	280	3.6%
Douglas	61	0.8%
Ferry	6	0.1%
Franklin	171	2.2%
Garfield	0	0.0%
Grant	195	2.5%
Grays Harbor	89	1.2%
Island	32	0.4%
Jefferson	28	0.4%
King	1,073	14.0%
Kitsap	344	4.5%
Kittitas	30	0.4%
Klickitat	29	0.4%
Lewis	108	1.4%
Lincoln	2	0.0%
Mason	98	1.3%
Okanogan	179	2.3%
Pacific	33	0.4%
Pend Oreille	8	0.1%
Pierce	753	9.8%
San Juan	10	0.1%
Skagit	173	2.3%
Skamania	25	0.3%
Snohomish	560	7.3%
Spokane	325	4.2%
Stevens	61	0.8%

The Caseload Forecast Council is not liable for errors or omissions in the manual, for sentences that may be inappropriately calculated as a result of a practitioner's or court's reliance on the manual, or for any other written or verbal information related to adult or juvenile sentencing. The scoring sheets are intended to provide assistance in most cases but does not cover all permutations of the scoring rules. If you find any errors or omissions, we encourage you to report them to the Caseload Forecast Council.

APPENDIX E – STATISTICAL SUMMARY OF WASHINGTON STATE FY2013 JUVENILE DISPOSITIONS

County	Number	Percentage
Thurston	507	6.6%
Wahkiakum	11	0.1%
Walla Walla	186	2.4%
Whatcom	263	3.4%
Whitman	9	0.1%
Yakima	404	5.3%
Grand Total	7,685	100.0%

Type of Court Disposition

The vast majority of dispositions (95%) were the result of guilty pleas; only 2% of dispositions involved offenders adjudicated guilty following a juvenile court hearing. The remaining dispositions (3%) were revoked deferred and "Alford" pleas.

Locus of Sanction

Most juvenile offenders are sanctioned at the local, county level (Figure 3). Only 8 percent (629) of FY2013 dispositions resulted in confinement in a state operated JRA facility. The average range of confinement for JRA commitments was 41 to 58 weeks (Table 4).

Figure 3. Locus of Sanction

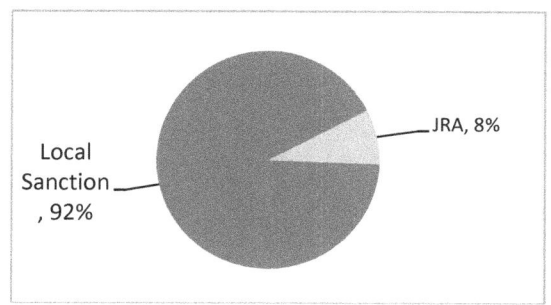

Table 4. Confinement Ordered by Placement Type

Placement Type	Average Sanction	
JRA	41 to 58	Weeks
County Detention	14.9	Days
Work Crew	4.6	Days
Electronic Monitoring	24.4	Days

Local Sanctions

"Local sanction" is the presumptive sentencing range for offenders at the lower end of the offense seriousness/prior adjudication score continuum. Most (92%) of FY2013 dispositions resulted in sentences to local sanctions at the county level.

Almost two thirds (62%) of youths sentenced to local sanctions were assigned some confinement in county detention, with an average sentence of 15 days. Another 33% received community supervision without detention. The remaining 5% received some other sanction (work crew, electronic home monitoring, etc.). The average order of electronic home monitoring was 24 days. The average work crew order was 5 days.

In addition, the courts ordered an average of 29 hours of community service per disposition.

The Caseload Forecast Council is not liable for errors or omissions in the manual, for sentences that may be inappropriately calculated as a result of a practitioner's or court's reliance on the manual, or for any other written or verbal information related to adult or juvenile sentencing. The scoring sheets are intended to provide assistance in most cases but does not cover all permutations of the scoring rules. If you find any errors or omissions, we encourage you to report them to the Caseload Forecast Council.

APPENDIX E – STATISTICAL SUMMARY OF WASHINGTON STATE FY2013 JUVENILE DISPOSITIONS

Figure 4. Local Sanction by Type

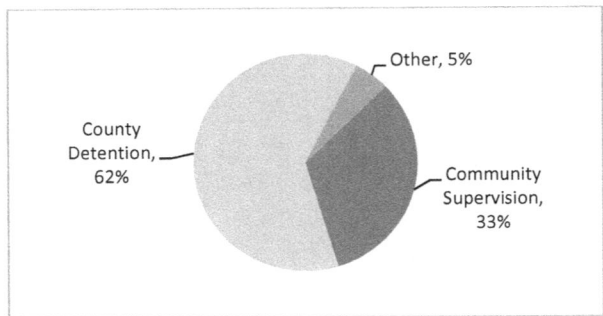

Felony and Non-felony Dispositions

Most FY2013 juvenile dispositions were for non-felony (gross misdemeanor and misdemeanor) offenses. Felonies accounted for less than a third of all dispositions (Table 5).

Table 5. Felony and Non-felony Dispositions

Offense	Number	Percent
Felony	2,259	29%
Gross Misdemeanor	3,766	49%
Misdemeanor	1,660	22%
Total	7,685	

Felony Offenses

There were 2,259 dispositions for felonies. Property crimes were the most common felonies committed by juveniles, with an average sanction of 9 to 12 weeks confinement. The second most common felonies were assaults, with an average sentence of 19 to 26 weeks confinement (Table 6). On average, felony dispositions included 6 months of community supervision in addition to any confinement.

Table 6. Average Confinement Ordered by Felony Category

Offense	N	Ave. Term (in Weeks)	
		Minimum	Maximum
Assault	360	18.8	25.8
Drug	178	5.1	7.1
Manslaughter	1	180.0	180.0
Murder 1	2	187.9	233.9
Other Felony	147	9.1	11.0
Property	1,203	8.5	11.7
Robbery	156	30.3	43.3
Sex	212	16.4	22.5
Total	2,259	12.4	17.0

Non-Felony Offenses

Over two thirds of FY2013 dispositions were for non-felony offenses. There were 3,766 gross misdemeanor dispositions, with an average sentence of 16 days confinement, and 1,660 misdemeanor dispositions, with an average sentence of 11 days confinement. The average community supervision imposed for gross misdemeanors and misdemeanors was 5 months.

The Caseload Forecast Council is not liable for errors or omissions in the manual, for sentences that may be inappropriately calculated as a result of a practitioner's or court's reliance on the manual, or for any other written or verbal information related to adult or juvenile sentencing. The scoring sheets are intended to provide assistance in most cases but does not cover all permutations of the scoring rules. If you find any errors or omissions, we encourage you to report them to the Caseload Forecast Council.

APPENDIX E – STATISTICAL SUMMARY OF WASHINGTON STATE FY2013 JUVENILE DISPOSITIONS

Table 7. Average Non-Felony Confinement Ordered

Offense	Number	Avg. Term (in Days)
Gross Misdemeanor	3,766	16.4
Misdemeanor	1,660	10.9
Total	5,426	14.7

Violent and Non-violent Offenses

The great majority (95%) of FY2013 juvenile dispositions were for non-violent offenses. Dispositions across all non-violent offenses carried an average sentence of 23 to 29 days confinement.

Table 8. Violent and Non-Violent Offense Dispositions

Offense	Number	Avg. Term
Serious Violent	8	208 to 258 Weeks
Violent	376	26 to 37 Weeks
Non-Violent	7,301	23 to 29 Days
Total	7,685	

Juvenile dispositions for "serious violent offenses"[317] were extremely rare in FY2013, accounting for only 8 (0.1%) of 7,685 dispositions. Dispositions for serious violent offenses carried an average range of 208 to 258 weeks confinement in JRA.[318]

There were an additional 376 dispositions for violent crimes, with an average sentence of 26 to 37 weeks confinement.

Figure 5. Violent and Non-Violent Dispositions

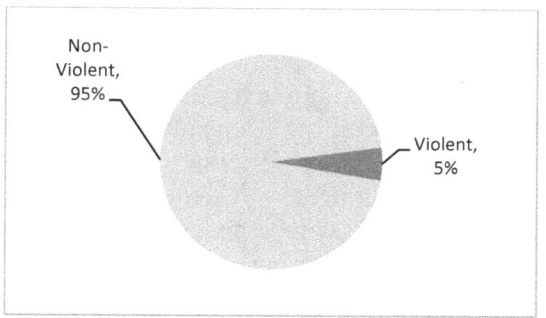

Sentencing Alternatives

The state juvenile code permits a number of alternatives to the standard presumptive sentencing ranges (Option A), depending on the current offense, criminal history, and treatment needs of the offender.

Special Sex Offender Disposition Alternative (SSODA)

During FY2013, 210 dispositions were imposed under the Special Sex Offender Disposition Alternative option. SSODA authorizes the court to suspend the standard range disposition and impose in-patient or outpatient treatment for certain sex offenses. The court may impose a number of special conditions as a prerequisite of the suspended

---

[317] "Serious violent offense" is a subcategory of violent offense and means:
(a)(i) Murder in the first degree;
(ii) Homicide by abuse;
(iii) Murder in the second degree;
(iv) Manslaughter in the first degree;
(v) Assault in the first degree;
(vi) Kidnapping in the first degree;
(vii) Rape in the first degree;
(viii) Assault of a child in the first degree; or
(ix) An attempt, criminal solicitation, or criminal conspiracy to commit one of these felonies; (RCW 9.94A.030(45))

[318] Most individuals under the age of 18 committing "serious violent offenses" are sentenced as adults and therefore are not technically juvenile offenders. These sentences are reported in a separate CFC publication: Statistical Summary of Adult Felony Sentencing: Fiscal Year 2013 available on the CFC website.

The Caseload Forecast Council is not liable for errors or omissions in the manual, for sentences that may be inappropriately calculated as a result of a practitioner's or court's reliance on the manual, or for any other written or verbal information related to adult or juvenile sentencing. The scoring sheets are intended to provide assistance in most cases but does not cover all permutations of the scoring rules. If you find any errors or omissions, we encourage you to report them to the Caseload Forecast Council.

APPENDIX E – STATISTICAL SUMMARY OF WASHINGTON STATE FY2013 JUVENILE DISPOSITIONS

disposition. SSODA dispositions carried an average confinement of 4 days, an average suspended range of confinement of 211 to 246 days, and an average of 17 months of community supervision.

Chemical Dependency Disposition Alternative (CDDA)

During FY2013, 247 dispositions were imposed under the Chemical Dependency Disposition Alternative option. The CDDA provides chemically dependent youth with an alternative disposition that includes drug or alcohol treatment. Chemical Dependency Alternatives involved an average confinement of 5 days, an average suspended range of confinement of 51 to 63 days, and an average of 7 months of community supervision.

Option-B Suspended Disposition

Option-B provides authority to the court to suspend a portion of the standard range confinement time in order for the offender to participate in a treatment or education program. The court imposed 38 Option-B suspended dispositions with an average confinement of 3 days, an average suspended range of confinement of 114 to 246 days, and an average of 12 months of community supervision.

Mental Health Disposition

The Mental Health option is rare in juvenile dispositions. There were 6 dispositions that were imposed under this option. It carried an average suspended range of confinement of 154 to 204 days, and 6 months of community supervision.

Table 9. Juvenile Disposition Alternatives

Option	N	Average Range of Confinement (days)			
		Confinement		Suspended	
		Min	Max	Min	Max
CDDA	247	4.7	4.7	50.8	62.8
Mental Health	6	-	-	153.8	204.0
Option B	38	2.8	2.8	114.2	245.7
SSODA	210	4.2	4.2	210.6	246.3

Manifest Injustice Dispositions

In addition to the alternatives described above, the court may depart from the standard range by imposing a manifest injustice disposition either above or below the standard range[319]. The CFC recorded 339 (4.4%) manifest injustice dispositions in fiscal year 2013. The majority of these dispositions (77.3%) were above the standard range (aggravated); 20.9% of manifest injustice dispositions were below the standard range (mitigated).

Table 10. Manifest Injustice Dispositions by Type

Type of Disposition	Number	Percentage
Aggravated	262	77.3%
Mitigated	71	20.9%
Within	6	1.8%
Total	339	100.0%

---

[319] The court may declare a "Manifest Injustice" and sentence outside the standard range when the facts and circumstances of a case or characteristics of the juvenile lead to the conclusion that dispositions ordered within the standard range would be manifestly unjust. The court's findings of a Manifest Injustice must be supported by clear and convincing evidence and its justification entered into the record.

The Caseload Forecast Council is not liable for errors or omissions in the manual, for sentences that may be inappropriately calculated as a result of a practitioner's or court's reliance on the manual, or for any other written or verbal information related to adult or juvenile sentencing. The scoring sheets are intended to provide assistance in most cases but does not cover all permutations of the scoring rules. If you find any errors or omissions, we encourage you to report them to the Caseload Forecast Council.

APPENDIX E – STATISTICAL SUMMARY OF WASHINGTON STATE FY2013 JUVENILE DISPOSITIONS

The most common reasons for mitigated manifest injustice dispositions were "other mitigating factor" and "all parties agree to mitigated sentence", while the most cited reasons for aggravated manifest injustice dispositions were "other aggravating factor" and "recent criminal history or failed to comply with diversion agreement" (Table 11).

Table 11. Manifest Injustice Reasons

Mitigating Reasons	Number
Other Mitigating Factor.	39
All parties agree to mitigated sentence (down).	11
Suffered mental or physical condition that reduced capability for the offense.	3
One year or more between current offense and prior offense.	2
The conduct neither caused nor threatened serious bodily injury or contemplated the conduct would.	2
Acted under strong and immediate provocation.	1
Aggravating Reasons	
Other Aggravating Factor.	235
Recent criminal history or failed to comply with diversion agreement.	142
All parties agree to aggravated sentence (up).	123
Standard range too lenient considering priors.	65
Other complaints resulting in diversions or guilty plea not listed in history.	40
Victim was particularly vulnerable.	26
Finding of sexual motivation.	11
No Reason Provided, inquiry made	8
While committing or fleeing from offense inflicted or attempted to inflict injury.	8
Heinous, cruel or depraved.	1
Leader of criminal enterprise.	1

Summary

This report details characteristics of the 7,685 FY2013 Washington State juvenile offender dispositions reported to the Caseload Forecast Council.

The picture presented is perhaps at odds with some of the perceptions held by the general public about juvenile offenders.

As the data show, over three quarters (76%) of the dispositions involved young males. Most offenders sentenced in juvenile court have little or no criminal history. In fact, approximately 80% of dispositions have no prior offenses.

Similarly, most offenders sentenced in court are there for relatively minor crimes. More than two thirds (71%) of the offenders sentenced in FY2013 were sentenced for offenses that were gross misdemeanors or misdemeanors.

Washington is among the small number of states with presumptive sentencing guidelines for juvenile offenders. Although courts have access to a variety of sentencing alternatives for offenders with specific treatment needs (sex offenders, chemical dependency, Option B, and mental health issues), the majority of offenders (93%) are sentenced under the presumptive sentencing guidelines.

One of the intents of the Washington juvenile code and its system of presumptive sentencing guidelines is to promote accountability and proportionality in the sentencing of juvenile offenders. The data in this report support the conclusion that these intents are being realized, at least to the extent that the severity

APPENDIX E – STATISTICAL SUMMARY OF WASHINGTON STATE FY2013 JUVENILE DISPOSITIONS

of sanctions ordered by the courts tend to increase with the seriousness of the offense and the extent of prior criminal history.

While the sentences of offenders were proportional to seriousness of current offense and criminal history, the population of offenders sentenced was disproportionately male and minority, when compared to the state population. There was significant racial/ethnic disproportionality in the sentenced population. Compared to the state as a whole, those adjudicated in FY2013 were more likely to be African American, Hispanic, or Native American. They were less likely to be Caucasian or Asian/Pacific Islander. African Americans were the most over-represented group in the population, with a coefficient of disproportionality of 4.5.

It is obviously beyond the scope of this report to determine the causes of gender and racial/ethnic disproportionality in the sentenced population. But the data are clear that it persists.

This report is updated annually. It, along with prior annual reports, is available on the CFC web site: WWW.CFC.WA.GOV.

The juvenile disposition data contained in this report come from Washington Disposition forms sent to the Caseload Forecast Council (CFC) by the courts. Data include all juvenile dispositions known to the CFC that were imposed between July 1, 2012, and June 30, 2013 (Fiscal Year 2013). Data elements entered into the CFC database and used in the report include race, gender, type of sentence, current offense, offense history, offender score, and the imposed terms of confinement and community supervision.

Comments or questions may be directed to:

John C. Steiger, PhD
Executive Director
Caseload Forecast Council
P.O. Box 40962
Olympia, WA 98504-0962
John.Steiger@cfc.wa.gov

The Caseload Forecast Council is not liable for errors or omissions in the manual, for sentences that may be inappropriately calculated as a result of a practitioner's or court's reliance on the manual, or for any other written or verbal information related to adult or juvenile sentencing. The scoring sheets are intended to provide assistance in most cases but does not cover all permutations of the scoring rules. If you find any errors or omissions, we encourage you to report them to the Caseload Forecast Council.

www.ingramcontent.com/pod-product-compliance
Lightning Source LLC
Chambersburg PA
CBHW080237180526
45167CB00006B/2308